New York Times **Best-Selling Author**

PETER GREENBERG

TRAVEL EDITOR FOR NBC'S *TODAY* SHOW

DON'T GO THERE!

THE TRAVEL DETECTIVE'S ESSENTIAL GUIDE TO THE MUST-MISS PLACES OF THE WORLD

SARIKA CHAWLA, CHIEF RESEARCH EDITOR

RODALE

Book design by Christopher Rhoads
Map page 95 courtesy of Ian Spiro, fastfoodmaps.com
Photo page 178 courtesy of Courtney Scott, http://abroadrview.blogspot.com
Photo page 250 courtesy of the City of Fountain, MN

ISBN-13: 978–1–60529–994–5

Distributed to the trade by Macmillan

LIVE YOUR WHOLE LIFE™

We've all had a trip that went horribly wrong, whether it was a flight from hell, a disastrous cruise ship journey, or a resort that made the Bates Motel look like a four-star palace.

If you've had an experience with an airline, hotel, cruise line, resort, or destination that was so bad you vowed never to go back, do the world a favor and share your story. After all, truly successful, meaningful travel is also about the places in the world *not* to visit. Share your experience on DontGoThere.org.

Contents

Acknowledgments

This book is based on my extensive travel experience as well as exhaustive research by Sarika Chawla, my chief research editor. A quick look at the Sources section of this book alone will give you a pretty good idea of the comprehensive nature and sheer volume of her research.

Sarika was supported by a team of dedicated staffers including Monique-Marie DeJong, Margaret Emery, Athena Arnot-Copenhaver, Dara Bramson, Matthew Calcara, Loretta Copeland, and Michelle Castillo.

Additional backup research was provided by Mike Day, Carly Goldsmith, Kaitlyn Voyce, Michelle Shearer, and Alix Proceviat, as well as Lauren Van Mullem, Brandi Andres, Michelle Fields, and Lindsay Schmitt.

Sarika and the team dug deep and cross-referenced scientific data as well as police files, consumer complaints, government reports, university studies, and eyewitness traveler accounts from all over the globe. The group literally went through boxes and boxes of background and supporting materials that had to be read, sourced, fact-checked, and then, finally, updated. And in some cases, translated.

Having said that, this book is also, by admission and intent, incomplete, as this list of must-miss places around the world evolves on a parallel path of the fast-growing world of citizen journalism, helped in no small part by the global village of the Internet and the ever-changing world of the travel business itself.

My special thanks go to Leigh Haber, my first editor at Rodale, who initially embraced this book, and to Karen Rinaldi, who has made this all happen. To Meredith Quinn, who handled the day-to-day editing, and Nancy Bailey, who kept this project on track. As always, thanks to my agent, Amy Rennert, for always believing in me and in the concept, and to Lyn Benjamin, for always believing in *us*.

Last but not least, I want to acknowledge my readers, so many of whom have been helpful in pointing me in the right direction—that is, to all the wrong places—based on their own experiences. And I want to encourage everyone to continue to alert me. Let me hear from you. Log on to DontGoThere.org and report in.

Introduction

I got the idea for this book years ago, in an unexpected way. I was at an editors' conference, and an Indiana newspaper's travel editor was at the podium explaining his philosophy of travel journalism. He commented, "We feel that if we don't have something nice to say about a place, we just won't say it."

I couldn't believe a professional journalist would make such a statement!

I immediately stood up and challenged him. "If that's your philosophy, you should resign," I said. "You're being irresponsible to your readers. What you are describing is a newspaper that is an advertising vehicle for the travel industry, and as such it has no credibility."

I didn't make a lot of friends that day.

Back then, much of travel journalism was defined by outright boosterism, and the traditional definition of a travel writer was a librarian looking for a free cruise. That kind of reporting and writing might be perfect for a small-town newspaper, but not for me. And not for you.

I felt then—and still feel now—that such behavior was inappropriate if we were to honestly and professionally report on what is arguably the largest industry in the world. There is no room in travel journalism for quid pro quo approaches to reporting.

From that moment, I've kept a running file of my own bad travel experiences.

For example, when I became a correspondent for *Newsweek,* I was stationed in Houston, Texas. And I fried during the summer. It was so hot that I put my bed up on blocks and moved it directly next to the air conditioner, put my pillow on the window unit, and, despite getting a stiff neck each night, slept—literally—on top of the AC. I spent weekend afternoons hanging by the ice rink at the Galleria shopping center, because it was the coolest place I could find.

I hated Houston. One particularly hot day, I decided to drive as far as I could until I found an ocean. The thermometer was over 100 degrees when I drove onto I-45 and headed south. I kept driving until I hit Galveston, excited to see a coastline . . . until I actually came upon it. What confronted me was one of the ugliest beachfronts I'd ever seen, with one of the dirtiest, oiliest beaches. I never even got out of the car; I simply turned it around and headed back to Houston.

Thankfully, Houston has gotten better for me. Galveston, though, remains on my Don't Go There List.

Whenever I come back from a trip, someone is bound to ask me where I've been. I tell them, and am often amazed by their response: "I don't want to go there. It's not on my list."

I worry about that "list." Who publishes it? I'm convinced that this "list" is actually compiled by a group of failed art history majors who—having studied paintings for years—feel bound and determined to finally see them in person and want everyone else to see the same things. No surprise, then, that Italy and France rank number one and two among American travelers as favorite places to go.

But there are other, perhaps more relevant, lists. Places we like, experiences that resonate deeply in our memories. There are the places we've always yearned to visit; fantasy locations from our youth; places we've heard about, read about, wondered about. . . .

And then there are the places we've always been warned about—by our friends and often by our own government: Cuba, Iran, Iraq, Libya, North Korea, and a host of other so-called bad lands.

This book isn't about any of these lists. You can always go to Italy and France, and if you know me, then you know I'm a proponent of traveling to the countries people think are forbidden. I've already been to many of those "no-no" countries.

I have visited every U.S. state multiple times and 151 of 196 countries around the world. And with each trip, my list continues to grow.

The result: *Don't Go There*—a book about places you *really* shouldn't go, and for good reasons.

You'll find my advice on overrated hotels and resorts, tourist traps, misleading brochures, and false advertising; and destinations that are crime-ridden, corrupt, or simply overpriced. And that's just for starters.

Then there are the cities that boast absurd nicknames, the most expensive cities, and destinations where you really can't breathe the air or drink the water.

How about dirty places, and destinations that . . . literally . . . stink?

Which brings me to the subject of . . . New Jersey. Even though Camden and Newark are compelling reasons all on their own not to go there, they don't hold enough weight to make you avoid the entire state. Yes, New Jersey has the highest auto-insurance cost, the highest property taxes, not to mention the largest petroleum containment area outside the Middle East . . . but there are equally compelling reasons to go to certain parts of the state.

(And, for the record, parts of every other U.S. state are subject to my don't-go-there advice.)

This book is all about proper perspective, and toward that end, *Don't Go There* will try to avoid the obvious.

So, while they may be referenced, I'm not going to tell you not to go to war zones, areas of civil disturbances, and other well-known hot spots, like Three Mile Island. You don't need me to tell you to stay away from Baghdad or Mogadishu.

I'll also stay away from U.S. State Department advisories and warnings. Again, I firmly believe that in most cases, the advisories alone do not paint a complete picture of compelling reasons not to go someplace.

Instead, I'll caution you against going to what I call the *not* spots, referenced by pollution, crime, corruption, highways of death, cancer clusters, even supersized fast-food consumption.

Hopefully, this book will do a more thorough job of detailing the real situation on the ground and what you're likely to encounter should you choose to go there.

Now, I know I will be accused of being unfairly subjective, and there will be claims that I inserted facts out of context, that I somehow have violated the spirit of travel journalism by not being a promoter of travel.

Well, guess what? I have never worked for the travel industry. I report on it—good (and sometimes very good), bad, and yes, quite often ugly. Travel writing is not about being part of a popularity contest. Like all other reporting, it's about presenting—not promoting—facts that allow people to make reasonably intelligent, independent decisions about the choices available to them.

This book attempts to promote nothing but awareness and common sense. Brochure language—syrupy words that end in *-st*—is verboten. You know the words: *best, prettiest, finest* . . . well, you get the picture. And that's the point: With Photoshop programs on computers, even the Love Canal can look like it's the loveliest, nicest, greatest . . . toxic waste site in America.

Is this book not objective? Of course it's not objective. Will some tourist boards and destination marketing folks attack it? Probably. But if you have a brochure that proudly proclaims your region to be the "land of opportunity," yet you have the highest unemployment rate in the state, I'd say you've got some explaining to do.

You can't be the "island of enchantment" and at the same time have one of the highest murder rates in the world. Well, you can call yourself that, but that's why I'm here to put things in proper, real-world perspective.

So, let's put it in perspective. When you read a chapter on polluted cities or corrupt governments or really bad airports, does that mean you should absolutely not go there? Not necessarily. I'd be the first to argue that travel is a right, and that any and all travel—no matter where—should never be restricted.

This book is all about creating, or at the very least redefining, your own personal travel IQ. Travel doesn't have to be about checking off boxes on your wish list. It's not a contest, and there are no prizes for winning the race. Instead, it may be time to be a contrarian traveler—to also value your travel based on where you *don't* go.

You probably know about a very successful book written by Patricia Schultz that lists the places to see before you die. Part of the reason for its success, I would suggest, is a sort of desperation on the part of many of us who feel compelled to go somewhere—perhaps anywhere—now, rather than later.

I understand that mentality. But as long as we're being desperate and worried about a ticking clock, then how about all the places you should probably die before you see . . . at least for now?

If you still want to go there, no points will be deducted from your final score, but don't say I didn't warn you. . . .

AIR POLLUTION

IF YOU GO THERE, DON'T BREATHE

Of course, there is no real scientific metric that can quantify the impact of bad air in small, medium, or large doses based on the time you spend at a destination as a traveler. But let's just say good air is in short supply in some places. As far as I'm concerned, you're going to want to miss them, or if you do go, hold your breath.

U.S. Cities

In May 2008, the American Lung Association released its *State of the Air* report, gathered from 700 U.S. counties' data for the years 2004 to 2006. The report measures three types of air pollution: short-term particle pollution, year-round particle pollution, and ozone pollution. The kind you should be concerned about is small particles (10 microns or smaller), which can get lodged deep in your lungs and even pass into your bloodstream. Even short-term, these particles can make breathing difficult and exacerbate preexisting conditions, such as asthma. Trust me, spending even a few days choking on soot, fumes, or carbon emissions is no treat.

The *State of the Air* report grades cities on a color-coded scale that ranges from green (healthy air) to purple (hazardous air). Here's what the researchers found.

- One in 10 people in the United States lives in areas with unhealthy levels of all three types of pollution.

THE MOST POLLUTED U.S. CITIES IN 2008

OZONE	SHORT-TERM PARTICLE POLLUTION	YEAR-ROUND PARTICLE POLLUTION
Los Angeles, CA	Pittsburgh, PA	Los Angeles, CA
Bakersfield, CA	Los Angeles, CA	Pittsburgh, PA
Visalia-Porterville, CA	Fresno, CA	Bakersfield, CA
Houston, TX	Bakersfield, CA	Birmingham, AL
Fresno-Madera, CA	Birmingham, AL	Visalia-Porterville, CA
Sacramento, CA	Logan, UT	Atlanta, GA
Dallas–Fort Worth, TX	Salt Lake City, UT	Cincinnati, OH
New York, NY–Newark, NJ	Sacramento, CA	Fresno-Madera, CA
Washington, DC–Baltimore, MD	Detroit, MI	Hanford-Corcoran, CA
Baton Rouge, LA	Washington, DC–Baltimore, MD	Detroit, MI

Source: *American Lung Association's 2008* State of the Air *report*

- Two of five U.S. residents live in counties that have unhealthy levels of either ozone or particle pollution.

- Nearly one-third of the U.S. population lives in areas with unhealthy levels of ozone.

- More than one-quarter of the people in the United States live in areas with unhealthy short-term levels of particle pollution.

- One in six people in the United States lives in areas with unhealthy year-round levels of particle pollution.

Also aiding in ranking the world's worst air-polluted cities is the Blacksmith Institute, a New York City–based independent environmental nongovernmental organization (NGO) that combats air pollution worldwide.

As you can see from the chart above, California is home to almost half of the cities that made it onto that list, and home to the two areas with the worst air quality in the United States: the San Joaquin Valley, in central California, and the city of Los Angeles, in Southern California. Let's take a look at some of the worst offenders in California, and in the rest of the country.

Arvin, California (San Joaquin Valley)

About 105 miles northwest of Los Angeles, you might be tempted to pull over to explore a quiet California farming community. Well, think again. The tiny city of Arvin, sequestered in the San Joaquin Valley 20 miles southeast of Bakersfield, doesn't so much cause pollution as bear the brunt of it, serving as the final destination of air pollution from bigger cities. Things have gotten so bad that the U.S. Environmental Protection Agency (EPA) has dubbed Arvin "the most polluted city in America." Now, that's a pretty frightening thought, considering that we're talking about an agricultural community of about 15,000 people.

So, where does all the bad air come from? It's deceiving. The reality is, the situation mostly boils down to geography. Located in the bowl-shaped San Joaquin Valley, Arvin collects wandering swaths of tainted air from San Francisco and Los Angeles. Add in heavy diesel pollution from the local agricultural industry and traffic on nearby Interstate 5 and you have the recipe for the nation's worst air quality.

Arvin also contends with the highest levels of ozone in its air. The EPA estimates that from 2004 to 2006, smog contributed to ozone levels that were above national acceptable averages (0.075 parts per million) about 73 days of the year—that's the highest rate in the country. (For comparison, San Francisco Bay's average exceeded acceptable levels only 4 days during the same period of time.)

Arvin residents have been advised to stay indoors when it's really bad— but because of the high number of field workers living in the city, this can be impossible, as families' entire livelihoods often depend on working outside. Kern County, which includes Arvin, has a childhood asthma rate of 17.5 percent, as compared with 12.2 percent nationwide. Things get so bad in Arvin that school systems often have to keep some kids inside during recess as they deal with runny noses, watery eyes, excessive coughing, and difficulty breathing. On the worst days, kids wear masks over their faces when they go outside—that is, if they're well enough to go outside in the first place.

Bakersfield, California (San Joaquin Valley)
Only 20 miles northwest of Arvin, Bakersfield has heavy traffic on Route 99 and Interstate 5. Add in heat and bowl-shaped geography, and you get some nasty air.

Ranked number two on the American Lung Association's list of the most ozone-polluted cities in the United States (behind Los Angeles but ahead of Visalia-Porterville, Houston, and Fresno-Madera), Bakersfield has more than 308,000 residents, making it the city with the highest population in Kern County, one of the fastest-growing regions in the country. Three years ago, there was a booming demand for building permits here, even though the population was already dense enough. As a result, construction pollution is becoming a real problem in Bakersfield and has undoubtedly contributed to the city's poor air quality.

Fresno, California (San Joaquin Valley)

In a frightening analogy, the Sierra Club says of Fresno, in central California, that "simply breathing in this area, one of the country's richest agricultural regions, is as bad as smoking a pack of cigarettes a day," especially for those who work primarily outdoors and live in the poorer neighborhoods located close to the highway.

Fresno has a bursting agricultural sector and a booming population—so its noxious air is getting to people on a daily basis. With a total population of 891,756 in Fresno County, more than 38 percent of those people (342,212 individuals) suffer from conditions such as pediatric asthma, adult asthma, chronic bronchitis, emphysema, cardiovascular disease, and diabetes, all of which are exacerbated by Fresno's fetid air and frequently hot weather.

Ranking in the top 10 in multiple air pollution categories, Fresno has some of the worst air in the country. According to the American Lung Association's 2008 *State of the Air* report, Fresno is the fifth-most-polluted city by ozone—specifically, Fresno received an ozone grade of F, with an average number of 96 days a year marked as orange ozone alert and 4 days spent on red alert for ozone. Additionally, Fresno has an average of 99 days when particulate matter is on orange alert and 15 days when it's in the red. Though Fresno has so far steered clear of the dreaded purple rating for air contamination, it still fails miserably.

Los Angeles, California

Since the American Lung Association first began compiling its now-integral *State of the Air* report in the late 1990s, Los Angeles has always been at the top of the list—and that's not a good thing.

But when the 2008 *State of the Air* was released, Los Angeles had a moment of jubilation when it slipped to the number two spot for the most polluted air in the country. After nearly a decade at the top, the Los Angeles region was dethroned by the Pittsburgh metropolitan area for the number one spot on the short-term particle list.

Despite its new, better ranking, Los Angeles still takes the soot cake with an overall grade of F from the American Lung Association. In the 2008 report, Los Angeles had, on average, 141 days in the orange alert zone for high ozone concentration, 26 days spent in the red zone, and 7 days spent in the most severe (purple) zone.

Because L.A. is surrounded by mountain ranges on three sides, the city's geography has as much to do with its poor air as do the world-famous, bumper-to-bumper traffic and warm weather, which exacerbate already-crappy air into a deadly accumulation of pollutants. Think about this: Los Angeles County has 9,935,475 residents, and 3,738,560 of those people live with the American Lung Association's standard list of conditions—pediatric asthma, adult asthma, chronic bronchitis, emphysema, cardiovascular disease, or diabetes.

Birmingham, Alabama

Birmingham is the largest city in Alabama, in the seat of Jefferson County—one of two counties in Alabama to receive a grade of F for air quality in 2008 (Shelby County being the other). One of the top 10 most polluted cities in the country, according to the American Lung Association, ranking fifth for short-term particle pollution, Birmingham is making its first appearance on the list for ozone pollution. And it's about time.

Of the 656,700 people in Jefferson County, 306,078 suffer from conditions such as asthma, bronchitis, diabetes, and heart disease. That's 47 percent of its population, and it's not as if those people just acquired those diseases this year.

Birmingham is bowl shaped (like Los Angeles and the San Joaquin Valley), encouraging poor air quality, with 98 days a year spent in the orange alert zone for particle pollution and 3 weeks spent in orange alert for high ozone levels.

Most of Birmingham's pollution can be attributed to its glory days as a one-industry steel town, which, according to City-Data.com, included automotive manufacturing and distribution, and machinery and industrial equipment production, all of which are pollutant-laden operations. But, with close access to the Warrior-Tombigbee River System, which joins the Tennessee-Tombigbee Waterway, Birmingham is still a shipping and transportation haven. City-Data.com notes that "eight airlines, five air cargo services, approximately 100 truck lines, four railroads, and more than ten barge lines" call Birmingham home. Undoubtedly, as Birmingham's transportation sector grows, pollution will get worse.

Detroit, Michigan

Forbes magazine says, "Detroit not only has a bad count in short-term particles but an undistinguished record in water pollution and other health

Top Asthma Capitals in 2008

1. Knoxville, Tennessee
2. Tulsa, Oklahoma
3. Milwaukee, Wisconsin
4. Atlanta, Georgia
5. Memphis, Tennessee
6. Allentown, Pennsylvania
7. Charlotte, North Carolina
8. Greenville, South Carolina
9. St. Louis, Missouri
10. Greensboro, North Carolina

hazards. The good news is that particle count appears to be improving. However, Motor City is built around cars and not public transportation, and the improvement doesn't look like it's moving very fast."

According to the 2008 *State of the Air* report, Detroit experiences an average of 3 days a year in the orange alert zone for high ozone levels but, luckily, has no red or purple days in the same category. For particle pollution, Detroit gets worse, experiencing an average of 1½ months in the orange alert zone and 4 days in the red zone.

And here's a good guess as to why Motor City deserves an overall grade of F for air quality, according to the American Lung Association. Let's run the numbers: Detroit has 911,402 of Wayne County's 1,971,853 people, and 46 percent of Detroit residents suffer from types of asthma or emphysema, diabetes, chronic bronchitis, or cardiovascular disease.

Pittsburgh, Pennsylvania

Back in 2003, writer Karen Roebuck described this city: "Perhaps the clearest thing about the air in the Pittsburgh area is that it's bad." She was right then, and, sadly, she's still right now.

Pittsburgh sits in southwestern Pennsylvania's Allegheny County, which has a population of about 1.2 million—more than 300,000 of whom reside in the city. In Allegheny County, the American Lung Association figures that 626,049 individuals suffer from diabetes and lung- and heart-related conditions.

Pittsburgh has an average of 13 days annually spent with ozone ratings in the orange alert category and 1 day in the red. In the extremely detrimen-

Eternal Flames

If you happen to be driving north on Route 61 through Pennsylvania, you might end up at a detour that takes you through an abandoned hill town . . . but what you may not know is that you're driving through an area that once was a thriving coal mining town—which now, with the few buildings that are left, barely qualifies as a ghost town. In May of 1962, a pile of garbage in Centralia, Pennsylvania, caught fire. Though the fire itself shouldn't have been a big deal, it ignited coalfields lying just below the surface, turning into a fire that has been burning continuously for more than 46 years. Appalling smoke and poisonous gases wander through skeletons of trees that have been turned the color of rust. And let's not forget the stench: The area smells like rotten eggs—a result of the hydrogen sulfide permeating the air.

For 20 years, people tried flushing the mines with water and drilling into the veins of coal to at least contain, if not extinguish, the fire. But the amount of coal in this stretch of land made this a losing battle. Even 25 years ago, the United States Office of Surface Mining (OSM) estimated that $663 million would be required to do the job. Finally, all efforts were abandoned, and so was the town. The fire has whittled this once-burgeoning mining community's population of 1,100 people to about 20, and nearly all the buildings have been razed. Some experts estimate that the fire could continue to burn for the next 100 years. Something to, uh, pass on to future generations!

tal particle pollution category, the city spends a whopping 156 days a year in orange alert and an average of 20 days in red.

In fact, when the 2008 *State of the Air* report was released, Janice Nolen, the American Lung Association's assistant vice president of national policy and advocacy, explained Pittsburgh's rise to the top: "It's not that Pittsburgh has gotten worse," she reported. "It's that Los Angeles has gotten better."

If you didn't guess already, Pittsburgh gets an overall grade of F from the American Lung Association.

International Cities

Ours isn't the only country that suffers from poor air quality—breathing overseas can be just as difficult. Even if you don't suffer long-term effects from heavily polluted air, you're likely to notice a difference in your breathing, lung capacity, and overall health while traveling abroad. This especially holds true for people who are elderly, pregnant, or very young. With the help of the Blacksmith Institute and the World Bank's World Development Indicators database, we came up with our list of places where simply going and breathing might hurt you.

Tianying, China

China may be the country worst off in terms of air quality, with 7 out of 10 of all the nation's cancer deaths related to pollution. And this is according to the Chinese government, so the numbers may actually be worse!

Located in Anhui Province in China's northeastern Rust Belt, Tianying is one of the myriad industrial cities throughout the country. More than one authoritative source has described it as one of the world's "hellholes," and in June 2000, the State Administration of Environmental Protection (SEPA) designated Tianying as one of China's top eight most polluted cities.

According to some estimates, the city's entire population of 140,000 people has potentially been affected by the extensive mining and ore processing that occurs in this city, and most of those affected suffer from lead and other heavy metal poisoning. Some of the worst symptoms of lead poisoning, most often experienced by Tianying's children and elderly, are lowered IQs, learning disabilities, eyesight problems, hearing impairment, and kidney malfunction. Not things you want to risk—even in the short term.

Tianying is the epicenter of the Chinese lead industry, producing half of the country's quantity. As a result, air and soil concentrations of the metal are 8.5 to 10 times the national health standards, and it is leaking into food sources such as wheat. Lead levels are sometimes 24 times Chinese acceptability standards—which is unfortunate, because it's not as if China is refusing to make changes. In fact, the country's restrictions on lead are much tighter than those in the United States.

Chongqing, China

You might be familiar with Chongqing as a starting point on the ever-popular Yangtze (Chang) River cruise. But what you may not know is that this is one of the fastest-growing urban centers in the world. With a population of more than three million and growing, Chongqing is one of the largest cities in China—and with its large amount of coal combustion by industry and power plants, it's one of the most polluted, too.

The majority of Chongqing's pollution comes from steel factories that crank out loads of automotive and machinery parts, and also dangerous levels of pollutants that immediately get trapped in the air.

Beijing, China

In 2007, Beijing saw 246 "blue sky" days (exactly what it sounds like). The year before that, there were 241 blue sky days. After the announcement that Beijing would host the 2008 Olympic Games, the world waited to see whether the city could clean up its act in time. By the time the Olympics rolled around, the city had reached its goal number of blue sky days . . . but we're still talking relative terms here. Beijing's pre-Olympic air quality, in terms of particle pollution, vehicle emissions, and smog, was even worse than that of Los Angeles in 1984, Atlanta in 1996, and Athens in 2004.

The World Health Organization lists Beijing's pollution levels as up to triple the recommended maximum. The city is home to 11.8 million people and a major coal industry and is blanketed by a thick layer of pollution year-round, but the levels of fine particulate matter (i.e., dust) and ozone skyrocket in the summertime.

So some 2008 athletes weren't about to take the risk. Case in point: The world's fastest long-distance runner, Haile Gebrselassie, announced that he would not compete in the Olympic marathon. Why? The Ethiopian athlete suffers from asthma and knew Beijing's air quality would inhibit his performance in the race. He did, however, run the 10,000-meter event . . . and came in sixth.

Other athletes combated the effects of pollution by donning masks when they arrived in Beijing for the games. That may work as a competition strategy, but what about the nearly 12 million people who live in Beijing on a daily basis?

Chongqing's ever-expanding skyline is a symbol of the city's economic success and growing population. But good luck finding that skyline. Even on favorable air days, a thick haze hangs over the city, and the only things you can clearly see in the sky are construction cranes working on new bridges and high-rises.

Cairo, Egypt

Do you know what gets me about the air pollution in Cairo? Even Cairo's tourism Web site cops to the city's flaws! Right there, along with the rest of the city's statistics, the site says, "Cairo has serious air pollution from motor vehicles and factories, which combine to make Cairo's air pollution level one of the highest in the world. Air quality is severe and comprises 2.1 percent of all deaths."

The air in Cairo causes people's eyes to water and sting, while their chests get clogged, meaning that taking a breath is a struggle. Lead particles aren't just airborne; they're also in the food and water. In fact, the amount of lead found in the dust on some of Cairo's playgrounds is significant enough to qualify the areas, under American standards, as hazardous waste sites.

As usual, industry is the main problem. Arab Abu Sayed, an industrial site just outside of downtown Cairo, is home to almost 200 mud-brick factories, Egypt's largest conglomeration of greenhouse-gas emitters. Though the capital city is making efforts to add green spaces and parks, the tourism site still warns of harmful air. And until that changes, I'll skip Cairo in favor of less-polluted parts of Egypt!

Delhi, India

At the number two spot on the World Bank's most-polluted list, Delhi, India, boasts a cornucopia of unhealthy air qualities, and one of the biggest culprits is vehicle emissions.

Though Delhi's air quality improved after public transportation was outfitted with compressed natural gas in 2002, the problem has returned with a vengeance. A recent boom in private vehicle ownership, plus the introduction of the world's cheapest car (the Nano, which costs about $2,500), has raised Delhi's air pollution closer to the levels of pre–compressed natural gas days, leaving locals with increased chances of contracting respiratory diseases such as chronic bronchial asthma and lung infections.

The main problem with private vehicles in Delhi is that they're backsliding. Cars made after 2005 that have the same engine size as cars a few years older emit more carbon monoxide than their predecessors. Fuel economies also have gotten worse, falling from 16 to 13 kilometers per liter. And the popularity of cost-effective diesel cars has had an adverse effect on the city's air quality. According to the Society of Indian Automobile Association Manufacturers, the annual rate of increase in diesel cars was twice that of petrol models; a third of the cars in Delhi were diesel as of 2006, and that number is expected to rise to half by 2010.

Calcutta, India

If you need a statistic to sum up the devastating effects of the air in Calcutta, try this: 70 percent of the city's population must cope with an array of respiratory disorders including lung cancer, asthma, and general breathing trouble. Currently ranked as the third-most-polluted city worldwide by the World Bank, Calcutta (also known as Kolkata) has overtaken Delhi as India's pollution capital.

Chittaranjan National Cancer Institute (CNCI), one of India's premier research bodies, spent 6 years investigating the realities of Calcutta's air pollution and published its findings in 2007. The institute found that Calcutta's high rates of lung cancer—18.4 cases per 100,000 people—directly related to the city's air pollution and far surpassed Delhi's rate of 13.34 cases per 100,000.

Apathy may be a big part of the problem. In 2006, only 300,000 registered vehicles turned up for emissions tests—that's out of 1.5 million registered cars in Calcutta.

Just how bad is it now? After CNCI published its findings in 2007, Calcutta's 11 city police stations received breathing machines, allowing policemen access to additional stores of oxygen as they work in the streets for hours on end. Think that's crazy? These oxygen concentrators are of the same caliber used by patients in hospitals. Still, things in Calcutta have gotten to the point where even that may not be enough to help in the long run, as deadly particulate matter may already be lodged deep within residents' lungs.

Mexico City, Mexico

Situated at an elevation of some 7,400 feet, Mexico City has long been Mexico's most polluted city, and it's certainly up there as one of the world's most polluted.

Mexico City has two problems: Its uniquely high altitude results in thinner air, and the city is surrounded on three sides by mountains. The World Health Organization claims that ozone levels there exceed acceptable standards up to 300 days of the year.

Scientists have given Mexico City the old college try, making concerted efforts to discover the causes of its continued pollution. Turns out that the problem is at the top of many official to-do lists, but with such ridiculous geography, it seems the city may be a lost cause.

Who's Smoking the Most?

Industry isn't the only culprit causing air pollution. People are lending a hand (and a lung), too.

The international research group Euromonitor International calculated how many cigarettes were sold in 2006. Each figure below is in billions.

Asia Pacific—577

Eastern Europe—443

Western Europe—383

Latin America—249

United States/Canada—210

Middle East/Africa—132

Australasia—20

In 1997, Mexico City underwent the first-ever detailed measurements of its air and corresponding pollutants. The results showed that the pollutants that caused "stinging eyes and lungs" were akin to those that plagued 1970s Los Angeles. Mexico City's pollution concentrations peaked at 9 a.m. and 7 p.m., with particle concentrations exceeding EPA acceptability standards seven times, one of those being more than triple the standard amount.

According to the Blacksmith Institute, the city has met four of the six air-quality requirements: lead, sulfur dioxide, carbon monoxide, and nitrogen oxides. Normally, this would be a good thing, but the two big ones—ozone and particulate matter—remain beyond acceptable standards.

Some good news: In June 2008, Mexico City launched a green project that will place extensive gardens on public rooftops to help combat air pollution. This urban reforestation project will start by covering the city's municipal transit authority building—that's 1,190 square meters—with shrubbery and plants. In addition to aesthetic improvement, the green project will help catch rainwater, insulate buildings, and capture particles before they reach the lungs of humans on city streets below.

WATER POLLUTION

DON'T DRINK THE WATER, REALLY

Every resort brochure shows pristine beaches. The sun is always setting at just the right place in the photo. The happy couple is always frolicking on the untouched sand. The size-2, surgically enhanced models can predictably be found posing in the water.

But before you take your next beach vacation, here are some must-miss water locations. But if you go, you might want to bring a haz-mat suit along with the sunscreen.

U.S. Sites

Great Pacific Garbage Patch

Attention, cruise passengers and long-distance boaters: Would you believe there's a great big floating island of trash in the Pacific Ocean?

Much of the plastic that we use and throw away winds up congregating in a trash pile that has been dubbed "the Great Pacific Garbage Patch" by Algalita Marine Research Foundation, a nonprofit environmental protection organization based in Long Beach, California.

Greenpeace, which calls the pile the "Trash Vortex," reports that 100 million tons of plastic is produced in the United States each year, much of which gets thrown away; 10 percent of it winds up floating in the ocean. About 20 percent of this trash comes from ships, and the rest comes from sources on land. About 3.5 million tons of garbage has ended up in the Garbage Patch, making it the size of Texas! Two whirlpools of plastic converge and connect with a "highway" of trash, causing more trash to come in than go out. However, how deep the debris extends is unknown.

Greenpeace says that at least 267 marine species have suffered from some kind of ingestion or entanglement with this giant mass of marine debris. Sunlight, salt water, and currents break down plastic, so between the pieces of trash floats microscopic plastic, which absorbs toxins like a sponge. Near the surface of the water alone, "the plastic outweighed plankton six to one," reported Steve Smith, formerly of Greenpeace, now at Futerra Sustainability Communications.

The patch dates back to the years following World War II, when we began relying on synthetic materials, and worsened in the 1980s and 1990s as we increased our use of plastic bottles and bags. What is alarming is that consumption of plastics worldwide is only increasing. This gathering of junk has an international flair—there are labels written both in English and in Asian languages. And this floating cesspool of trash isn't just not going anywhere; it's getting bigger.

While the Garbage Patch will hardly be a pit stop on your next trip to Japan, there are plenty of beaches in Hawaii that are directly in its path.

Kamilo Beach, Hawaii

This is truly one of the trashiest beaches in the world, covered in an endless swath of plastic. Located at the southernmost point on Hawaii's Big Island, it once was a location where native Hawaiians gathered logs for canoes, but now it houses a large amalgam of plastic debris, thanks to the trade winds.

Shark Attacks

Before you go for a dip, keep in mind that bacteria aren't the only dangerous threat. Cue the *Jaws* theme song, because some locations are fraught with shark attacks.

The United States mainland and waters in Hawaii traditionally account for nearly half of the world's shark attacks, but you can pretty much count on Florida to lead the pack, with 32 attacks in 2007, up from 23 in 2006.

Known as the "World's Shark-Bite Capital" for 2007, Volusia County, Florida (which includes Daytona Beach), had 17 incidents. And the beach you want to watch out for is New Smyrna Beach.

Adam Walters, a consultant for Greenpeace International, explained that as currents sweep along the beach, a new type of sand, consisting of small plastic fragments washed ashore, forms a layer on top of the beach's real sand.

Kahuku Beach, Hawaii

Trash continually washes ashore on this Honolulu beach, making it the last place you'd want to go suntanning or swimming. In fact, the only reason to venture here is to research how plastic affects our environment.

Nets, tires, golf balls, and buoys from boats languish on this beach. Though cleanups occasionally occur, it's impossible to keep the beach plastic- and garbage-free. Don't believe me? A Greenpeace team once found 410 golf balls and spelled out the word *TRASH*—with each letter measuring at least a foot across.

Okay, so a couple of beaches may be affected by an environmental disaster located far out in the Pacific. But what about waters that are a little closer to home?

Onondaga Lake, Syracuse, New York

Just about 1 mile by 4.6 miles, this small lake in Syracuse, New York, is something very special. It is, according to Joseph Heath, general counsel for the Onondaga Nation, the most polluted lake in the United States. Now, that's saying a lot.

Containing about 35 billion gallons of water, Onondaga has "suffered from a century of industrial dumping" and contains high levels of phosphorus, ammonia, nitrate, and bacterial contamination resulting from water runoff after storms.

For years, the city of Syracuse dumped sewage into the lake, while other pollutants, such as polychlorinated biphenyls (PCB) waste, which flows from a tributary, also affected the quality of the water.

One of the biggest polluters of the lake was Honeywell International, a multibillion-dollar corporation that included Solvay Process Company and Allied Chemical. In 1884, Solvay Process Company began producing sodium carbonate, or soda ash, on the lake's western shores, which resulted in salty by-products being dumped into the water at the rate of up to 6 million gallons a day, raising the levels of chloride, calcium, and sodium. Later, Allied Chemical and Dye Company produced chlorine, which involved using mercury cells that—you guessed it—ended up in the lake. According to the New York State Department of Environmental Protection, between 1956 and 1970, an estimated 165,000 pounds of mercury was dumped into Onondaga's waters.

This once-pristine lake used to be a major fishing spot, but when mercury was found in the lake's waters in 1970, fishing was banned altogether. In the past 5 years, mercury levels in fish have increased threefold, and the fish are affected beyond federal food standards. According to the nonprofit organization Onondaga Lake Partnership, approximately 7 million cubic yards of the lake sediments are contaminated with mercury— 100 to 400 tons in the lake bottom alone, penetrating at least 25 feet deep. Because the bottom of the lake is so polluted, it is its very own Superfund—part of the EPA's National Priorities list for hazardous substances, pollutants, and contaminants. The lake, in total, has eight septic Superfund sites.

Lake Pontchartrain, Louisiana

It seems that this lake just can't get a break. Until a major restoration began in the early 1990s, it was referred to as a "cesspool" for almost a half century. The last time the lake was healthy enough for swimming was in the early 1960s. According to Carlton Dufrechou, executive director of the Lake Pontchartrain Basin Foundation, "Fifteen years ago the lake was a mess all the time," mostly from storm-water runoff and sewage overflows from New Orleans, untreated sewage discharged from growing suburban communities, agricultural discharges, and industries such as dredging the lake's bottom for shells used in construction of roads.

However, because of the efforts of countless individuals, organizations, and agencies, the lake made a near-miraculous recovery and was suitable for swimming again by 2000. Then, in 2005, Hurricane Katrina's floodwaters polluted the 630-square-mile Lake Pontchartrain with an over-200-million-gallon stew of contaminants, including sewage, the contents of underground storage tanks, household and industrial chemicals, and oil and gas. Amazingly, once the polluted floodwaters were pumped out, the lake sprang back to health in just 3 months. However, in April 2008, the lake's clarity "went down the tubes" when the Bonnet Carré Spillway was opened to allow the Mississippi River to drain into the lake after heavy rains and spring floods upstream.

Dufrechou described the lake's condition then as "chocolate milk." Two months later, Lake Pontchartrain experienced three algae blooms. That summer, Mother Nature let the river cure itself, and in mid-July, algae was no longer visible, the lake's clarity was improving, fish were returning, and even a few dolphins and manatees were sighted.

Lake Champlain, Vermont

In 1999, two dogs died after ingesting Lake Champlain's blue-green algae-covered water. How bad is that?

According to the Conservation Law Foundation, Lake Champlain in Vermont has been polluted with an abundance of phosphorus for the past 30 years, and it's only getting worse in several parts of the lake. The main culprit responsible for the high phosphorus levels is urban development.

You Left Your *What* in San Francisco?

Here's something gross that you probably didn't know about: sewage spills in San Francisco Bay.

That's right, on January 31, 2008, a worker failed to set up enough pumps to handle all the water in the Mill Valley plant, causing nearly three million gallons of partially treated sewage and storm water to spill off the Marin County coast and into Richardson Bay, part of San Francisco Bay. The next month, a pump failure at San Quentin prison caused 1,500 gallons of raw sewage to spill into the bay.

And that's not all. According to center director Brooke Langston, of the Richardson Bay Audubon Center & Sanctuary, more than 107 sewage spills—each exceeding 1,000 gallons—contaminated San Francisco Bay in 2007. And that wasn't even the bulk of it—spills of less than 1,000 gallons went unreported. Why is this happening? In general, outdated infrastructure leads to failing and malfunctioning pumps. The good news is that, after those two large spills in early 2008, the rules were changed so that all spills containing sewage have to be reported within 2 hours.

After the January spill, warnings were posted in San Francisco and Marin counties at beaches such as Crissy Field, Baker Beach, China Beach, and Aquatic Park. In the first 2 months of 2008, beaches were closed for about 4 days. Similarly, area beaches were closed for more than a week in 2007 when a cargo ship smashed into the Bay Bridge, dumping 58,000 gallons of fuel, which affected 40 miles of beaches.

The water often looks cloudy and green and smells foul, due to algae blooms, and the depletion of the lake's oxygen has affected fish. During dry, hot weather, the blue-green algae actually can become toxic. Beaches along the lake are frequently closed in order to safeguard human and animal health, but Essex Beach in New York State has been permanently closed.

If you think that's bad, consider this: According to the Vermont Natural Resources Council, 126 rivers and lakes in Vermont don't meet the normal minimum water-quality standards, and storm-water runoff tarnishes the water quality of 26 streams. These bodies of water actually are deemed "impaired" because of the amount of pollution they possess. Contaminants include sediment, nutrients such as phosphorus and nitrogen, toxics, and pathogens, which are known to cause disease in humans. Bottom line: Don't plan on swimming or even catching fish in these waters.

Gulf Coast States

If you have a sensitive stomach, you may want to skip this section. What would you say about a flesh-eating bacteria that exists near our nation's shores?

In 2004, three Houston men were infected with the bacteria *Vibrio vulnificus* while wade-fishing in the Gulf of Mexico near Galveston and Port O'Connor. One victim, a 38-year-old man, was reportedly in the water for only about 15 minutes and ended up in the hospital 2 days later. Another victim had to have part of his leg amputated and suffered kidney failure.

V. vulnificus is naturally present in warm seawater, particularly in Gulf Coast states. The Texas Department of Health expects *V. vulnificus* to be located everywhere in the Gulf of Mexico, since these organisms thrive in warm, salty water, and levels increase as temperatures rise.

V. vulnificus is closely related to the bacteria that causes cholera. People who are healthy but ingest *V. vulnificus* may experience vomiting, diarrhea, and abdominal pain. For those who have compromised immune systems, especially those with liver disease, *V. vulnificus* can infect the bloodstream, resulting in fever and chills, decreased blood pressure (also known as septic shock), and large, fluid-filled blisters and skin lesions.

People can become infected with the bacteria if they have an open wound that becomes exposed to contaminated seawater. Phyllis Kozarsky, MD, a professor of medicine and infectious diseases at Emory University School of

Medicine and an expert on *V. vulnificus,* says, "The bacteria gets in there and sets up shop." Severely painful, it can rapidly spread through the body's tissues, causing skin to blister and become red, hot, and very tender. Blackened areas of dead skin and underlying tissues can develop. Those infected may have a fever as well. If someone comes down with these symptoms, he or she should immediately head to a hospital and be evaluated.

The bacteria can also be ingested by eating raw or poorly cooked contaminated seafood, especially oysters. In fact, *V. vulnificus* is the cause of 95 percent of all seafood-related deaths in the United States. Because mollusks, such as oysters, are filter feeders, Dr. Kozarsky says they can "develop high concentrations of bacteria from water."

So where are the infections happening?

Before 2007, the bacteria was not tracked nationally, but the CDC and the states of Alabama, Florida, Louisiana, Mississippi, and Texas collaborated to survey the number of infections breaking out in the Gulf Coast region.

In 2007, Texas reported 26 cases of *V. vulnificus* infection. Eleven stemmed from water contact, 12 resulted from eating shellfish, and three were from unknown causes or from other types of exposure. Most cases occurred in highly visited fishing and swimming areas.

According to the Florida Department of Health, there were a total of 22 cases of *V. vulnificus* in that state in 2007. Ten of those were exposures through wounds, seven resulted from eating oysters, four were from unknown exposures, and one was from ingesting clams.

After Hurricane Katrina in 2005, the CDC discovered 22 new cases of

Lake Washington, Mississippi

According to the Mississippi Department of Environmental Quality, polluted runoff is the leading cause of water-quality problems in Mississippi, and Lake Washington may be one of the most harmful sources of water pollution in the state. The EPA reports that each year, erosion dumps some 12 tons of soil per acre into the lake, along with pesticides and fertilizers that stimulate algae growth. Locals noticed the dramatic effect in the summer of 1990, when a rare blue-green algae bloomed across the lake's stagnant water and gathered on the shores. The algae produced deadly toxins that killed 14 dogs that drank the lake water.

V. vulnificus illness, five of which were fatal, among residents or displaced residents of Mississippi and Louisiana.

Dr. Kozarsky's advice? If your immune system is compromised or you have cuts, scrapes, or scratches on your skin, ask your medical provider whether you should go swimming in the Gulf Coast region, which includes Louisiana, Texas, and the Mexican coast. And don't eat raw shellfish from these areas. Or, just take my advice and don't go there!

Now consider this: There are currently no state departments of health that regularly test for the bacteria in order to warn people against swimming or fishing in the waters. How scary is that?

Anacostia River, Washington, DC

The pollution in the Anacostia River has been called "the waste of Congress." The river starts with tributaries located in Prince George's and Montgomery counties in Maryland, and the river's headwater begins in Bladensburg, Maryland, merging with the Potomac River at Hanes Point and eventually running out into Chesapeake Bay.

The Anacostia is dubbed "the Forgotten River," because most people associate the Potomac with Washington, DC. But when the city was erected between the two rivers, the Anacostia was navigable, used for transportation and shipping goods and services.

Over the years, many of the trees growing along the river were cut down. As a result, contaminated water from the streets and highways now flows into the river, adding dangerous chemicals and carcinogens to the 40 feet of silt already lining the river's bottom. Some researchers consider the silt to be a catch-22, because although it causes the contaminants to remain stagnant in the river, the silt also keeps them from traveling farther, and thus prevents more harm downriver.

The carcinogens in the silt harm the river's fish, which are often infected with noticeable bulbous tumors as a result. Even more alarming: Some people still fish in this river. (Hint: If a fish caught in the Anacostia can double as a nightlight, it's probably best not to eat it.)

Due to the city's antiquated sewer system, snowmelt or even an inch of rain affects the river, traveling into drains to the water and sewage overflow and flushing the water-sewage amalgam into the river. Activists for the river hope to encourage using rain barrels, planting more trees, planting rain guards, and laying permeable pavers so that water seeps into the soil and directly into the water table, instead of flowing to the drains and into the river.

If you were to capture an aerial photo of where the Anacostia and the Potomac meet, you would actually see a line where brown water and blue water meet—the brown being the Anacostia. Now, that's an image you won't see in tourist brochures!

Santa Fe River, New Mexico

You don't have to worry about what fish you might catch in this river—the huge issue here is that the Santa Fe River is threatened by a serious lack of water.

For the past 20 years, the river has been mostly dried up—overgrown with weeds, littered with trash, eroded, blocked by upstream dams that collect water from the mountains. City wells have affected the water table so much that it cannot sustain the river while supplying water to the city of Santa Fe.

City, county, and state governments are budgeting millions of dollars to create parks and trails along the river channel, dubbing their efforts "river restoration." However, if water isn't included in this endeavor, the restoration will be null and void. The City of Santa Fe controls the majority of the river's water, and at the very least needs to restore a trickle.

The river starts in the Sangre de Cristo Mountains and flows 46 miles before reaching the Rio Grande. The first dam was built in 1881, and the river hasn't been the same since—and for the past 20 years, it has been used as a drainage ditch for storm water and to fill reservoirs, so it fails to function as a river in many reaches. The river has been frequently turned off and on, depending on the city's water-system demands, and at one point was shut off almost completely.

Though the river once fed fertile land, the water table sank and caused wells to reach deeper. Many water-dependent plants and animals, local springs, and subsurface aquifers have disappeared almost entirely. On the riverbanks, invasive species such as the Siberian elm are crowding native species, including cottonwoods and willows.

Longtime residents recall fishing in the river for trout, splashing in swimming holes, and even ice-skating, but over time this has pretty much come to an end.

Bottom line: No water, no fish . . . why would you ever go?

Iowa River, Iowa

The nonprofit group American Rivers listed the Iowa River as the third-most-endangered river in America in 2007, and that's saying something. Although the federal Clean Water Act exists, it is weakly enforced here, as the state has not implemented key provisions or allocated appropriate funds to its Department of Natural Resources.

Communities rely on the river for drinking water and recreation, but several polluters have destroyed the river with toxins, nitrates, phosphorus, viruses, bacteria, pathogens, and untreated sewage. Some causes of the pollution are concentrated animal feeding operations (CAFOs), municipal and industrial wastewater treatment facilities, and small rural communities that don't have public sewers. A recent decrease in the freshwater mussel population has been an indicator of high pollution levels, especially since freshwater mussels tend to be more sensitive to pollutants than are other marine life.

The river is easily accessible because it runs through the center of the state, so you might want to go for a stroll along the banks of the murky brown water, but definitely skip that swim!

Kinnickinnic River, Wisconsin

Although the local community has joined together in spirit to restore this river, there is no funding to bring it back to life. The Kinnickinnic River basin, a Milwaukee watershed, covers nearly 850 square miles, and more than 1.5 million people depend on it for day-to-day use. The actual river covers 33 square miles, eventually flowing into the Milwaukee Estuary and Lake Michigan. Sounds great, right? Well, get this: The Milwaukee Estuary and 2.8 miles of the river have been deemed a federal Area of Concern (AoC), due to toxins and the river's urbanization.

Concrete channels, diminishing natural vegetation and stream banks, sewer overflows, and industrial contamination all threaten the river. Polluted storm-water runoff also harms the Kinnickinnic, placing it squarely on American Rivers' 2007 list of the most endangered rivers in America. Plus, toxic pollution created during the rapid urban development between the 1900s and the 1970s has formed into toxic sediments that still poison the river's waters and marine population. The Kinnickinnic now has the smallest fish diversity within the Milwaukee Estuary, and levels of toxins here rival those where fish have cancer.

The communities around the river—which include some of the poorest in Milwaukee—are left with poor-quality drinking water. The boating industry,

Before You Go to Any Beach . . .

To determine the level of water contamination at beaches, local public health officials take samples of the water for analysis. Information they gather is sent to the U.S. EPA and Natural Resources Defense Council (NRDC), where the samples are tested for bacterial, human, and animal waste contamination. On average, 7 percent of the samples collected at beaches nationwide violate public health standards. Depending on the beach, samples are taken daily, weekly, or monthly to monitor conditions.

If you're traveling to a beach, make sure to find out whether it is regularly monitored and whether it has any advisories or closures. This information can be found, among other places, in the NRDC's annual *Testing the Waters* report. Do be aware that a lag time between collecting water samples and posting advisories or closings does exist, since samples must incubate and be tested.

Keep in mind, though, that beaches are not tested for every type of contamination. So, before you take a dive, check to see if the water looks and smells clean. Do you see trash floating in the water or any pet waste on the beach? If so, it's a very bad sign. Swimming in contaminated water can cause you to contract gastroenteritis (stomach flu).

According to the NRDC, "Evidence suggests that current water quality criteria may not be adequate to protect swimmers from all pathogens. Exposure to even a small number of virus particles can cause infection."

Beach closings stem primarily from high bacteria levels, rainfall and storm-water runoff, and events such as sewage leaks. Turns out, in 2007, the number of closing and advisory days at ocean, bay, and Great Lake beaches reached 22,571 days nationwide—the second-highest level since the NRDC began tracking these events 18 years ago.

Based on water-quality tests and public notifications at U.S. beaches (oceans, bays, and Great Lake shores), here are some of the NRDC's worst offenders in 2007 (by percentage exceeding national standards).

Shired Island, Dixie County, Florida	72%
Cedar Island, Taylor County, Florida	66%
Villa Angela State Park, Cuyahoga County, Ohio	64%
Pennoyer Park Beach, Kenosha County, Wisconsin	63%
Euclid State Park, Cuyahoga County, Ohio	59%
Hagen's Cove, Taylor County, Florida	59%
Keaton Beach, Taylor County, Florida	59%
Jackson Park Beach, Cook County, Illinois	56%
Hancock, Ocean County, New Jersey	56%
Doheny State Beach–North Beach, Orange County, California	55%

huge in this area, is also suffering, because the accumulation of contaminated sediment greatly affects recreational and commercial activities.

Neglect is really the main culprit here, and until the government pulls together the funding to bring the Kinnickinnic back to its natural state, my advice is just don't go there.

Neuse River, North Carolina

The Neuse River is threatened by poorly planned development. Large hog operations in the watershed affect this river, and if new plans for development are approved, human sewage, storm-water runoff, and habitat destruction will also cause damage. Because coastal development has started traveling inland, there has been an increase in urbanization in the area's headwaters.

The river, which has more than 3,400 miles of tributaries, starts near Durham and travels 250 miles through Raleigh, flowing into Pamlico Sound. The waters have been polluted for decades, endangering many local species and affecting tourism-friendly activities such as kayaking and sailing. Even scarier, the river has affected the water in Falls Lake, which provides drinking water for 400,000 residents near Raleigh.

The Coastal Plain is home to millions of hogs living in concentrated animal feeding operations, and their waste has overwhelmed the river with nitrogen, phosphorus, and ammonia. The high levels of these nutrients cause an excessive amount of algal buildup, which decreases the water's oxygen and causes outbreaks of *Pfiesteria,* which kills fish and is very harmful to humans.

Although there have been state- and federally mandated pollution reductions, the Neuse River has benefited very little. If more development occurs along the river and its tributaries, any improvements that have been made will be destroyed.

International Sites

Pattaya, Thailand

This used to be a beautiful beach, but I'd avoid it now. Rampant development and intentional neglect of the environment have combined to ruin this place. How did it happen? The answer is simple: Raw sewage continues to be pumped into the sea.

Even when the Thai government passed stricter environmental laws, greedy developers found ways around them. For example, one provision of the law requires that the owners of any new building project with more than 60 units provide adequate sewage and wastewater treatment for the property. Sounds promising. But 300-unit apartment and condo complexes were built, and many of them were still pumping directly from the toilets to the sea.

How did this happen? It's simple—and terrible: The developers sold off pieces of the 300-unit properties in 59-unit blocks, thus circumventing the law. I won't go there. And neither should you, until they clean it all up.

Aral Sea, Uzbekistan

Located between Uzbekistan and an autonomous region of Kazakhstan known as Karakalpakstan, the Aral Sea is a true environmental catastrophe, but no one seems to be paying attention.

Turns out, pollution isn't the main destroyer of the sea (although it's a big part of it); draining is the true culprit. Two main rivers, the Syr Dar'ya and Amu Dar'ya, normally replenish the sea, but they have, since the 1960s, instead been diverted for irrigation uses.

Uzbekistan is the world's second-largest cotton exporter, and since cotton is the world's thirstiest crop—it takes about 2,500 gallons of water to produce just 1 pound of Uzbek cotton—this export nearly sucks the Aral Sea dry. On top of that, toxic dust storms carrying more than 40 million tons of salt-laden particles and chemicals, such as pesticides, blow across the Aral region, drying things out even more.

As the Aral Sea diminished, all 24 native fish species disappeared. The sea once boasted a booming fishing industry, but now it's virtually eradicated. If you were to travel today to some of the areas that were once covered by water, you would see former fishing vessels lying on the bare earth, with camels in the background.

The polluted waters that remain severely harm the well-being of Karakalpakstan's population, and the lack of basic health care has allowed many diseases to fester. Most sources of drinking water do not meet basic standards, and because salt levels are more than four times the World Health Organization's guidelines for acceptability, 40 percent of the population of Karakalpakstan has no access to safe drinking water. If people are exposed to chronic levels of salty drinking water, they can suffer from high blood pressure and kidney and urinary tract diseases.

King River, Australia

The King River is thought to be one of the most polluted rivers in Australia. The Queen River, which feeds into the King, was long used as a dumping ground for the Mount Lyell copper mine in Tasmania. Between 1922 and 1995, the river saw about 1.5 million tons of sulfidic tailings, or ore-washing residue, flow into the river each year. The mine closed in 1995, which greatly alleviated the problem, but the damage from heavy metal poisoning was already done. Almost all aquatic life in the lower King River and the Queen River is dead.

The endpoint of the King River has several dead zones—areas that cannot support any life. Anytime the sediment is disturbed, such as during heavy rainfall, a major fish kill follows.

Part of the Queen River runs through Queenstown, where, because of acid rain, the soil has been contaminated with heavy metals, so virtually no living flora can be found. The hills and valleys are bare, and instead of grass, you see channels of erosion that, oddly enough, resemble the surface of the moon. Revegetation could help alleviate the problem, but the city of Queenstown is largely against this option because the moonscape nature of this region has generated a large amount of tourist traffic.

For now, the King River remains in bad shape, but officials are aiming to rehabilitate marine life in the lower part of the river by neutralizing or removing acid drainage altogether, removing copper, and releasing clean water into the river. But whether the river will ever again sustain normal life remains to be seen.

Groundwater and Coastal Water, Bangladesh

Bangladesh suffers from two types of water pollution: saline contamination and arsenic issues. The coastal zone water technically isn't polluted, but it has a large amount of saline contamination due to the rising sea level. This destroys agriculture and contaminates drinking water, but the zone is also complicated by minor arsenic and iron problems.

Noncoastal zones, however, suffer from severe arsenic issues. Groundwater is extracted for irrigation purposes, and this is where the arsenic develops, resulting in arsenic poisoning in many residents.

Here's how arsenic contamination happens: One of the minerals found in the region's dirt is iron, which sometimes turns into iron oxide, or rust. The rust forms a thin coating on rock particles, and the coating soaks up arsenic from river water. The rock particles then travel downstream and congregate either in the sea or in the river's delta soil and deposit in the Bengal delta. Arsenic is then released into the water.

According to the Royal Society of Chemistry, arsenic found in drinking water is now affecting millions of people in West Bengal and Bangladesh. Arsenic poisoning can cause skin cancer and a large growth of keratin on the feet. For more than 20 years, people living in West Bengal and Bangladesh have tapped into groundwater for drinking by using tube wells, which contain some of the most dire water-quality problems history has ever seen.

Citarum River, Jakarta, Indonesia

Fed by the Citarum River, the West Tarum Canal in Jakarta is in "poor condition," reported the Asian Development Bank (ADB) in February 2007.

The canal provides 80 percent of Jakarta's freshwater supply. "Water pollution is a critical problem in the Citarum river basin, with much of the pollution coming from industrial and urban uses in Bandung, from where it moves down the river," reports ADB.

The 200-mile river is peppered with more than 500 factories, many of which produce chemically treated textiles. During industrialization in the 1980s, factories dumped anything they wanted into the river.

About 20 years ago, the once-flowing river was a prime location for fishermen, but now it's choked by the domestic waste of nine million people and hundreds of factories. The river is thick with rubbish because of the lack of a waste collection service and is navigated by locals, who sift through the filth to salvage anything of minute value—risking contracting a disease.

One of the biggest concerns about the area is that two rivers, one being the Citarum, feed Lake Saguling, where the French constructed the largest power generator in West Java. As contaminants and garbage increasingly bog the river down, experts predict that the generator will malfunction. Bottom line: Anything nasty gets dumped into the river. And it's about to get nastier.

Sarno River, Italy

The Sarno River is extremely polluted. It flows for 15 miles from the Sarno mountain slopes, crossing three provinces, and flows into the Bay of Naples, whose basin covers nearly 500 square miles.

A 2005 study by the University of Naples confirmed that the Sarno River has been violated by pollution for more than 30 years, and high levels of pollutants, such as heavy metals, lurk in the river. Industries including tomato processing, tanneries, and chemical manufacturing contribute to the industrial pollution of the river. Untreated agricultural waste is also dumped.

The chances that residents living in the basin will contract degenerative digestive or respiratory illnesses, bacterial infections, or abnormal cell growth have slowly but steadily increased.

But listen up: Even if you're a tourist, you might be affected. Since the river's polluted waters travel into the Bay of Naples, surrounding seawater is contaminated—and the nearby beaches get polluted as well.

TOXIC PLACES

WHO'S TOXIC NOW?

There are some places that are—or have been—so polluted by toxins that people have died from breathing the air or drinking the water.

Domestically, organizations such as the Sierra Club and Greenpeace and government agencies like the Environmental Protection Agency (EPA) have helped identify these locations, but naming them is only about one-tenth of the battle. Fixing them has been the hardest part.

Internationally, the situation is worse. Remember Chernobyl? Bhopal? Well, those are just two examples out of hundreds, if not thousands, of locations where people have suffered horrifically from toxic pollutants caused by that lethal combination of human error, big-business greed, and government apathy and collusion. One of the leading organizations that identify and combat toxic pollution in developing nations is the Blacksmith Institute. Based on its findings, those of the EPA, and my own travels through some desolate sites, I came up with my list of some of the most toxic places in the world.

U.S. Sites

Cancer Alley

Just the term *Cancer Alley* should be enough to make you turn back, but it all depends on where you're going in the first place. The Mississippi River industrial corridor runs about 80 miles from just northwest of Baton Rouge,

Louisiana, to New Orleans, with giant companies such as Georgia Gulf, Dow, and Shell Chemicals lining the route. Now, whether belching smokestacks and chemical waste leaching into the soil have led directly to elevated levels of cancer in this area is still, technically, up for debate—but the anecdotal evidence is pretty frightening.

According to Rick Hind, legislative director for Greenpeace, there is "an enormous amount of polluting industry sitting on top of communities. . . . For example, Dow Chemical in Baton Rouge has a legal permit to put 550 million gallons of wastewater in the Mississippi River a day."

But developing cancer from contaminated water isn't the only risk—the fear of a Bhopal-like industrial accident is very real here, particularly with the presence of acutely poisonous gases such as ammonia and chlorine. These communities have public service announcements showing how to protect yourself in case of an industrial accident: Reserve a room in the house, turn off the air-conditioning and heating, and put wet towels on the windowsills and any gaps around the doors. Then turn on the radio to see when it's safe to go out.

Still, evacuation plans are sketchy at best, because nobody trusts them. And no one knows what to do first. Think about it—if there are contaminants in the air and a mother has kids in school, should she leave the house to get them, or keep them in the school? If the accident is big enough, it may not even matter.

Take a look at the Mississippi River, and chances are you won't see many kayakers or sailors navigating the mighty waters, past industrial clusters spewing toxic fumes and waste. The days of Huck Finn are no longer.

Hanford, Washington

The first time I visited this area of southeastern Washington State, I couldn't help but notice that the high-school football team's uniforms showed the unmistakable image of a nuclear mushroom cloud. And while that might have been in questionable taste, it did reflect the reality that the Hanford nuclear reactor site employed so many locals.

The complex was built by the federal government in 1943 to produce plutonium for our country's nuclear weapons and played an enormous role in America's history, starting with the Manhattan Project and supplying the plutonium used in the Trinity test site in New Mexico (the first nuclear explosion) and in Nagasaki in 1945.

For decades, the Hanford Site, which sits next to the Columbia River, spewed pollutants, particularly the radioactive element iodine-131, into the air and water. According to the Department of Energy's Hanford offices (the Richland Operations Office and the Office of River Protection), over the course of 50 years, the site produced 450 billion gallons of liquid waste—both radioactive contaminants and hazardous chemicals—that contaminated the groundwater.

In 2005, six people diagnosed with thyroid diseases who lived downwind of the site were chosen to represent their neighbors during a bellwether trial against Hanford contractors, including DuPont (which operated Hanford from 1943 to 1946) and General Electric (which ran it from 1946 to 1965). After 3 days of deliberations, the jury returned with a favorable verdict for two of the plaintiffs, awarding them a total of about $500,000. Three of the cases were dismissed, meaning that the judge found that the plaintiffs' illnesses probably weren't caused by Hanford emissions; the sixth case was deadlocked and declared a mistrial.

In April 2008, a major ruling by the Ninth U.S. Circuit Court of Appeals opened the door for about 2,000 residents who lived downwind of the site between World War II and the start of the cold war to sue the Hanford contractors for radiation damages.

Even though the last of the reactors was decommissioned in 1987, cleanup at Hanford is still decades away from being completed. But, get this, now Hanford offers free public tours of the facilities, for which you can sign up at www5.hanford.gov/publictours. Chances are you won't get sick on a tour—visitors are kept a good distance away—but my advice is, just don't go there!

Indian Point Nuclear Power Plant

You thought nuclear waste was an issue only in vast, far-off places? Try talking to someone in Westchester County, New York. The Indian Point Energy Center, a nuclear power plant on 239 acres of land in the town of Buchanan, 25 miles north of New York City, is a sore subject for many living nearby.

One of Indian Point's three reactors has been decommissioned, but Units 2 and 3, which were built in 1974 and 1976, respectively, still function. The reactors are owned by Entergy Nuclear Operations and provide about 30 percent of the electricity used in the New York City metro area. Great—but

Apex, North Carolina

Industrial accidents, while damaging, usually affect only those in the immediate vicinity, but what about when the public is adversely affected? That was the case on October 5, 2006, in Apex, North Carolina, located west of Raleigh, when residents were forced to evacuate their homes after a fire at a nearby hazardous materials plant. The Environmental Quality plant was a storage facility for hundreds of 55-gallon drums of flammable and combustible materials, such as benzene, mercury, potassium cyanide, and other materials that ignited and sent out toxic fumes over the town. More than 16,000 people were urged to evacuate, and more than 100 were hospitalized with respiratory problems.

An investigation of the accident by the U.S. Chemical Safety and Hazard Investigation Board (CSB) found, among other issues, that this facility wasn't required to be equipped with fire or smoke detection sensors nor monitored after hours. The only items of fire control equipment in place were portable fire extinguishers.

Accidents happen, but this wasn't the only major industrial incident in North Carolina. On January 29, 2003, an explosion occurred in the Kinston-based West Pharmaceuticals Services rubber-manufacturing plant. According to the CSB, the explosion of combustible polyethylene dust injured 38 people, including two firefighters and six employees.

Some good news: Following the 2006 event, the governor formed a Hazardous Materials Task Force to examine the regulations for hazardous waste storage facilities, which became the basis of changes that finally were enacted in June 2007. The measures included more-frequent inspections and stricter monitoring of hazardous waste storage, as well as a requirement that companies inform emergency responders about chemicals that are being stored.

they're also leaking cesium, strontium, and tritium into the groundwater and the Hudson River.

And if that's not bad enough, the plant lies directly under the path of the planes that flew into the World Trade Center on 9/11 and is now also perceived as an enormous terrorist target.

The fears of nuclear waste, a major industrial accident, or a terrorist strike in a densely populated area are what motivated groups such as the Sierra Club, Westchester Citizen's Awareness Networks, and the States of New York and Connecticut to file petitions in March 2007 to halt the move

Butte, Montana

The Berkeley Pit in Butte, Montana, an open-pit copper mine, spans an area of close to a mile and a half and is nearly 1,780 feet deep. The water it now contains is contaminated with toxic chemicals and heavy metals. But get this: There's a viewing platform for tourists, and you actually have to *pay* to see this pollution-laden landmark. Need I say more?

that would relicense Indian Point for another 20 years. The case is still pending, reported legal counselor Susan Shapiro.

Consider this sobering fact: 8 percent of the U.S. population lives within 50 miles of Indian Point. For any nuclear accident, the peak fatality zone falls within a 17-mile radius; the peak injury zone is within a 50-mile radius. For Indian Point, the peak injury zone includes New York City (except Staten Island), Westchester County, Connecticut's Fairfield County, and parts of New Jersey's Bergen and Passaic counties. When the Indian Point nuclear reactors were built, the nearby population was a lot less dense, but now there are 21 million people living within an hour's drive.

The real problems? There is no workable or fixable evacuation plan, and many experts argue that the aging systems and structures of the plant no longer perform properly to protect public health and safety. Even with an emergency evacuation plan, an evacuation would take almost 10 hours—about 8 hours too long for most residents.

The Union of Concerned Scientists, a leading nonprofit organization of

Love Canal, New York

To put it bluntly, the Love Canal in Niagara Falls, New York, is not a lovely place. In 1978 a resident posted a sign saying, "Give me liberty. I've already got death." In 1979 the EPA reported that residents were experiencing an alarmingly high rate of miscarriages. It was soon discovered that the town was located on toxic waste. In 2004, it was removed from the EPA's Superfund list of most toxic places, but it still remains on my list of places not to visit.

Picher, Oklahoma

It sounds like the plot of a maudlin film, but for the residents of Picher, in northeastern Oklahoma, the fate of this dying mining town is all too real. Once home to a prosperous industry based on lead and zinc, Picher is also home to Tar Creek, named a Superfund site by the EPA for its high levels of pollution. (A Superfund site is an area targeted by the environmental policy the government enacted to protect communities from abandoned toxic waste sites.) Also, enormous piles of mining waste called chat—several hundred feet tall and many acres wide—were poisoning the air and water. Meanwhile, a recent federal study found that the abandoned mines were at risk of cave-ins. And that was enough for the government to step in and buy out residents. According to reports, the town's population has dwindled from 20,000 to about 800 people.

To make matters even worse for those remaining, an F4 tornado blew through Picher on May 10, 2008, killing six people and injuring another 150. The town was devastated, with homes torn apart, and the storm blew lead and other toxic materials off the towering chat piles. Talk about a town that can't get a break.

There is one good thing that comes out of Picher these days, and that's a story of human compassion. One local resident, Gary Linderman, has vowed to be the last man standing in Picher (earning the nickname "Lights Out Linderman"). Why? Because he's the town pharmacist.

scientists and citizens formed at MIT in 1969, conducted a study that was published in a 2004 report entitled *Chernobyl on the Hudson? The Health and Economic Impacts of a Terrorist Attack at the Indian Point Nuclear Plant*. If either Indian Point nuclear reactor were attacked, the result would be catastrophic.

The study surveyed what might happen within the 50-mile peak injury radius based on various possible weather conditions. The result? Within 7 days, approximately 3,500 people would die of acute radiation syndrome, based on analyses of 95 percent of possible weather conditions. The remaining 5 percent of weather conditions—the worst-case scenarios—would result in approximately 44,000 deaths.

The estimated number of long-term deaths, usually cancer related, within a 50-mile radius is "almost 100,000" in 95 percent of weather conditions and more than 500,000 in worst-case weather scenarios.

Toms River, New Jersey

Now one of the fastest-growing cities in New Jersey, Toms River has the dubious honor of being home to one of the largest cancer clusters in the world. Between 1979 and 2000, the township of Toms River had 112 cases of cancer in children up to the age of 19, according to the New Jersey Department of Health and Senior Services. That's 23 percent higher than expected in a population of 84,000 people.

A 2003 update of a 1997 study from the department entitled *Childhood Cancer Incidence Health Consultation: A Review and Analysis of Cancer Registry Data, 1979–1995 for Dover Township (Ocean County)* reported that childhood cancer was significantly higher in Toms River, particularly leukemia and brain and central nervous system cancers in female children under the age of 5.

The presumed cause: massive contamination from the dye-manufacturing plant Ciba-Geigy Chemical Corporation (now known as Ciba Specialty Chemicals Corporation), which operated from 1952 to 1990. According to the EPA, sludge and chemical process wastes were stored underground in thousands of drums, which then leached into the groundwater. Other

Sylvester, West Virginia

It should come as no surprise that West Virginia is plagued with a long legacy of pollution and chronic disease associated with coal mining. But a 2008 study put those facts on paper when it reported that in counties where coal is still mined, residents have a 70 percent increased risk of developing kidney disease; a 64 percent increased risk of chronic pulmonary disease, such as emphysema; and a 30 percent greater likelihood of high blood pressure. And then there's the town of Sylvester. Back in 1998, the Elk Run Mining Company, a subsidiary of Massey Energy, installed a coal preparation plant. Within a month, prevailing winds blanketed the entire town in a thick layer of black coal dust. For years, residents—namely two women known as the Dustbuster Sisters—battled Massey Energy to control its emissions. The good guys eventually had a small victory in 2002, when the mining company was ordered to install a gigantic nylon dome over its coal piles—though West Virginia taxpayers had to foot the bill. Did the dome help? Somewhat—but both residents and visitors still report ongoing problems with coal dust invading the town. If you still want to go there, you might want to reconsider wearing that white shirt or pantsuit.

companies, such as Union Carbide Corporation, which was based in nearby Bound Brook, and United Water Toms River, were also cited in a settlement with the families of Toms River regarding childhood cancers. By 1983, Toms River was added to the National Priorities List as one of the most hazardous waste sites in America.

Today, the toxic wells in Toms River have officially been cleaned up, soil treatment continues, and the site has some of the most stringent water testing regulations in the state of New Jersey. But is it too soon to return?

International Sites

Bhopal, India

You may have heard of Bhopal, India, the site of one of the worst industrial disasters in history. On the night of December 2, 1984, a Union Carbide pesticide factory leaked 24 tons of methyl isocyanate and 35 tons of toxic gases when none of the six safety systems in place managed to stop the leak. The gas spread throughout the city for more than 2 hours, killing 350 people almost immediately. Bodies lay on the streets, thousands of unidentified corpses were burned in mass funeral pyres, and hundreds of thousands of survivors suffered permanent damage to their eyes and lungs.

Although statistics vary, the most accepted death toll came from Amnesty International in a 2004 report entitled *Summary of Clouds of Injustice— Bhopal Disaster 20 Years On*. According to the report, within 2 to 3 days of the leak, more than 7,000 people died, and many more were injured. It's estimated that 15,000 more people have died over the past 20 years from illnesses related to gas exposure, and more than 100,000 people continue to suffer birth defects, genetic defects, and chronic illnesses. According to Greenpeace, more than 20,000 people still live close to the factory site.

"The company was polluting the site with pesticides and heavy metals long before the 1984 gas disaster," explained Aquene Freechild, of the Boston-based Environmental Health Fund, which works with the International Campaign for Justice in Bhopal. "After the horrific gas leak, it abandoned the site and never cleaned it up. Carbide never notified the residents that the soil and drinking water were poisoned."

Today, you can walk around Bhopal and see almost no signs of its grisly history. But step anywhere near the old Union Carbide factory and the acrid smell will make it all too real.

Chernobyl, Ukraine

Okay, I've already heard all the jokes about deer that glow in the dark, but the reason I still include Chernobyl on the list is that, like Hanford, it's now giving tours. Are they kidding?

No, they're not. It's a revenue generator. But what else does it generate?

You're probably familiar with a few of the most toxic sites in the world—and Chernobyl certainly tops that list. The April 26, 1986, Chernobyl disaster was the worst nuclear power plant accident in history. One of four nuclear reactors exploded, releasing radioactive fallout that was 100 times greater than that of the atomic bombs dropped on Nagasaki and Hiroshima. The official death toll from the immediate blast is 31.

A radioactive cloud spewed over Belarus, Ukraine, and western Russia (specifically, towns such as Bryansk, Kaluga, Orel, and Tula), and winds spread radioactive mists over Europe (particularly then Czechoslovakia, Hungary, Poland, Romania, and what was formerly Yugoslavia) and North America. A practically never-ending list of toxic materials, including cesium-137, plutonium, strontium, and uranium, smothered the area.

A landmark report entitled *Chernobyl: The True Scale of the Accident* was released in 2005 by the Chernobyl Forum, which is made up of eight UN agencies, including the World Health Organization and the International Atomic Energy Agency. The 600-page report, which involved the work of hundreds of international scientists, economists, and health experts, stated that fewer than 50 deaths, mostly of rescue workers with high levels of exposure, have been directly related to radiation poisoning caused by the incident. But, among the millions who were exposed to the radiation, as many as 4,000 people may die of related conditions, such as thyroid cancer.

For more than 20 years, Chernobyl and neighboring Prypiat remained virtual ghost towns—at least a 20-mile radius surrounding the plant has been deemed a "forbidden zone," unsafe for human habitation on account of radiation levels. Outside of that toxic radius, radiation levels are, for the most part, acceptable, although radioactive hot spots do still exist. Levels of radiation can also vary wildly within areas because of wind and rain patterns at the time of the accident. In recent years, some former residents have started returning to their homes.

Is it safe to go there? Who knows? But if you're bold or stupid, or both, you can take the daylong Chernobyl tour from Kiev, which includes a visit to Reactor 4, the town of Prypiat, and the Chernobyl Scientific Center.

Dzerzhinsk, Russia

Once a major site for cold war–era chemical-weapon manufacturing, this city of 300,000, located about 250 miles east of Moscow, is still one of Russia's major chemical production sites, and its residents are suffering from the effects. In 2007, the Blacksmith Institute released a report that listed Dzerzhinsk as one of its top 10 most polluted cities in the world. In 2004, the city earned the dubious distinction of being named "the Most Chemically Polluted Place in the World" by *Guinness World Records*. That's right, worse than Chernobyl.

The city continues to be affected by the industrial chemicals that soaked into the local water and soil, including arsenic, lead, sarin, and a nerve agent known as VX gas. And the chemical production hasn't ended. According to the Blacksmith Institute, a quarter of the city's population still works at factories that produce toxic materials. Blacksmith reports that in 2003, the death rate exceed the birth rate by 260 percent, and the average life expectancy is reported to be 42 years for men and 47 for women.

If, for some reason, you find yourself wandering around the Dzerzhinsk area (you'll know you're there by the burnt, metallic smell), there are three parts of town that you definitely want to avoid: Gavrilovka, about 2 miles from a former tetraethyl lead production facility, where the groundwater is poisoned by high levels of lead, arsenic, and other toxins; Piri, where the drinking water has high levels of ferrous-organic and fecal bacteria; and the Volosyanikha Canal, where industrial waste has been dumped since the 1930s, saturating the water with arsenic, chromium, lead, and mercury, among other contaminants.

Kabwe, Zambia

Zambia is an amazing country: It borders Victoria Falls, and scientists have found fossils of some of the earliest humans here. But Zambia's second-largest city, Kabwe, reflects another legacy: staggering levels of toxic pollution. Poisonous heavy metals are rampant, thanks to a long history of essentially unregulated mining and smelting operations.

Although the lead mine was closed in 1994, heavy metals have leached into the soil and water supply, dust particles clog the air, and the city is littered with piles of scrap metal and exposed quarries. Children are especially at risk of lead poisoning, as early exposure can lead to long-term effects. Local children have had an average of 60 to 120, and up to 300, micrograms of lead per deciliter of blood. The acceptable limit is 10 micrograms.

The good news is that Zambia was recently granted $50 million from various funds, primarily the World Bank, to help remove the hazardous materials. How long the cleanup will take, however, remains to be seen.

La Oroya, Peru

The legacy of La Oroya is not a pleasant one—99 percent of the children in this city of 35,000 have elevated blood levels of lead, probably impairing them for life. This was the finding of the Director General of Environmental Health in Peru in 1999, while a survey the same year by the Ministry of Health found that blood lead levels among local children were triple the limit set by the World Health Organization (WHO).

Blanketed by a layer of gray dust, La Oroya has been a metal-mining town since 1922. It's the second-largest smelting operation in Latin America, producing gold, silver, and lead, meaning there have been decades of toxic emissions and waste contamination. Between the runoff from the slag heap and tons of lead dust, sulfur dioxide, and other pollutants belching from the smelters, these toxins are poisoning the air, water, ground, and livestock.

Oxfam International, a nonprofit nongovernmental organization (NGO) dedicated to promoting social justice, advocacy, and emergency preparedness, reports that a scientist recently calculated that the projected cancer rate in La Oroya is 2,000 times higher than the maximum level considered acceptable by the U.S. EPA. From the story of a 6-year-old girl who stopped growing due to lead poisoning to reports of livestock simply dropping dead in their tracks, the effects of the metal-smelting plant seem endless.

Oh, and that smelting operation? It's owned by an American company. The Missouri-based Doe Run Peru Corporation bought the plant in 1997. According to Oxfam America, the company has received four extensions of a government-induced compliance plan, which would reduce the quantities of toxins released by the plant. Interesting when you note a 2001 study that showed an alarming rise in blood lead levels in the town of Herculaneum, Missouri, where Doe Run also runs a lead smelter. When the study was released, the U.S. government ordered Doe Run to comply with national air-quality standards, which it did. Unfortunately, La Oroya isn't getting that same treatment.

Linfen, China

China may claim to have cleaned up its act in time for the 2008 Olympics, but I'm not buying it. I'm also not inhaling it or drinking it. And neither is the World Bank, which lists the 20 most polluted cities in the world—16 of which are in . . . China. And the city of Linfen is near the top of the list.

So how bad is bad in China? Located in northern China's coal belt, Linfen is suffering from the effects of the coal-mining industry in Shanxi Province—take one look and you'll see what I mean. Even in daytime, the combination of soot and auto emissions means that it's almost always dark in Linfen. Drivers keep their headlights on all day; residents walk around with face masks on; a layer of black dust coats nearly everything; even the nearby Sushui River runs black.

Linfen has suffered from the region's fast-growing industrial development of coal mines, and steel factories and refineries act with little to no regulation. Shanxi Province produces about 600 million tons of coal each year, which accounts for about a quarter of China's total coal output.

High rates of lung cancer and respiratory diseases are not exactly a surprise, but what about arsenic and lead poisoning? Not only is the air toxic in Linfen, but the city's well water has been contaminated by industrial waste that includes arsenic, carbon monoxide, lead, nitrogen oxide, and sulfur dioxide.

The government is finally stepping in to limit total coal output, shutting down highly polluting operations and replacing them with cleaner and more efficient facilities. But the damage has been done, and while Linfen tends to get the most attention, there are plenty of other cities that suffer from similar or worse pollution problems—Datong, Taiyuan, and Yangquan, to name a few. If you go, take an oxygen mask and your own supply of water. I'm serious.

Sukinda and Vapi, India

Though it's among the most infamous, Bhopal isn't the only toxic site in India. Just take a look at the towns of Sukinda and Vapi, both of which made the Blacksmith Institute's list of the top 10 polluted places in the world.

The Sukinda Valley, located in the state of Orissa, on India's east coast, is home to 97 percent of the country's chromite ore deposits and 2.6 million people. Sukinda has 12 operating mines that reportedly run with little to no environmental management. The waters of this valley contain carcinogenic hexavalent chromium compounds, courtesy of 30 million tons of waste rock lining the Brahmani River. In spite of limited treatment facilities, the river continues to be the main source of water for residents.

The result? Drinking water and dust that are poisoned by hexavalent chromium, which has caused gastrointestinal bleeding, lung infections, asthma, and even tuberculosis. According to the Orissa Voluntary Health Association, 84.75 percent of deaths in the mining areas and 86.42 percent of deaths in nearby villages are related to chromium.

Hoping to secure a more in-depth and official examination of the Brahmani River region, and to install an effective treatment plan for the hundreds of thousands of water sources that are contaminated by the mine industry, the Parliament of India met with the Committee on Petitions (a grievance committee composed of publicly elected representatives) in March 2006 to address these issues, among others. According to the document that resulted—Parliament's 127th *Report in the Action Taken by the Ministry of Environment and Forests*—the Sukinda region has been poisoned by "effluent discharge" from "heavy and medium industries" to the extent that "the entire stretch of the Brahmani River from Rourkela to the sea has been highly polluted." Their recommendation? To treat man-made sewage and wastewater before it's discharged into the river and examine the "carrying capacity" of the region before establishing more industry. But there's not much going on to alleviate the pollution that has already damaged this region.

And in Vapi, located in the western state of Gujarat, it's a different story with the same ending. The manufacturing industry, rather than mining, is destroying the environment and affecting the health of locals. Within a 250-mile industrial belt, there are more than a thousand tanneries and factories manufacturing pesticides, fertilizer, dyes, and much more, and those facilities spew toxins such as lead, mercury, and zinc into the groundwater.

In 1994, the Central Pollution Control Board of India, a Delhi-based arm of the Ministry of Environment & Forests, deemed that Vapi was "critically polluted." Think about it. Residents who drink the contaminated water have reportedly suffered from respiratory diseases; skin diseases; lung, skin, and throat cancers; infertility; and spontaneous abortions. Still want to go there?

Sumgait, Azerbaijan; Norilsk, Russia; and Mailuu-Suu, Kyrgyzstan

Unfortunately, the effects of Soviet-era industry aren't limited to towns surrounding Moscow. As far south as Sumgait, Azerbaijan; as far east as Mailuu-Suu, Kyrgyzstan; and all the way up to the Siberian city of Norilsk, industrial pollutants continue to affect residents to this day.

(continued on page 44)

Mercer's Dirtiest Cities

Mercer Human Resource Consulting publishes annual Health and Sanitation Rankings, part of its yearly *Quality of Living* report. Each city is scored against New York City, which has an index score of 100. (The lower the score, the worse off the city is.)

According to Mercer's 2007 report, the top 10 dirtiest cities in the world are . . .

1. **Baku, Azerbaijan**—Mercer Health and Sanitation Index score: **27.6**
   Baku is the center of Azerbaijan's oil industry and is heavily polluted by oil refineries and petrochemical plants. Oil leaks have poisoned the Baku Bay, diminishing once-lucrative caviar and sturgeon supplies.

2. **Dhaka, Bangladesh—29.6**
   Traffic congestion is one of the leading causes of Dhaka's poor air quality. During the dry season, lead concentration in the air here is among the highest in the world. This has been compounded by the city's population explosion, with the number of residents nearly quadrupling to 12 million in the past 25 years. (The World Bank named this the city with the highest population growth in the world.) Dyeing, tanning, and pesticide factories, among others, are polluting the groundwater and rivers, causing irreversible damage.

3. **Antananarivo, Madagascar—30.1**
   Madagascar's capital city, formerly known as Tananarive, is also a victim of rapid urban growth—current population estimates are about 2 million, in a city that was built for about 500,000. Traffic congestion, garbage-filled lakes, and waste dumping into the West Indian Ocean are just a few of the polluting factors in this city.

4. **Port-au-Prince, Haiti—34**
   Blackened, smoggy air; crushing traffic jams; plastic debris on the beaches; destroyed mangrove forests eroding the coastline . . . the problems that plague Port-au-Prince seem never-ending. When you factor in the city's immense poverty and crime, it really does become a prime candidate for a must-miss destination.

5. **Mexico City, Mexico—37.7**
   Located in a volcanic valley, Mexico City is plagued by immense industry and heavy traffic that have caused a layer of brown smog

to settle over the city. The government replaced leaded gasoline with unleaded and has made efforts to curb emissions by limiting traffic and, on occasion, taking emergency measures to ban private vehicles altogether. But the city's high altitude, bowl-like geography, and intense sunlight all intensify existing pollutants to create some of the most unbreathable air in the world.

6. Addis Ababa, Ethiopia—37.9

A lack of waste-removal infrastructure has led to immense pollution of Addis Ababa's waters. There is trash and debris floating in the rivers, along with a nasty sludge of sewage, industrial chemicals, and heavy metals. Meanwhile, vehicle emissions and wood burning contribute to heavy air pollution and smog that choke the city.

7. Mumbai, India—38.2

With a population of more than 15 million people, this congested city is suffocating from overcrowding and pollution caused by rapid urban growth. Vehicular pollution, mounds of burning garbage, and one of the largest industrial zones in all of Asia release toxic materials that hang over the city like a thick blanket.

8. Baghdad, Iraq—39

As if you needed another reason to stay away from Baghdad . . . military-based pollutants, burning oil wells, dense traffic spewing lead dust into the atmosphere, and sewage waste are just a few of the factors that make this city so toxic. Now consider the fact that the Tigris River, often the only option for drinking water, has become a deadly stew of raw sewage, oil, chemicals, and heavy metals. Still thinking of booking that plane ticket?

9. Almaty, Kazakhstan—39.1

Industrial pollution from oil production, chemical plants, and mining, along with vehicle emissions from old, poorly maintained cars, has produced a cloud of smog that you can see hanging over the city. Dust, benzapyrene, lead, and sulfur dioxide are some of the major components.

10. Brazzaville, Republic of the Congo—39.1

Not to be confused with the neighboring Democratic Republic of the Congo, this former French colony is marred by corrupt leadership and immense poverty, which only exacerbate the pollution caused by the region's rich oil industry. Raw sewage also threatens the coastal waters.

The city of Sumgait, a major industrial epicenter that sits on the west coast of the Caspian Sea, was established in the 1950s with more than 40 factories producing chemicals such as chlorine, pesticides, and synthetic rubber. According to the Blacksmith Institute, those factories released between 70,000 and 120,000 tons of harmful emissions each year, while untreated sewage and sludge containing mercury were dumped "haphazardly" since the city's inception. A recent study commissioned by the United Nations Development Program, WHO, the Azerbaijani Health Ministry, and the University of Alberta found shockingly high levels of cancer in Sumgait that were 22 to 51 percent greater than in the rest of the country.

The air and water, imbued with toxic levels of heavy metals, may have already affected the city's population of 275,000. A cemetery in Sumgait even has a devastatingly grim children-only section, reserved for those children who suffered from bone disease, genetic defects, and mental retardation caused by the toxic environment.

Though Sumgait no longer maintains the same dangerously high output as in its Soviet heyday, about 20 percent of the city's factories still operate.

Things aren't much better in Mailuu-Suu, Kyrgyzstan, where uranium ore mining and processing factories produced the uranium that was used in the first Soviet atomic bomb. Cancer rates in the town's dwindling population are twice that of the rest of Kyrgyzstan. To make matters worse, 1.96 million cubic meters of radioactive mining waste sits in giant piles. There has been some recent movement to isolate these wastes and improve the country's disaster preparedness and response, but the existing piles are under the constant threat of the area's high seismic activity. Landslides have already knocked down several waste sites, and trust me, you don't want to be there when it happens again.

Norilsk, about as far north into Russia as you can get, was once a slave-labor camp but is now the world's largest heavy metals smelting complex. When the snow turns black from pollution, it's time get out! The Norilsk Nickel plant is the leading culprit here, producing nickel and palladium, and is the biggest air polluter in Russia—which says a lot. And if you need any more reasons to skip that winter journey to Norilsk, consider that from December to January, it's dark for about 6 weeks straight!

MOST DEPRESSED AND DEPRESSING DESTINATIONS

What if a place is just so depressing that its residents are depressed as a result?

There's really no good way to measure how depressing a location is, but we certainly can look at the places with the highest suicide rates and go from there.

World Health Organization (WHO) figures show that a suicide takes place somewhere in the world every 40 seconds. In 2007, the CDC released its most recent figures showing which states have the most suicides, and quite a few of the places that top the list happen to suffer from some pretty depressing weather conditions, isolation, and boredom, which leads to depression, which leads to . . . you get the picture.

Look at it this way: If the place is depressing and its people are depressed, you just might catch the, uh, fever! Ever notice how bad you suddenly feel when you're around people who are depressed? You want to get out of there, right? So, consider this a red-flag warning as I introduce you to . . .

America's Suicide Capitals

Montana

Could Big Sky Country also be big die country? Indeed, Montana was the state with the highest rate of suicide (22 per 100,000 people)—double the national average of 11 per 100,000 people—and has never dropped out of the top five in the past 20 years. It seems that Montana's state slogan, "the last best place," has been sadly misinterpreted by many of its residents. Montana's vast emptiness allows people to detach themselves easily, which may provide a quick path to social isolation, a major suicide risk factor.

But where in Montana do the most people kill themselves? Between 2000 and 2006, the area with the highest rate of suicide was Yellowstone County, with 161 cases. Oh, and I forgot to mention that most suicide prevention experts trace the high death rate in Montana to easy access to, you guessed it, firearms. Two-thirds of the suicides in Montana are committed with guns, compared with one-half nationally.

Nevada

The first thing that comes to mind when you think of Nevada is probably its most visible claim to fame: Las Vegas . . . lights, money, excitement. But according to the CDC, Nevada ranked second in the country for the

(continued)

highest suicide rates in 2005, with 480 total suicides—a rate of 19.9 per 100,000 people.

According to Nevada's Office of Suicide Prevention, suicide is the sixth leading cause of death for Nevadans—above homicide and HIV/AIDS. And, interestingly enough, Nevada's senior citizens over the age of 60 have the highest suicide rate in the nation. Talk about cashing out. . . .

Alaska

How happy can you be when you have to dress in layers? Well, it's not the cold that makes people kill themselves in the 49th state. What puts Alaska's suicide rate so high on the map: lack of sunlight.

During winter, the area above the Arctic Circle experiences near-24-hour darkness, which has been linked to depression, lethargy, and a sense of hopelessness.

Alaska ranks third in the country for the highest suicide rate, with 19.7 such deaths per 100,000 people. Suicide is the second leading cause of death, behind unintentional injuries, for the 15-to-34 age group and the third leading cause for the 10-to-14 and 35-to-44 age groups.

A majority of suicides in the study (58 percent) occurred in urban communities—Anchorage, Fairbanks, Juneau, Palmer/Wasilla, Sitka, Kodiak, and Ketchikan.

New Mexico and Wyoming

New Mexico and Wyoming are tied for fourth in the country in suicide rates, each with 17.7 suicides per 100,000 residents.

The New Mexico Suicide Prevention Coalition (NMSPC) reports that New Mexico consistently ranks among the top five states in the United States in suicide rates, particularly among the male population. In fact, suicide is the third leading cause of death among New Mexico's youth.

What's even more disturbing: The report revealed that 14.5 percent of adolescents in New Mexico said they had attempted suicide in 2003, and 21 percent had seriously considered killing themselves in the previous 12 months.

Though Wyoming is the least populous U.S. state, with just over half a million residents, its people, like Montana's, suffer from a vast, isolated landscape, lack of access to mental health facilities, and a penchant for firearms.

Suicide Bridges

More than 1,300 recorded suicides have taken place at the Golden Gate Bridge in San Francisco, which makes it the top death bridge in the world.

At Seattle's 167-foot-high Aurora Bridge, officially known as the George Washington Memorial Bridge, more than 40 people have committed suicide in the past decade, contributing to a total of more than 230 since the bridge was built in 1932. In 2006, nine people killed themselves by jumping from the bridge, tying 1972 as the deadliest year. Even worse, some jumpers don't land in the water . . . they hit the parking lot or nearby grounds below. Some good news: State officials are now considering installing a "suicide prevention fence" on the bridge.

Another famous suicide bridge, the San Diego–Coronado Bridge in San Diego, was built in 1969, and since then, more than 230 people have jumped from it to their deaths. The upside, if you can call it that, is that not everyone who jumps off the bridge dies—about 10 people have survived the 200-foot fall.

Manhattan Tourism Sites

Why kill yourself in a place where you're more likely to get hit by a taxi anyway? Answer: Because of a perverted sense of history and place.

Researchers say it's a phenomenon called "suicide tourism": choosing a memorable place to do the deed. According to a 2007 study from Cornell University, between 1990 and 2004, there were 274 suicides in Manhattan by nonresidents, and that represented more than 10 percent of all suicides committed in Manhattan.

A report from American Public Health Associated states that "the most common methods of suicide for the Manhattan nonresidents were long fall, hanging, overdose, drowning, and firearms; the most common locations included hotels and commercial buildings, followed by outside locations such as bridges, parks, and streets."

The Empire State Building, George Washington Bridge, and Times Square were among the most common spots.

Depression and Suicide Abroad

Lithuania

Lithuania has had a long-standing reputation as suicide central . . . but is it an epidemic? That's what some experts suggested after looking at the aftereffects of Soviet domination followed by a widespread economic crisis.

Lithuania continues to have one of the highest rates of suicide in the Baltics. Though statistics vary, it's estimated that there were 30 suicides per 100,000 people in 2006. Even more frightening statistics suggest that an average of 30 people kill themselves per week, out of a small population of 3.5 million.

(continued)

MOST DEPRESSED AND DEPRESSING DESTINATIONS—*Continued*

Russia

What screams depression more than a country whose average person consumed 15 liters of alcohol a year?

Remember 1985, when Gorbachev launched a massive anti-alcohol campaign? Consumption-per-person limits were set at a half liter per month.

At the time, Gorbachev's short-lived perestroika had perhaps the most positive affect on suicide rates in the country's history. According to a Harvard University study, male suicides in Russia fell 44 percent during the mid-'80s. A 2001 study calls perestroika "history's most effective suicide preventive program for men." Which it was. But it didn't last long.

Suicides in Russia have skyrocketed since 1990, the tail end of Soviet rule, when the rate was 26.4 per 100,000 citizens. Now, it's up to 70.6 per 100,000 men and 11.9 per 100,000 women. Looks like people are back to drinking again. . . .

Belarus

Belarus has one of the highest suicide rates in the world, 33.5 per 100,000 residents, to be exact. The high number of suicides might lead you to believe that folks have decided to kill themselves before the radiation ends their lives.

But before you blame it on the possibility that people might actually glow in the dark, know that depression in Belarus is closely linked to an outrageously large consumption of alcohol. A recent study by Grodno State Medical University in Belarus revealed that "it seems quite likely a substantial proportion of suicide in Belarus is due to acute effect of binge drinking." Cheers!

Estonia

It's amazing what independence from communism can create. One 2004 study looked at suicide rates of native Estonians, Russian immigrants in Estonia, and Russians living in Russia, comparing rates before and after the fall of the Soviet Union and during the subsequent Estonian independence.

In the Soviet era, the Russian immigrants in Estonia had the lowest suicide rates of the three groups. While, on the one hand, immigration is an accepted risk factor for suicide, Russians living in Estonia—though the minority—had higher earning power, lived in better housing, were able to maintain their sense of ethnic identity, and generally enjoyed privileged status.

But after Estonian independence in 1991, Russian immigrants had to adapt to new conditions, study Estonian as an official language, and apply for citizenship, forcing them into that category of displaced immigrants who are at a higher risk of suicide.

Now add in the fact that after independence, Estonia as a whole was left in a shambles—we're talking bread lines and out-of-control inflation, meaning that native Estonians and Russian immigrants alike suffered from years of a depressed economy. Suicides in Estonia have soared, now reaching 33.2 per 100,000 people. The good news is that since Estonia joined the EU, the nation's economy is well on its way to stabilizing, which may soon result in lower suicide rates.

Hungary

Much of old Eastern Europe is generally thought to be dark and depressing, so it should be no big surprise that Eastern European legend Hungary is high on my depressed and depressing list. According to WHO, Hungary's suicide rate is 400 per one million residents, and the country held the title for the highest suicide rate worldwide until recently. More than 2,800 people commit suicide each year in Hungary, but some researchers say that number might actually be much higher.

China

Though not in the top 10, China has some interesting situations going on: With a population nearing 1.3 billion, you'd think city dwellers, living with constant claustrophobia, would lead the international suicide race. But instead, it's those who live in rural areas who are ahead. And here's a real surprise: Three times more women than men commit suicide.

The Beijing Suicide Research and Prevention Center has found that family disputes, coping with disease, and economic hardship are the highest-ranked suicide factors in the country.

And here's another interesting development from a country that also holds notorious records for pollution: 58 percent of all of China's suicides were accomplished by ingesting—get this—pesticides!

Chapter 4

PLACES THAT REALLY STINK

Let's not mince words. Hold your nose. Really hold your nose. Then, turn the other way and run, don't walk. . . . Here are some places that really *stink*. Between massive factory farms breeding livestock and industrial zones spewing out foul toxins, there are some towns that smell so bad . . . well, just trust me, even if you're driving through with the windows rolled all the way up, it's not enough. This qualifies as not only a "don't go there," but a "don't even go *near* there!"

Often hiding between larger cities, these stinky places are nuisances that can sneak up on unsuspecting travelers driving between destinations. Sure, you might not visit these places on purpose, but if you don't choose your routes carefully, you may be hit with the stinking consequences.

Factory Farms

Over the past 20 years, the United States' animal production industry has become more concentrated than ever before. The industrial livestock sector now focuses on "factory" animal production, which houses hogs, cattle, and poultry in concentrated animal feeding operations (CAFOs)—cages and pens designed to fit as many animals in as small an area as possible.

According to the Center for Food Safety, all the livestock in the United States produces 250,000 pounds of you-know-what per second. That's 25 pounds of manure per cow per day. And, instead of using sewer systems to manage the loads of excrement, CAFOs often spray liquefied manure onto croplands under the conspicuous guise of "fertilizer."

Can you say *ew*?

In February 1995, the Raleigh, North Carolina–based *News & Observer* ran a Pulitzer Prize–winning exposé by Joby Warrick and Pat Stith on one of the largest hog production companies in the world, Smithfield Farms. Following a 7-month investigation, the series put the problem with factory farms into perspective: Imagine "a city as big as New York suddenly grafted onto North Carolina's Coastal Plain. Double it. Now imagine that this city has no sewage treatment plants. All the wastes from 15 million inhabitants are simply flushed into open pits and sprayed onto fields. Turn those humans into hogs, and you don't have to imagine at all. It's already here."

So . . . how stinky is it?

Animal factories' odors can easily travel 8 to 10 miles from the largest of these types of facilities. And, as Scott Dye, national program director of the Sierra Club's Water Sentinels program, puts it, "even if you aren't anticipating it, the odiferous slap to the senses is something no one can ignore."

Drive through a town with a factory farm and you, too, will be hit with the nauseating concoction of gases, including ammonia and hydrogen sulfide, that results from massive quantities of manure and decaying

Factory Hog Farms

The top-ranking states in terms of the number of factory hog farms:

Iowa—3,876

Minnesota—1,624

North Carolina—1,404

Illinois—970

Indiana—788

Nebraska—574

Ohio—413

Missouri—404

Pennsylvania—315

South Dakota—257

Source: *factoryfarmmap.org/*

carcasses—in some cases, as you'll see, dumped illegally beside farms, or stored in leaky holding pits that have their own set of odors.

Here's a sampling of some of the stinkiest places we could sniff out.

Putnam County, Missouri

Scott Dye used to describe his hometown as "paradise," but now he has to get creative: "It's like living in a place with bushes outside of the door with a gremlin ready to clobber you over the head with the stinky stick."

Tour de Stench

The emissions from chicken CAFOs in western Kentucky are so bad and such a potential health threat that Aloma Dew, an organizer with the Sierra Club, has put together a sensory education program called the Tour de Stench.

Sponsored by the Cumberland (Kentucky) chapter of the Sierra Club, among others, the tour takes participants through three counties in western Kentucky that have suffered heavily from factory farms. The tour is meant to raise awareness of factory farms and their effects on communities.

"Inevitably, people start gagging," says Dew. "But just think of the people who have to live there all the time. It's inescapable. Residents are left feeling very helpless." Some locals have family land dating back to the late 1700s, including a cemetery complete with gravestones from Kentucky's settlement period. Moving camp, even if it were easy, is often not an option, either emotionally or economically.

During the tour, which is free of charge, you'll be taken by car or van to see just how close people actually live to these places. In fact, you'll even see a sign that says, "Welcome to Chickenshitville—Follow Your Nose to Our House," as you approach one home that has 25 giant chicken houses as its neighbor. The tour covers three or four destinations along the way, including residents' homes near chicken houses and huge waste piles made up of chicken manure and dead birds. The tour travels past the Tyson hatchery, processing plant, freezer and transportation facility, and grain storage area. You'll talk with the neighbors of these smelly facilities and catch a whiff of the smell they're exposed to almost daily. There are few regulations on these facilities, and most of those are not enforced, so locals are captive to the odor, flies, bugs, rodents, and harmful emissions caused by these huge warehouses of chickens.

Don't believe me (or them)? Sign up for the Tour de Stench yourself by e-mailing aloma.dew@sierraclub.org.

Dye grew up on a 340-acre family farm in north central Missouri, about 4½ miles out of Unionville in Putnam County, that had been in his family since his grandfather's birth in the last year of the Civil War. But Dye doesn't live there anymore—at least not since the hog barons moved in.

In the early 1990s, Dye's family farm quickly became surrounded by what the hog industry calls "finishing houses"—barns that grow pigs from 55-pound adolescents to 250-pound porkers ready for slaughter. These 72 structures feature nine holding pits—lagoons—which some in the community have described as "festering shit-holes."

Dye once observed one such drained cesspool, and can attest that the generically termed "manure" that gathers there is everything and then some. At the bottom of one pit, he recalls a combination of horrifying sludge, including but not limited to dead piglets and hog bones; hypodermic needles and glass containers used to administer any number of hormones and antibiotics to hogs; thousands of tons of built-up fecal matter; rubber gloves; and drug remnants referred to as "dope."

In too high a concentration, manure as fertilizer is no longer beneficial; instead, it becomes toxic—soaked with nitrogen, which, if it gets into the rivers, can literally suffocate the ecosystems. And these associated occurrences rudely announce themselves right under your nose.

Though Unionville itself is not necessarily the culprit here, wind patterns blow the factory farm stench all over Putnam County. Unionville sits right at the intersection of Highways 5 and 136, and the closest main veins to Unionville are I-35 to the east and I-172 to the west, so stick to these options and surpass Unionville entirely if you have any sympathy for your sense of smell.

Hereford, Texas

Hereford, Texas, is proudly called by many in this region "the Saudi Arabia of cattle manure," with more than 3.5 million meat and dairy cows within a 100-mile radius of the city. With just 14,500 people calling Hereford home, that means there are about 241 cows for every human living in town.

With quaint hotels, various horse shows, and historic spots, Hereford is a subdued diversion from nearby Amarillo but otherwise doesn't have much to offer, unless you count odor as a commodity. As the locals like to say about Hereford and its cows, "It's the smell of money."

Located in the Panhandle of Texas and banking on the vast quantities of manure these cows produce, Hereford is graced with ethanol plants that are fueled by the cow manure, which in turn helps convert corn into an economically viable alternative to oil. And that's what really makes Hereford reek. Among some of Texas's proposed ethanol conversion plants, Hereford features one site owned by Panda Ethanol that was just fired up in late 2007. Now up and running, it uses 1 billion pounds of manure to fuel its plant per year, thus replacing 1,000 barrels of oil per day.

But just because Hereford has created an amicable relationship between the livestock and alternative energy sectors, it by no means serves up a good time for those visiting. In Hereford, barns brimming with cattle urine and manure churn out the infamous "smell of money."

Hereford is about 50 miles southwest of Amarillo. Hereford Municipal Airport is northeast of the city on Highway 60. If you're driving through the Panhandle, stick to I-40, which hits Amarillo, running east and west—and, most important, north—of Hereford. If north-south is your route, use I-27, which sits to the east of Hereford, ultimately connecting with Lubbock from Amarillo. South of Hereford are I-20 and I-10, which will get you to California or the deepest bayous of Louisiana, should you want them.

New Bern, North Carolina

Just how bad can the stink be along North Carolina's Neuse River, near the city of New Bern? "Like a slap in the face," says Rick Dove, a North Carolina resident for 32 years. As an attorney, retired Marine Corps colonel, and former official riverkeeper of the Neuse, Dove took water samples and kept close observations of ecosystems in and around the river via boat and plane. But perhaps most important, he *knows* this river intimately and can judge its condition in the blink of an eye.

In 1991, Dove and his son, working together in their self-made commercial fishing business, began to watch the Neuse River deteriorate right before their eyes.

"The stench was unbearable," recalls Dove. Fish that were still alive started rotting away, with visible holes through their bodies. And get this: Dove and his son began developing the same lesions on their own skin, sim-

Bridgewater, Maine

One of Bridgewater, Maine's claims to fame is the double-decker outhouse attached to the Town Hall. Isn't one stinky outhouse bad enough? Unless you really, really gotta go, forget about visiting Uncle John.

ply from coming in contact with the toxic waters. He and his son also claim to have experienced memory loss and severe difficulty breathing.

"Fish got sick, we got sick—and then we knew the Neuse was sick," says Dove.

Due to the placement of large industrial swine production facilities perilously close to rivers and nearby poor, residential communities, overwhelming amounts of putrid contaminants were regularly spilling into the Neuse and its surrounding tributaries.

Dove, who has testified before Congress three times about this problem, says there are more than 10 million hogs in eastern North Carolina alone, producing fecal waste that is literally deadly, not to mention unimaginably stinky, with unearthly quantities of hydrogen sulfide and ammonia. A consensus among scientists allows that even very low concentrations of hydrogen sulfide can have irreversible, long-term effects on people's brain function.

A study conducted by Dr. Mark Sobsey, a professor of environmental sciences and engineering at the University of North Carolina School of Public Health, discovered that the fecal matter these hogs produce each day surpasses that of humans by a voluminous ratio of 10:1. That means the hogs in North Carolina make more waste than all the citizens, combined, currently residing in California, New Hampshire, New York, North Carolina, North Dakota, Pennsylvania, and Texas. The numbers speak for themselves, but with such extreme quantities of reeking excrement, you'd have to smell it to believe it. Or, even better, please just take my word for it!

If you're driving north-south on I-95 and smell something terrible, just look east toward North Carolina's most environmentally sensitive area, which is also where you'll begin to inhale the awful odor of the hog factories, with gagging following quickly thereafter. Please, keep driving. Don't go there.

Factories and Industry

Cedar Rapids, Iowa

Some people call Cedar Rapids "the City of Five Seasons," where the fifth is "time to enjoy the other four."

Well, Cedar Rapids also has an unofficial nickname: "the City of Five Smells."

Ogden, Utah

Apparently, the smell emanating from the American Nutrition pet-food processing plant in Ogden was so bad in 2007 that the city purchased a Nasal Ranger to crack down on the plant. The Ranger, a specialized tool that looks like a bullhorn people can hold to their noses to increase olfactory sensitivity, was bought for $1,475 and will help volunteers detect high levels of noxious nuisances while also keeping air quality in check.

Cedar Rapids, the second-largest city in Iowa, is home to many grain processing plants, including General Mills and Quaker Oats, which is the largest cereal plant in the world. In Cedar Rapids, most people claim the smells emanating from processing plants are more or less innocuous, pleasantly redolent of Cap'n Crunch's Crunch Berries or oatmeal, though some days these sites can offer up a miasma of odors.

Burnt corn; stale, rotting garbage; and overcooked oatmeal are some of the more overpowering smells that combine into one nasty stench. Cedar Rapids is also home to the food manufacturing sites of Archer Daniels Midland (ADM), Cargill, and Ralston Foods. You'll know when you get close to the town: It will beckon you with clouds of smoke emanating from the industrial center, followed by the smell.

To add insult to injury, at least 100 blocks in Cedar Rapids were underwater when the Cedar River flooded in June 2008. And weeks later, the debris and garbage remaining from the flood began piling up, so much that officials had to reopen the formerly closed Cedar Rapids landfill (once known as Mount Trashmore) to accommodate what equated to four football fields, or 2 years' worth, of trash. Any way you put it, Cedar Rapids stinks. The city sits, unfortunately, on the connector route I-380, between Iowa City, on I-80, and Waterloo, on Highway 20. If you find yourself in that area, stay on I-80 to get to Des Moines, and take I-35 north if you need it. Avoid I-380.

Spring Valley Lake and Victorville, California

Ever since the Nutro pet-food processing plant was installed in Spring Valley Lake, California, in March 2006, people have been pummeled with unbearable odors. If you've smelled your dog's kibble, you can probably guess that the process required to form chunks of meat and veggies into hard kernels is going to be a stinky one.

Alarmingly close to residential areas, the Nutro plant has been the top priority for the Mojave Desert Air Quality Management District, where community relations and education manager Violette Roberts has helped to expedite odor abatement in and around Spring Valley Lake—without lengthy legal action.

Barely 1 month after the Nutro plant was installed, nuisance complaints started cascading into the district offices. Between May 2006, when the complaints started surfacing, and February 2008, the district tallied 4,566 in all. Roberts clarifies that "a lot of these are repeat complaints," but in the month of March 2008 alone, the district's own staff person dedicated solely to documenting complaints tallied 174 of them.

As with many of the other stinky places, the stench in Spring Valley is temperamental and depends greatly on the winds—but someone is always getting the smell.

Since the plant was first installed in 2006, a much taller ventilation stack has replaced the older one, to spit out the odorous fumes much higher into the atmosphere, and this has helped Spring Valley greatly improve the stench. The good news is that Nutro plans to install a "regenerative thermal oxidizer," or RTO, which is expected to get rid of the smell almost altogether. Recent testing and commissioning of odor control equipment at the plant showed that the fix appears to be working well.

Spring Valley is about 80 miles northeast of Los Angeles and is virtually unavoidable if you're driving from L.A. to Las Vegas, as I-15 is the main route between those two cities, and Spring Valley sits right in the way. In order to miss this area on your drive, you can take Highway 247 south out of Barstow (which you'll hit if you're on I-15) and then take Highway 18 out of Lucerne Valley, which spits out in San Bernardino. It'll take longer, but it's a surefire way to avoid the stench of Spring Valley.

Lewiston, Idaho

Lewiston, Idaho, has a long history of being one of the western United States' stinkiest cities, despite its prime location near the Pacific Northwest, just 11 miles from the Nez Perce National Historical Park. Situated relatively close to the downtown area of Lewiston (Nez Perce County) and Clarkston, Washington, sits the menacing Potlatch Corporation pulp and paper mill. Although Lewiston's stench, like Hereford's, is the smell of money for locals, it doesn't make a traveler's experience driving through it any better.

The odor of Lewiston has a lot to do with where it's placed geographically, with little ventilation. In the early to mid-1990s, an air sampling taken in the Lewiston-Clarkston Valley showed chloroform and benzene in levels considered by experts to be harmful to humans.

In 2003, the EPA reported that Potlatch emitted 350 tons of methanol, 62 tons of ammonia, 38 tons of acetaldehyde, and 5 tons of methyl ethyl ketone a year—and the truth is, none of that stuff smells very good.

For the brave-nosed and irony-loving traveler, Lewiston has a Scenic Byway, U.S. 12, running right through it. But if you want to avoid the town—and you should—while you're motoring through the West, chasing the wide-open-spaces experience, make sure that, if you're coming from, say, Boise, Idaho, you stay on I-84 and later hook into more significant roads such as Highway 395 and I-90, which would be the easiest way to avoid the whole area.

Williamsburg, Michigan

Tucked between Elk Lake and Grand Traverse Bay is a great pit stop for the road trip through Michigan's watery regions: Williamsburg, Michigan, is off the beaten path, with rolling hills and a handful of old-fashioned bed-and-breakfasts. It's hard to imagine that life in the once-pristine township is no bowl of cherries.

In January 2006, Bill O'Brien, of the *Traverse City Record-Eagle,* reported on the fetid odors emanating from Williamsburg Receiving and Storage's fruit-processing plant, a place where fresh cherries are turned into delectable maraschino cherries. Turns out that the simple maraschino packs a pretty pungent stench, which may help explain why the locals plan outdoor parties but don't stay outside for long.

The reason: a horrible smell coming from the plant's industrial wastewater site, composed of ferocious quantities of sulfites and salt used in processing the cherries. Imagine a 5-million-gallon, football-field-size lagoon of stagnant wastewater. Welcome to Williamsburg.

In November 2005, the cherry plant's wastewater site spilled nearly one million gallons of the stuff directly into the parking lot of the plant, eventually contaminating local wetlands, as well as drinking-water wells in residential areas. The Michigan Department of Environmental Quality (DEQ) sent inspectors to the area, and as O'Brien reported, one staff member noted that the smell "would knock you over." The DEQ and a group of neighboring property owners sued Williamsburg Receiving and Storage over the environmental problems and reached a negotiated settlement in May 2006 that included $150,000 in fines payable to the state, plus payments to some of the neighboring property owners. The number of complaints over the stink has dropped since then, but the state continues to evaluate the effects of the spill and contamination of the nearby groundwater and soil. Until that's cleared up, I suggest staying away.

The town is about 12 miles east of Traverse City and about 40 miles north of Cadillac. If you want to head north from Cadillac, stick with Highway 115, which coincides with Highway 37 at Mesick. Take 37 north into Traverse City in order to miss Williamsburg. Or, just to be safe, take 115 all the way to the coast of Lake Michigan for a more scenic drive.

International Honorable Mentions

Taean County, South Korea

Residents of Taean County, South Korea, just 95 miles southwest of Seoul, were horrified by the worst oil spill in the nation's history on December 7, 2007. Home to wildlife, fish farms, and even a national park, Taean County will be hard pressed to encourage tourists—previously numbering in the millions—to return for a visit.

The *New York Times* covered the disaster, noting that officials and volunteers managing the spill have called the odors "stomach churning" and

---

Rotorua, New Zealand

Home to constantly emitting sulfuric gases, Rotorua is the self-proclaimed stink capital of the world—in fact, it calls itself "Sulfur City." You want to smell rotten eggs endlessly? You've come to the right place. This geothermally active region is actually a major tourist destination for its steaming geysers, otherworldly pools of bubbling mineral lakes, and healing mud baths. But don't pack your Prada for this trip. The smell of sulfur not only will overpower you during your stay, but will stick to your clothes through several washings! Is it worth a visit? For the first-time tourist, perhaps yes, with the cautions mentioned above. Worth a second visit? No.

Naples, the Stinkiest Place on Earth? Sometimes

Lots of organized tours to Italy go to or through Naples, the third-largest city in the country, where people usually visit to see Mount Vesuvius and interesting Roman ruins. But they'll also see something that the brochures don't mention: piles of festering filth and trash. In Naples and the surrounding Campania region, the waste disposal industry is Mafia run, specifically by the Camorra, with often disastrous consequences and no way to cut through the red tape. The city goes through cycles when it is literally drowning in garbage.

Things really came to a head when collectors stopped picking up the trash in Naples on December 21, 2007 . . . and didn't come back until early to mid-January 2008! A few months later, the European Union filed suit against Italy for failure to dispose of the massive piles of garbage in Naples. In the meantime, residents were surrounded by heaping mounds of moldering trash, and many took to burning the piles, which created a toxic hazard and an overwhelming stench. And that wasn't the first time this happened: The region's dumps hit maximum capacity more than a decade ago, causing the problem to arise almost on an annual basis.

Local officials have yet to announce a yearly garbage festival in an attempt to attract curious, unwitting tourists, but that might be their only salvation. Speaking of salvation: Save yourself and don't go there.

have consequently suffered nausea and headaches. Fish farms, oyster clusters, and clam beds are coated in layers of the stuff.

Ironically, just 1 week before the spill, the South Korean town of Yosu had won a bid to host an international event entitled Expo, expected to occur in 2012 and highlighting a theme of "the living ocean and coast"—a phrase that planners hoped would encourage a heightened environmental awareness in Asia. The slick has been accumulating since the December onslaught, and even the 7,000 people working around the clock to cope with the disaster were not enough. Looks like that nauseating stench will linger for quite some time.

Dharavi Slum, Mumbai, India

Dharavi, one of the largest slums in Asia, located in the middle of India's financial center of Mumbai, is replete with open sewers, cramped housing facilities, and poor sanitation, although electricity and plumbing do exist. Oddly enough, because of its booming economy, it's become a bizarre, absurd paradox. It's one of the world's dirtiest urban areas, but also one of the fastest growing.

In July 2006, the U.K.'s *Independent* covered the slum, describing it as "a tour of scents" and adding, "Turn a corner and the smell of soap is abruptly replaced by the stink of an open sewer. Around the next corner it is replaced by the delicious smell of a biscuit factory. Beyond that there is suddenly the unbearable stench of drying goat hides at the tanners, so strong it makes you gag." You can decide to go or not, but once you're there, you have no control over what you'll smell.

Want to see it for yourself? You can take a tour of the Dharavi slum through Reality Tours and Travel (realitytoursandtravel.com). This tour takes you through the slum in small groups, with no cameras allowed, for a firsthand perspective on how the locals live. Controversial? Yes. Voyeuristic? Maybe. Educational? Certainly. Disgusting? Count on it.

Chapter 5

NATURAL DISASTERS

HURRICANES, TORNADOES, EARTHQUAKES, OH MY!

Unless you're getting combat pay from the Weather Channel, there are dozens of places you should avoid if you don't want to be hit with tornadoes, hurricanes, floods, and other weather phenomena.

With occasional exceptions—such as the tornado that ripped through downtown Atlanta in March 2008, causing $150 million in damage—bad weather does have recognized geographic targets, patterns, and seasons.

Let's start with hurricanes.

Hurricanes

To date, Hurricane Katrina, in 2005, was the biggest natural disaster in U.S. history, and the emergency response to it was one of our government's biggest failures.

More than 1,700 people died in Hurricane Katrina and in the resulting floods, with damage estimated to have cost as much as $81.2 billion.

But what other areas would suffer a similar fate if a Category 5 hurricane were to rip through town? What about a Category 4? Or 3?

For travelers, the areas you're likely to be concerned with during hurricane season are the Caribbean, southern Florida, Louisiana, Texas, and the East Coast. Though hurricane season varies by region, it officially runs from

June 1 through November 30; the threat of major hurricanes peaks as you travel eastward from August to October.

According to the National Weather Service, you want to start worrying when you're facing a Category 3, which involves 111 to 130 mph winds that can destroy mobile homes and cause some damage to small buildings. A Category 4 hurricane reaches 131 to 155 mph winds and can destroy roofs, erode beaches, and cause floods that reach inland. A Category 5 essentially will devastate an area, and you definitely don't want to be there when it strikes!

Outer Banks, North Carolina

Off the coast of North Carolina, about 100 miles of barrier islands make up a long, thin chain known as the Outer Banks.

The islands have a year-round population of about 33,518, but that number swells to more than 300,000 in the summer months as visitors flock to expansive beaches, an abundance of outdoor activities, and the wild, undeveloped landscapes of the nationally conserved areas. In fact, the 70-mile Cape Hatteras National Seashore, in the middle of the Outer Banks, is our country's first National Seashore.

But, as the National Park Service suggests (rather ominously), "On these narrow barrier islands, things never stay the same." The waters of the Outer Banks have long been known for their volatility. This area is where the cold waters of the Labrador Current meet the warm waters of the Gulf Stream. One result is a wonderful biodiversity of marine life; the other is a life-threatening environment for ships. Sailors who have faced the opposing currents, heavy fogs, and dangerous shoals have nicknamed the area "the Graveyard of the Atlantic."

In the Outer Banks, peak hurricane season is August through October. But in recent years, some big storms have hit as early as late July.

North Carolina and the Outer Banks are no strangers to hurricanes. According to HurricaneCity.com, hurricanes and tropical storms have hit the islands of Cape Hatteras 55 times since 1871. The islands jut out into the Atlantic in such a way that they are, in fact, one of the most hurricane-prone areas in the world.

Being one of the lowest coastal areas in the country, the islands, which are nothing more than ribbons of sand, suffer major erosion during severe storms. It's estimated that the 93-mile stretch from Cape Hatteras to the Virginia state line averages 4.7 feet of erosion annually. Hurricanes can speed up this process, and with global warming increasing the frequency and strength of storms, things aren't getting any better. In a bad storm, a hurricane can wash away 20 feet or more of beach.

When Hurricane Isabel struck in 2003, it opened a 1,700-foot-wide inlet through Hatteras Island, cutting off Hatteras Village from the rest of the island for several months. The Pamlico Sound's waters became saltier, threatening the habitat for crabs, fish, and oysters.

Local officials spend millions of dollars to keep the sand where it is, employing measures such as sandbags and sand replenishment, but houses that were built 200 to 300 yards from the ocean now have water lapping at their porches. All it will take is one Category 5 hurricane and those homes are going for a permanent swim.

A lot of North Carolinians remember Hurricane Fran, which killed 37 people in 1996, 24 in North Carolina alone, and was considered to be the worst local disaster at the time. But that record was wiped out on September 16, 1999, when Hurricane Floyd struck near Cape Fear, inflicting more than $3 billion in damage in North Carolina and nearly 60 fatalities.

Still want to risk a visit during the summer? Keep in mind that even with early warning, evacuation routes clog quickly, because many towns and villages have only one road to get you in . . . and out. Everyone then has to cross the 2.5-mile Bonner Bridge, which has linked Hatteras to the rest of the cape for nearly 50 years. In the summertime, as many as 10,000 vehicles cross the bridge daily, and it is the only evacuation route from Hatteras during a hurricane.

Did I mention the bridge is also sagging? It sits loosely on a bed of sand and has been corroded by salt water and rust. Bottom line: North Carolina's Outer Banks are due for another pounding, and a new bridge is well overdue.

But North Carolina is hardly the most hurricane-prone state in the country—Florida, for example, far outranks it.

South Florida

"Florida is the most hurricane vulnerable and the most hit state of all," said Ken Kaye, a senior writer for the *South Florida Sun-Sentinel*. "For Florida residents, living here is like being a bunch of bowling pins, waiting for someone to roll a ball across the Atlantic. And those balls keep on coming."

Kaye reported that between 1851 and 2006, Florida was hit almost twice as many times as any other hurricane-prone state—113 hits in all, 37 of which were considered to be major (Category 3 or above).

According to HurricaneCity.com, Florida has 12 of the top 25 most affected hurricane cities, including Delray Beach, Boca Raton, Miami, Fort Lauderdale, and Key West.

The biggest evacuation challenge: the Keys. "Throughout most of the Keys, there is only one road to and from the mainland," explains Kaye. "It's a two-lane highway, and all it takes is one minor accident for it to be clogged. When a storm is coming, it's bumper-to-bumper cars all the way up to Miami."

As a result, hurricane evacuation orders come early in the Keys. Still, what would happen if the area were in the direct line of a powerful Category 4 or 5 storm?

In 2006, scientists at the National Hurricane Center conducted simulations to determine a realistic forecast of what would happen if South Florida were hit by hurricanes stronger than Wilma and Katrina. (Both were Category 1 or 2 storms when they passed through the area.) The scientists simulated the effects of a Category 3 Hurricane Katrina, with 125 mph winds, and a Category 4 Wilma, with 150 mph winds and a "disastrously lazy forward speed of only 3 mph."

The result? "Seven feet of seawater swamps Key Biscayne and 45 miles of coastline from Miami Beach to Deerfield Beach," reported the *Miami Herald*. "Saltwater surges through some houses in Hollywood, Coconut Grove and elsewhere. Waist-deep freshwater blankets vast regions of suburban Broward and Miami-Dade counties. Ferocious winds crush tens of thousands of roofs and gut numerous office buildings. Residents who defy orders to evacuate skyscrapers in Miami Beach, on Hollywood's beach and along Miami's downtown corridors could be blown out of their apartments. Power outages persist for months rather than weeks."

And the irony, of course, is that Fort Lauderdale continues to promote itself as "the Venice of America." If these predictions ever pan out, they might be right! Come to think of it, San Antonio also promotes itself as "the Venice of America." Here's a news bulletin: There's only one real Venice. It's in Italy. Live with it.

Bahamas

If you're planning to go to the Bahamas between June 1 and November 30, I have just two words of advice: travel insurance.

Ever since the dramatic 2004 hurricane season, when Hurricanes Frances and Jeanne pummeled the Bahamas, some hotels and resorts in the

Bahamas, as well as parts of the Caribbean and Jamaica, have heavily promoted their "hurricane guarantees," which basically say that visitors can cancel their vacation during a hurricane with a no-penalty refund. Some offer complete refunds or vouchers for the entirety of your vacation; others offer a refund or voucher for the nights lost due to a late arrival or early departure. Sounds nice, but is it too good to be true? Let's take a look.

- The guarantee doesn't apply if there is a hurricane watch before you leave home. So, if you're without travel insurance and a hurricane is bearing down on your Grand Bahama Island vacation, you can't skip the trip and expect to cash in on your hurricane guarantee.

- Policies kick in only when the National Hurricane Service (NHS) officially deems a storm a hurricane, when the sustained wind speeds reach 74 mph or above. If you depart before the hurricane is officially identified, you're out of luck.

- In most cases, the storm has to hit your resort directly for the guarantee to be valid.

- A hurricane guarantee certainly doesn't apply to your airfare and won't cover any additional expenses you might incur if you're stuck on the island.

- If your vacation is scheduled after a hurricane hits, and if the hotel or resort claims to be open during your reservation, they can—and probably will—deny any cancellation waiver. If the airport is open but your airline hasn't resumed service to the island, you're not covered, either.

- And last, but certainly not least, is a little caveat that's buried in every hurricane guarantee: "This offer is subject to change and may be withdrawn at any time without notice." Like . . . *when there is a hurricane?*

Galveston, Texas

I'm sorry. Unless you like ugly, oily beaches and a totally unimpressive waterfront, Galveston, Texas, is a definite don't-go-there destination. Here's another reason not to go: "People are not supposed to live on a sandbar," wrote historian Gary Cartwright about Galveston, "and the fact that they choose to live on this one tells you something about the collective psyche."

Those who choose to live in places like the island city of Galveston are

Indianola, Texas

Once a thriving port town on the Gulf Coast, Indianola finally succumbed to a series of natural disasters that ultimately made it impossible to rebuild.

In 1875, the city boasted a healthy population of about 5,000; Indianola was the second-largest port in Texas and a major military depot. On September 15, a hurricane razed the city and killed anywhere from 150 to 300 residents. The locals gathered up the debris and rebuilt, vowing that the city would be stronger than ever; 11 years later, on August 19, 1886, another hurricane struck, followed by a fire. This time, rebuilding wasn't an option. Storm erosion has submerged much of the former city under water, and Indianola is nothing more than a ghost town, with about 125 residents remaining.

fully aware of the risks, just as Los Angeles residents accept the possibility of earthquakes and Midwesterners are used to regular tornado sirens.

With an island's rugged beauty comes great vulnerability, and Galveston is no exception. Why? For one thing, it's located smack in the middle of the Gulf Coast. Second, it's attached to the nearest big city, Houston, only by a causeway, a toll bridge, and ferryboat service on the east end of the city.

"Getting people out of Galveston isn't the problem, but Interstate 45 feeds into Houston, with other roads leading into it, so you can get grid-lock," says Heber Taylor, editor of the *Galveston County Daily News*. "During Hurricane Rita, there were reports that people were on the road for 23 hours trying to get out; there was massive gridlock."

In summer, the population can grow from 60,000 to more than 100,000. (Imagine being stuck with all those people on that oily, ugly beach!) That's an awful lot of cars to exit the island, fast, when a hurricane approaches.

Galveston made history back on September 8, 1900, when a hurricane flooded the city, killing thousands (anywhere from 6,000 to 12,000) and nearly wiping it out entirely. Was it a message from the gods that maybe even they thought that people should leave and never return?

Message not received. After that storm, locals took it upon themselves to build a 10-mile-long, 17-foot-high concrete seawall to protect the city from flooding and storm surges, jacked up all the buildings, and pumped a slurry of sand and water behind the seawall to raise the island.

More than a century later, the wall is still holding. But how long can Galveston hold on? When Category 2 Hurricane Ike swept through the island in September 2008, it left behind another path of devastation and despair. For the more than 2,000 residents who refused to evacuate, the real horror wasn't the storm itself, but its aftermath. We're talking no running water, no electricity, no gas, and limited emergency care. Officials urged them to leave. For those who evacuated, the same officials warned "don't return." Residents—either way you look at it—didn't have much of a choice.

But you do have a choice when it comes to Galveston, even in good weather. Hurricanes notwithstanding, there's still that oily beach!

Grand Cayman

"Devastation beyond imagination." That was the headline of the Cayman Net News after Hurricane Ivan tore through Grand Cayman Island on September 12, 2004. Roofless, gutted buildings; flattened trees; washed-up graves—it was a nightmarish scene that lasted for months.

Here's something you won't find in the brochures. According to HurricaneCity.com, the Cayman Islands are affected by hurricanes every 2.21 years. In fact, the Cayman Islands are the most affected islands in the site's database.

Although not the most recent storm, Hurricane Ivan was the worst hurricane to hit the island in more than 80 years. It took months for the local infrastructure, such as power and water, to recover, and years before the island returned to its prehurricane state. If you're willing to take the risk with your tropical vacation, remember that hurricane season runs from June through November, and the highest-risk months are August through November. And if you want to stay dry, skip the rainy season, which hits from May through November.

Tornadoes

Tornadoes are complex creatures and need certain conditions in order to form. Tornado season is mainly in spring and summer, when warm, moist winds from the Gulf of Mexico move north to meet the colder, drier Canadian winds that are moving south. And that's why the Great Plains are so prone to tornadoes, particularly along the infamous Tornado Alley, which includes Iowa, Kansas, Nebraska, Oklahoma, and Texas.

The Fujita Scale (F Scale) measures a tornado's intensity, although in 2007 the National Weather Service announced that it would be using the Enhanced Fujita Scale (EF Scale) to more accurately assess wind speeds. All you need to know is this: An F0 is no big deal, causing light damage such as overturned signs and broken tree branches; an F3 can rip off roofs, uproot trees, and overturn vehicles as large as trains. An F5? We're talking almost unimaginable devastation, like that of the tornado that flattened the town of Greensburg, Kansas, in 2007.

The thing about tornadoes is that they're notoriously unpredictable. So, if you don't want to be at the wrong place at the wrong time, your best bet is just don't go there.

Oklahoma City–Moore, Oklahoma

Even if it seems unfair to single out a city based on its geography, it's hard to ignore the fact that Oklahoma City lies within the heart of Tornado Alley, earning it the dubious honor of being one of the most tornado-prone cities in America. According to the National Oceanic and Atmospheric Administration (NOAA) National Weather Service Forecast Office in Norman, Oklahoma, the peak month for tornadoes throughout the Plains is May, with frequent occurrences also in April and June.

How many tornadoes are we talking about?

"We average about 50 tornadoes per year," said News 9 meteorologist Gary England, of local CBS affiliate KWTV. "On May 3, 1999, we had almost 70 in 1 day. We measured the strongest winds on the face of the earth, 300-plus mph with just one of the tornadoes, which was known as an F5." This tornado moved through Moore and Oklahoma City, turning out to be the costliest and most violent in history worldwide, and the deadliest ever for the Oklahoma City area.

"I wouldn't move to Moore," laughs England.

But the good news, he says, is that sirens sound when a tornado is spotted or shows up on radar, and residents usually get at least a 10-minute warning. What that means is you head for shelter immediately and hope that you took out the full insurance on your rental car, because it probably won't be there—or recognizable—when you emerge.

But that's assuming you even get the warning. Consider the case of Anniston, Alabama.

Anniston, Alabama

After a series of tornadoes pounded Kansas, Missouri, and Tennessee on May 4, 2003, killing 37 people, the American Meteorological Survey (AMS) used the opportunity to survey public response to tornado warnings given to the residents of homes that sustained F4 or F5 damage.

Turns out, in many tornado-prone areas, residents don't listen for sirens. They stay tuned to their radios or televisions to alert them. But what if the radios don't broadcast the alerts?

Welcome to the world of radio-station consolidation and automated broadcasting. I'm talking about the world of radio behemoths like Clear Channel. When local stations were purchased by large media giants and switched to canned programming, it often meant the end of local, breaking news and any human opportunity to interrupt programming with news alerts.

In January 2008, as foul weather moved into the Anniston area, residents reached for their radios and tuned to WDNG-AM 1450. Instead of warnings of the impending tornado, what they got was what one listener later described as the continuation of a taped talk-radio rant about the shortcomings of John McCain and Mike Huckabee. Fortunately, had there been a major disaster, the emergency broadcast system would have overridden any radio programming, but in the end, the storm passed with little damage and no injuries.

Still, the lesson remains: Unless you're driving a car equipped with Doppler radar, you might want to avoid Anniston during tornado season.

Jackson, Tennessee

Jackson's Convention & Visitors Bureau proudly displays the state motto, "The stage is set for you." But in reality, that stage has been set twice: first for crime and then for tornadoes. The city did itself proud by emerging from being number 10 on the dreaded Morgan Quitno list of the Most Dangerous Cities in the United States for 2006 to off the list completely the next year. But there's not much they can do about the tornadoes.

Located between Nashville and Memphis in west Tennessee, this little city, population just over 60,000, is the place to avoid come tornado season. The irony is that Tennessee isn't even in Tornado Alley, but somehow it seems that the town of Jackson in Madison County is often the wrong place at all the wrong times.

Jackson and surrounding communities were devastated when a tornado ripped through the city on February 5, 2008. The twister was part of an outbreak of 82 confirmed tornadoes that killed at least 58 people in Tennessee, Alabama, Arkansas, and Kentucky.

This was the third major tornado to hit Jackson in 10 years. On May 4, 2003, a massive outbreak of supercells destroyed communities in Tennessee, Arkansas, Kansas, and Missouri, and killed at least 11 people in Madison

Aurora, Nebraska

"The possibilities are endless," boasts the official Web site of Aurora, Nebraska. Turns out that's something of an exaggeration, unless you're talking about tornadoes, severe thunderstorms, and the possibility of getting clonked by hail the size of a bowling ball.

That's right, the quiet little city of Aurora, about an hour west of Lincoln and home to a population of 4,225, may not offer a lot touristwise, but it holds the honor of having the largest hailstone ever recorded in the United States.

The hailstone, which had a 7-inch diameter and an 18.75-inch circumference (about the size of a soccer ball), dropped from the sky during a thunderstorm on June 22, 2003. That particular stone didn't cause any damage, but according to NOAA, the storm caused about $500,000 in property damage and $1 million in crop damage across the county. The hailstones left craters up to 14 inches wide and 3 inches deep.

If you dare to venture to Aurora in the summertime, the good news is that death by hailstone is actually quite rare. But in a state that suffers an average of 40 tornadoes a year and has the highest annual hail frequency in the country (on par with southeastern Wyoming and northeastern Colorado), don't say I didn't warn you!

County alone. Prior to that, January 17, 1999, brought one of the most severe tornado outbreaks ever recorded in that month. That night, Jackson was actually hit by two tornadoes, killing six people in the county and destroying hundreds of homes and public buildings.

Bottom line: Tornado season is a threat in both spring and winter. That's right, there's a regular tornado season, which starts in March and reaches full pitch in May, and then, as history has shown, there's a secondary tornado season in November and December. And recently, January and February have been surprisingly active; in fact, February 2008 set a record with 148 tornadoes, beating the old record of 83 twisters in 1971. For some perspective, the 30-year average for February is 23.

Floods

It sounds like the plot of a bad disaster film, but massive flooding is a real threat in some parts of the world. And with ever-rising sea levels, for some places, it's already too late.

Tuvalu Islands

You know things are bad when a tiny island nation threatens to sue the United States and Australia for greenhouse-gas emissions.

Tuvalu, a Polynesian island in the Pacific Ocean, is made up of a group of atolls and reef islands. It has long been a tourist destination for those looking for a more off-the-beaten-path Polynesian resort, but probably not for much longer. It's not the smallest nation in the world (Vatican City, Monaco, and Nauru have it beat), but it is the second-lowest-lying country in the world (behind the Maldives), which makes it prone to disaster. The highest point on Tuvalu reaches only about 16 feet, and rising sea levels are threatening the very being of the island and its people. "It could be the most fascinating example of sea-level rise," said Steve Smith, a spokesman for Futerra Sustainability Communications.

Even the Honorable Saufatu Sopoanga, former prime minister of Tuvalu, wrote an essay about it in 2004 entitled "Stop My Nation Vanishing," published in the United Nations Environment Programme's magazine, *Our Planet.*

"What we see in Tuvalu is marginally higher (peak) sea levels when tides are highest," he writes. "This means annual high tides are creeping further and further ashore. There is crop damage from previously unseen levels of saltwater intrusion. There is a higher incidence of wave washover during storms or periods of strong tidal activity."

But his advice was never heeded: The King Tide, the highest tides of the year, flooded the island's main road in January 2008. Leaders have already approached New Zealand and Australia to form a contingency plan to relocate islanders before the island disappears. With just over 12,000 locals still remaining, the Tuvalu government has made an agreement that allows 75 Tuvaluans to relocate to New Zealand each year.

San Francisco Bay, California

Don't go to . . . San Francisco? Well, at the very least, you may want to avoid this area during a heavy rainstorm. (Keep in mind, the rainy season is from November to March.) Rising sea levels are threatening San Francisco Bay in astounding proportions.

What's going on? The San Joaquin River flows north, the Sacramento River flows south, and they meet in the Sacramento–San Joaquin River Delta, which is almost entirely below sea level.

The delta covers about 1,153 square miles, but we're talking about 280 square miles of low-level land that's at risk, with potential flooding in major areas around San Francisco Bay, including downtown San Francisco, both the San Francisco and Oakland airports, and virtually all of Silicon Valley.

Between 1850 and 1960, San Francisco Bay was filled in with land at an average rate of 4 square miles a year to create more ground for industry and homes. As a result, the bay rose 7 inches in the past 150 years.

Things may be happening sooner than we expect. The U.S. Geological Survey (USGS) reports that during the winter of 1997–98, high winds, heavy rains, and abnormally high tides caused by El Niño "wreaked havoc" on the San Francisco Bay Area. The report read, "The Pacific Ocean surged over parking lots and the coastal highway at San Francisco's Ocean Beach, and whitecaps up to six feet high splashed over the city's waterfront Embarcadero for the first time in recent memory. Elsewhere, U.S. Highway 101 north of the Golden Gate Bridge was flooded by as much as 4 feet of water from San Francisco Bay, and other low-lying areas around the bay were also swamped, forcing hundreds of people to flee their homes."

Tack on another El Niño anomaly after the rise in California's temperatures, and you've got trouble.

Shishmaref, Alaska

Talk about don't go there—the indigenous people of Shishmaref, Alaska, can't even go to their *own* place. They're on their way out. The 400-year-old little Alaskan village built on the permafrost of Sarichef Island is finding its coast melting, and melting sea ice is making the area increasingly vulnerable to storm surges and erosion. In addition, one storm brought 90 mph winds, toppling cliff sides and eroding at least 50 feet of ground. A bigger storm could effectively wipe out the entire community.

The water from the surrounding Chukchi Sea is advancing toward this village and putting the 600 residents in a precarious situation. It's estimated that the entire village will disappear within decades. In fact, more than half the residents of the nearby village of Kivalina were forced to evacuate as recently as September 13, 2007, when a storm sent 3- to 4-foot-high surges into the town. One thing is for sure: The future of Shishmaref will tell a cautionary tale of global warming and its devastating effects on our communities.

Organizations such as the San Francisco Bay Conservation and Development Commission, a committee of government-appointed members and citizens, are working to develop a regional strategy that will incorporate protective measures such as levees, dikes, wetland restoration, and new seawalls.

International Risks

Bangladesh

When it comes to vulnerability to natural disasters, Bangladesh stands out among the rest. Cyclones, earthquakes, floods, and the occasional drought pummel this little country too often for comfort.

In 2006, the Earth Institute's Center for Hazards and Risk Research (CHRR) at Columbia University, the World Bank, the Norwegian Geotechnical Institute, and other partners produced a report entitled *Natural Disaster Hotspots: A Global Risk Analysis*. These high-risk areas were identified in order to help develop safety nets and technologies to prevent future deaths.

According to Art Lerner-Lam, director of CHRR, "Bangladesh loses a very large fraction of its land every year due to flooding. . . . However, ever since the floods in the 1960s and 1970s when Bangladesh was split off from Pakistan, the government has been putting [flood control] measures into place. It's very impressive how they've progressed." Some of those measures include building earthen embankments and drainage areas.

The problem with Bangladesh can be summed up in three words: location, location, location. Bangladesh is susceptible to cyclones that emerge from the Bay of Bengal.

Approximately 90 percent of this coastal country sits less than 32 feet above sea level, and much of the country lies low and flat between the Ganges and Brahmaputra rivers, making it vulnerable to annual flooding—especially during monsoon season, from June to October. Tack on earthquakes from the Himalayas and rising sea levels from climate change, and you have prime conditions for a catastrophic natural disaster.

The country was devastated in 2007 by monsoon season, which killed more than 200 people in Bangladesh and 1,550 in India. In September 1998, one of the worst floods in modern history submerged about 66 percent of the country, killing more than 1,000 and rendering another 30 million residents homeless as hundreds of thousands of houses were washed away. Before that, a cyclone killed an estimated 300,000 in 1970, and in April 1991, more than 130,000 were killed by cyclone-related flooding.

Indonesia

Indonesia is fast becoming one of the most natural-disaster-prone areas in the world, and there's really no season that is safe from risk. According to the Earth Institute, the southern and western islands, such as Java and Sumatra, are at extreme risk of "droughts, earthquakes, floods, landslides, and volcanoes."

Indonesia, home to 129 active volcanoes, is located on the Pacific Ring of Fire, a geologically active circular area of the Pacific basin that is prone to earthquakes and volcanic eruptions. In fact, 90 percent of the world's earthquakes occur along the Ring of Fire. The second-most seismically active region in the Pacific Ocean is the Alpide Belt, which runs from Java all the way to the Atlantic—and this was the area where a massive earthquake struck on December 26, 2004. The world was stunned when the 9.0-magnitude earthquake off the west coast of Sumatra triggered a series of tsunamis of up to 50 feet. It was the deadliest tsunami in recorded history, killing tens of thousands of residents and tourists.

Still tempted to go?

Even worse, Indonesia also suffers from "man-made" disasters that threaten its inhabitants. Environmentalists say that illegal deforestation is causing flash flooding—the lack of vegetation allows tropical downpours to flood large regions. And, though not a natural disaster, this has made things worse: On May 28, 2006, in the Porong subdistrict of Sidoarjo in East Java, a team drilling for natural gas caused a massive explosion—leading to a torrent of hot, steaming mud and gas that still flows to this day and has forced more than 50,000 people from their homes.

India

Monsoons, floods, droughts, windstorms, and earthquakes: It seems that you can expect a natural disaster in India at any given time of the year.

According to the Earth Institute, you're more likely to see droughts in the northwestern region of India, toward the Pakistani border, which encompasses such cities as Jodhpur and Ahmedabad; meanwhile, floods are more prevalent in the eastern part of the country. The Indian Ocean earthquake in 2004 caused the devastating tsunami that demolished India's eastern coastal areas, especially the state of Tamil Nadu. It was an unusual occurrence in this region, but one that continues to resonate.

If you're planning a visit, watch out for the months of June through September. That's when you're likely—okay, just about guaranteed—to be drenched by monsoons, suffer unbearably hot weather, and risk running right into a cyclone. During this season, nearly all of the country will get soaked, including the western coast, which includes the resort area of Goa; New Delhi, in central India; and Calcutta, on the eastern side.

Most Overdue for a Pounding

New York, New York

Turns out, the eastern seaboard is long overdue for a major hurricane, and New York City could bear the brunt of it. Hurricane Gloria in 1985 caused some damage on parts of Long Island but dropped only about 3.5 inches of rain in Central Park. The last major hurricane to hit the area was way back in 1938, when the "Long Island Express" sent a 15-foot storm tide over Long Island, demolishing parts of the Hamptons and killing 29 people in that area.

New York City is at risk of a major storm surge because of its geographic position in the Atlantic Ocean—something called the New York Bight, the sharp bend where New York meets New Jersey. According to the USGS, the New York Bight area has a "moderate to high" level of coastal vulnerability. A study conducted by a computerized model known as SLOSH (Sea, Lake and Overland Surges from Hurricanes), developed by the Federal Emergency Management Agency, the U.S. Army Corps of Engineers, and the National Weather Service, found that the bight would amplify the effects of the storm surge of even a moderate hurricane.

According to a lecture by hurricane expert Nicholas Coch, PhD, a professor at Queens College, "Whenever a hurricane comes up here, you add one category to it because we're in the worst possible place in the world to be." New York City, he pointed out, is the only major U.S. city to have been hit by a major hurricane three times (in 1821, 1893, and 1938). "The hurricanes that hit you will go hundreds of miles inland," he said.

Meteorologists say that if a major hurricane hits anywhere near New York City, sea levels could rise by 25 feet. And if that happens, you want to be as far away as possible from lower Manhattan, Brooklyn, and Jersey City.

Southern California

This is probably no big surprise, but Southern California is due for a major earthquake on the San Andreas Fault, and this one could devastate Los Angeles.

At a 2007 news conference at the University of Southern California, seismologists said that the southernmost section of the fault has not ruptured in more than 300 years and is about 150 years overdue. In 2008, the USGS in Pasadena, California, calculated that there is a 99.7 percent chance that a quake of magnitude 6.7 or larger will strike California in the next 30 years.

Scientists still can't precisely predict exactly where in California the quake will happen, but the odds are higher that a quake will hit Southern California than northern California.

San Diego State University seismologist and professor Kim Bak Olsen, PhD, used supercomputers to conduct a three-dimensional simulation of a San Andreas Fault earthquake. The first of its kind, the simulation showed that if the fault broke from south to north, Los Angeles could suffer from a massive 2-minute quake, leading to seismic waves becoming trapped in sedimentary basins under the city.

Let's just say that you don't want to be anywhere near Los Angeles County when it happens. The 1994 Northridge Earthquake was magnitude 6.7, killed 72 people, injured more than 9,000, and caused $25 billion in damage in the metropolitan area. I lived through it . . . but my house didn't. It was totaled. Almost instantaneously, it became a split-level. And then it had to be bulldozed.

Cumbre Vieja, Canary Islands

We know enough to fear overdue volcanic eruptions, but what about a volcano that's overdue to collapse? Cumbre Vieja is the most active volcanic ridge on the volcanic La Palma Island in Spain's Canary Islands, off the coast of Africa. Scientists fear that Cumbre Vieja's collapse will cause a tsunami that will push massive waves all the way across the Atlantic within hours.

Sounds like a doomsday movie, doesn't it? Well, according to the Benfield UCL Hazard Research Centre, a U.K.-based organization that conducts natural hazard and risk research as part of University College London, a 1949 eruption caused Cumbre Vieja's western flank to detach itself from the rest of the volcano, opening up a crack almost 2.5 miles long. Studies conflict over whether a landslide will occur in smaller pieces or one big block, but most conclude the same thing: Something major *will* happen.

The Benfield UCL Hazard Research Centre and the University of California, Santa Cruz, modeled a worst-case scenario: The west flank of Cumbre Vieja could collapse in a matter of minutes, causing waves nearly 3,000 feet high. Waves as high as 320 feet would crest over the Canary Islands and the West Saharan coast, and waves over 85 feet high would reach the north coast of Brazil. Substantial waves would strike the Atlantic coasts of Britain, Spain, Portugal, and France. Florida and the Caribbean would be hit by waves 65 to 82 feet high, just 9 hours after the landslide.

Would you want to be there when it happens? Didn't think so.

Yellowstone National Park, Wyoming

Turns out, the central part of the park, the Yellowstone Caldera, a crater that reaches 47 miles in width, has been moving upward since mid-2004 at a rate of up to 3 inches per year, faster than ever before.

The last major eruption in Yellowstone was 640,000 years ago. That was a long time ago, but today, scientists refer to "the Beast" that growls in the belly of Yellowstone. A 2005 USGS report on volcanic threats points out that this geothermally active region has experienced "recurrent earthquake swarms and ground deformation (uplift & subsidence)" and "changes in hydrothermal features."

The truth is, Yellowstone is hardly the most threatening active volcano in America. The USGS bestowed that title on Kilauea in Hawaii, followed by Mount St. Helens and Mount Rainier in Washington State. But what sets Yellowstone apart is the sheer number of visitors that descend every year: 2007 logged a record-setting 3.15 million visitors.

Is Yellowstone overdue for a big one? Scientists truly don't know for sure. Simply put, Yellowstone's long volcanic history and roiling magma beneath the caldera mean that it's entirely possible . . . we just don't know when.

Mount Taranaki, New Zealand

New Zealand is known for its beautiful vistas, notably the stunning Mount Taranaki, which dominates the landscape of the North Island.

But what if that island were covered in a layer of ash? This volcano has been so quiet that residents have gotten used to its inactivity, but as it turns out, there has been more activity than originally thought. According to vulcanologist Shane Cronin, PhD, of the Institute of Natural Resources at Massey University in Palmerston North, New Zealand, the volcano has had activity once every 90 years on average for the past 9,000 years, with a major eruption every 500 years. Research shows that the last major eruption was in 1655, and there were smaller eruptions in 1755 and probably in the early 1800s. And that kind of activity is far more frequent than they thought.

If this massive volcano, which stands 8,260 feet high, were to erupt, the lava flow wouldn't be the biggest problem—the ash cloud would cut power and water supplies, damage acres of crops, and disrupt all airline flight paths over the North Island, closing Auckland Airport. And when you consider that this volcano has been active for at least 130,000 years, a peaceful 200-odd years doesn't mean we're safe from another eruption. According to a report published in July 2007 by Cronin and other researchers, if we assume that the most recent eruption was in 1854, there's a good likelihood of its happening again in the next 50 years.

Himalayas

An enormous 7.6-magnitude earthquake rocked the Pakistan-India border in 2005, killing more than 100,000 people; a 7.7-magnitude quake devastated the city of Bhuj in Gujarat, India, in January 2001; and a quake of magnitude 6.6 hit the town of Chamoli, India, in 1999. The geologically unstable Himalayas have been the source of much devastation, and the worst may be yet to come.

The Himalayas were created more than 50 million years ago, when the Indian subcontinent collided with Asia. The subcontinent continues to butt against Asia at a rate of about 2 centimeters per year. And, according to seismologist Roger Bilham, PhD, of the University of Colorado, the Himalayas have suffered more great earthquakes than previously thought, and another big one is long overdue.

A 2001 study called "Himalayan Seismic Hazard," by Bilham and others in conjunction with the Indian Institute for Astrophysics in Bangalore, pointed out that "earthquakes in the Himalayan region occurred in 1803, 1833, 1897, 1905, 1934 and 1950."

And the biggest concern regarding this impending quake? The death toll could be massive, reported the study: "The population of India has doubled since the last great Himalayan earthquake in 1950. The urban population in

Is Anywhere Safe?

Slate.com has issued a totally unscientific—but entertaining—list that rates which U.S. states and locations within those states are the safest when it comes to natural disasters.

Want to steer clear of hurricanes, floods, and tornadoes?

Then head to . . . Storrs, Connecticut. Slate based its findings on a study of every federal disaster declaration from 1965 through 2004 and the number of people who died as a result of those disasters. The three safest states (translation: the states with the fewest federal disaster declarations): Connecticut, Massachusetts, and Rhode Island.

the Ganges Plain has increased by a factor of ten since the 1905 earthquake. . . . Today, about 50 million people are at risk from great Himalayan earthquakes, many of them in towns and villages in the Ganges plain. The capital cities of Bangladesh, Bhutan, India, Nepal, and Pakistan and several other cities with more than a million inhabitants are vulnerable to damage from some of these future earthquakes."

DISEASE CAPITALS

CATCHY, HUH?

I've always said that the destination has become incidental to the experience. But when it comes to your health, you do need to research the destination first to reassure yourself that your "experience" won't land you in the hospital . . . or worse.

The following is not so much a guide to where not to go, but a heads-up on where you need to be aware of the risks. After all, if you're traveling to West Africa, you know you're going to need to be vaccinated for yellow fever. But in some cases, certain diseases are cropping up in places that you may not expect—HIV in Eastern Europe and drug-resistant malaria in Southeast Asia, for example. Of course, common sense rules in most situations: At least 4 to 6 weeks before you depart, see your doctor to get any necessary vaccines, and wherever you travel, don't have unprotected sex, don't share needles, and please . . . skip the tattoos.

Sometimes, health issues that take center stage in the media are overblown and exaggerated—SARS; hand, foot, and mouth disease; mad cow disease; and the avian flu being recent examples.

SARS, which killed a total of 774 people between 2002 and 2003 (the most recent outbreak), didn't stop me from going to Hong Kong during that time period; hand, foot, and mouth and mad cow diseases don't stop me from visiting the United Kingdom (and there are no cows frothing at the mouth waiting for me at the airport); and the avian flu, which has killed 243 since 2003, didn't stop me from traveling throughout Asia that year. And the dreaded Ebola hasn't stopped me from traveling to Uganda, ever.

Indeed, Ebola is one disease you really don't want to catch. It is a deadly virus that is transmitted through direct contact with the blood or bodily fluids of an infected person or animal, or through dirty needles. Symptoms include high fever, headaches, muscle aches, stomach pain, fatigue, and diarrhea, and if it's not caught early, the virus is likely to cause failure of all major organs. There are four strains of the disease, including Ebola Reston, which is not fatal to humans.

The thing about Ebola is that there are few surprises in where it shows up. It's primarily found in sub-Saharan Africa, though there were some cases of the Ebola Reston strain in quarantine rooms of primate facilities in Texas and Virginia, originating with monkeys that were imported from the Philippines.

According to the U.S. Centers for Disease Control and Prevention (CDC), some of the most recent Ebola scares include a 2007 outbreak of Ebola hemorrhagic fever in the district of Bundibugyo, Uganda, where the disease infected 148 people and killed 37. Also in 2007, there was an outbreak in the Democratic Republic of the Congo, which infected 264 people and killed 187.

But it's important to put this disease, as with SARS, the avian flu, and mad cow disease, in perspective. If you look at the numbers, Ebola killed fewer than 200 people in the world last year. The more widespread influenza, on the other hand, is responsible for more than 30,000 deaths in the United States every year.

The numbers speak loudly here. Proper personal hygiene and, where appropriate, vaccinations, along with basic intuition, are usually more than enough to give you the confidence to go to these areas.

The same applies to other diseases and health challenges.

HIV/AIDS

There's no place in the world that's free of infectious disease, but in most parts of the world, common sense goes a long way, particularly when it comes to STDs. The CDC's Division of Global Migration and Quarantine studies the relationship between travel and disease, and STDs are at the top of the list. The reason: Even today, more and more people still indulge in casual and unprotected sex when they're traveling.

According to the CDC, the risk for international travelers is not so much where you go, but what you do when you get there. Bottom line? Don't go there without a condom, and just say no to drugs.

UNAIDS, the Joint United Nations Programme on HIV/AIDS, estimates that as of 2007, an estimated 33 million people were living with HIV/AIDS worldwide. And as rates have risen—sometimes exponentially—the disease has started significantly affecting communities other than the usual gay community. The heterosexual population is being infected at alarming rates.

There are few places in the world where HIV/AIDS is not a problem. Infection rates are rising in countries such as India, Indonesia, and Vietnam; but you may be surprised to know that some of the greatest increases in HIV infection are now in Eastern Europe and Central Asia. UNAIDS estimates that in 2007, 1.6 million people were living with HIV in Eastern Europe and Central Asia, compared with 630,000 in 2001. That's an increase of 150 percent!

Russia and the Ukraine made up the majority of the area's cases in 2006, with 66 percent and 21 percent, respectively, of the total number of cases. In Central Asia, Uzbekistan had the largest rate of HIV infections, with 2,205 cases in 2006, but there have also been rapidly growing numbers in Azerbaijan, Georgia, Kazakhstan, Kyrgyzstan, and Tajikistan. The primary source of infection has been an increase in the use of shared drug needles.

According to AVERT, a U.K.-based international HIV and AIDS charity, the 2006 rates of HIV diagnoses in Eastern Europe were as follows.

EASTERN EUROPEAN COUNTRY	HIV DIAGNOSES IN 2006	RATE PER MILLION IN 2006	TOTAL HIV CASES, END OF 2006
Armenia	66	21.9	429
Azerbaijan	242	28.6	965
Belarus	733	75.6	7,747
Estonia	668	504.2	5,731
Georgia	276	62.2	1,156
Kazakhstan	1,745	117.8	7,402
Kyrgyzstan	244	45.8	1,070
Latvia	299	130.3	3,631
Lithuania	100	29.3	1,200
Republic of Moldova	621	148.0	3,464
Russian Federation†	39,207	275.1	369,187
Tajikistan	204	31.0	710
Turkmenistan	0	0.0	2
Ukraine†	13,256	288.3	91,057
Uzbekistan	2,205	81.7	10,015
Total	59,866	–	503,766

†Excluding mother-to-child cases.
Source: *avert.org/eurosum.htm*

As bad as these numbers may seem, nothing compares with what's happening in sub-Saharan Africa, where the AIDS epidemic continues to rage. UNAIDS estimates that 22.5 million of the 770.3 million people in that region are living with HIV—and, unlike in other parts of the world, the majority are women, at a rate of 61 percent. HIV continues to be the largest cause of death in Africa—in 2007, 2.1 million people died of AIDS worldwide, and 1.6 million of those were in sub-Saharan Africa. That's more than three-quarters!

HIV rates vary greatly among African countries: Kenya is seeing some decline in new infections, and in Senegal and Somalia, fewer than 1 percent of adults are infected; South Africa has the largest number of infections in the *world* (including adults and children), with an estimated 5.5 million people (of about 47 million total) living with HIV; Swaziland, though it, too, is seeing a decline in new infections, still has the greatest number of adult cases in the world, with 26.1 percent living with HIV; the rate in the Central African Republic is among the highest in the region, with 6.2 percent of people living with HIV; in Western Africa, cases are rising in Cameroon, Gabon, and the Ivory Coast. Nigeria has had relatively low incidence, but rates have risen from 2 percent of the adult population in 1993 to 3.9 percent in 2005.

Does that mean you should be afraid to visit a country where HIV is on the rise? Of course not. But it never hurts to be armed with knowledge.

Cholera

This deadly disease is transmitted by the so-called fecal-oral route, through ingesting *Vibrio cholerae* bacteria, which can be found in contaminated water and undercooked food. Cholera is endemic to India, Africa, the Mediterranean, South and Central America, Mexico, and the United States.

In most cases, travelers who follow the rule of thumb "Cook it, boil it, peel it, or forget it" will be just fine—but you know as well as I do that for adventurous eaters, it's not always easy to follow those rules!

The World Health Organization (WHO) reports that while about 75 percent of people infected with cholera don't develop any symptoms, it is an extremely virulent disease that can kill healthy adults sometimes within hours. Those who do develop symptoms can suffer from watery diarrhea, vomiting, and leg cramps, leading to a rapid loss of body fluids, resulting in dehydration, shock, and even death. Moreover, the pathogens can remain in feces and potentially infect others for up to 14 days.

There are some instances in which cholera outbreaks are almost inevitable, and you simply don't want to be there when it happens. Bangladesh is one of those unlucky countries that suffer from all the circumstances that breed the deadly bacteria: unsanitary conditions, poor water sanitation, and overcrowding. Cholera epidemics happen annually here, during and after the floods of monsoon season, which runs from July through September.

Did you know that cholera is also a major concern in Vietnam? Since 2007, Vietnam has been battling outbreaks of the disease, and according to WHO, Vietnam's Ministry of Health reported 2,490 cases of severe acute watery diarrhea between March 5 and April 22, 2008, alone—377 of those tested positive for *Vibrio cholerae*. Up to 20 provinces and municipalities in the country have been infected, particularly in Hanoi. Fortunately, no deaths have been reported.

The Ministry of Health has been pointing its finger at a few likely causes of the most recent outbreak, which included consuming improperly cleaned raw vegetables, tainted shrimp sauce, and, oh yeah, dog meat.

My advice? Feel free to go to Hanoi, but be wary of what you put in your mouth when you wander along Nhat Tan Street in the Tây Hồ District . . . it's known as Dog-Meat Street for a reason.

Dengue Fever

You may not have heard of this one, but it's a big problem in more than 100 countries around the world, particularly in warm, tropical climates. Dengue fever, which can be fatal in some cases, is transmitted by mosquitoes. Symptoms include headaches, fever, intense joint pain, and rash.

In 2008, WHO reported that two-fifths of the world's population is at risk of the disease, and there may be as many as 50 million infections worldwide each year. Back in 1970, only nine countries had dengue epidemics—today, it's about four times as many. This massive increase is being blamed on both human population growth and the effects of global warming on mosquito habitats.

Because dengue is associated with tropical climates, you may not be surprised to hear about outbreaks in Southeast Asia and Africa . . . but don't forget about Latin America.

According to the Pan American Health Organization, an international public health agency that is the World Health Organization's regional office for the Americas, during 2007 there were some noticeable outbreaks:

Brazil: 210,580

Mexico: 40,559

Paraguay: 6,137

Puerto Rico: 3,111

The mosquito that transmits dengue fever is actually the same one that transmits yellow fever—another acute viral disease. The only difference is that there is an effective vaccine for yellow fever, but not for dengue. Your best bet to avoid contracting this unpleasant disease is to simply avoid mosquito bites: Wear long sleeves and long pants; stay indoors when mosquitoes are most active, in the early morning and late afternoon into the evening; apply insect repellent that contains DEET; and use mosquito nets at night.

Malaria

Another mosquito-borne disease, malaria is possibly the most notorious of all. It's transmitted by different mosquitoes than dengue and yellow fever but occurs in similar tropical climates. The disease exists in more than 90 countries worldwide and is among the leading causes of death, particularly in developing countries. Symptoms include high fever, severe chills, vomiting, anemia, and jaundice, and if it's not treated, malaria can become deadly by disrupting the blood supply to vital organs. Though it's both preventable and curable with antimalarial drugs such as chloroquine, quinine, mefloquine, and halofantrine, WHO's *World Malaria Report 2005* stated some sobering facts:

- At the end of 2004, some 3.2 billion people in 107 countries and territories lived in areas at risk of malaria transmission.
- Between 350 million and 500 million clinical episodes of malaria occur every year.
- About 60 percent of malaria cases worldwide and more than 80 percent of malaria deaths worldwide occur in sub-Saharan Africa.
- Every year, malaria causes at least one million deaths, about 90 percent of which are African children.
- A child dies of malaria every 30 seconds.

Although most cases occur in sub-Saharan Africa, malaria can also be found in Central and South America, the island of Hispaniola, the Middle East, the Indian subcontinent, Southeast Asia, and parts of Oceania, such as

Papua New Guinea. And things may be getting worse. Drug-resistant malaria is now cropping up around the world, and it's drastically hindering progress to control the spread of the disease. Though drug-resistant malaria can now be found occasionally in sub-Saharan Africa, the Amazon region of South America, and the Indian subcontinent, it's really been a problem recently in southern China and in the border areas of Thailand, Cambodia, and Myanmar. The reasons for the appearance of this scary disease are manifold but include an increase in population movement and the use of lower-quality drugs that don't entirely kill off the malaria parasites.

Human intervention may be spreading the problem even more. In June 2007, the *Los Angeles Times* ran an article by Edmund Sanders entitled "Malaria's Sting Spreads As Temperatures Rise," which exposed how global warming has affected formerly "malaria-free" zones. For example, the high altitude and cooler temperatures of villages around Mount Kenya were once uninhabitable to malaria-carrying mosquitoes—the town of Thangathi, in particular, sits 6,000 feet high with temperatures often dropping below 65°F. But since 2001, malaria cases in this region have nearly doubled, reaching more than 200,000, second only to pneumonia.

If that weren't bad enough, studies in the Amazon rain forest, on both the Brazilian and Peruvian sides, have shown a link between deforestation and a rise in malaria. One study found that numbers of *Anopheles darlingi*, the Amazon's primary malaria-spreading mosquito, were nearly 200 times greater in deforested locations than in other parts of the rain forest.

There have also been some "surprise" cases of malaria, such as the 2006 outbreak in Kingston, Jamaica, that infected more than 200 people—it was the first such outbreak in the area in more than 40 years.

The CDC recommends taking Lariam (a brand name for mefloquine) before heading to areas susceptible to malaria, but experience has shown me that there are better options. I've seen too many people airlifted out of Africa due to the side effects of that drug! Instead, check with your doctor, and with his or her consent, take Malarone instead.

Hepatitis B

This is a big one. Hepatitis B is caused by a virus that attacks the liver, and can lead to cirrhosis, liver cancer, liver failure, and death. Three-quarters of the world's population live in areas where there are high levels of hepatitis B infection, according to WHO. The good news, though, is that there is a vaccine to prevent the viral infection, and not everyone who has hepatitis B needs treatment. However, once you start showing acute symptoms, such as vomiting, right-side abdominal pain (near the liver), yellowness of the skin and/or whites of the eyes, and dark urine, chances are it's too late for anti-viral medications to help.

Hepatitis B is transmitted through infected body fluids—and sexual intercourse is the leading cause of transmission, though the virus can remain in blood for about a week even after it leaves the body, such as, say, on a razor blade. About two billion people worldwide have been infected with hepatitis B, and most develop a natural immunity after the initial infection. Despite that, there are approximately 350 million people worldwide living with lifelong, chronic infection.

The disease is especially problematic in China. The Asian Liver Center, a nonprofit organization associated with Stanford University, addresses the high occurrence of hepatitis B and liver cancer in Asians, reporting that about one in 10 people in China are chronically infected with the virus—that equals about 130 million people and about one-third of the total number of cases worldwide! (In comparison, HIV affects about 40 million worldwide.)

In 2002, the Chinese government implemented a countrywide vaccination program for newborns, but the continued use of dirty needles and the number of breast-feeding mothers who unknowingly pass the virus on to their children are among the leading causes of transmission. Lack of health care, poor education about the disease, and heavy discrimination against carriers all compound the problem.

Other areas that are high-risk for hepatitis B are the rest of Asia (excluding Japan), sub-Saharan Africa, the Amazon basin, parts of the Middle East, and some parts of Eastern Europe. Most countries worldwide now mandate that the hepatitis B vaccine be part of the national immunization program, but in developing countries—particularly in sub-Saharan Africa and parts of Asia—the price of the vaccine is prohibitively expensive. Fortunately, the hepatitis B vaccine will soon be available in these countries with the assistance of the Global Alliance for Vaccines and Immunization and the Global Fund for Children's Vaccines.

Hepatitis C

Though the name is similar to that of hepatitis B, this disease is usually spread through sharing infected needles or during blood transfusions, but is rarely sexually transmitted. The scariest part is that while a traveler's risk of contracting this infection is generally low, there is no vaccine available. And the disease can often be asymptomatic, though it can lead to scarring of the liver, cirrhosis, and, in worst-case scenarios, complete liver failure.

About 3 percent (170 million to 200 million) of the world's population has been infected with this virus. Though it's more common in parts of Africa and Asia, hepatitis C is most prevalent in Egypt.

In 2008, Sustainable Sciences Institute (SSI), an international nonprofit organization that helps develop epidemiological research in developing areas, reported that an estimated 10 to 13 percent of Egypt's 73 million–plus population is infected with hepatitis C and/or has the antibody in their system. (Compare that to 1.8 percent in the United States.) And that's somewhat of an improvement! In the 1980s, 22 percent of Egypt's population was infected, but an increased population and better awareness of how the disease is transmitted have helped lower that number.

Why is the disease so prevalent in Egypt? In the late 1970s and early 1980s, government health workers used dirty needles to treat millions of farmers and other rural people who were suffering from bilharzia, or schistosomiasis, a debilitating waterborne parasitic disease that can cause liver and intestinal damage. This was, in fact, one of the greatest tragedies of modern medicine, in which the government—through sheer negligence—infected millions of people with a life-threatening disease.

Again, the good news is that the risk of a traveler contracting this disease is low. But on the off chance that you require a blood transfusion while traveling in Egypt, this is the kind of information that you need to know ahead of time.

Lyme Disease

Here's a disease that travelers need to watch out for—actually, you may even have to watch out for it in your own backyard! Lyme disease is transmitted through a deer tick bite, which first manifests itself as a circular rash with a clear center. Other symptoms are flulike: fever, headache, and muscle or joint pains. Early-stage Lyme disease can be treated with oral antibiotics, but it can't always be eradicated, and in some cases, the diagnosis can come too late. Within weeks or months of receiving an untreated bite, you may suffer from debilitating effects such as meningitis, encephalitis, and facial palsy.

Ticks that transmit Lyme disease are prevalent in the northeastern United States, in states such as Connecticut (the illness was named after the town of Old Lyme!), New York, Rhode Island, and Vermont. But the risk also exists in Minnesota, northern California, and Wisconsin. And . . . Austria?

That's right, ticks that transmit Lyme disease exist in Europe, although instead of deer ticks, the discase is transmitted by the sheep tick (or castor bean tick), which can be found in forested areas of eastern Austria and Scandinavia, in particular. As in the United States, transmission season tends to be from March to September. Once again, use common sense: If you're planning on hiking in the Viennese suburbs or even in your own hometown, wear long pants, use insect repellent, and examine yourself for ticks afterward. It's as easy as that.

Toxoplasmosis

What would you say about a parasite that makes men dumb and women sexy? (That only sounds half bad to me.) Well, it turns out that a common parasite known as *Toxoplasma gondii,* which is carried by more than 60 million men, women, and children in the United States, may have those effects.

Humans are usually infected with this parasite by accidentally ingesting parasite eggs from infected cats (such as by cleaning the litter box and putting your hands to your mouth) or by eating raw or undercooked meat that

---

Connecticut's Cancer Clusters

According to the American Cancer Society, Connecticut has one of the highest rates of breast cancer in the nation, ranking first for breast cancer and third in the nation for urinary bladder cancer and non-Hodgkin's lymphoma in 2002. It was second in the nation for the highest overall cancer risks among females. The Connecticut Breast Cancer Coalition Foundation estimates that there are 37,000 breast-cancer survivors in the state each year and approximately 4,000 Connecticut women will be diagnosed with breast cancer and DCIS (ductal carcinoma in situ) this year. Barry Boyd, MD, of Greenwich Hospital, suggests that these high cancer rates are in part a direct reflection of the lifestyle in the northeastern United States; there are more full-time working women who lead a fast-paced lifestyle, delay childbearing, and don't breast-feed.

Delaware's Cancer Battle

Delaware's cancer death rate was third in the nation in 2002. In the late 1990s, nearly 3,800 Delawareans were diagnosed with cancer, and more than 1,700 died of it. Delaware's *News Journal* reported in 2008 that state officials had identified eight areas in the state with abnormally high cancer rates. Based on studies done between 2000 and 2004, the cancer rate in these clusters was 10 to 45 percent above the national average. And while the correlation hasn't been proven, perhaps it comes as no surprise that those eight clusters are all located just north of companies that emit chemicals into the air, water, and land.

contains the parasite. It can cause flulike symptoms in people with compromised immune systems and can be passed on by a pregnant woman to an unborn child, possibly leading to miscarriage, or to vision loss or seizures later in the child's life. Researchers have long thought that the parasite is harmless to healthy carriers.

But a study from Australia is saying otherwise. In the December 2006 issue of *Australasian Science,* Nicky Boulter, DPhil, an infectious-disease researcher with the University of Technology, Sydney, reported that "Infected men have lower IQs, achieve a lower level of education and have shorter attention spans. They are also more likely to break rules and take risks, be more independent, more anti-social, suspicious, jealous and morose, and are deemed less attractive to women." However, he wrote, "infected women tend to be more outgoing, friendly, more promiscuous, and are considered more attractive to men compared with non-infected controls." The bottom line, he said, is that "it can make men behave like alley cats and women behave like sex kittens."

There's not a whole lot you can do to avoid this disease during your travels (and with symptoms like that, maybe you don't want to avoid it). *Toxoplasma gondii* exists worldwide, so all I can say is, keep away from the cat feces!

SUPERSIZE ME . . . NOT

There was a time, not too long ago, when I knew the location of almost every McDonald's within a 200-mile radius of wherever I happened to be. Not a pretty picture. And then I got to know certain destinations by their proximity to fast food. Ocean City, Maryland; Virginia Beach, Virginia; and Myrtle Beach, South Carolina: the deep-fried franchise capitals of my fast-food memories. In retrospect, it was cultural and nutritional evidence in the growing argument for not going there.

But these destinations are hardly alone. In 2006, the market research and consulting firm Sandelman & Associates conducted a survey to determine which cities in America are the biggest consumers of fast food. The firm looked at 61 major cities to determine what percentage of fast-food users patronized a quick-service restaurant 12 or more times a month. Some, such as Oklahoma City, weren't big surprises. But Greenville, North Carolina?

Greenville, North Carolina

That's right, this town with a population of about 72,000 topped the list for fast-food consumption. In 2006, 59 percent of fast-food consumers in Greenville patronized a quick-service restaurant 12 or more times *a month* over the course of a year. (The national average is 42 percent.) Specifically, those who consume fast food indulged in their cholesterol-and-fat festival a whopping 23.9 times per month—that's almost 5 days a week!

Known as a college town and a shopping destination, the 31.8-square-mile zone has at least four Burger Kings, three KFCs, seven McDonald's, seven Subways (and an eighth on the way), two Taco Bells, five Wendy's, and dozens of other regional quick-service restaurants.

Perhaps it should be no surprise that fast food is practically a way of life here: The first Hardee's restaurant opened its doors in Greenville in 1961. This fast-food chain is known as the "Home of the Thickburger" (910 calories, 64 grams of fat) and boasts items such as the Monster Thickburger (1,420 calories, 108 grams of fat) and signature Made-from-Scratch Biscuits (370 calories, 23 grams of fat). To date, there are now four Hardee's in Greenville.

If you really want to see this town in action, don't miss the annual Hardee's Thickburger Eating Contest, in which hungry participants down as many ⅓-pound burgers as possible in 12 minutes, 50 seconds. The most recent winner managed to inhale 6⅓ burgers!

McAllen, Texas

Next on this list is good old McAllen, in Hidalgo County, South Texas. Fifty-eight percent of residents here have the dubious honor of dining at fast-food joints more than 12 times a month—in fact, according to Sandelman, these residents' visits number as many as 25 in a month!

With a current population of about 126,000, McAllen is actually one of the fastest-growing cities in the United States, with multinational corporations and Fortune 500s setting up shop there. But you wouldn't know it by looking at the city's dining options, which include a bevy of taco shops, chicken shacks, and burger joints, along with the occasional Red Lobster and Olive Garden.

But perhaps some additional fast-food restaurants are just what this town needs. In May 2008, Texas posted unemployment rates of 4.5 percent, with the highest rates in the McAllen-Edinburg-Mission area, at 6.1 percent.

Oklahoma City, Oklahoma

This capital city is hardly known as a great foodie destination. And with fast-food users visiting places like McDonald's and Burger King almost 21 times a month on average, it's clear that its residents agree.

And Oklahoma City is no stranger to this list, either. It has appeared on Sandelman's top-10 fast-food consumer list three times before: in 1999, 2003, and 2006.

But, hey, if you want a taste of some authentic Oklahoma City cuisine, head to . . . Sonic? That's right, the fast-food drive-in franchise is based here (it actually started in Shawnee, Oklahoma) and is home to such treats as the Sonic Burger (25 grams of fat) and the don't-miss, 44-ounce cherry slush. Talk about supersizing! At least the servers are getting some exercise—they roller-skate out to your car.

But there is hope for this city: In late 2007, the mayor of Oklahoma City decided that enough was enough and put the city on a diet. Mayor Mick Cornett (who's dropped 38 pounds since 2007) challenged the city to shed a million pounds as its New Year's resolution. Check out thiscityisgoingonadiet.com if you don't believe me.

El Paso, Texas

Maybe you should just stay away from Texas altogether. As well as making up a good chunk of top fast-food consumers, Texas is pretty much the hub of fat cities, according to *Men's Fitness*. Using several months' worth of data on exercise habits, gym usage, and the availability of green spaces and good weather, the magazine composed a list of the Fattest Cities in America. Six of 2008's top 10 cities came from the state where bigger is better. Besides Arlington and San Antonio, number four was Fort Worth; number five, El Paso; number six, Dallas; and number 10, Houston. The Texas Department of State

(continued)

SUPERSIZE ME . . . NOT—*Continued*

Health Services reported that in 2007, nearly 66 percent of Texas adults were overweight or obese.

Sandelman found that El Paso residents visited fast-food joints an average of 21 times a month. And it shows. Back in 2002, a group called the Pan American Health Organization, an arm of the World Health Organization (WHO), found that 67.8 percent of women and 76.6 percent of men in El Paso were overweight or obese.

And trust me, it can't be getting any better. Take a drive through El Paso (it's not exactly a walking town) and you'll see a rich mix of culinary feasts . . . from fast-food Mexican joints to McDonald's, Wendy's, and Carl's Jr.'s.

San Antonio, Texas

One of San Antonio's claims to fame is its chili, dating back to the 19th century, when "chili queens" would set up shop in the town square to dish out spicy dishes to locals. But it seems that the locals aren't chowing down on fiber-rich beans and metabolism-inducing peppers these days. In this Texas city, Sandelman found that 48 percent of frequent quick-service users had patronized fast-food restaurants 12 or more times in the past month. Among all quick-service patrons, 20 percent made at least 12 fast-food stops a month. To make matters worse, San Antonio also ranked number three on the *Men's Fitness* list of Fattest Cities in America, behind Las Vegas and Arlington, Texas.

Morgantown, West Virginia

When it comes to fast-food consumption, a medal of honor should be bestowed on one small West Virginia town. Tucked in the northeast corner of the state, Morgantown is one of the smallest cities in the country, at 9.8 square miles. And in this tiny town you'll find Applebee's, Arby's, Blimpie, Burger King, Chick-fil-A, KFC, Little Caesars, Long John Silver's, McDonald's, Panera Bread, Papa John's, Pizza Hut, Ruby Tuesday, Sbarro, Subway, and Taco Bell . . . some with more than one location!

More Fast-Food Tidbits

• South Los Angeles has more fast-food restaurants than any other part of Los Angeles County. In 2007, city councilwoman Jan Perry called for a moratorium on opening any more fast-food outlets in this area for at least 2 years; in July 2008, the L.A. City Council passed the proposal for 1 year, with two possible 6-month extensions.

• According to the CDC, 17 percent of adolescents nationwide ages 12 to 19 years are overweight, as are 19 percent of children ages 6 to 11—up from a study from the 1990s.

• WHO estimates that there are currently 1.6 billion overweight adults in the world . . . and that number is growing.

• In 2007, WHO estimated that the island nation of Nauru in the South Pacific has the highest percentage of overweight people, with 94.5 percent of its adult population ages 15 and older classified as overweight. Behind it are the Federated States of Micronesia, Cook Islands, Niue, and Tonga, all of which have obesity rates over 90 percent.

• The United States has the most McDonald's locations per capita (0.43 per 10,000 people). Second is New Zealand, followed by Canada, Australia, and Japan.

• Yum! Brands, Inc., based in Louisville, Kentucky, is the world's largest restaurant company, with more than 35,000 restaurants in more than 110 countries and territories. It owns KFC, Long John Silver's, Pizza Hut, and Taco Bell.

Want to see a real fast-food nation? Check out this U.S. map showing the locations of 10 different fast-food chains.

WORST AIRLINES

THE ULTIMATE DOWNGRADE

People ask me all the time, "What's your favorite airline?" The answer is, it depends on where I'm going. Or, perhaps more appropriately, where I'm *trying* to go.

Also, considering how many airlines have ceased to operate in the past few years—or are operating under Chapter 11 bankruptcy protection—it's tough to have a favorite airline when we now define a successful airline by which can lose money . . . *longer.*

But there are other factors that help determine whether an airline is worth a second—or even a first—try.

On-Time Arrival Rates

One of the most important things to consider before booking your ticket is whether an airline can actually get you to your destination on time!

Overall, a shocking number of airlines find it tough to land at New York's LaGuardia on time. In April 2008, Northwest managed to land on time there only 44.9 percent of the time; Frontier Airlines, 45.1 percent of the time; JetBlue, 45.8 percent; ExpressJet, 46.6 percent; and American Airlines arrived on time at LaGuardia 49.9 percent of the time. Oh, and if you find yourself on Mesa Airlines, make sure you bring a book—only 33.3 percent of Mesa's flights to LaGuardia manage to get there on time.

Based on the most recent 2008 statistics, some other must-avoid airline/destination combinations are . . .

Worst On-Time Arrivals

Here are the worst on-time arrival percentages by airline (of 20 reporting airlines), from April 2007 to April 2008.

1. Atlantic Southeast: 66.0
2. American: 67.2
3. American Eagle: 68.6
4. United: 69.4
5. Comair: 69.5
6. Northwest: 70.8
7. JetBlue: 73.2
8. Alaska: 73.4
9. Mesa: 73.5
10. ExpressJet: 73.8

United to Miami—on-time arrival rate of only 37.1 percent

Comair to Tampa—only 38.2 of them arrive on time.

Mesa Airlines to Boston—44.6 percent on time

American Eagle to Atlanta—45.6 percent on-time rate

Northwest to Newark—55.5 percent on time

Okay, that's all well and good, but what are the specific *flights* that you should avoid? Turns out, there are plenty of them. See the chart on page 98.

The Lost-Luggage Blues

With the growing movement to charge passengers for checking bags, somehow we're paying the airlines to lose our luggage . . . when they used to do it for free! (This is why I FedEx my bags when I travel.) "Mishandled" bags, whether they are lost, damaged, delayed, or pilfered, translate into a big pain for travelers. In 2007, there were a total of 4,419,654 mishandled bags, or 7.03 per 1,000 passengers, for U.S. domestic flights. In the first quarter of 2008 alone, there were 987,897 mishandled bags, at a rate of 6.81 per 1,000 travelers. That quarter, the worst of the worst were . . .

Atlantic Southeast Airlines—Delta's small regional carrier managed to mishandle 38,449 bags in this period. That's 13.16 bags for every 1,000 passengers.

MOST DELAYED FLIGHTS

Here are the top 10 flights that arrived late 70 percent of the time or more in the first quarter of 2008 (January through March).

CARRIER	FLIGHT NUMBER	ORIGIN	DESTINATION
Mesa	7124	Chicago O'Hare International	Central Wisconsin Airport
Mesa	7177	Chicago O'Hare International	Des Moines International
United	334	Chicago O'Hare International	Port Columbus International (Ohio)
ExpressJet	1223	Newark Liberty International	Chicago O'Hare International
SkyWest	6380	San Francisco International	Boise
United	1204	Chicago O'Hare International	Pittsburgh International
JetBlue	1297	Logan International (Boston)	Pittsburgh International
ExpressJet	2979	Bradley International (Windsor Locks, CT)	Newark Liberty International
Mesa	7155	Chicago O'Hare International	Abraham Lincoln Capital (Springfield, IL)
Mesa	7212	Chicago O'Hare International	Piedmont Triad International (Greensboro, NC)

American Eagle Airlines—Don't bother checking your bags on this regional carrier. It mishandles 13.08 bags for every 1,000 passengers. That translates into 51,084 in a 3-month period!

Pinnacle Airlines—Another small airline that mishandles more than its fair share of bags—we're talking 12.07 for every 1,000 passengers, or 28,834 total.

Skywest Airlines—This company has more in common with Atlantic Southeast than just its parent company. Skywest, too, mishandles luggage at sky-high rates: 11.5 for every 1,000 passengers, or 58,960 total in the first quarter.

Mesa Airlines—Last but certainly not least is good old Mesa, which mishandled 9.92 bags per 1,000 people. Hey, at least it's under 10 percent!

But remember, these numbers are just for the United States. Turns out, Portugal's TAP is the worst of the European airlines: In 2007, it reported 27.8 mishandled bags per 1,000 passengers (about 23,000 bags). Coming in a close second (and getting worse every year) is British Airways, which mishandled a whopping 26.5 bags per 1,000 passengers (about 114,000 pieces). KLM and Alitalia followed with 19.7 (about 46,000 and nearly 51,000

SCHEDULED DEPARTURE TIME	NUMBER OF FLIGHTS DELAYED	TOTAL OPERATIONS	PERCENTAGE NOT ON TIME	AVERAGE MINUTES OF DELAY (LATE FLIGHTS ONLY)
1955	29	32	90.63	37.76
1900	32	36	88.89	48.22
1900	36	41	87.80	60.53
1845	33	38	86.84	85.39
1253	32	37	86.49	58.50
1850	29	34	85.29	74.97
1755	34	40	85.00	59.79
1550	34	40	85.00	59.76
1625	33	39	84.62	95.15
1400	31	37	83.78	43.03

bags, respectively), Air France with 17.6 (almost 104,000 items), and BMI with 17.0 (almost 8,900 bags). The European average, according to the Air Transport Users Council, was 16.6 per 1,000 passengers.

And let's never forget the total disaster of Terminal 5 at Heathrow, in which thousands of bags were lost, mishandled, or otherwise delayed when British Airways opened its new London terminal in March 2008. The airline actually filled up planes with luggage of passengers traveling to continental Europe and flew the bags to Italy to sort them out there.

For reasons of basic sanity, I always avoid flying to Heathrow if I have to check bags—especially if I have to connect there for an onward flight. If I absolutely have no choice but to fly through Heathrow, I give myself (and my luggage) 5 hours to make the flight connection, otherwise I stand an excellent chance of never seeing my bags. I apply the same 5-hour rule to changing flights at Charles de Gaulle in Paris. Anything under 5 hours and luggage just won't connect. Most airlines will book you with 90-minute or 2-hour connect times through both of these airports. They're smoking crack—don't do it!

Bumped Passengers

If you're planning on flying with these airlines, you may be sitting around the airport for quite some time after you're bumped from your flight, so

Don't Let Fido Go There

There are no reliable statistics on the number of animals that are lost, injured, or killed on domestic flights, but anecdotal evidence suggests that airlines do manage to have a substantial number of "incidents" when it comes to passengers' pets—so think twice before bringing your dog or cat on your flight.

American Airlines

In January 2008, a pug named Puji flying from San Juan, Puerto Rico, to Orlando showed up dead. With their short noses, pugs are notoriously bad fliers because of potential breathing problems, but the good news is that the owner's second pug made it to Florida safe and sound.

In March 2008, a 6-year-old feline named Charlie the Cat made it from El Paso to Dallas–Fort Worth in one piece, but when the crew went to load him onto a flight to Philadelphia, he was dead. A necropsy showed that the kitty had some issues with his lungs, heart, and liver.

The following month, on April 2, a dog named Sundi flying from San Juan to Fort Lauderdale and a cat named Diablo flying from JFK to San Francisco were both dead on arrival. The dog may have suffered from renal disease and chronic emphysema, which may have led to respiratory distress. The cat? Well, the owner—who brought the body home for burial!—says it was just old.

Delta Air Lines

Remember the old Monty Python sketch with the line "Look, matey, I know a dead parrot when I see one, and I'm looking at one right now"? In April 2008, ramp agents working on the ground may have reenacted that scene when they discovered the frozen body of an African gray parrot that had flown on Delta from Miami via Atlanta to Orange County, California (and boy, were his wings tired!). The airline came up empty-handed when it tried to figure out why the bird had frozen to death.

Another breed that doesn't do well in the air is the English bulldog . . . as evidenced by the fate of a 3-year-old dog that died en route to Medford, Oregon, from Atlanta via Salt Lake City. (Incidentally, it was the same day the parrot died.) Heatstroke was the likely cause of his demise.

Alaska Airlines

In January 2008, a dog flying from Seattle to Ketchikan, Alaska, showed up deceased—no cause given, but here's a tip: Don't send your dog to Alaska in the dead of winter!

bring along some entertainment. In the first quarter of 2008, Atlantic Southeast Airlines took the lead when it came to involuntarily bumping its passengers: 2,807 fliers were booted from their seats, or 5.22 per 10,000 passengers. Next up was Pinnacle Airlines, which bumped 4.71 per 10,000. Next, Comair, with 4.48, and American Eagle, with 2.79.

The Bottom Line on Airline Seats

I've sat in some of the worst airline seats imaginable—seat 35E on a 767 comes to mind, or the middle seat in the last row on any 747. And let's not forget the old seats on Aeroflot or the Chinese airline CAAC in the 1970s. Or the time I was on an EgyptAir flight in 1981 and the seat in front of me collapsed during takeoff, filling the cabin with thousands of toxic dust particles.

So, what has changed in all these years? Not much.

Still, when it comes to bad seats, almost nothing can compare with the agony of flying with your knees pressed firmly against your chest. A good way to figure out if your knees are going to be doubling as your tray table is to take a look at something called the seat pitch, which is the space between the back of a seat and the back of the one behind it. For some perspective, the seat pitch of Cathay Pacific's plush first-class seats on a Boeing 747-400 is 79 inches; easyJet's Airbus A319 has only one class of service, with 29 inches of space per seat.

Another major factor in whether you're in for a comfortable or a cramped ride is, of course, the seat width, or the amount of space between a seat's armrests. To have a fighting chance of keeping your elbow from jabbing the person in the seat next to yours, you're going to need at least 18 inches of space.

We checked in with our friends at SeatGuru.com to figure out which airlines scored the lowest.

Spirit Airlines

Not only does this airline have some of the worst customer service I've ever seen (translation: none), but Spirit adds insult to injury by charging you $15 for an exit-row seat, $10 for an aisle or window, and $5 for a middle seat. If you're unfortunate enough to fly on Spirit's Airbus A321, sitting anywhere but in the first row will award you a seat pitch of 28 inches and a 17-inch seat width. They call those seats "Deluxe Leather Class." I call them downright inhumane.

American Airlines

I fly American a lot, but there are certain short-haul, regional routes that involve minuscule aircraft that I try to avoid. One such plane is the Aerospatiale/Alenia ATR 72, which is often flown by American Eagle between Miami and Nassau, Bahamas. This commuter craft features cramped, uncomfortable seats that have a pitch of 32 inches and a width of 18.7 inches. Your best bet is to try to snag a seat in the first row, which is the emergency exit row.

Northwest Airlines

High fuel prices do have some benefits. Northwest maintains a fleet of DC-9s, most of which are more than 30 years old! Rising fuel prices in 2008 finally pushed the airline to cut more than a quarter of the gas-guzzling aircraft from its fleet, from 92 to 68. But if you're still unfortunate enough to end up on one of those planes, probably on a short-haul flight between cities like Minneapolis and Minot, North Dakota, you can expect to squeeze yourself into economy seats with a 30-inch pitch and 17-inch width. Definitely avoid the last two rows and the seats in front of the emergency exits, as they have limited recline.

It's unlikely that you'll find yourself on a Saab 340 aircraft, unless you happen to be flying from, say, LaGuardia to Ithaca. But if you do end up on this 11-row prop plane, do yourself a favor and don't take seat 11B. (You can't miss it, as it's the only B seat on the plane.) Most of the aircraft is in a one-two configuration, meaning that A seats are on one side of the plane, while Cs and Ds are on the other. But in the very last row, there are four seats—four very small seats, each 16 inches wide, that barely recline and are crunched against the restroom. The main advantage of 11B is if you're 7 feet tall—you'll essentially have the entire aisle as legroom.

Ryanair

This Dublin-based carrier is one of the many low-cost airlines that have proliferated throughout Europe since the EU deregulated airlines in the early 1990s. Though I'll give it major points for offering a truly budget option for travelers throughout Europe, this airline takes "no-frills rule" to the extreme. Ryanair's fleet of Boeing 737s have a seat pitch of 30 inches, and, worst of all, on some aircraft, the seats don't even recline. That's right, in a move to pass savings along to customers, the airline ordered a fleet of Boeing aircraft that skipped the reclining seats, Velcro headrests, window shades, and seat pockets.

But my biggest pet peeve with budget airlines like Ryanair and easyJet is when they hide the nickel-and-diming in fine print. Case in point: If you plan on checking any more than 15 kilograms (about 33 pounds) of luggage, you'll have to shell out about $25 *per kilogram* over the allotted weight. If you're not careful, you might have to take out a second mortgage for what should have been a $20 flight!

Banned Airlines

Now, what about the airlines that you really don't want to fly because they're simply too dangerous?

In the United States, the FAA has its own list of airlines it won't allow to fly into America. The FAA's International Aviation Safety Assessments (IASA) program dictates that under most circumstances, certain countries are banned from serving the United States using their own aircraft and crews. And those countries, as of July 24, 2008, are . . .

Bangladesh

Belize

Bulgaria

Democratic Republic of the Congo (formerly Zaire)

Gambia

Ghana

Guyana

Haiti

Honduras

Indonesia

Ivory Coast

Kiribati

Nauru

Nicaragua

Paraguay

Philippines

Serbia and Montenegro (formerly Republic of Yugoslavia)

Swaziland

Ukraine

Uruguay

Zimbabwe

In 2006, the European Union, along with Norway and Switzerland, banned 92 airlines from landing at European airports, arguing that they use old, obsolete, or poorly maintained aircraft and fail to meet minimum safety standards.

In some cases, certain countries had their entire commercial air fleets banned from flying into Europe—that includes the Democratic Republic of the Congo, Equatorial Guinea, Liberia, Sierra Leone, and Swaziland. According to the EU, these five African countries lack proper regulatory oversight, resulting in the near-total ban.

Jacques Barrot, then vice president of the European Commission in charge of transportation, cited examples such as the Congo, which is still trying to develop a credible aviation safety system that could monitor its vast fleet, much of which is composed of converted Soviet warplanes. These planes often suffer from serious safety deficiencies, according to the EU's transport commission.

The bottom line: Even though you probably won't encounter one of these airlines in the European Union—or the United States, for that matter—you may come across them elsewhere. And it pays to know which airlines have been blacklisted for safety reasons!

Afghanistan
Ariana Afghan Airlines

Angola
Taag Angola Airlines

Bangladesh
Air Bangladesh

Comoros

Air Service Comores

Democratic People's Republic of Korea (North Korea)

Air Koryo

Democratic Republic of the Congo

African Air Services

Africa One

Aigle Aviation

Air Beni

Air Boyoma

Air Infini

Air Kasai

Air Navette

Air Tropiques

Bel Glob Airlines

Blue Airlines

Bravo Air Congo

Business Aviation S.P.R.L.

Butembo Airlines

Cargo Bull Aviation

Cetraca Aviation Service

CHC Stellavia

Comair

Compagnie Africaine D'aviation

Doren Air Congo

El Sam Airlift

Espace Aviation Service

Filair

Free Airlines

Galaxy Incorporation

Goma Express

Gomair

Great Lake Business Company

Hewa Bora Airways

International Trans Air Business

Katanga Airways

Kivu Air

Lignes Aeriennes Congolaises

Malila Airlift

Malu Aviation

Mango Airlines

Piva Airlines

Rwakabika Bushi Express

Safari Logistics

Safe Air Company

Services Air

Sun Air Services

Tembo Air Services

Thom's Airways

TMK Air Commuter

Tracep Congo

Trans Air Cargo Service

Transports Aeriens Congolais

Virunga Air Charter

Wimbi Dira Airways

Zaabu International

Equatorial Guinea

Ceiba Intercontinental

Cronos Airlines

Euroguineana de Aviacion y Transportes

General Work Aviacion

GETRA—Guinea Ecuatorial de Transportes Aereos

Guinea Airways

Utage—Union de Transport Aereo de Guinea Ecuatorial

Indonesia

Airfast Indonesia

Air Pacific Utama

Asco Nusa Air Transport

Asi Pudjiastuti

Atlas Deltasatya

Aviastar Mandiri

Balai Kalibrasi Fasitas Penerbangan

Dabi Air Nusantara

Deraya Air Taxi

Derazona Air Service

Dirgantara Air Service

Eastindo

Ekspres Transportasi Antar Benua

Garuda Indonesia

Gatari Air Service

Helizona

Indonesia Air Asia

Indonesia Air Transport

Intan Angkasa Air Service

Kartika Airlines

Kura-Kura Aviation

Linus Airways

Lion Mentari Airlines

Mandala Airlines

Manunggal Air Service

Megantara Airlines

Merpati Nusantara

Metro Batavia

National Utility Helicopter

Pelita Air Service

Penerbangan Angkasa Semesta

Pura Wisata Baruna

Republic Express Airlines

Riau Airlines

Sampurna Air Nusantara

Sayap Garuda Indah

SMAC

Sriwijaya Air

Survei Udara Penas

Transwisata Prima Aviation

Travel Expres Airlines

Travira Utama

Trigana Air Service

Tri MG Intra Airlines

Wing Abadi Nusantara

Kyrgyz Republic

Air Manas

Artik Avia

Asia Alpha Airways

Avia Traffic Company

Bistair-Fez Bishkek

Click Airways

Dames

Eastok Avia

Esen Air

Golden Rule Airlines

Itek Air

Kyrgyz Trans Avia

Kyrgyzstan Airlines

Max Avia

OHS Avia

S Group Aviation

Sky Gate International Aviation

Sky Way Air

Tenir Airlines

Trast Aero

Valor Air

Liberia

All carriers

Republic of Gabon

Air Services SA

Air Tourist (Allegiance)

Nationale et Regionale Transport (Nationale)

Nouvelle Air Affaires Gabon

SCD Aviation

Sky Gabon

Solenta Aviation

Rwanda

Silverback Cargo Freighters

Sierra Leone

Air Rum, Ltd.

Bellview Airlines (S/L) Ltd.

Destiny Air Services, Ltd.

Heavylift Cargo

Orange Air Sierra Leone Ltd.

Paramount Airlines, Ltd.

Seven Four Eight Air Services Ltd.

Teebah Airways

Sudan

Air West Co. Ltd.

Swaziland

Aero Africa (Pty) Ltd.

Jet Africa Swaziland

Royal Swazi National Airways Corporation

Scan Air Charter

Swazi Express Airways

Swaziland Airlink

Ukraine

Ukraine Cargo Airways

Ukrainian Mediterranean Airlines

Volare Aviation Enterprise

Chapter 8

WORST AIRPORTS

FALSE IMPRISONMENT

When you're figuring out the time it takes to get somewhere, consider that actual flying time, on average, constitutes as little as 20 percent of your total journey door-to-door. Let's call our search for airports to avoid "the *slowest* common denominator."

Domestic

Chicago, Illinois: O'Haro International

Poor Chicagoans. When it comes to airport choices, it's basically bad (Midway) and worse (O'Hare). Between weather and delusional flight scheduling, traveling in and out of Chicago is pretty hopeless. As the second-busiest airport in America (behind Atlanta's Hartsfield-Jackson), O'Hare already suffers from acute overcrowding—whether it's in the parking lot, in the terminal, or in the skies. In 2007, O'Hare handled more than 76 million passengers and more than 926,000 aircraft operations, and, according to the Department of Transportation, it also ranked at the bottom in three categories: late aircraft, air traffic control, and cancellations. Midway Airport, one of the fastest-growing airports in the country, served about 19 million travelers in 2007, so it's not much better than O'Hare these days.

Alternate airport: General Mitchell International Airport in Milwaukee (Chicago's third, secret airport)

Miami, Florida: Miami International

On a good day, it's pretty bad at the appropriately initialed MIA. On a bad day, it's like the last flight out of Saigon.

With terminals that seem to have been designed by René Magritte in consultation with Franz Kafka, plus sloppy signage throughout, many travelers find themselves on an endless odyssey through the airport to their gate. (Case in point: A sign at one of the exits just outside the airport once read "Escape to the City.") Massive construction also factors into the mess: A $6.2 billion plan—now under way—will add four runways and several new taxiways; increase space for parking; expand the terminal from 3.5 million to 7.4 million square feet; and increase the numbers of gates, ticket counters, and kiosks. These renovations were scheduled to be completed by 2005 but have been pushed (tentatively) to summer 2011. Thankfully, the new South Terminal has already opened for business and has helped ease the stress on the old North Terminal. The idea is that Miami will no longer be the worst-rated hellhole of an airport once the renovations are complete, but I'll believe that when I see it.

Alternate airports: Palm Beach International, Fort Lauderdale–Hollywood International

Cincinnati, Ohio: Cincinnati/Northern Kentucky International

Somewhat unexpectedly, Cincinnati has long been America's most expensive airport in terms of airfares, thanks to Delta's stranglehold over it. (No competition means higher fares.) According to the DOT's 2008 *Domestic Airline Fares Consumer Report,* fliers here paid an average of 96.2 percent more than travelers at other airports for flights of similar lengths.

To get an idea of just how outrageously expensive Cincinnati/Northern Kentucky airport is, passengers flying out of the next two most expensive airports—Eagle, Colorado, and Fargo, North Dakota—pay 36.7 percent and 26.6 percent more than the average fare, respectively. These airports are comparatively tiny, so one might expect them to be expensive, but Cincinnati, being a major metropolitan international airport, has no excuse.

Alternate airports: Columbus Regional (14.6 percent below average cost), Dayton International (7.6 percent below average cost), Louisville International (0.4 percent below average cost)

Atlanta, Georgia

Welcome to the world of chronic delays. Atlanta's Hartsfield-Jackson is the most time-draining airport, accounting for 1.9 *million* minutes of delays each year. This is, in fact, the busiest airport in America, trumping even O'Hare. More than 89 million passengers passed through Hartsfield-Jackson in 2007, up 5 percent from the previous year.

If you're stuck in the airport—and, trust me, there's a good chance you will be—and find yourself in need of some entertainment, some relatively perverse entertainment actually, don't miss (in fact you *can't* miss) the smoking "lounges" in various terminals. Look through the often nicotine- and tar-stained windows and you'll see hapless smoking travelers, like caged animals waiting for feeding time. It's a pathetic sight to watch. Either the airport should become entirely nonsmoking, or there needs to be a better solution for smokers. As it is now, this is cruel and unusual punishment, both for the people inside and for those of us peering in as we walk by.

Alternate airport: Chattanooga Metropolitan (especially if plans for a high-speed train to Atlanta go through)

New York, New York: LaGuardia

The race for the title of New York City's worst airport is quite competitive. JFK, Newark Liberty, and LaGuardia are all delay-plagued, and just about anyone flying into or out of New York City has their own flight-delay horror stories. But I have to give the award to LaGuardia. In the past 4 years, I have yet to depart on a flight from LaGuardia that actually left on time. Yes, there were occasional flights that actually pushed back from the gate on time, but that's (sometimes literally) as far as we got, or as close as we got to an on-time departure.

LaGuardia may have been voted "greatest airport in the world" in 1960, but the world has changed a lot since then—unfortunately, LaGuardia hasn't. These days, the nearly 70-year-old airport just struggles—and when the airport struggles, we suffer.

Oh, and if you're looking for comfort or style, look elsewhere—with the totally outdated decor (both inside and out), you'll feel as if you're traveling back in time. As one traveler told me, "I've been to elementary-school cafeterias with more ambience."

Alternate airport: Long Island MacArthur

The Most Delayed Airports

The Department of Transportation's Bureau of Transportation Statistics compiles monthly reports on which airports have the most delayed flights. But what you need to remember is that it's not just about the offending airport—it's also about the time of day that you're planning to travel. Why? Because when you have airlines scheduling for competitive—not intelligent—reasons, you're going to have 84 flights scheduled to depart at 8 a.m. while there are only two runways. You do the math.

Keep in mind that when it comes to delays, you want to look at the arrival time, not the scheduled departure. For one thing, it's easier to fake statistics for flight departures, because once the plane pulls away from the gate, it's considered to have "departed," even if you're sitting on the ground for the next 10 hours. Also, and call me crazy, I don't really care if my plane sits on the runway for 30 minutes before departure . . . just get me to my destination on time!

Of the major international airports, here are the worst of the bunch and the times that you should *not* plan to arrive. (Figures are for April 2008, unless otherwise noted.)

New York LaGuardia

Average on-time rate: 56 percent

Okay, things can be pretty bad at LaGuardia throughout the day, but you definitely want to plan an early-morning arrival. Flights scheduled to arrive between 7 a.m. and 7:59 a.m. arrive on time 81.7 percent of the time, and it goes steadily downhill from there. By noon, only 61 percent of scheduled flights are on time, and by 10 p.m., it's a dismal 41 percent on-time rate. That last figure is, in fact, the lowest on-time arrival rate of any reporting airport, and that's saying something!

Newark Liberty International

Average on-time rate: 68.7 percent

This one often tops the charts as having the worst on-time arrival rate, and things aren't looking up. Like most other airports, Newark starts the day off strong, with an 82.1 percent on-time arrival rate between 6 a.m. and 6:59 a.m. But come afternoon, watch out. By 2 p.m., we're talking about 64.8 percent, dropping to 58.9 percent by 4 p.m. and 54.3 percent around 8 p.m.

Miami International

Average on-time rate: 71.2 percent

Miami airport is also a pretty pathetic scene when it comes to arrivals. Although things start off relatively strong—90.9 percent on-time rate for flights scheduled to arrive between 7 a.m. and 7:59 a.m.—things get worse fast. By noon, you're looking at a 72.2 percent on-time arrival rate; by 4 p.m., it's 63.8 percent. Things pick up a bit in the evening, but then drop back down to a sad 48.3 percent on-time arrival rate at 10 p.m.

Dallas–Fort Worth International

Average on-time rate: 71.3 percent

Although DFW is an enormous, efficiently run airport, its on-time statistics are telling. It comes out of the gate strong, with an 82 percent on-time rate, but steadily declines throughout the day, until the last flights in are on time only 59.4 percent of the time.

John F. Kennedy International

Average on-time rate: 72.3 percent

Between LaGuardia, Newark, and now JFK, there's a reason that I prefer to fly out of Long Island MacArthur in Islip whenever possible. For one of the busiest airports in the country, JFK has a pretty bleak on-time arrival rate, dropping as low as 60.2 percent between 6 p.m. and 7:59 p.m. You're better off planning your arrival between 9 a.m. and noon, when the on-time rate is at least 85 percent.

Okay, so that's 1 month's statistics . . . but what's been happening over the course of a year? Well, we added it up. The worst-performing major airports for on-time arrivals over the course of 6 months (November 2007 through April 2008) are . . .

Miami (MIA): 65.8%

New York LaGuardia (LGA): 61.9%

Chicago O'Hare (ORD): 60.1%

San Francisco (SFO): 58.4%

Newark (EWR): 51.4%

What does that tell you? Bad weather, of course, plays a huge factor in all this. When there's snow in Chicago and fog in San Francisco . . . just don't go there!

International

Moscow, Russia: Sheremetyevo International

Moscow's main (but not only) international airport, Sheremetyevo, maintains the worst aspects of its Soviet days, with poor customer service; corruption; a dank, dirty, and depressing atmosphere; inadequate seating; and mile-long lines. To make matters worse, the airport also features some of the downfalls of modern-day Russia—namely, astronomical prices.

Don't laugh, but my advice to anyone flying out of Moscow is, bring toilet paper. You're going to get stuck at the airport, you're going to have to go to the bathroom, and, since the Russians' idea of toilet paper is quite different from ours, you're going to need it! Also, bring dollars. Just about everyone at this airport has his or her hand out, and the people looking to be paid off are usually the folks who control whether or not you get out of the airport.

Alternate airports: There are three other airports in Moscow to choose from, but unfortunately, none are much better.

Manila, Philippines: Ninoy Aquino International

Maybe it just seems that corruption is endemic at Aquino airport and there are plenty of people waiting at every turn to scam you, but it's when you try to catch a cab outside that things can get ugly.

Many travelers, especially first-timers, complain of a sort of "taxi mafia." Basically, cab drivers from the city who drop off passengers at the airport aren't allowed to pick up travelers leaving the airport—that privilege is extended to only a handful of very expensive accredited cabs. So taking a

Don't Land There

The Courchevel Altiport, located in the middle of the French Alps, is only a few dozen yards away from the ski slopes. The runway is 1,760 feet long (a more comforting length would be close to 6,000 feet, and you *really* want it to be 9,000), and it has an 18.66 percent steepness gradient. Pilots who manage to land there safely come away with lifelong bragging rights.

cab from the airport into the city will cost two to three times as much as going the other direction.

On top of that, the incompetence of the airport's administration is breathtaking. Construction on the new Terminal 3 began in 1997 and was supposed to be completed in 2002. Today, thanks to shoddy construction that necessitated repairs and renovations before it could be put to use, Terminal 3 has yet to open, and costs continue to rise. In fact, it looks unlikely that the terminal will open anytime soon.

Alternate airport: Clark International is much newer and has runways so long that a space shuttle could land there.

Dakar, Senegal: Leopold Sedar Senghor International

This airport will make you wish that Dakar wasn't West Africa's major regional hub. But if you're traveling to West Africa, chances are you'll stop there.

My friend Patrick Smith, of Salon.com's Ask the Pilot column, wrote of this airport: "There is only squalor, an unnerving sense of confinement, and to some extent, danger." He called it the world's worst. I wouldn't go that far, but let's just say if Dakar is a stopover, try above all to make it a quick one. And whatever you do, don't check bags through on connecting flights.

Alternate airport: Unfortunately, there's no other option here.

Paris, France: Charles de Gaulle International

Here, the problem isn't the smell (though some complain that bathrooms regularly do stink), the corruption (some say airport employees' arrogance is worse), or the crowds (there are regular bottlenecks at certain transfer points). Rather, the consensus seems to be that this airport is just a poorly designed mess.

At de Gaulle, the French seem to have adopted a decidedly surrealist approach to signage, especially in some of the older terminals. And the problems happen when you try to transfer flights. There's no easy way to connect without going outside and trying to find a bus (wherever that may be) that actually will take you to the correct terminal. And when you get to that terminal, the lines can be so long that you can easily miss your flight. As for your connecting luggage, *c'est la vie!*

Alternate airports: Paris-Orly, Paris-Beauvais

The World's Scariest Runways

The U.K.'s *Sunday Times* asked pilots to nominate some of the world's scariest airport runways. Here are some of the most colorful—and frightening—responses.

Tioman Island, Malaysia

"You'll fly straight at a mountain until you see individual leaves, then turn right through 90 degrees and point the nose at the end of the strip. Hit the brakes hard to stop before you hit the cliff. Note the arrester wires on the runway as you alight from the plane. Ask to see photos of the pilot's children before takeoff."

Tegucigalpa, Honduras

"This is a horribly bumpy flight through clouds, with high peaks either side of you, a last-minute tight left turn into a man-made gap in the mountain range, then a steep dive and a controlled crash landing onto a postage-stamp runway."

Goma, Democratic Republic of the Congo

"Not only is a third of the runway inoperable because of the active and smoky volcano, but there's a town at the other end, then one of the deepest lakes in Africa. (Good news: There are no crocs in it. Bad news: That's because the water is too poisonous.) Congolese safety and medical standards aren't great, either."

Dutch Harbor, Alaska

"Any airport in Alaska is terrifying in winter: absolute darkness, snow, and wind. The last time I flew into Dutch Harbor, it took 30 years off my life. We came in sideways, touched wheels to tarmac, then flew round again. And again. And again. The captain said, 'Fourth time's a charm.'"

São Paulo, Brazil: Congonhas International

São Paulo International Airport has long been among Brazil's busiest. More recently, it's also earned a reputation for being one of Brazil's—and the world's—most dangerous.

In 2007, TAM Flight 3054 tried to land in wet, rainy weather and ended up sliding off the runway and crashing into a building adjacent to

Uralsk, Kazakhstan

"I flew in 3 weeks ago. I have never experienced a landing like it. The runway appeared to be overgrown with weeds, and the surface was like a poorly maintained B road in an ex-mining region [in the] north of England."

Arequipa, Peru

"There's a 5,791-meter volcano at the end of the runway. The altitude means planes have to reach nearly double their sea-level stalling speed to take off . . . before banking sharply to avoid the volcano."

Catalina Island, California

"Even in a small twin-engine plane, this tiny hilltop airstrip is worrying. As with the deck of an aircraft carrier, you fly off the end of the runway, over a cliff, and into the air."

Guatemala City, Guatemala

"It starts at 1,503 meters and ends at 1,476, via 1,478, 1,494, and 1,484, in that order! It's a novel takeoff experience: The thrusting of the engines is aided by the flapping of the wings."

Lukla, Nepal

"It's 527 meters long and 20 meters wide, with an incline of 11.75 degrees. On landing, the pilot appears to try to park the plane in the mountain, rather than on it."

Skardu, Pakistan

"There is a corkscrew approach, and all you see out the window is mountainsides swirling around. I had no idea what was going on until we hit the ground."

the airport. With 187 casualties on the plane and 12 more on the ground, this crash currently ranks as the worst in Brazilian history in terms of fatalities. Just a day before, two planes slid off wet runways, and not long before that, a Boeing 737 narrowly avoided a crash. Other wayward flights have damaged cars and taxis, barbecue stands, apartments, supermarkets, and more.

There are two related problems at Congonhas. First, while the airport's location was on the edge of the city when it was built, sprawling, crowded São Paulo has since expanded, surrounding the airport on all sides. Because of that, it has been impossible to lengthen the facility's original runways, which are too short for big, modern jets.

Alternate airport: Sadly, there really isn't one. Guarulhos International is far too busy and crowded to be a viable alternative.

EXPENSIVE CITIES

What's the most expensive city in the world? Surprise—it's Moscow, according to Mercer International, an international human resources consulting firm that releases an annual cost-of-living survey. The survey covers 143 cities around the world and measures the comparative costs of more than 200 items, including food, housing, transportation, household goods, and entertainment. London rose to second place, followed by Seoul, Tokyo, and Hong Kong.

TOP 20 MOST EXPENSIVE CITIES (2007)

CITY	FORMER RANKING (MARCH 2006)
1. Moscow	1
2. London	5
3. Seoul	2
4. Tokyo	3
5. Hong Kong	4
6. Copenhagen	8
7. Geneva	7
8. Osaka	6
9. Zurich	9
10. Oslo	10 (tie)
11. Milan	13
12. St. Petersburg	12
13. Paris	15
14. Singapore	17
15. New York	10 (tie)
16. Dublin	18
17. Tel Aviv	24
18. Rome	21 (tie)
19. Vienna	21 (tie)
20. Beijing	14

But what does that mean in real figures? When you look at the specific costs of some of the basics, Hong Kong, Tokyo, and New York wind up trumping Moscow. All figures on the following pages are in U.S. dollars, as of 2007; purchase prices reflect those of medium-priced establishments.

(continued)

EXPENSIVE CITIES—Continued

COST-OF-LIVING COMPARISONS FOR SELECTED CITIES

CITY	RENT OF AN UNFURNISHED LUXURY TWO-BEDROOM APARTMENT (PER MONTH)	BUS OR SUBWAY RIDE
Hong Kong	8,957.88	0.72
Tokyo	4,101.69	2.57
New York	4,000.00	2.00
Moscow	4,000.00	NA
London	3,888.78	5.83
Seoul	3,425.24	0.95
Singapore	3,142.49	1.18
Tel Aviv	3,000.00	1.25
Geneva	2,869.09	2.62
Beijing	2,840.00	NA
Paris	2,634.36	1.85
Milan	2,634.35	1.32
Osaka	2,563.55	1.71
Chicago	2,400.00	2.00
Copenhagen	2,298.89	3.36
Zurich	2,295.27	3.12
San Francisco	2,200.00	1.50
Rome	2,041.63	1.32
Sydney	2,037.29	1.96
Oslo	2,026.41	4.86
Miami	2,000.00	1.68
St. Petersburg	2,000.00	NA
Amsterdam	1,975.77	2.10
Vienna	1,844.05	2.31
Madrid	1,844.04	1.46
Washington, DC	1,700.00	1.25
Warsaw	1,580.61	0.82
Dublin	1,580.61	1.98
Seattle	1,500.00	1.50
Zagreb	1,448.90	NA
Brussels	1,448.90	1.98
Prague	1,448.90	0.80
Buenos Aires	1,400.00	0.35
Atlanta	1,400.00	1.75

MUSIC CD	1 ISSUE OF INTERNATIONAL DAILY NEWSPAPER	1 CUP OF COFFEE, INCLUDING SERVICE	FAST-FOOD HAMBURGER MEAL
12.67	2.82	5.12	2.98
15.81	1.28	4.53	5.39
17.42	1.63	3.75	5.70
24.83	6.30	6.11	4.80
25.26	2.33	3.89	7.56
14.21	2.12	5.83	4.67
13.68	2.49	4.26	3.86
16.62	2.85	4.10	7.81
24.51	3.12	3.52	9.35
21.95	4.01	4.51	2.64
22.38	2.90	3.03	8.17
26.34	2.90	4.21	7.51
21.36	1.28	4.49	5.38
19.00	1.33	3.50	5.00
27.23	3.18	4.95	9.72
22.87	3.12	3.69	9.35
18.44	1.00	3.50	4.80
25.69	2.90	2.90	7.51
19.54	3.52	2.74	5.06
27.40	3.57	4.70	10.54
16.11	1.50	3.00	5.57
22.13	7.64	3.82	4.49
28.97	3.29	3.62	7.17
23.70	3.03	3.82	6.78
26.35	3.03	3.03	8.13
17.97	1.50	2.95	4.50
24.36	3.89	3.05	4.63
26.35	2.76	3.95	8.56
15.65	1.50	2.75	4.89
24.95	3.60	4.49	5.04
25.00	2.90	4.08	7.45
28.06	2.33	3.69	4.63
11.30	5.81	1.77	4.36
16.99	1.50	3.75	4.13

(continued)

EXPENSIVE CITIES—*Continued*

Hong Kong, Tokyo, New York, and Moscow may come out on top, but there are plenty of other places that are proving to be out of control when it comes to basic travel costs. Each year, the *Economist* puts out its Big Mac Index, which compares the cost of a McDonald's Big Mac, equalized into U.S. dol-

BIG MAC INDEX

COUNTRY	BIG MAC PRICE (IN U.S. DOLLARS)
Iceland	7.44
Norway	6.63
Switzerland	5.05
Denmark	4.84
Sweden	4.59
Great Britain	3.90
European Union	3.82
United States	3.22
Turkey	3.22
Canada	3.08
Chile	3.07
Colombia	3.06
Brazil	3.01
Hungary	3.00
Peru	2.97
United Arab Emirates	2.72
Australia	2.67
Mexico	2.66
Argentina	2.65
Latvia	2.52
Estonia	2.49
Lithuania	2.45
Czech Republic	2.41
Saudi Arabia	2.40

lars, in various nations. The most expensive country, according to this source? Iceland. That's right, head to Reykjavik and your Big Mac may cost you a whopping $7.44. That's very pricey secret sauce. Coming in second is Norway, so make sure you've got your wallet when you fly into Oslo.

COUNTRY	BIG MAC PRICE (IN U.S. DOLLARS)
Singapore	2.34
Japan	2.31
Pakistan	2.31
Poland	2.29
Taiwan	2.28
Costa Rica	2.18
Uruguay	2.17
South Africa	2.14
Slovakia	2.13
South Korea	2.08
Paraguay	1.90
Russia	1.85
Thailand	1.78
Indonesia	1.75
Sri Lanka	1.75
Philippines	1.74
Ukraine	1.71
Egypt	1.60
Venezuela	1.58
Malaysia	1.57
Hong Kong	1.54
New Zealand	1.43
China	1.41

(continued)

EXPENSIVE CITIES—Continued

Want a sense of how much you're going to pay for travel-specific costs? Check out this price comparison of some of the most expensive cities, provided by Wisconsin-based Runzheimer International, a management

AVERAGE TRAVEL COSTS IN SELECTED CITIES (IN U.S. DOLLARS)

	BREAKFAST*	LUNCH*	DINNER*
Geneva	37.29	37.68	60.12
Zurich	31.36	43.16	59.60
Copenhagen	29.35	30.28	52.87
Oslo	22.97	36.41	52.39
Moscow	33.20	30.15	54.41
London	40.92	32.99	60.33
Hong Kong	30.46	28.84	58.87
Tokyo	29.02	26.53	57.60
Seoul	33.19	49.28	55.85
Los Angeles	21.65	20.19	42.82
San Francisco	23.55	19.78	46.64
San Jose/Silicon Valley	20.84	17.23	34.93
Washington, DC	21.25	21.88	42.35
New York	29.77	25.82	53.40

* Food prices reflect full meals (excluding desserts and cocktails) at restaurants within hotels and in business areas. Reported data include all applicable taxes and a 15 percent gratuity.

** Lodging costs include tax and reflect year-round published rates at properties frequented by business travelers. In some international locations, data are not available for all three property types (deluxe, first class, and economy); in these cases, all rates are averaged together to provide a composite value.

Want to know what you're going to pay for the basics? Check out this comparison chart of U.S. cities from Runzheimer. Get your hair cut in Los

COST COMPARISON FOR BASIC NEEDS IN U.S. CITIES

LOCATION	MEN'S HAIRCUT	TUBE OF TOOTHPASTE	SOFT DRINK	BOTTLED WATER	SHAMPOO
Atlanta	20.17	2.17	1.87	2.10	0.99
Boston	27.33	2.64	1.82	2.24	0.98
Chicago	20.22	3.06	1.47	2.33	1.16
Honolulu	18.92	3.46	1.83	2.18	0.95
Los Angeles	18.59	2.94	1.48	2.13	1.18

consulting firm that provides workforce mobility solutions relating to business vehicles, relocation, travel management, corporate aircraft, and virtual office programs. And whatever you do, stay out of the cabs in Oslo, Tokyo, and London.

CORPORATE LODGING (1 NIGHT, FIRST-CLASS, SINGLE OCCUPANCY)**	TAXI (AIRPORT TO DOWNTOWN)†	DAILY CAR RENTAL‡
400.44	34.69	139.97
360.94	50.87	135.52
303.20	4.96	177.30
298.19	102.57	201.65
468.22	35.00	120.64
403.23	93.40	151.84
351.00	44.90	81.95
213.31	234.72	82.62
298.48	15.90	66.17
196.95	37.50	77.15
203.30	36.50	98.24
163.17	17.50	90.42
278.59	11.50	74.57
350.95	24.00	66.80

† Transportation data include the typical cost of a taxicab between the airport and downtown for a single passenger, and the retail price of shuttle service between the airport and downtown.

‡ Prices reflect the average rate for a nondiscounted, unlimited-mileage, 1-day car rental from an airport and include taxes and fees.

Angeles, but not Washington, DC. Buy a bottle of shampoo in Honolulu, but stay away from the toothpaste in San Francisco. All prices below are in U.S. dollars.

LOCATION	MEN'S HAIRCUT	TUBE OF TOOTHPASTE	SOFT DRINK	BOTTLED WATER	SHAMPOO
Manhattan	38.67	3.91	1.99	2.99	1.27
Miami	20.67	3.13	1.40	2.47	1.02
San Francisco	24.90	3.93	1.72	2.61	1.62
Washington, DC	44.69	2.76	1.50	2.14	1.16
Washington, MD	27.83	2.80	1.54	2.53	0.98
Washington, VA	33.22	2.99	1.98	2.24	1.76

WORST HOTELS

PAGING NORMAN BATES

What makes a good hotel? The criteria that actually matter might surprise you. It's not the thread count of the sheets. Or the size of the room. Or how many different designer soaps, lotions, and potions are displayed on the bathroom vanity. It's not about the view out the window, either. After all, how much time do you really spend in your hotel room, other than to sleep and shower? Not much.

The real differentiators are basic: safety, cleanliness, location, light in the room, connectivity, and great water pressure in the shower.

One thing that will keep me from returning to a hotel is nickel-and-diming. When a hotel quotes you its room rates, that should be it when it comes to charges. Any hotel that adds resort fees, "hospitality" fees, or mandatory-tip-to-the-bellman fees gets put on my future Don't Go There List. When a hotel charges $6 for a small bottle of water or installs infrared-sensor, Darth Vader–type minibars, I'm out of there.

But when a hotel practices full disclosure and transparency, and doesn't treat each corner of a room as an individual profit center, then I'm likely to return again and again.

And if someone is actually nice to me at the hotel—if someone understands the concept of service to the point where he or she actually anticipates my needs and follows through to meet them—I become loyal forever.

Speaking of loyalty, most of us have a myriad of loyalty program cards for airlines and hotels, but what keeps us coming back to hotels isn't frequent-stay programs or branding. The bottom line is that when it comes to real hotel loyalty, it's about telling the truth, and it's about basics—in design, function, and service. End of discussion.

But then again . . . not necessarily. Let's not forget the brochure mentality. Anyone who has read my other books or has seen me on the *Today* show knows that I don't trust brochures or brochure language. And neither should you. When a hotel claims to be oceanside, you'll probably have to cross a four-lane highway to get there. The B&B is quaint? Expect a doll-size bed in your pint-size room. European-style? Broken plumbing in your shared bathroom.

One of the best glossaries of brochure language translation I've ever found was written years ago by an innkeeper, Charles Hillestad. These are some of the most commonly used misleading phrases that I always watch out for in hotel and B&B brochures, and you should, too.

AIR-CONDITIONED: Windowpanes broken

ANTIQUES: Used furniture

AUTHENTIC: They couldn't afford to rip it out and replace it.

COZY: Your suitcase has more square footage than your room.

ELEGANT: Even the Venetian blinds have tassels.

FREE-SPIRITED: Bathing suits are optional in the hot tub.

GARRET: A place to bump your head

INN: Hotel, motel, home stay, restaurant, or anything at all with rooms

INSPECTED: In 1942

LUXURIOUS: Towels will actually fit around your waist.

NEWLY REFURBISHED: In 1942

ONCE IN A LIFETIME: No one ever returns.

ORIGINAL: Unpainted

RUSTIC: The plumbing is out back.

My favorite on this list is Charles's translation of "once in a lifetime," because it says so much about the travel experience. Hotels don't make money when we stay there once—they only really make money when we return, and of course, when we tell our friends.

So . . . would I return to the hotel in Honolulu that advertised it was just "steps from the beach"? Well, I counted—it was a mile away. That's a lot of steps. When they said "ocean view," I didn't think I'd have to bring binoculars.

How many times have you returned from a trip, only to tell your friends not to go to a particular hotel because your experience just was not what was advertised?

Sometimes it takes a lot of people spreading the bad word in order for things to turn around. Take the example of the Grand Hotel of Wildwood Crest in New Jersey, which was anything but grand. In 2002, after approximately 43 complaints were filed with the New Jersey Division of Consumer Affairs, the state actually sued the hotel for misleading consumers through false advertising. The advertising—and the hotel's brochures—made the claim that the rooms and facilities were clean, well maintained, and luxurious. But when guests arrived, according to the official complaint, they discovered that the hotel was "filthy" and "foul-smelling," and "lacked air-conditioning in certain areas." Some complained about puddles of standing water infested with bugs, and one woman found that the halls were "so foul-smelling that she held her breath each time she walked down them." The hotel later settled with the state and paid restitution to the guests.

It's also possible that brochure language can simply be lost in translation. One Italian hotel's brochure promised that "you'll sleep as soundly and peacefully as on your deathbed." Now, there's a hotel where guests check in but don't check out!

Of course, there are other reasons not to go to a hotel. . . .

Legionnaires' Disease

Have you heard the one about Legionnaires' disease in hotel rooms? In March 2008, visitors staying at the Quality Suites in Orlando had to pack up and leave after two guests were hospitalized in Pinellas County with Legionnaires' disease. The 154-room hotel, located in a highly touristed area near Universal Studios and SeaWorld, was fully booked, so hundreds of guests were forced to find another place to stay when the hotel voluntarily shut down.

County health inspectors closed the pool and hot tub while looking for factors that could have led to the growth of bacteria. What they found were dirty air filters and standing water in drip pans from air conditioners in about two dozen rooms. The hotel voluntarily fixed the problems and is now back open for business. But my big concern is that when this disease rears its ugly head in hotels, it's almost always a result of sheer neglect—which is definitely *not* among my criteria for a good hotel. If the staff doesn't properly maintain and clean equipment, who knows when there might be another outbreak?

Legionnaires' disease (LD), according to the CDC, is an infection usually caused by the bacteria *Legionella,* which often results in pneumonia. The disease was identified in 1976, when an outbreak of pneumonia occurred among attendees of an American Legion convention in Philadelphia. It's contracted through contaminated mist or vapor, which means large air-conditioning units and public hot tubs are high-risk conductors. Each year, between 8,000 and 18,000 people are hospitalized with LD in the United States, and between 5 percent and 30 percent of those cases are fatal. People who have a higher risk of LD include smokers, the elderly, people with chronic lung disease, and those with weakened immune systems because of disease or medications.

As it turns out, LD is more common in hotels than people realize; victims typically contract the illness through a whirlpool or sauna, or, even more disturbingly, in the shower. There have also been cases originating in buildings with large cooling towers in which the contaminated drip can enter through a window or through the air-conditioning system. The result? Hotels can easily be breeding grounds for this deadly disease.

About 97 percent of LD cases go undetected, so someone might stay in a hotel, then unknowingly return home sick. Even if the person goes to a doctor, the doctor may not diagnose LD or order the appropriate tests. Why? Because the symptoms are similar to those of pneumonia and other lung conditions. Of the cases that are diagnosed and reported, very few can be traced back to the hotel where the disease was acquired.

That said, here are some recent cases that were traced to hotels:

- In Ocean City, Maryland, in 2003, the Worcester County Health Department, the Maryland Department of Health and Mental Hygiene, and the CDC conducted an investigation when two guests at the **Princess Royale** contracted LD days after checking out of the hotel. One later died of the disease. After examining dozens of other reports of people who got sick after visiting Ocean City, the CDC found that at least 50 of them had had exposure to the hotel. Seven cases of LD were confirmed among that group, and one possible case was discovered between October 2003 and February 2004. The common source was the potable water supply.

- The **Cortina Inn** in Killington, Vermont, was shut down in April 2008 after state health officials traced at least two cases of LD to the hotel. A third case had some connection to the property, but its direct correlation couldn't be determined. According to a report from the Vermont Department of Health, after the cases were confirmed to be LD, the hotel was inspected and samples were taken from several areas, including the pool and spa, and the showerhead and faucet in one victim's room. The results from all four of those sources confirmed the presence of *Legionella pneumophila,* indicating a public health hazard. This wasn't the Cortina's first infraction: A hotel whirlpool was the source of two cases of LD back in 1985. And get this: In June 2008, the hotel was shut down *again* after the bacteria was rediscovered, although no new cases of LD were reported. The Connecticut-based corporation that owns the hotel filed for bankruptcy in the same month.

- **The Islander Resort,** formerly known as the Seagarden Inn, in Daytona Beach, Florida, was temporarily closed in February 2006 when three guests contracted LD, probably from the indoor spa, during a January stay. One victim, an 82-year-old woman, later died. The hotel is back open for business, but I'll leave it up to you whether you want to go there!

Dirtiest Hotels

Not surprisingly, I've stayed in more than my fair share of dirty hotels. Here's a list of my top seven dirtiest hotels . . . in the past 3 years.

1. Miami International Airport Hotel, Miami, Florida—I'd rather sleep in the terminal.

2. Westin Los Angeles Airport, Los Angeles, California—They've really let it slip. The corner suites have balcony hot tubs so you can look out and watch planes take off. Just don't look in the hot tubs.

3. The Adolphus, Dallas, Texas—This was once a favorite of mine, but after years of neglect, it's gotten shabby and dirty.

4. Wyndham Palm Springs, Palm Springs, California—Can you say "spring break" with no cleanup?

5. Las Vegas Hilton, Las Vegas, Nevada—It may say Hilton on the door, but cleanliness of the rooms is a gamble.

6. Hyatt Regency, Atlanta, Georgia—This old, tired convention hotel needs a convention of maids to check in.

7. Hilton Paris, Paris, France—It's in a great location, but the management is just running a holding pattern while the owners try to sell the hotel. Want to know why there have been no buyers? The hotel isn't exactly putting on its best face.

TripAdvisor, one of the leading user-generated review Web sites, has compiled user reviews to create a list of the top 10 dirtiest hotels in America, and trust me . . . you don't want to go there, either.

If you have your doubts about trusting a user-generated Web site, don't worry; I did, too. According to Brooke Ferencsik, a spokesperson for TripAdvisor, the site has three methods of vetting which posts go up. A team made up of dozens of quality-assurance specialists trained in fraud detection reads every review before it's posted. The site also utilizes automated filter tools that detect certain patterns and language that give away a suspect post. And, finally, the Web site's community of travelers tends to speak for itself—their passion is pretty renowned, and they'll often flag something that doesn't smell right. Plus, the sheer volume of reviews usually gives travelers a more complete picture of the property.

My team and I cut through layers of red tape to track down government health-inspection reports and pulled out the facts you need to know. Inspection reports will tell you whether a hotel is a threat to public health, and user reviews will recount real experiences of real people.

Between consulting TripAdvisor's findings and checking out government reports, we got the scoop on what's going on in some of the worst hotels in America.

1. Hotel Carter, New York, New York

You have to be pretty bad to earn the title of Dirtiest Hotel in America. But to be in the top two for 3 years running? Now, that's a problem.

Times Square might have reinvented itself as an upscale destination, but the 700-room Hotel Carter—which rightly bills itself as affordable (about

$100 a night) and centrally located within the tourist hub—is a throwback to the city's seedier days. And it has a sordid past to prove it.

In August 2007, a hotel maid got an unwelcome surprise when she found the dead body of a young woman, wrapped in garbage bags, under the bed. Police later charged a fugitive sex offender with the murder, saying that the 35-year-old had beaten and strangled the 22-year-old aspiring model and hidden her under the bed in his room. The two had met online, and at the time of the murder, the girl had been living in a Chelsea-area housing project and working as a call girl.

That's not all. A few years before, a building engineer died in a freak elevator accident. And in 1999, a clerk at the hotel was charged with killing his coworker with a knife and a hammer during a fight at the front desk. In 1987, the body of a partially clothed woman with her hands tied behind her back was discovered in the hotel's rear courtyard, apparently having been pushed out of a window. Back in 1983, a 25-day-old baby was beaten to death by her father at the hotel.

Cursed? Maybe. Dirty? Yes. Recent TripAdvisor reviews range from "The hotel was a dump. . . . They never cleaned the rooms. My parents had some cookies in their room and some rats or mice ate it [sic] during the first night. The bathroom were [sic] covered with black stain. It was horrible!" to higher praise that begins with "Perfect for our stay" but then admits, "The sheets were never changed during our 4-night stay." Stained sheets, filthy bathrooms, broken phones, and peeling wallpaper are just a few of the complaints. But the good news is, if you stay for less than 30 minutes, you get your money back!

2. Ramada Inn by the Falls, Niagara Falls, New York

Well, no need to worry about this one. The hotel closed its doors after making the dirtiest-hotels list!

3. Days Inn Vanderbilt/Music Row, Nashville, Tennessee

Some people will put up with a lot for a $99-a-night room that's in the middle of all the action. But when you're faced with "dirty, sticky carpets" and stained mattresses, and when the only "plus side," according to one reviewer, is the absence of roaches or other insects, you know you don't want to go there.

Now, here's the funny part: We checked in with the Metro Public Health Department in Tennessee, and an inspector was sent out the very next day! And when inspector Tommy Eubanks came back with the report, guess what? The hotel failed. It scored 69 percent, with three critical violations, including hair and food crumbs in the beds, at least one nonworking smoke detector, and improper storage of toxic items.

The story didn't end there. A month after the surprise inspection, the Days Inn began operating as a West End Lodge. The same inspector then made another unannounced visit and granted the hotel a passing score of 72—but noted that one of its buildings was shut down. Well, the latest word is that the property is closing its doors for good at the end of 2008 . . . and the building is scheduled for demolition. And I say, good riddance!

4. Red Carpet Inn, Fort Lauderdale, Florida

Out of 88 reviews on TripAdvisor, the best compliment that anyone could give this hotel was "not that bad."

Surprisingly, there was only one inspection of the property prompted by a consumer complaint in the past 2 years. That one, filed by the Florida Department of Business & Professional Regulation on May 1, 2007, didn't come up with anything. But other standard reports in 2007 and 2008 turned up items such as standing water on guest-room floors, and dust and debris in a bedroom.

Just for fun, here are a few other comments about this hotel:

"Bugs, drugs, and pubic hair," said one eloquent reviewer on TripAdvisor.

"This is the most disgusting property that we have ever visited," said one user of HotelGuide.net.

"Everything was terrible," posted another woman on TravelPost.com. "This was the worst hotel/motel experience I've ever had in my travels. . . . The online picture is completely deceiving. The place was a dump."

Still want to trust those inspection reports?

5. Regency Inn & Suites, New York, New York

This Penn Station–area hotel attracts a big international crowd, and there are angry rants and complaints in multiple languages to prove it. "NO vayas nunca a este hotel" ("Never go to this hotel"), cried one visitor from Madrid. While the majority of folks vowed never to return, other guests have said the hotel is worth the few bucks they paid for the stay, or that it wasn't as bad as they feared.

Unfortunately, we couldn't pull up the inspection reports for this property. Why? Because there weren't any! According to the New York City Department of Health and Mental Hygiene and the Department of Housing

Preservation and Development, there is no agency in New York State that inspects hotels on a regular basis. They claim that the Health Department will inspect a hotel based on complaints that are potential health hazards. But even when supplied with names of specific hotels with complaints of bugs, mold, and general filth, they refused to check into any records. Way to go, New York.

6. St. Augustine Beachfront Resort, St. Augustine, Florida

Out of nine inspections of this property from 2006 to 2008, six were based on complaints, and the resort met standards the first time around in only four of the inspections. Soiled and wet carpets, holes in the outer walls, and moldlike growth (whatever that means!) were just some of the findings. One particularly disturbing report, filed in September 2007, found 18 critical violations and 24 other observations—including a "fictitious room rate posted," a broken smoke detector, a locked fire extinguisher box missing the breaking device, and repeat violations involving a leaking roof.

Of course, guests unfortunate enough to stay at this beach "resort" could have saved themselves the trouble had they done their research ahead of time. "The Most, Horrible Hotel EVER!!!" wrote one unlucky patron in April 2008, though that guest did note that the hotel was currently being renovated.

And there's the one post that says it all: "Worst FL experience ever!"

7. Travel Inn Civic/Medical Center, Miami, Florida

This one, interestingly, didn't show up in the quest for inspection reports. Why? Well, it changed ownership and now operates as a Rodeway Inn. Did that have anything to do with the claims of cockroaches (both live and dead), filthy linens, dirty floors, broken toilets, moldy walls, and, oh yeah, lice? My guess is . . . very likely. The Rodeway Inn claims that it's going through extensive renovations. Hey, it can only get better from where it started.

8. Eden Roc Motel, Wildwood, New Jersey

"Eden Crock!" "Filth!" "Worst place in town," shout the headlines of reviews of Wildwood, New Jersey's Eden Roc Motel. From the dumpy lobby to clogged bathroom drains to stained sheets, this $90-a-night motel certainly seems to deserve its place among the 10 dirtiest hotels.

Osaka's Love Hotels

Japan has a host of unusual offerings for its visitors, such as "Love Hotels." It seems, though, that many of these hotels are adorned more with crazy fetishes than with affectionate embellishments. Some rooms have been created to resemble igloos, doctors' offices, and pirate ships. The Hotel Adonis in Osaka has the Library Room—but this space doesn't conjure dim, romantic corners where the likes of Shakespeare, Milton, and Wordsworth are shelved. Instead, the room looks stuffy and out-of-date and appears to boast shelves of bland law books from the 1980s. Stick to making out in your local library.

According to New Jersey's Department of Community Affairs, Bureau of Housing Inspection, hotels are inspected once every 5 years unless there's a complaint—and Eden Roc hasn't received any complaints since its last inspection, in 2005. Now, consider this: That one department inspects *all* the hotels, motels, condos, and townhouses in the entire state of New Jersey—we're talking hundreds of thousands of buildings with three units or more. It took weeks of due diligence and three different departments even to find someone who could provide the inspection reports (and someone finally did, a very lovely and helpful woman named Pat)—so, for the average consumer to file a complaint, it probably takes a Herculean effort.

As the inspection reports indicate, in 2005 the Eden Roc suffered from mold in guest rooms and a lack of carbon monoxide alarms. Not so bad, but after reading those reviews, I'll still skip that trip to the Eden Roc Motel.

9. Days Inn Lancaster, Lancaster, Pennsylvania

A dirty hotel in Amish country? That just seems wrong. But it's true—this Days Inn, which is now operating under the Rodeway Inn brand as Inn at Lancaster, has visitor reports of bugs, filth, and horrible customer service—and that's just the tip of the iceberg. Like New York State, parts of Pennsylvania don't regulate or monitor hotels. (Restaurants and swimming pools are covered by the Department of Agriculture and the Department of Health, respectively.)

That said, the folks at Manheim Township (who preferred to remain anonymous) said that every year, they receive five or six complaints, usually bug-related, about this one hotel. But each time the township follows up with the hotel, it seems that the management has done "just enough" to pass inspection. And, because this is an independently owned franchise, the parent company has no obligation or authority over the facility.

10. Pacific Sands Motel, Santa Monica, California

Despite its coveted Santa Monica address, the 58-room Pacific Sands Motel has a pretty dirty reputation. Stained floors, rusty drain covers, cockroaches, and possible bed bugs were just a few of the customer complaints.

The Los Angeles County Environmental Health Department provided the recent inspection reports for this hotel. Surprisingly, there was only one confirmation of bed bugs—so why was the health department called out four separate times to check for them? In all, there were seven incident reports from December 2006 to January 2008, including complaints concerning bed bugs, broken plumbing, and unsanitary bathroom conditions.

Better Business Bureau Complaints

TripAdvisor's list was so much fun that we decided to look beyond the Web in our search for bad hotels. Turns out, there are plenty. The Better Business Bureau (BBB) handed us reports on some of consumers' most-complained-about hotels. And believe me, for every person who takes the time to contact the BBB, you can reasonably assume that there are dozens more who had equally bad experiences but didn't complain.

Sandpiper Beacon Beach Resort, Panama City, Florida

Folks at the BBB serving northwest Florida provided a gem of a hotel: the Sandpiper Beacon Beach Resort in Panama City, Florida. In 36 months, the hotel, which ironically markets itself as "The Fun Place," had 50 complaints, 47 of which were unanswered. Reported problems included issues with advertising, contracts, billing and collection, sales practices, customer service, products, and refunds and exchanges.

Between 2006 and early 2008, the Florida Department of Business & Professional Regulation responded to six complaints and conducted two standard lodging inspections; three of those eight actions required follow-up inspections. The major violations included broken and disabled fire equipment and threadbare, unclean bedding.

If that's not enough to turn you off, perhaps the hotel's appalling customer service is. The Sandpiper is considered to be a "party hotel" for spring breakers, so some shabbiness in its quality can be expected, even forgiven. But then you hear the case of KayCee Chapman, a high-school student from Tennessee who stayed at the Sandpiper with three friends in May 2007. "They accused us of having a keg in the bathtub," she said when we interviewed her. "We came back from shopping one afternoon, and we were locked out, with a note on the door saying that we had to go see the front desk. They said the bathtub was cracked and flooded the room below. Since the room was in my name, they said I had to pay $2,000 for the bathtub or I'd go to jail."

The police were called and the guests were absolved, after having been locked out of their room for 5 hours. Two nights later, they were awoken at 3 a.m. by a security guard pounding on the door, accusing the sleeping guests of making too much noise. "The lights were off, and we were in our pajamas. We were obviously sleeping, but he didn't believe us." Chapman had to go to the front desk, where the manager told her that the group was about to be kicked out, again. "He decided that he would give us 'one more chance' to stay. At that point, I just wanted to get home, but we stayed another night." The final straw? The hotel refused to return her deposit.

Rodeway Inn, Wisconsin Dells, Wisconsin

With a history of unanswered complaints and horrible customer service, the Rodeway Inn in Wisconsin Dells received the Wisconsin BBB's F rating—its worst possible rating. That was one we just had to investigate.

According to the Sauk County Health Department, this hotel, formerly known as the Diamond Hotel, is on the radar, with housekeeping and maintenance issues as the primary factors. The health-inspection reports on this hotel showed evidence of cockroaches, cracked windows, mold in the shower of the pool restroom, and dirty rooms. (Regarding the latter, the report noted "new staff in training." Training for what? How to vacuum under a bed?)

A young woman named Joy Williams, who had booked four rooms for New Year's Eve 2007, was accidentally charged for a fifth room, and when she went to the front desk to complain, the woman behind the counter "freaked out on me right away," said Williams. "She said, 'You're such an idiot.'" Williams continued, "It was a horrible place. It looked like they hadn't ever vacuumed the stairs, and we were afraid to sit on the bed. The bed didn't have a fitted sheet; there were black marks all over the sheets. The front desk was not organized at all and had receipts lying everywhere. There were blankets over the windows. It looked really trashy." Stains on the sheets, bare electrical wiring, and cobwebs were among other complaints filed with the Better Business Bureau.

Bed Bugs!

Over the past few years, the media has been in a frenzy over the topic of bed bugs in hotels. In fact, there has been a sharp rise in the number of bed bug reports—anywhere from a 70 percent to a 150 percent increase, depending on your source. Adult bed bugs are reddish and about the size of an apple seed; the eggs are pale, almost clear, and about a millimeter long. The adults feed at night and leave red, itchy bumps similar to mosquito bites on skin. The thing about bed bugs is that they can strike anywhere, not just in low-budget or unsanitary hotels.

Case in point: The deluxe **Mandarin Oriental Hyde Park, London,** was sued in 2007 by a couple claiming several million dollars in damages after allegedly suffering hundreds of bed bug bites. In this posh Knightsbridge hotel, where room rates *start* at £245 a night (that's almost $500) in the low season, attorney Sidney Bluming and his wife, Cynthia, certainly weren't expecting nightly attacks by the little buggers during their 5-night stay.

With swollen, itchy skin, the Blumings returned home, only to realize that the bed bugs were hiding out in their luggage and clothing, and infesting their Manhattan apartment. The couple claimed that they had to discard much of their furniture and many personal items (in a recently renovated apartment, no less) and fumigate the home to rid themselves of the pests. The Blumings sued the hotel for fraud, deceptive trade practice, negligence, recklessness, nuisance, and intentional infliction of emotional distress.

According to a statement released by the couple's lawyer, Michael Weinstein, of the Newark, New Jersey–based firm Robertson Freilich Bruno & Cohen, after the Blumings returned home and consulted their doctors and an oncologist, ". . . the hotel withheld from them for nearly a week the knowledge that bed bug infestation was to blame." The hotel general manager and a third-party exterminator ultimately admitted that there were bed bugs embedded in the headboard of the couple's hotel room. When we contacted the hotel ourselves, they came back with the statement "We can confirm that a regrettable, but isolated, incident of infestation occurred in May 2006 within one guestroom at our London property."

Fortunately, there have been no cases since, but that doesn't mean it won't happen again.

Stone Inn's, Siloam Springs, Arkansas

Another bed bug case was settled around February 27, 2008, after Rose M. Pagley-Brown sued the Stone Inn's in Siloam Springs, Arkansas, claiming that she was infested by hundreds of bed bugs during her stay. The suit alleged negligence and sought damages for pain and mental anguish, embarrassment and humiliation, medical bills, and other expenses—the woman claimed that she suffered from recurring nightmares of bed bugs feeding on her while she slept once she returned home. She even brought some sample bed bugs down to the front desk, but the motel owner denied that there was any problem. The suit was settled out of court.

Hotel Pennsylvania, New York, New York

The Hotel Pennsylvania claims to be "the World's Most Popular Hotel." Maybe, if you're talking about popularity with bed bugs.

While it certainly enjoyed its glory days, this "popular hotel" is now nothing more than a two-star accommodation, where room rates start at about $138 a night, in a four-star location (sort of—that part of town isn't exactly high end, but the hotel is located across the street from Penn Station and Madison Square Garden and is also close to Macy's).

Hotel owners had to pony up nearly $100,000 to six victims after two Swiss women claimed that they were bitten from "head to toe" during their 2005 stay. To make matters worse, the women's attorney, Adam Sattler, noted, "As soon as they approached the counter to check out, before they were even able to say anything, the person behind the counter said, 'We know it, bed bugs.' That tells me that the hotel knew about it."

If all goes according to plan, this "historic hotel" is slated for demolition in 2011. And that's not soon enough for me!

Comfort Inn & Suites, Los Angeles, California

Bugs, bugs, and more bugs. This Hollywood hotel is a great value, starting at $100 a night, and is located near some of the major Los Angeles sites—but there may be other "guests" in your room.

Health inspectors found six dead cockroach nymphs in the eating and storage areas of the hotel in July 2006 after a guest complaint. The good news is that no live roaches were reported at that time. Later that summer, a complaint over bed bugs was found to be "justified" in room 335. Less than a year later, a bed bug was found on the bed in unit 306. And then, guess what? Two weeks later, bed bugs were discovered in two rooms on the second floor.

And if that's not enough, check out some of the user reviews from 2008: "Bed Bugs! Beware! Beware!" wrote one TripAdvisor reviewer. "Just ok; plus a bug problem," wrote another. Seems that this problem has been going on for quite some time, with no indication that it's going away anytime soon.

Chapter 10

WORST CRUISES

SHIPS OF FOOLS

In general, cruising is very safe. As you're reading this, more than 80,000 of your fellow Americans are at sea. And nothing has happened. Most of them are having a good time. And many of them will cruise again—the business enjoys a high percentage of repeat customers. Despite that, there are cruise customers who have had horrible experiences while onboard. And lots of the cruise ships those unhappy people went on are repeat offenders, so there are vessels on which you do *not* want to sail. But what are the metrics, the warning signs, for avoiding certain cruise ships?

It gets down to full disclosure, transparency, and commitment to the environment.

Cleanliness Is Next to Godliness—How Viruses Spread on Cruise Ships

Viral gastroenteritis is an infection caused by a variety of viruses, resulting in inflammation of the stomach and small and large intestines, which causes vomiting and diarrhea. People most commonly contract a norovirus (or Norwalk-like virus), which is often misleadingly referred to as stomach flu. (The illness is not caused by the influenza virus.)

But its other nickname is one that's all too accurate: the cruise-ship virus. The confined nature of shipboard life makes ships the proverbial petri dish at sea—the perfect breeding ground for a communicable disease.

Around 23 million Americans become infected with norovirus each year without even setting foot on a ship, but because ships are required to report gastrointestinal (GI) illnesses to the CDC, these incidents garner media attention. An outbreak is defined as 3 percent or more of the ship's population having a GI incident. (This could range from a dozen to a couple of hundred people, depending on the ship's capacity.)

There have always been viral outbreaks on cruise ships. The number of cases was relatively stable in general—six or seven outbreaks per year—until 2002, when the figures exploded. In 4 months, from September to the end of that year, cruise ships reported 22 outbreaks affecting 1,350 passengers and 218 crew members.

Cruise lines are often quick to blame passengers for bringing the illness aboard with them, but the statistics speak otherwise. It seems that certain ships and certain cruise lines appear more prone to outbreaks than others. For example, *Royal Odyssey* in March 1997 and *Regal Princess* in 1998 each had three successive cruises reporting illnesses traced to a Norwalk-like virus. Is it the ships themselves, their design, or the mix of crew

CRUISE SHIPS WITH THREE OR MORE REPORTED ILLNESS OUTBREAKS, 2002–2007

SHIP (CRUISE LINE)	TOTAL OUTBREAKS
Ryndam (Holland America)	7
Amsterdam (Holland America)	5
Regal Princess (Princess)	5
Sun Princess (Princess)	5
Veendam (Holland America)	5
Island Princess (Princess)	4
Norwegian Crown (Norwegian)	4
Queen Elizabeth II (Cunard)	4
Seven Seas Mariner (Regent)	4
Volendam (Holland America)	4
Constellation (Celebrity)	3
Norwegian Dream (Norwegian)	3
Norwegian Sun (Norwegian)	3
Royal Princess (Princess)	3
Serenade of the Seas (Royal Caribbean)	3
Zenith (Celebrity)	3
Mercury (Celebrity)	2

Source: *Centers for Disease Control and Prevention*

members acting as reservoirs for the illness? Even if a worker is quarantined and returns to work after 48 to 72 hours of being symptom-free, the virus could still be in the person's system, keeping him or her contagious for as long as 2 weeks!

Vessel Sanitation Program

On cruises, it's all about the high-touch areas, such as the buffet and the shuffleboard cues, and human interaction, including shaking hands.

In 1975, in response to several large GI disease outbreaks on cruise ships, the CDC established the Vessel Sanitation Program (VSP), a joint effort with the cruise industry to achieve better sanitation and to minimize the risk of GI disease on cruise ships. The VSP staff conducts surprise (although whether they're really a surprise is debatable) sanitation inspections twice a year on U.S.-bound cruise ships with international itineraries carrying 13 or more passengers.

The VSP inspectors look at many factors that contribute to ship cleanliness and sanitation, including water supply storage; disinfection of spas and hot tubs; food handling, preparation, and storage; personal hygiene and sanitation practices of the crew; and environmental and public health practice training. Inspection scores of 85 or lower (out of 100) are unsatisfactory. The Green Sheet Report is a list of the most recent cruise ship inspection scores and is available online to the public at cdc.gov/nceh/vsp. Bottom line: If a ship scores below 85, think twice before booking!

And make sure you don't just look at the score—read the specific violations, too. You probably want to know whether your lamb shank is stored at the right temperature and whether there's mold in your ice machine. Check out these examples of low-scoring ships.

Cruise Ship: *Stad Amsterdam*   **Score: 56**

Cruise line: Stad Amsterdam
Inspection date: 03/29/07
Violations included:

- Major water violations, such as not testing the potable-water distribution system for *E. coli*—something that is supposed to be done four times a month; also, unavailable documentation of cleaning, disinfection, and flushing of the potable-water tanks

- Serving noncommercially caught fish to passengers and crew
- High refrigerator temperatures, leading to improper storage of potentially hazardous foods
- Unclean dishes; dishes left in upright positions with pooled water
- No schedule for pest management, no record of sticky trap placement, no plan for pest inspection

Cruise Ship: *Nautilus Explorer*   **Score: 74**
Cruise line: Lever Diving
Inspection date: 06/24/2007
Violations included:

- Amount of chlorine injected into the potable water not properly controlled or analyzed
- Four monthly *E. coli* tests on the water distribution system not conducted
- No hourly monitoring of the whirlpool
- Open/preparation date of food, rather than the discard date, being used for date marking
- Reuse of difficult-to-clean, single-use spice containers
- Pitted and scored cutting boards, making cleaning difficult; kitchen items soiled with food debris
- Debris in storage containers for clean utensils and pots

Cruise Ship: *Pride of Aloha*   **Score: 78**
Cruise line: Norwegian Cruise Lines
Inspection date: 12/21/07
Violations included:

- Unsatisfactory chlorine levels in the whirlpool
- Food preparation dates incorrectly marked (a week off) in refrigerators
- Incorrect refrigerator cooling standards, causing a potential for food cross-contamination
- Residue on food contact surfaces, utensils, dishes, and a meat grinder

"All Hurl the Queen!"

In December 2007, the 90,000-ton liner *Queen Victoria* was christened in a lavish ceremony by Camilla Parker Bowles, the Duchess of Cornwall and wife of Prince Charles, in a long-standing tradition of having royals (or, in her case, a near royal) bless the Cunard Queen luxury liners. What they didn't expect was for that blessing to become a curse.

With more than 2,000 worldwide guests in attendance at the ceremony, the champagne bottle failed to smash against the bow—a bad omen in the world of maritime christening. Nicknamed the "Curse of Camilla," this moniker came true, as only a few weeks later the *Queen Victoria* was struck down by norovirus—nearly 80 passengers out of around 3,000 on the ship suffered serious vomiting, stomach cramps, and diarrhea.

- Occasional inaccessibility of staff hand-washing facilities
- Numerous live insect larvae in pooled water in a beverage station's technical space

Cruise Ship: *Amadea*   **Score: 84**

Cruise line: V. Ships Leisure USA
Inspection date: 04/04/2008
Violations included:

- No shield or barrier between the Havana Club's hand-washing sink and the area where juices and mixers are stored during service

- Sponges used throughout the ship for wiping after having cleaned food-contact and non-food-contact surfaces

- Heavily grease- and dirt-soiled kitchen areas and equipment in the Amadea Restaurant; black mold buildup on the bulkhead at the deck juncture; one "filth fly" noted in preparation room

- Public restrooms in the spa area equipped only with air hand dryers, requiring passengers to exit by using their bare hands on the door handle

- Four Seasons Restaurant galley staff handling carrots without wearing gloves, and placing the carrots in a large pan for storage. The carrots were said to be for cooking, but because of the large volume, they might also have been served raw.

Pillage and Steal: The Modern-Day Jack Sparrow

Not a month goes by without reports of fires, on-ship violence, sinking ships, and people overboard.

Dramatic photographs shocked the world in late 2007 as the *Explorer,* a cruise ship sailing near Antarctica, sank off the South Shetland Islands after hitting an unidentified object. More than 150 passengers and crew took refuge on lifeboats.

Sounds pretty bad, and sometimes cruise ships might seem like a veritable, dangerous soap opera, but the numbers of these incidents are still relatively low. Except in one area . . .

What about cruise ships being attacked by . . . pirates? No, it's not your next organized excursion at sea. This is real.

The International Maritime Bureau (IMB) Piracy Reporting Centre reports that piracy is on the rise: Reported piracy incidents went up 10 percent, from 239 in 2006 to 263 in 2007; in the first 6 months of 2008, there were 114 incidents worldwide.

Somalia and the nearby Gulf of Aden are perhaps the most high-profile spots for piracy, and incidents are on the rise. The country does not have a navy, leaving the 1,880-mile coast—the longest in Africa—vulnerable. Given its proximity to key shipping routes that connect with the Red Sea and the Indian Ocean, this is a major problem.

In 2007, there were a total of 31 piracy incidents (both attacks and attempted attacks) reported in Somalia, up drastically from 10 in the previous year. Somalia also saw the most kidnappings of any region that year—at least 154 people were held hostage in 11 different hijackings. In the first half of 2008, there were 5 incidents off the coast of Somalia and 19 in the Gulf of Aden/Red Sea region.

The last attack on a major cruise ship occurred in November 2005, when the *Seabourn Spirit* was attacked by Somali pirates firing automatic weapons and rocket-propelled grenades. The ship was on a 16-day cruise from Egypt to Kenya and was carrying 151 passengers (48 of whom were American) and 161 crew members. Only one crew member was injured, and the ship was eventually able to outrun the pirates before they could board the ship.

More recently, in April 2008, Somali pirates hijacked the French luxury yacht *Le Ponant* as it sailed from the Seychelles to the Mediterranean Sea through the Gulf of Aden, located between Somalia and Yemen. The 30 crew members onboard spent a week in captivity before being freed; six pirates were captured by French military forces.

Despite that, Somalia can't hold a candle—or perhaps a dagger—to Nigeria when it comes to piracy. In 2007, there were a total of 42 incidents, including 25 "actual" attacks (versus attempted attacks)—a dramatic increase from 12 the year prior. Most of the incidents were centered around the port of Lagos and the Niger Delta region. In the first half of 2008, there were 18 incidents . . . and counting.

Nickel-and-Diming on Cruise Ships

Of course, that kind of modern-day piracy isn't the only thievery you want to watch out for. The real pillaging of cruise passengers comes in the form of onboard revenue.

Before the skyrocketing costs of fuel changed the bottom line, most airlines could actually make a profit if their load factors (how much of an airplane's passenger-carrying capacity is filled) averaged around 68 percent. Hotels make a profit at around 72 percent. Cruise lines? It might surprise you to learn that most cruise-line business models show their ships beginning to make profits when they're . . . 102 percent full! That's a lot of cabins to fill.

Because of the massive frenzy of new shipbuilding, cruise lines have even more cabins to fill and large debts to service. Companies have structured their business models not to make money on the cabins, so they have to do whatever they can to lower fares to make sure that those cabins are always filled. Although you may not believe it, the discounted cabin rate you're quoted before booking is the real thing, since it's the best way for cruise lines to make sure that you (and as many of your friends as possible) get onboard.

Cruise lines make their *real* money when you leave your cabin to take a shore excursion; dine at premium restaurants; or visit the bar, the spa, the casino, the onboard shopping, the rock-climbing wall, the ice-skating rink, the ship's photographer, and, well, you get the picture. It's a big *ka-ching!* at sea.

These extra costs can easily exceed your original quoted cruise fare; they can even triple it. In fact, there's a lively competition out there between onboard and onshore spending. The locals in many cruise destinations complain that cruise ships take the lion's share of their passengers' money by the time the ship docks. With passengers already bottomed out, there's very little onshore spending.

So how does this happen, you ask?

If you book a cruise expecting it to be all-inclusive, think again. First, consider the tips you're expected to leave the maid and the bartender—and don't forget your cabin steward and butler, dining-room stewards, busboy, table captain, head waiter, maitre d', wine steward, baggage handler, tour guide, hairdresser, masseuse . . . and so on and so on.

Then there are those additional charges that can, in effect, double your cruise fare. Expect to pay for everything from bottled water to sodas to alcohol, which is usually where they really get you. And if you plan on skipping the buffet or 6 p.m. dinnertime, those specialty restaurants, cafés, and ice-cream shops are going to cost you. For example, on several of Royal Caribbean's ships, a meal surcharge at its signature Italian restaurant, Portofino, will set you back $20 to $25 per person! And while Ben & Jerry's was born from bohemian roots, that doesn't mean your ice cream is free. Expect to pay "market prices" for your sundae.

Then there are shore excursions—from city tours to dogsledding—perhaps the most profitable revenue generator on cruise ships. On Norwegian Cruise Lines, a 5-hour tour of Volcanoes National Park on Hawaii's Big Island is $37 per adult, and given that it's just a bus tour, this is a big profit maker. How about a helicopter glacier trek in Alaska? Expect to shell out up to $500 per person on any cruise line, and that figure includes a huge markup as well.

As a result, you need to budget accordingly. One way to gauge how much you might spend on a cruise is to look at how old your ship is. An older ship won't cost you as much, because the cruise line hasn't been able to physically add on more revenue generators.

But how about a newer ship? Count on spending at least 2½ times what you paid for your cabin, per person. Cruise ships built in the late 1990s and early 2000s are larger, devoting considerably more space to income generators such as shops, cafés, activities, casinos, and bars.

Make sure you read the fine print and the charges for each and every profit center onboard your ship to estimate what you might be spending on extras each day. And just do the math. If the total cost of activities you think you might do is shocking, don't go there. Pick another ship. Or skip the ship-offered shore excursions. Instead, find another couple onboard and the name of a hotel in a particular port city you'd like to explore. As your own tour group, call the hotel's concierge to arrange for a car and driver—you'll save lots of money.

Safety on Cruise Ships

Cruise Lines International Association (CLIA), the official trade organization for cruise lines in North America, claims that passenger safety and security are the cruise industry's highest priorities, and that a cruise ship is inherently secure because it is like a gated community, with 24-hour surveillance and a controlled environment. In order to maintain this secure environment, cruise lines have established strict ship security procedures that are, in part, outlined in internationally agreed-upon measures set forth by the International Maritime Organization (IMO). Ships are also designed according to safety standards set by the IMO and the U.S. Coast Guard.

However, as the cruise industry continues to grow, new concerns are being addressed with regard to passenger safety, particularly for passengers in foreign waters.

"There has been little or no oversight or accountability [for] the safety and security of these citizens," said U.S. Rep. Doris Matsui (D-Calif.), who recently called for an amendment to existing legislation that protects American citizens onboard cruise ships. "There have been a number of high-profile cases in the news of passengers falling overboard, passengers gone missing, and passengers being victims of sexual assaults."

Sexual and physical assaults on cruise ships were the leading crimes reported to and investigated by the FBI on the high seas over the past 5 years, and the government is starting to pay attention.

Back in 1999, the International Council of Cruise Lines (now part of CLIA) issued the following statement: "A passenger is safer on a cruise ship than in urban or rural America." And a review of FBI annual crime statistics supports this: The number of reported shoreside aggravated sexual assaults occurring in urban or rural communities is at least 20 to 50 times greater than the total number of all reported shipboard assaults of any type. In fact, the rate of sexual assault on cruise lines is—at worst—half the U.S. rate of forcible rape. The cruise industry claims that the rate of sexual assault on cruise ships is 17.6 per 100,000, as compared with a U.S. rate of 32.2 per 100,000.

However, numbers can be deceiving. Using the industry's own figures, one is as much as 50 percent more likely to be sexually assaulted on a cruise ship than on land. That number was derived by looking at the number of passengers traveling each day on Royal Caribbean International (RCI).

(That cruise line was chosen as a sample because reliable numbers were readily available.) The figures for sexual assault and sex-related incidents on RCI between 2003 and 2005, as provided by a civil suit and later published in the *Los Angeles Times*, were 81 sexual assault cases, 52 cases of "inappropriate touching," 28 cases of sexual battery, 99 cases of sexual harassment, and 13 cases specified as "other." Based on these numbers, it was concluded that the rate of sexual assault on cruise ships is actually 48.065 per 100,000. Either the industry lied in 1999 and again in 2006, or the problem of sexual assault has gotten out of control.

On April 24, 2008, the U.S. House of Representatives passed a bill that includes plans for a national database of crimes that occur on cruise ships. The provision was included as an amendment to the Coast Guard Reauthorization Act, sponsored by Rep. Matsui and cosponsored by Reps. Ted Poe (R-Tex.), Christopher Shays (R-Conn.), and Carolyn Maloney (D-N.Y.). It is supported by the Rape, Abuse & Incest National Network, National Alliance to End Sexual Violence, National Center for Victims of Crime, Pennsylvania Coalition Against Rape, and National Organization for Victim Assistance.

Said Rep. Matsui in a public statement: "One of my constituents was the victim of a brutal assault while on a cruise vacation. She turned to me for help after the cruise line had provided little or no support, and has since been a true advocate in making the government aware of this gross oversight in the safety of vacationing American citizens."

The online database will be maintained by the Secretary of the Coast Guard and will keep a numerical tally of deaths, missing persons, and reported crimes on cruise ships. The online crime statistics will be updated quarterly and broken up by cruise line. Cruise lines will be required to include a link to the online database on their Web sites.

If this database gets up and running—and if it is available to the public—it will become an essential barometer for picking which cruise ship to avoid.

The Cruise Industry and Pollution

Perhaps the most concerning effect of cruising is the amount of pollution that each and every cruise ship leaves in its wake. The cruise industry is quick to point out the initiatives it has implemented and the awards it has received in what is essentially a pat on the back for improving standards.

How Wasteful Is Your Cruise Ship?

"To the cruise ship industry, a key issue is demonstrating to the public that cruising is safe and healthy for passengers and the tourist communities that are visited by their ships. Cruise ships carrying several thousand passengers and crew have been compared to 'floating cities,' in part because the volume of wastes produced and requiring disposal is greater than that of many small cities on land. . . . Those wastes, if not properly treated and disposed of, can pose risks to human health, welfare, and the environment. Environmental advocates have raised concerns about the adequacy of existing laws for managing these wastes, and suggest that enforcement of existing laws is weak."

From the Congressional Research Service report Cruise Ship Pollution: Background, Laws and Regulations, and Key Issues, February 2008

This report also details that during a typical 1-week voyage, a large cruise ship (with 3,000 passengers and crew) is estimated to generate . . .

- 210,000 gallons of sewage
- 1 million gallons of gray water
- More than 130 gallons of hazardous waste
- 8 tons of solid waste
- 25,000 gallons of oily bilgewater

The average cruise ship carries 600 crew members and 1,400 passengers. On average, passengers on a cruise ship each account for about 7.7 pounds of garbage daily—compared with the 1.7 pounds generated by a person residing onshore.

For some perspective on air pollution, a single cargo ship coming into New York Harbor can release as much pollution as 350,000 current-model-year cars driving for 1 hour. In Los Angeles/Long Beach, the 16 container ships in port each day produce as many smog-forming emissions as one million cars. In one port visit, a single cruise ship generates the same amount of emissions as more than 12,400 cars.

But that doesn't change the fact that these floating cities leave behind monumental amounts of trash, wastewater, and fumes.

According to the United Nations Atlas of the Oceans, some of the environmental impacts of cruise tourism involve the following.

- Air pollution through the emission of sulfur-rich exhaust fumes
- Infrastructure damage due to the development of ship construction sites as well as new berthing areas and deeper channels and ports
- Damage caused by anchors and pollution through use of toxic paints and antifouling agents
- Overcrowding of particular destinations with tourists for a short period of time. On Easter Island, for example, it is common for 800 to 900 people to disembark within a few hours for bus tours to see the archaeological sites, making a huge impact on the island's fragile environment.
- Excessive water consumption and environmental pressures to produce high quantities of food
- Waste including sewage, oils, garbage, plastics, and hazardous substances

The U.S. Coast Guard is responsible for enforcing regulations regarding ocean dumping from vessels. It is illegal to dump plastic refuse and garbage mixed with plastic anywhere at sea. Dumping nonplastic trash and other forms of garbage is restricted, usually ranging from 3 to 25 miles offshore, depending on the region. These regulations apply to all U.S. vessels and to foreign vessels operating in U.S. waters up to 200 miles offshore.

But it's not necessarily the dumping of plastic or garbage that has the greatest environmental impact; it's the discharge of wastewater into our oceans.

There are three types of wastewater: bilgewater, black water, and gray water. Bilgewater is a collection of water, oily engine fluids, lubricants, cleaning fluids, and other wastes that accumulate in the lowest part of a vessel. Black water refers to human waste from toilets and, on some ships, includes wastewater from medical facilities onboard. Gray water comes from showers and sinks.

A section of the Clean Water Act requires that vessels with installed toilet facilities be equipped with an operable marine sanitation device (MSD) to treat the sewage. However, the industry is not required to monitor or report MSD discharges to either the government or the public.

There are no restrictions on the release of gray water in oceans. Current state and federal antipollution laws allow cruise ships to dump treated black water if the ship is stationary or if it's within 3 miles of shore (except for California and Alaska). Once ships are 3 miles from shore, they can dump untreated sewage anywhere (except in the Alexander Archipelago in Alaska, where treated sewage and gray water may be discharged only while cruise ships are under way, traveling at least 6 knots).

But there have been plenty of cases in which cruise lines decided not to follow the rules. Regency Cruises, Palm Beach Cruises, Discovery Cruise Line, Celebrity Cruises, Dolphin Cruise Lines, Princess Cruises, and the Holland America Line have all been fined for illegally discharging oil, garbage, paint, plastic, ballast water, and food waste into the waters of Alaska and/or the Caribbean. Between 1993 and 1998 alone, there were 87 confirmed cases, and those cruise lines paid more than $30 million in fines.

In July 1999, this problem garnered national attention when Royal Caribbean Cruises Ltd. (now known as Royal Caribbean International), the world's second-largest cruise line, pleaded guilty to routinely dumping oil and chemicals from ships in coastal waters around the United States. The $18 million fine was the largest ever to be paid by a cruise line in connection with polluting U.S. waters.

The company later pleaded guilty to 21 felony counts and entered into a plea agreement for dumping hazardous chemicals in New York Harbor, as well as oil and toxic chemicals in Miami, the Virgin Islands, Los Angeles, and the Inside Passage in Alaska, and for lying to the coast guard about continuing to dump pollutants after promising to stop after the previous conviction.

The guilty ships in RCCL's case were the *Sovereign of the Seas*, the *Majesty of the Seas*, the *Grandeur of the Seas*, the *Song of Norway*, the *Sun Viking*, the *Monarch of the Seas*, the *Nordic Empress*, and the *Nordic Prince*.

"It worked like this," reported former U.S. Attorney General Janet Reno. "The company's cruise ships were rigged with secret bypass pipes. Engineers on the ships used the pipes to dump their bilge waste overboard, often in the darkness of night . . . and to make matters worse, the company routinely falsified the ship's logs so much so that its own employees referred to the logs with a Norwegian term meaning 'Fairy Tale Book.' . . . They dumped everywhere. At sea, in port, and in sensitive environmental areas, even in the shadow of the company's executive suites, they didn't care. We expect the laws to be enforced. . . . If people flim-flam us, they should expect the consequences. And the message is our waters are far more fragile than people give credit for and we have got to stop messing them up if we want to preserve the way [of] life for our children and our grandchildren."

RCCL also pleaded guilty to deliberately dumping many other types of pollutants, including hazardous chemicals from photo processing equipment, dry-cleaning shops, and printing presses into the water from the ships' sinks and showers, which, as gray water, is routinely, and legally, discharged into the oceans.

More recently, in December 2004, Holland America was fined $200,000 and had to pay $500,000 in restitution after its vessel the *Ryndam* discharged sewage into Juneau Harbor in 2002. The cruise line also paid $1.3 million to improve the ship's handling of waste.

In November 2006, Celebrity Cruises was fined $100,000 after its vessel the *Mercury* dumped 500,000 gallons of untreated wastewater in the Puget Sound and the connecting Strait of Juan de Fuca. Even worse, the cruise line denied it, until shipboard documents revealed that the waste had, in fact, been dumped 10 times over 9 days the previous year.

In June 2007, Princess Cruises was fined about $1.57 million after the *Sea Diamond* sank off the coast of Santorini 2 months earlier . . . because about 450 tons of fuel and lubricants sank along with it.

The good news is that states such as Alaska, Washington, and California have taken the lead in environmental monitoring, enforcement of environmental laws, and passenger safety when it comes to cruise ships.

In Alaska, Democratic state representative Beth Kerttula and Republican state senator Rick Halford introduced almost identical bills in 2000, requiring full monitoring and reporting of ship discharges. The Alaska Cruise Ship Initiative (now called the Commercial Passenger Vessel Environmental Compliance Program) passed in both Alaska's house of representatives and senate in 2001. Some of the new regulations include requiring large passenger vessels to sample treated sewage and gray water discharges on a bimonthly basis, implementing a vessel-tracking system to home in on offending cruise ships, and even having official "ocean rangers" aboard large ships for the duration of the cruise to verify environmental compliance.

Based on the success of Alaska's initiatives, Washington followed in March 2005, as a state law to protect Puget Sound from cruise ship wastes and sewage passed in the House unanimously. The bill, proposed by Democratic Rep. Mary Lou Dickerson, tightens restrictions concerning wastewater and sewage discharges, and also empowers the state to independently test cruise ship effluents and treatment equipment.

In 2008, Democratic California senator Joe Simitian introduced a similar bill to protect California waters from cruise ship pollution. It also protects cruise ship passengers from crimes on the high seas and coordinates with Department of Homeland Security agencies to be a first line of defense against terrorist attacks in U.S. ports of call. To date, the bill is pending.

The real bottom line here is that if your cruise ship doesn't have an entire deck devoted to waste management, don't go there. If it has a high incidence of reported sex crimes, don't go there. If it hasn't passed sanitation inspection or has marginal scores, don't go there. And unless you follow my rules for realistically budgeting your cruise, then . . . don't go there!

DANGEROUS TRAINS

HARD TO KEEP TRACK

Did you know that every 90 minutes in the United States, there is a train accident? What about the fact that more people are killed in railroad crossing accidents each year than in commercial airline accidents?

And to think you thought more people died in train derailments.

But when a train does jump the tracks, it's not pretty.

Train Accidents

Train Derailments

A train derailment is, well, exactly what it sounds like. You may remember the case in April 2008 in Shandong, China, when a Beijing-to-Qingdao train derailed due to excessive speed and collided with another passenger train traveling in the opposite direction. More than 70 people were killed, and another 400-plus were injured in this tragic accident.

In the United States, there were a total of 2,301 derailed trains in 2005; in 2006, there were 2,172; and in 2007, numbers dropped to 1,883. The good news is that passenger-carrying trains such as Amtrak suffered only a fraction of those derailments (29 in 2007). The bad news is that any derailed train, no matter which company it belongs to, can have devastating effects on surrounding communities.

Take the case of the "San Bernardino train disaster," which took place back in 1989. A Southern Pacific train derailed on May 12 and plowed into a residential area, killing two train crew members and two residents, and destroying seven houses. The train itself was crushed. To make matters much, much worse, 13 days later, a gas pipe near the train tracks burst, killing two people and destroying 11 homes.

Perhaps the most helpful information is knowing where trains, both passenger and freight, derail most. Texas, which has more miles of track than any other state, leads the nation, with 230 of the 1,883 derailments in 2007; the majority of the Texas incidents took place in Harris County (which encompasses Houston). Illinois came second, with 151 derailments, primarily in Cook County; and California came third, with 110, nearly 21 percent of which were in San Bernardino County. Union Pacific trains were involved in the most derailments, followed by BNSF Railway Corporation.

Some of the major causes of train derailments are rails that are broken or misaligned and faulty wheels on the train. But, interestingly enough, heat can also play a factor in derailments: High summer temperatures in the United States tend to lead to "rail kinks," in which tracks expand and buckle, causing them to go out of gauge. And believe me, it's a train wreck when that happens.

Trespassing Accidents

Here's another surprising figure: About 500 people a year are killed in trespassing accidents (excluding highway-rail incidents—more on those later). Trespassing occurs when a person is traveling beside or on the tracks other than at a marked crossing, whether it's on foot, bicycle, or skis, in a car, or

Are You Fit for Train Travel?

As if crashes and derailments weren't enough to worry about, what about being fit enough for train travel? In 2006, an elderly Hong Kong man died after suffering from altitude sickness while riding the highest railway in the world—the Lhasa Express, from Qinghai to Tibet, a route that reaches altitudes of more than 16,000 feet. The man fell ill during the 26-hour journey to Tibet and, against the doctor's orders, checked out of a Lhasa hospital and climbed aboard the next train back to Qinghai. Early in the return journey, he suffered a heart attack and died soon after.

There's *What* Riding on That Train?

A train collision is one thing, but what happens when that train contains hazardous materials? On May 17, 2008, more than 3,000 residents of Lafayette, Louisiana, were evacuated when six cars of a BNSF train derailed and spilled as much as 10,000 gallons of hydrochloric acid. A toxic cloud spread over the city, and at least five people were hospitalized. Hydrochloric acid can cause skin and eye irritation and, in some cases, respiratory failure. No one suffered long-lasting injury, but in my opinion, those residents were just plain lucky. Not to mention the tourists who just happened to be passing by that day.

in any other vehicle. In 2007 there were 473 trespassing-related deaths, in 2006 there were 518, and in 2005 there were 463.

As you might expect, when a trespasser is killed by an oncoming train, it's usually considered the fault of the victim. After all, the victim was trespassing on private property (tracks are owned by the railroad companies), releasing the railroad from any liability.

Two families disagreed with this in 2000, when their daughters were killed by an oncoming Amtrak train. Rebecca and Rachel Marturello, at 14 and 11, respectively, and Rebecca's best friend, Zandra Lafley, 13, were walking on a railroad trestle over the Green River in Kent, Washington, near a popular bike trail and swimming hole. According to reports, Rebecca was nearly across the trestle when she heard the train whistle; she ran and leapt to safety, while the other two girls tried to run across the track, jumped onto the adjoining track, and then, perhaps out of confusion, crossed back onto the track that was in the path of the oncoming train.

The families of the two girls filed a wrongful death suit against Amtrak. The district court originally found insufficient evidence that the engineer had been wantonly careless, but in 2005, the Ninth U.S. Circuit Court of Appeals reversed that ruling.

The reason? The engineer had been alerted before the accident that there were children on the tracks—apparently playing "chicken." He thought he saw them jumping back and forth between the east- and westbound tracks, so he applied the brakes, dropping the train's speed from about 79 mph to 65 mph, and then continued over the trestle at that speed. He thought the girls were in the clear before he hit them. They obviously weren't.

Where are these trespassing fatalities happening? Primarily in California, with 79 out of 473 deaths in 2007, mostly in Los Angeles County. And the railroad company involved? Amtrak, with a whopping 30 fatalities in that state. Second is Texas, with 47 deaths, primarily in Harris County, but this time it's Union Pacific that leads, with 30 of those deaths.

Highway-Railroad Grade Crossings

Here's another statistic that may surprise you. Every year, between 300 and 400 people die at highway-railroad crossings, and more than 1,000 are injured. This is of particular interest to anyone considering renting a car. When it comes to safety, it's not just about unfamiliar highways—it's also about railroad crossings.

A highway-rail crossing incident refers to any impact between a train and a highway user at a designated crossing site (such as a road, walkway, or sidewalk). The reason they're calculated separately from other train accident reports is that when a train runs into a car or pedestrian at a designated crossing site, it's considered to be a traffic accident, not a train problem.

According to the most recent Federal Railroad Administration *Railroad Safety Statistics* report, the number of highway-rail accidents has declined steadily over the past several years. This is in part due to a long-term plan from the Department of Transportation called the National Rail Safety Action Plan, which has addressed safety issues on many highway-rail grade crossings.

However, with 300 to 400 deaths still happening every year, averaging out to almost one death every day, it's still not an acceptable number.

HIGHWAY-RAIL ACCIDENTS

	INCIDENTS	DEATHS	INJURIES
1997	3,865	461	1,540
1998	3,508	431	1,303
1999	3,489	402	1,396
2000	3,502	425	1,219
2001	3,237	421	1,157
2002	3,077	357	999
2003	2,977	334	1,035
2004	3,079	372	1,094
2005	3,058	358	1,052
2006	2,937	369	1,065
2007	2,749	338	1,034

Source: *Federal Railroad Administration*

Whether it's a situation of a driver trying to beat the train, visibility of the track being obscured, or a crossing gate malfunctioning, the railroad companies and safety advocacy groups butt heads over who is at fault. And in the majority of cases, the driver is blamed in final reports.

Back in 1997, one Ohio family formed Angels on Track, a nonprofit organization dedicated to improving grade crossings in the state and raising awareness nationwide, after their 16-year-old son was killed in a grade crossing accident. Vicky and Dennis Moore's older son, Jason, was driving on a rural road with younger brother Ryan and four friends in the car; the car was struck by a Conrail freight train, instantly killing Ryan and two others.

"The reason my son was killed was because railroad crossing safety is not a priority," said Vicky Moore. "It does not get the attention it deserves, and it only becomes a priority after someone is killed."

The track that the Moores' sons crossed was not protected by a gate, only a wooden crossbuck (the white, X-shaped "Railroad Crossing" sign), and the approach to the crossing was down a steep slope with "overgrown vegetation [that] restricted the view of approaching trains." The driver inched forward to see if a train was coming, and by the time he had clear visibility, the car nose was on the track. "By the time he could see, the train came from the left," said Moore. The train struck the rear of the vehicle, killing all three passengers in the backseat.

Truth and Consequences

In 1999, two Illinois families lost teenage sons when the car they were driving was hit by an Amtrak train traveling at 78 mph through a grade crossing. The official report was that the boys had tried to circumvent the automated gate, and the local paper reported that the gate was functioning properly, based on the accident report submitted to the Department of Transportation (DOT). As it turned out, eyewitnesses reported what really happened: The automated gate actually remained upright before, during, and after the accident—a railroad employee had shut off the power to the gate the day before. Even more horrifying, he informed his employer of this after the accident, but no one from the railroad came forward. Oh, and the entire thing was caught on video by a camera installed at the gate—although the DOT initially reported that the camera was broken. Soon after, an Amtrak representative showed up at the home of one of the families and, without admitting any fault, resolved the matter financially.

When Stupidity Leads to Tragedy

One of the worst train crashes in Southern California took place in 2005, and this one was entirely, unequivocally due to human error. But it wasn't the conductor who was at fault—it was a suicidal man who made a decision that cost 11 lives. Juan Manuel Alvarez, 25, parked his Jeep on the Metrolink commuter rail tracks at the border of Glendale and Los Angeles. As he saw the train coming, he changed his mind and walked away, leaving the Jeep on the tracks. A minute later, the Metrolink train derailed, ran into a northbound Metrolink commuter train, and then crashed into a parked Union Pacific train. Eleven people were killed and more than 180 were injured. In June 2008, Alvarez was convicted on 11 counts of first-degree murder, and that August, he was sentenced to 11 life sentences.

And perhaps worst of all, this wasn't the first fatality or injury at that crossing—eight people had died and many more had been injured at the same site since 1975. There had been an accident just 1 week before the Moores' collision, and 1 month prior, a man was killed at the same crossing. Was each case really the fault of the driver?

Since trains have the right of way at crossings, it is accepted that all accidents are caused by motorists failing to yield. The important question should be, *Why* do motorists fail to yield to approaching trains? In many cases, they just couldn't see or hear the trains.

Although gated crossings have been found to be safer than "passive" crossings—those marked with stop signs or crossbucks—only 27 percent of 144,738 public crossings and a handful of the 94,817 private crossings are equipped with gates.

In 2007, there were 338 fatalities at highway-rail crossings. Most were in California, with 47 deaths—Amtrak was involved in 23 of those fatalities, and Union Pacific in 9. In Texas, 20 of the 34 fatalities involved Union Pacific. And Florida saw 21 deaths, 11 of which involved Amtrak.

Now, assuming the train doesn't hit you or someone else, or simply derail, there's the embarrassing little subject of on-time performance.

On-Time Train Performance

I'm a big fan of train travel . . . when it makes sense. For example, the Pacific Surfliner between Los Angeles and San Diego is not only convenient, but also a beautiful ride. The Acela Express on the East Coast, between Boston, New York City, Philadelphia, and Washington, DC, is almost always a better bet than flying. Don't believe me? I challenge you to a race between New York and Washington—I'll take the train, and you can either fly or drive. I'll win with the train almost every time, I won't be sitting with my knees against my neck, and I won't have to take my shoes off in the process.

That's the good news. But when it comes to on-time performance, Amtrak has a dismal record. And it's not necessarily Amtrak's fault. The problem is that Amtrak doesn't own the rails over which it rolls—the freight train companies own the tracks. As a result, passenger trains are often forced to pull aside as hundred-car freight trains lumber by.

The worst punctuality offenders (and this is according to Amtrak), are as follows:

HISTORICAL ON-TIME PERFORMANCE

TRAIN SERVICE	JUNE 2008	PRECEDING 12 MONTHS
Missouri Routes	15.8%	20.1%
Texas Eagle	1.7%	16.8%
California Zephyr	36.7%	29.1%
Vermonter	6.7%	24.5%
Sunset Limited	19.2%	28.8%
Michigan Services	25.3%	29.3%

Source: *Amtrak*

Okay, so let's take the Texas Eagle's pathetic performance as an example. This train travels between Chicago, St. Louis, Dallas, San Antonio, and Los Angeles. In June 2008, 50.8 percent of delays stemmed from the railroad infrastructure, including maintenance work and functional problems with tracks or signals. And 38.4 percent of the time, the holdup had to do with "train interference," i.e., delays related to other train movements in the area, whether it's freight, commuter, or even other Amtrak trains getting in the way. For the Texas Eagle, the majority of the time (89.8 percent) it was a Union Pacific train that caused the delay. Only 4.6 percent of the time was it a passenger-related delay, meaning that a train was held up at the station assisting an ill or injured party or waiting for passengers to board or get off.

Of the two trains that cover the Texas Eagle route, train numbers 21 and 22, you definitely want to stay away from the 22—it was on time just 3 *percent* of the time over the course of a year.

How about the California Zephyr, which travels from Chicago to Denver to Emeryville, California? It's one of the most scenic rides you can take, traveling through the Rockies and the Sierra Nevada, but when you consider that it was on time only 29.1 percent of the time in June 2008, well, you'd better bring a few books along.

The primary reason for the California Zephyr's delays is interference by other trains—namely those owned by Union Pacific and Burlington Northern Santa Fe. But coming a close second are problems with the tracks and signals, mostly the ones owned by Union Pacific. Of the two trains that cover this route, train numbers 5 and 6, it's the latter you want to watch out for: It was on schedule only 18.1 percent of the time, as compared to 40.1 percent for the former.

There's not a lot you can do about train delays except arm yourself with information. Fortunately, Amtrak, in full acceptance of its flaws, actually posts historical on-time performance for each of its trains on its Web site, Amtrak.com. So if you know that a train is late more than 80 percent of the time, you may want to try your luck with flying.

HIGHWAYS
OF DEATH

GOD'S NOT YOUR COPILOT

When it comes to driving, it's not enough to say, "Don't go there." You need to fine-tune things, as in "Don't go there *this* way." It's not just the difference between interstates and two-lane country roads—it's the specific safety factors of individual roads throughout the United States and around the world. Every highway, every road, every thoroughfare has its own set of odds. Some roads are slightly riskier than others. Some are slightly less risky than average. And then there are the truly dangerous highways, where you are inevitably flirting with death the minute the rubber hits the road.

So, before you hit the ground running, plan your trips to do everything possible to avoid these roads.

Dangerous Rural Roads

The danger of rural roads is manifold. They are more likely to have one narrow lane going in each direction, limited shoulders, sharp curves, exposed hazards, pavement drop-offs, steep slopes, and limited clear zones along roadsides. Though these roads once served the original purposes just fine, recent jumps in population, commuting time, and commercial deliveries have led to increased use of them—and they weren't built to accommodate so much traffic! In fact, one study by the Washington, DC–based nonprofit group The Road Information Program (TRIP) found that in one recent 12-year period, travel on rural roads increased by 27 percent for all vehicles and by 32 percent for large commercial trucks.

The biggest risk, TRIP discovered, was motorists trying to negotiate curves on these rural roads—you're 6½ times more likely to be killed negotiating a curve on a rural, noninterstate road than on all other roads. Between 1999 and 2003, 58 percent of all vehicle occupants killed in rural, noninterstate accidents died in crashes that involved an attempt to negotiate a curve, compared with 9 percent on all roads.

Herewith, a list of some of the most dangerous rural roads—the ones you want to avoid if at all possible.

Alabama

Take a look at U.S. Route 431, between Seale and Eufaula (north of Dothan), a north-south route that's about 30 miles long. The roadside scenery here is strange—the most striking element being a series of white crosses, one for each fatality that has occurred along this rural run. Fireman Paul Hartgrove, of the Pittsview Fire Department, began erecting these crosses several years ago to commemorate the deceased while making drivers aware of the dangers on this narrow, two-lane road.

The Alabama Department of Transportation reports that the road is in the process of being widened from two lanes to four. But history indicates that this has been the case, or the intention, for the past 30 years.

To make matters worse, Route 431 is part of the drive south to Panama City, Florida, a major spring-break and family destination, and the stretch between Seale and Eufaula is about the worst in terms of hills and curves.

South Carolina

Let's start out with the really bad news: The traffic fatality rate on South Carolina's rural, noninterstate roads is the highest in the nation. We're talking 52 percent higher than the national average!

In plain numbers: In 2005, there were 2.21 traffic fatalities per 100 million miles of travel in the state, compared with the national average of 1.45. That translates to an average of 1,044 traffic-crash fatalities a year, and that means that someone is dying on a South Carolina road every 8 hours.

A whopping 72 percent of the deaths in 2005 took place on rural roads, even though only about 34 percent of all the state's travel occurs on those roads. Rural road accidents in South Carolina usually involve vehicles

SOUTH CAROLINA'S MOST DANGEROUS ROADS, 2002–2006

COUNTY	ROUTE	FATAL CRASHES	INJURY CRASHES	ROAD LENGTH (IN MILES)	PERSONS KILLED	PERSONS INJURED
Florence	29	3	3,173	7.32	3	254
Beaufort	474	1	24	2.07	1	28
Spartanburg	55	4	37	11.27	4	55
Aiken	779	4	5	4.84	5	16
Charleston	54	9	119	15.03	16	185
Charleston	20	10	314	17.35	12	459
Greenville	541	2	26	6.48	2	31
Florence	35	6	39	8.85	11	94
Horry	1121	1	27	1.72	1	32
Laurens	43	2	16	6.5	2	22

Source: *South Carolina Department of Transportation*

running off the road and colliding with a fixed object, such as a tree or pole.

South Carolina's Department of Transportation compiled a list of the state's roads, both rural and urban, with high crash rates from 2002 to 2006. As the chart shows, the number one deadliest road was the 7-mile section of Route 29 in Florence County, which experienced three traffic fatalities and 254 serious injuries during that time period.

North Carolina

While visiting North Carolina, you might want to literally steer clear of Graham County, where, once a crash occurs, a motorist is more likely to be injured or killed than anywhere else in the state.

One of the biggest contributors to Graham County's grim statistics is a stretch of U.S. 129 known as the Tail of the Dragon. This road boasts 318 curves between Tabcat Creek and Deal's Gap, at the border of North Carolina and Tennessee—that's only 11.1 miles! That element alone attracts motorcycle and sports car enthusiasts, many of whom consider this one of the greatest driving roads in the world. Between 2003 and 2006, there were 19 crashes, including one fatal crash and 10 injury accidents.

It gets worse. In addition to offering the best chance of being injured or killed, Graham County is also number one on the list of the five most dangerous counties for motorcycles. The Tail of the Dragon was cited as a major contributor, especially as more and more inexperienced bikers are taking to the road.

Montana

U.S. Route 2 winds across the northern part of the United States for a stunning 2,579 miles through some of the nation's most scenic areas. And the stretch going across Montana is no exception, since it passes through Glacier National Park. But with beautiful northern mountain scenery come some treacherous roads.

You'll see a good example of this on the road between the western Montana town of Kalispell and the Idaho border. Here, the steep, curvy, two-lane mountain road sees heavy traffic, which includes commercial trucks and vacationers' RVs. Montana's harsh winters can often mean blizzard conditions in the mountains, obscured visibility, black ice, and high winds. Combine those factors with speed limits of 70 mph and you have a recipe for disaster.

According to Kalispell's *Daily Inter Lake* newspaper, in 2007, Flathead County led the state in traffic fatalities, with 25 crashes that killed 26 people in a single year. That number had dropped from 30 deaths in 2006 but was up from 17 in 2005 and 19 in 2004. Montana Highway Patrol captain Clancy King blamed seat-belt violations for many of the preventable deaths.

Also in Montana, beware of the 100-odd miles of Route 93 between Kalispell and Missoula, with some of the worst sections about halfway down, in Polson. You'll know you've crossed into the danger zone when you see the local bumper sticker that says, "Pray for me, I drive Hwy 93!" Some parts of the road are under construction to add passing lanes and straighten out deadly curves, but because it runs through reservations and Forest Service land, this has been a long and difficult process to complete.

Hazardous Highways

Just because rural roads are small and winding doesn't mean they're the only risky roads. Check out these dangerous thoroughfares that you may encounter in your travels.

Florida

U.S. Route 19 in Florida, a main corridor for north-south travel in Pinellas County, has had its share of tragedies. The Florida Highway Patrol did a study between 1998 and 2003 showing that the 30-mile stretch between Pasco County and Pinellas County averaged about 52 deaths a year.

And it hasn't gotten much better: According to the Department of Transportation, between 2004 and 2006, there were a stunning 5,919 crashes,

45 fatalities, and 5,222 injuries. That's right, we're talking an average of 2,000 crashes a year for the entire Pinellas U.S. 19 corridor and more than 60 crashes per mile per year.

Things were so bad that the county organized a U.S. 19 task force in 2002 to identify the key problems with the road. These included vehicles speeding and running red lights, and frequent school bus stops. Florida's Department of Transportation is now working with Pinellas County to add sidewalks all along the route, countdown pedestrian signals at intersections, and intersection crosswalk markings.

Arizona

There are a number of trouble spots in Arizona. U.S. Route 93 between Wickenburg and the Hoover Dam sees heavy traffic but, despite ongoing improvements, is still only two lanes in many sections. There were 18 fatalities on this 40-mile stretch of road in 2005.

The problem isn't just the conditions of the road—it's the bigger picture of the Arizona environment. In the central and southern parts of the state, the extreme heat in the summer months, sometimes topping 100 degrees even in May, does more than just inflict simple wear and tear on cars. People may be unprepared to drive in a desert environment, meaning they have no water or food in case of delays. Those dangerous desert areas include all of I-10 and I-8, both of which have desolate stretches with few resources if you get in trouble.

Meanwhile, plummeting temperatures in northern Arizona also can cause unexpected messes when travelers aren't expecting snow and ice. Those spots include I-40 from New Mexico to around Kingman, where there are drops in elevation, and the northern part of I-17. Those extreme temperature changes can occur all the way from late November to early March.

So, bottom line: Be prepared for anything when you're driving through Arizona.

California

Highway 1

Arguably the most beautiful road in California, Highway 1 is also the deadliest. Winding coastal roads, sheer cliffs, wildfires, falling rocks, and mud slides are just a few of the dangers that face drivers who tackle this route.

The stretch from San Luis Obispo to Big Sur and Monterey is recognized as one of the riskiest of the entire coastal drive. According to the California Highway Patrol, from 2005 to 2007, this stretch saw 234 collisions, 11 of which were fatal and 97 of which caused injuries.

State Route 138

Also in California, but a little lesser known, is State Route 138, which runs east-west from Route 5 near Gorman to Route 14 near Lancaster. Although stretches of it have been developed over the past few years, the majority of the rural road remains a heart-stopping, winding, hilly, and undivided two-lane road that has been the site of multiple fatal accidents. According to the California Highway Patrol, from 2005 to 2007, there were 1,722 collisions along the entire length of SR 138, 35 of which were fatal and 734 of which resulted in injuries.

Though it's technically a rural route, SR 138 sees heavy traffic, as it's the main thoroughfare for residents of the Antelope Valley and surrounding areas to reach I-15 and other parts of the Inland Empire. It is also a popular bypass road on the way from Los Angeles to Las Vegas.

COLORADO CLOSURES (FROM SEPTEMBER TO APRIL)

	SEMI-TRUCK–RELATED ENTIRE ROAD CLOSURE	SEMI-TRUCK–RELATED LANE CLOSURE	ACCIDENT–RELATED ENTIRE ROAD CLOSURE
2004–2005	8:50	52:06	75:19
2005–2006	8:54	110:20	86:19
2006–2007	15:09	114:39	72:49
2007–2008	14:09	276:19	159:57

Source: *Colorado Department of Transportation*

Things got so bad in 2007 that the state shut down the road due to . . . road rage. That's right. California invested $46 million to widen the road, but the construction made for some seriously pissed-off commuters. The California Department of Transportation allowed drivers to use the road only during rush hour in the summer of 2006, one direction at a time, led by escort vehicles. The result? Some major road rage. BB pellets, flying burritos, and threats of shootings were just a few examples of what happened that summer. It wasn't until the job was finished that the road reopened to normal traffic.

Recently, one section between the Los Angeles County line and I-15 has now been realigned and widened, and has an added truck climbing lane designed specifically for trucks that travel more slowly than other vehicles when driving uphill.

So, what parts of SR 138 do you want to avoid? The 15-mile section from Palmdale east to Pearblossom is still pretty treacherous, with especially heavy traffic heading to Las Vegas on the weekends. The worst culprits are speeding drivers who attempt to pass illegally on this two-lane highway . . . driving head-on into oncoming traffic.

Colorado

Interstate 70 in Colorado is a beautiful—and notorious—road. With ski season come heavy snows and resort-bound skiers. Add those together and you get bottlenecking, road closures, and accidents. According to the numbers for 2007, the stretch of this immensely popular route between the Eisenhower Tunnel (about 60 miles west of Denver) and Vail sees as many as 38,000 vehicles in the peak winter and summer months.

In the first half of 2008, I-70 from C-470 (west of Denver) to Vail saw 18 fatal crashes, killing 21 people. Even with these disturbing figures, car crashes aren't necessarily the issue you have to worry about here; road

ACCIDENT–RELATED LANE CLOSURE	WEATHER–RELATED ENTIRE ROAD CLOSURE	WEATHER–RELATED LANE CLOSURE
33:49	15:06	0:00
45:12	25:39	22:23
90:01	72:47	8:04
93:32	86:32	0:00

closures are. And it's been going on for years. The Colorado DOT reported the above 4-year comparison of closure times on I-70 between the Eisenhower Tunnel and Vail as a result of semi-truck accidents, auto accidents, and weather.

While these numbers are hard to grasp, keep in mind that even a minor fender bender can cause a chain reaction that closes down the road, putting your Vail vacation in jeopardy.

Nevada

Nevada is an interesting case because its population and vehicle travel are increasing at the fastest rate in the country. Nevada's population has more than doubled since 1990, from 1.2 million that year to 2.5 million in 2006—that's an increase of 108 percent. Within that period of time, the number of cars on the road increased 103 percent! More cars on the road translates to more-frequent accidents, particularly when the infrastructure wasn't built to support big numbers.

TRIP released a study in March 2008 entitled *Getting Home Safely: An Analysis of Highway Safety in Nevada*. It showed that Nevada had 395 traffic fatalities in 2004, 427 in 2005, 431 in 2006, and 371 in 2007.

Those numbers mean that, on average, one person is killed every 22 hours in traffic crashes on Nevada's roads. According to the report, the number one most dangerous road in the state is in Clark County, on a section of State Route 159. This 13-mile stretch had nine fatalities and 72 injury-causing accidents between 2003 and 2006.

The good news, if you can call it that, is that this particular segment isn't a high-density traffic area. So, if you're only in the state to hit Las Vegas, chances are you won't travel this section, which starts at Blue Diamond Road where it meets SR 160 and curves toward Red Rock Canyon National Conservation Area and eastward to Las Vegas.

Nevada Roadway Locations with the Highest Serious Accident Rates, 2003–2006

COUNTY	ROAD	INJURY CRASHES	FATAL CRASHES	FATALITIES
Churchill County	SR 117 from mile point (MP) 0 to 5.2	10	1	3
Clark County	SR 160 from MP 12.2 to 43.2	126	23	23
Clark County	SR 159 from MP 1.4 to 14.1	72	7	9
Clark County	East Owens Ave. at Pecos Rd.	20	3	3
Clark County	Spring Mountain Rd. at Jones Blvd.	35	2	2
Clark County	SR 604 from MP 13 to 25.9	34	2	2
Clark County	Jones Blvd. at Hacienda Ave.	24	2	2
Douglas County	SR 88 from MP 0 to 7.1	48	2	2
Douglas County	U.S. 50 from MP 7 to 12.2	41	2	2
Washoe County	Oddie Blvd. at Sullivan Ln.	22	0	0

Source: *tripnet.org/Nevada_Safety_Report_March2008.pdf*

"It's a desert area, and your biggest risk out there is a burro strike," Nevada Department of Transportation spokesman Bob McKenzie said. That's right, a burro strike, as in driving into a burro!

According to Truckers

Who knows the roads better than truckers? *Overdrive* magazine does an annual survey of about 375 truckers to find out which roads are the worst in America. Criteria can vary—from poor road quality to high tolls to the worst rest stops.

So which interstate highways do you want to avoid, according to truckers?

1. I-10, Louisiana

2. I-80, Pennsylvania

3. I-40, Arkansas

4. I-5, California

5. I-40, Oklahoma

For several years running, Pennsylvania's I-80 was at the top of the list. Does its number-two ranking now mean things are better? Not necessarily. If you go west to east from about the 265-mile marker, near White Haven, all the way to New Jersey, about 45 miles later, don't expect any changes— that part hasn't been improved in years. It's still narrow, and it's one of the most accident-prone areas in Pennsylvania.

According to the Pennsylvania Department of Transportation (PennDOT), that area is, in fact, the most heavily traveled section of the entire I-80 corridor in Pennsylvania, particularly eastbound from the Stroudsburg area (about 5 miles from the New Jersey border). Traffic here varies from 54,800 to 73,000 vehicles a day, even with a reduced speed limit of 50 mph and police enforcement to deter aggressive drivers. According to PennDOT, speeding, aggressive driving, and driving under the influence are the primary causes of traffic crashes. Between 2002 and 2006, from Exit 304 to just west of the New Jersey border, there were 424 accidents, including three that led to fatalities, 11 that caused major injuries, and 104 involving minor injuries.

So, if things are so bad there, how did Louisiana climb its way to the top of the list? Well, after Katrina swept through, I-10 between Lake Charles

United States Road Assessment Program

Now, here's something useful. The AAA Foundation for Traffic Safety launched a pilot program called the United States Road Assessment Program (usRAP). Similar programs currently exist in Europe, Australia, and New Zealand.

The organization analyzes crash data based on road segments, correlating features such as the number of lanes, guardrail presence, and roadside clearance. Based on this information, usRAP generates Road Protection Scores and plots them on color-coded maps. So far, usRAP has analyzed roads in Florida, Iowa, Michigan and New Jersey, and is working on those in Illinois, Kentucky, New Mexico, and Utah.

"The idea is that travelers can know where the four-star roads are in the community," said Peter Kissinger, president of the Foundation for Traffic Safety. "In the future, you'll be able to tell your vehicle navigation system that you want to get from point A to point B on the safest route."

You can find the maps at usrap.us.

and New Orleans was left with major road issues, including uneven grades. Anyone driving over that stretch had better pay attention—the road needs a lot of work.

And Arkansas? The worst spots of I-40 are around the White River Bridge. Though the state has improved parts of the roads (widening it to three and four lanes each way), they continue to squeeze much of the traffic into two of those lanes, with trucks running in the center and right lanes, competing for space with passenger cars. Good luck passing.

Let's not forget Michigan, which didn't even make the worst five roads on the truckers' list. Watch out for the last 20 miles of U.S. 31 before it hits I-75 by the Mackinac Bridge, where you can expect your car to shake from the rough roads for at least 6 or 7 miles.

International Roads

Let's start with the hard numbers. The World Health Organization (WHO) estimates that 1.2 million people die in road accidents worldwide every year and that road crashes are the leading cause of death for healthy people ages 10 to 24 worldwide. U.S. State Department figures say that more than 200 Americans are killed in road accidents abroad each year—but that doesn't include those who are injured but not killed; people who leave the country and die later; the military; diplomats; victims who are medically evacuated back to the United States before dying; or numbers that are . . . not reported.

One of the leading organizations working toward promoting international road safety is the Association for Safe International Road Travel (ASIRT), an NGO that was founded by Maryland resident Rochelle Sobel after she lost her 25-year-old son, Aron, in a bus crash in Turkey in 1995. He was killed along with 22 other passengers on Milas-Soke Road of the Bodrum Izmir Highway—a 35-year-old road known by the government to be a deadly stretch. Her son was a medical student in his senior year at the University of Maryland and was completing his medical rotation by volunteering in a Turkish hospital. The police said the bus driver was speeding down the wrong lane of a wet, winding, two-lane road that had no guardrail, even after passengers asked him to slow down. The bus hit oncoming traffic head-on and plunged off the road into a ravine.

In 2002, ASIRT began working with the State Department to track how many Americans are killed in traffic accidents abroad. ASIRT also works with foreign governments to improve their roads, and publishes *Road Travel*

Reports for 150 different foreign countries, with descriptions of dangerous roads in that country, rules of the road, transportation options, and embassy contacts.

Although the following is by no means a complete list of the dangerous roads, they are among the worst in the world.

North Yungas Road, Bolivia

It's officially the most dangerous road in the world. North Yungas Road, which runs about 40 miles from La Paz to Coroico, was anointed as such by the Inter-American Development Bank in 1995, because the year before resulted in no less than 26 vehicles plummeting off the side of the road and into the canyon. Now, whether this Latin American economic lending bank has the authority to grant such a title is up for debate, but no one seems to object to the name.

Yungas Road was built by Paraguayan prisoners during the 1932–1935 war between Bolivia and Paraguay, to connect the rain forest of northern Bolivia to the capital city of La Paz. The road drops from an elevation of 14,000 feet to about 1,000 feet . . . quickly.

Carved into the side of the mountain, it is known for its extremely narrow single lane, with no pavement after the first few miles and sheer half-mile drops with no guardrails to keep you from toppling off the mountain. Add to that heavy fogs and frequent downpours, cascading waterfalls, gaping potholes, local drivers praying before they set off, crosses commemorating those who died, and, oh yeah, barking wild dogs along the way.

Bolivia's worst-ever accident took place on this road in 1983. A produce truck tumbled off the edge, killing the driver and 100 passengers.

This terrifying road has claimed lives as recently as April 2008, when an SUV carrying 13 passengers collided with a group of bicyclists, killing a 22-year-old British cyclist. The SUV rolled down an embankment at least 300 feet and killed eight people onboard. Two other cyclists and five passengers were injured. This was, in fact, the second death of a foreign cyclist in 1 week on the same road—days earlier, a California man fell off his bicycle and over a cliff to his death.

Michael Liebreich, a former member of the British Olympic ski team and an outdoor enthusiast, recalls his experience mountain biking down Yungas Road in 2004. Looking back, he says he realized, "You'd either have to have a failure of knowledge or a failure of judgment to ride down this road for fun." After just a few miles on the road, he and his fellow travelers came

Dangerous Curves Ahead

Writer Courtney Scott sent this gem to me while she was on the road in Italy: "While driving between Treviso and Venice, Italy, on the Il Terraglio road, be on the lookout for one of the funniest highway warning signs I've ever seen. The highway is lined with trattorias,  bars, villas, and apartments, and by day it's seemingly ordinary. But by night it's a sexed-up superhighway filled with prostitutes. On some nights, it's not unusual to count dozens of them on the sides of the road, jumping into and out of cars. So the highway department decided to be, uh, helpful in posting this sign."

across dozens of other bikers and vehicles at a spot where a Frenchwoman had tumbled 50 meters over a cliff. Liebreich and other riders attempted to rescue the woman amid the chaos, but she was pronounced dead soon after. Liebreich and his team turned around, having covered only about 5 kilometers, vowing never to return.

"On this road, you're going past memorials of people who died; it's not enjoyable, and it doesn't add to my pleasure that people have died here," Liebreich said. "It's not fair for the people who have to drive on the road. It's an appalling road, and there are people who grapple with it in their daily lives, and then you've got these stupid investment bankers on their mountain bikes."

While a new, safer bypass to connect La Paz and Coroico was finally unveiled in 2006, the older road continues to be a major thoroughfare for commuters, buses, and trucks to reach the Yungas region, and also is a draw for thrill-seeking mountain bike riders and curious foreign drivers. New rules state that during peak hours, uphill drivers have right of way, so if you're heading downhill, you'll have to scoot toward the precarious edge.

If you visit Bolivia, chances are you'll be solicited by adventure companies hawking "gravity-assisted mountain biking" down Yungas Road. Let me go on the record as saying, don't go there!

Nairobi, Kenya

In Kenya, ASIRT estimates that 3,000 people die in road crashes annually; that's 41 deaths per 100 million vehicle kilometers traveled, compared with

2.27 deaths per million kilometers (or 1.41 deaths per million miles) in the United States. But that number may not be accurate—improper reporting, bribery, and a tangled bureaucratic system make it nearly impossible to track down the correct numbers. ASIRT-Kenya documented numerous unsuccessful attempts to access data through calls, e-mails, and canceled meetings with the various governmental offices involved, including the Ministry of Transport, Police Headquarters, and Traffic Headquarters.

Everything from speeding to recklessness to overloaded vehicles to driving under the influence is among the culprits in Kenya. Most of the main roads are in ill repair and are dangerous. The dirt roads in the most rural areas are safer, because they're too rough for speeding. With cars in need of repair, lack of adequate safety belts in *matatus* (minibuses that are the primary form of public transportation), traffic congestion, deteriorating roads, lack of road shoulders and signage, poor lighting and road markings, roadside crime, and myths about road safety, the roads are more challenging and dangerous than in developed counties. Overall, it's not pleasant driving around.

One road to watch out for is the stretch from Nairobi to Mombasa—a heavily trafficked route that some tourists opt to traverse by car or bus. This 285-mile road can take about 7 to 8 hours to drive, and the bus ride has been known to take up to 11 hours! (For some perspective, we're talking about a road that's shorter than the distance between Boston and Philadelphia.) There are some nicely paved sections that you'll fly through before encountering several bumpy, pothole-filled stretches, along with a convoy of buses, trucks, and matatus that zoom dangerously downhill toward Mombasa.

My advice? Take the train. It's not as fast, or even as cheap, as flying, but you'll be able to get an early-morning close-up view of the countryside and villages along the way.

Another extremely dangerous road runs from Nairobi to Nakuru in Kenya's Rift Valley, a popular route for safari-bound travelers. The road is a two-lane highway with a long escarpment—a steep downhill slope—with no turnoff section for cars or trucks. It's packed with overcrowded buses and matatus, cars, trucks, bicyclists, and even pedestrians in some areas. Commonly, speeding turns into a competition to overtake other vehicles, and drivers frequently underestimate the conditions and their ability to pass, causing head-on collisions and rollovers almost daily. There are no guardrails on the escarpment, and one can see the cars, buses, and trucks that have careered off the steep cliff.

Although traffic rules are good in Kenya, they are not enforced well. The police set up roadblocks in the same places each day and wave vehicles over to apply road rules seemingly at random and often for *kitu kidogo* (a bribe). However, there are virtually no police vehicles patrolling the highways or using speed monitors to catch the truly dangerous drivers. At night, people often drive without their headlights, due to a belief that it saves on fuel consumption.

Important tips to road travelers in Kenya: Always speak up (or change drivers) if the driver is not driving safely, and always wear your seat belt. Not only is it likely to save your life in a crash, but it can save your back when you're on the incredibly bumpy roads in game parks. Going carelessly over bumps can cause spinal compression fractures in people with osteoporosis. In general, flying to your destinations in Kenya tends to be much safer than driving.

Mexico

Spectacular scenery and authentic roadside food make the road to Baja a worthwhile journey. And Highway 1 is not exactly a bandit-ridden, third-world dirt track—the 1,000-mile road is mostly paved, with plenty of travelers hitting major stops such as Tijuana and Ensenada. Farther south, though, the drive can be treacherous, with narrow, sharply curving stretches, few guardrails, steep drop-offs, plentiful speed bumps, large trucks bearing down on you at night with bright headlights, and *vados*—deep dips in the road that fill completely with water when it rains.

But there's another concern on Mex 1, and it's not the road itself. It's the crime. Corrupt police, armed robberies, and carjackings are not uncommon, and if you call for help, you can't always trust who shows up—the police in Mexico aren't necessarily going to be on your side.

Gary Graham, a journalist/photographer who also operates fly-fishing tours in Baja, described situations such as criminals posing as police officers, road workers flagging down targeted vehicles, and even would-be thieves dropping rocks onto cars from an overpass between Tijuana and Ensenada—when you pull over, that's when they get you.

A case in 2007 made headlines when three surfers were pulled over by police (who may or may not have been the real thing) just half a mile from the border. According to their account in *Surfer* magazine, the trio was nonchalant when first pulled over, expecting to pay the "$40 Mexican cop shakedown." But things took a turn for the terrifying when their car was swarmed by armed men demanding that they get out of the truck; at gunpoint, the surfers were dragged toward a 100-foot cliff and forced to crawl down the steep drop. Thankfully, they weren't shot and managed to climb their way to safety, only to encounter a near-kidnapping while in a taxi heading back toward the U.S. border. Not surprisingly, one of the surfers said emphatically that he will never drive to Baja again.

Mex 1 is pretty much unavoidable if you're driving through the Baja Peninsula, but you definitely don't want to do it at night. Keep photocopies of your vehicle registration so you don't have to hand over the original. And Graham said that if a cop asks for his driver's license, "I just flat refuse to give it over—although I don't recommend that to everyone. But I'll tell the police that I'll follow them to the station or ride with them if someone can follow in my car." Or, you can take my advice and don't go there!

Honorable Mentions

South Africa

The statistics here are frightening. The number of fatal crashes increased 6 percent, from 11,736 in 2005 to 12,454 in 2006. Compare that with the United States, which had 38,588 fatal crashes in 2006 and has almost six times the population. In South Africa, the number of fatalities per 100 million vehicle kilometers increased by 7 percent (to 11.75) between 2005 and 2006. The majority of these accidents were hit-and-run, but a good percentage were related to overtaking other vehicles, followed by a small number of failures to stop or yield, unsafe turning maneuvers, and cases of poor visibility and following distance.

There is a plethora of bad roads throughout South Africa, but one standout area is the Mpumalanga Province. This province borders Swaziland and Mozambique, and is home to the popular Kruger National Park. The area has some of the country's worst roads, with single carriageways with short passing lanes and random, heavy rains in the summertime.

Spain

Though there are plenty of countries in the EU to pick on when it comes to road safety, Spain is certainly up there. In the nation itself, there are 3.1 fatalities per 100 million vehicle kilometers (compared with 1.0 fatalities in the United States), and multiple roads that experience high rates of crashes.

Carretera Nacional N-340, the main highway and backbone of the beautiful Costa del Sol, is one of the most dangerous roads in Europe, with an average of 100 fatalities per year. One of the major causes of crashes? Drunk driving. Combine that with tourists who are unaccustomed to driving on the right side of the road, plus heavy rains, and you've got a lot of accidents waiting to happen.

Although it's officially a highway, the Costa del Sol is more of a city street that runs along the entire coast, through towns and villages—and with that, you get high volumes of traffic and pedestrians. One of the most dangerous stretches of the Costa del Sol runs east from Marbella for about 35 miles to Málaga; this segment has a high road crash rate and accounts for more road fatalities than any other N-340 section in the province of Málaga. The portion of the Costa del Sol heading west from Marbella to San Pedro averages 30 road crashes per year per kilometer and is known ominously as Carretera de la Muerte, the "Highway of Death."

For the sake of adventure, I won't give this road a total thumbs-down, but it's definitely one where you want to drive carefully and be aware of other drivers.

Highway 16, Canada

"Highway of Tears" is the nickname of Highway 16, an isolated road that spans 425 miles from the Rocky Mountains to the Pacific Ocean in British Columbia. With only a few small towns along the way, vast portions of this road pass through stretches where there is absolutely nothing—and yet it's a crucial artery for northerners.

Because there's a lack of reliable and accessible public transportation, hitchhiking is common along this road. Though reports vary, it's estimated that 43 women have been found murdered along this highway over the past 3 decades; dozens of others have disappeared along stretches of the road, and the worst part is, no one knows why.

Families of missing women have complained that the disappearance of indigenous Canadian women is often not taken seriously by local authorities. "Only in 2002, after the disappearance of a 26-year-old non-Indigenous woman, Nicola Hoar, while hitchhiking along a road that connects Prince George and Smithers, did media attention focus on the unsolved murders and other disappearances," said a 2004 report from Amnesty International Canada.

My advice should be obvious on this one: Don't go there to hitchhike!

DRUNKEST PLACES

Alcohol-Related Car Accidents

The leading cause of death for people ages 2 to 34 years in the United States is motor vehicle crashes. Alcohol-related car accidents kill someone every 31 minutes and nonfatally injure someone every 2 minutes.

According to the National Highway Transportation Safety Administration (NHTSA), 42,642 people were killed in motor vehicle crashes in 2006, and 17,602 (41 percent) of those incidents were alcohol-related. Of those traffic fatalities, 15,121 involved at least one driver, passenger, or nonoccupant who had a blood alcohol concentration (BAC) of 0.08 or greater.

As you might expect, the rate of alcohol-related fatal crashes is more than three times higher at night than during the day (59 percent versus 18 percent). For all crashes, the alcohol involvement rate is five times higher at night (16 percent versus 3 percent).

As bad as those statistics are, we're just getting started. The real key for travelers is *where* these crashes are occurring.

If you look at alcohol-related accidents, you must take into consideration the BAC of *everyone* involved, not just the driver. After all, an impaired passenger or pedestrian can be just as high-risk as an impaired driver behind the wheel.

According to the NHTSA's Fatality Analysis Reporting System, here are the five states that had the highest percentages of fatal crashes involving a passenger, driver, or pedestrian with a BAC of 0.08 or higher in 2006.

STATE	TOTAL CRASHES INVOLVING BAC 0.08+		TOTAL KILLED IN ALCOHOL-RELATED CRASHES		TOTAL KILLED IN ALL CRASHES
	NUMBER	PERCENTAGE OF ALL FATAL CRASHES	NUMBER	PERCENTAGE OF FATALITIES FROM ALL CRASHES	NUMBER
South Carolina	463	45	523	50	1,037
Hawaii	71	44	84	52	161
Wisconsin	319	44	364	50	724
Montana	114	43	126	48	263
Texas	1,487	43	1,677	48	3,475

(continued)

DRUNKEST PLACES—*Continued*

"Dangerously Drunk" Cities

In December 2007, researchers at *Men's Health* magazine compiled this list of the "Most Dangerously Drunk" cities in the United States.

1. Denver, Colorado
2. Anchorage, Alaska
3. Colorado Springs, Colorado
4. Omaha, Nebraska
5. Fargo, North Dakota
6. San Antonio, Texas
7. Austin, Texas
8. Fresno, California
9. Lubbock, Texas
10. Milwaukee, Wisconsin

The magazine looked beyond just drunk-driving statistics and focused on a bigger health picture: factors such as annual death rates due to alcoholic liver disease, CDC reports of how many residents are downing five or more drinks in a sitting, FBI statistics on drunk-driving arrests, the U.S. Department of Transportation's numbers on fatal accidents involving intoxicated motorists, and the Mothers Against Drunk Driving report card on state efforts to cut down on excessive drinking.

Some of the results are surprising. Hard-partying Austin? Sure. Fargo, North Dakota? Who knew? Let's check in to see what's going on in a few of the cities on the list.

Austin, Texas

Austin is definitely one city where you want to be extra careful when the bars close down.

In 2007, the Austin Police Department reported the majority of alcohol-related collisions on Friday night/Saturday morning between midnight and 3:59 a.m.—with bar closing times smack in the middle, at 2 a.m. Of the 496 auto accidents that occurred on Saturdays in 2007, 223 of them were in this time window.

In general, you want to use your common sense: Sixth Street is Austin's hub, so once the bars let out, you can expect drunken revelers to spill onto the streets and into their cars. The police department also provided me the intersections that you definitely want to avoid when the bars close—five or more alcohol-related collisions occurred at each of these spots in 2007.

LOCATION	NUMBER OF ALCOHOL-RELATED COLLISIONS
Koenig and Airport	6
I-35 SB Service Rd. and Stassney	6
9515 Lamar N (by Rundberg)	6
Riverside and Tinnin Ford (also Burton)	5
Cameron (Dessau) and Rundberg	5
Airport and Oak Springs	5
5600 Congress Ave. (at W. Stassney)	5

Even without a collision, people driving while intoxicated (DWI) are a major problem in the Austin area. The majority of DWI arrests also occurred between midnight and 3:59 a.m. in 2007, accounting for 972 out of 1,614 total Saturday arrests that year.

Here are the locations where more than 18 DWI arrests occurred in 2007.

LOCATION	NUMBER OF DWIS
800 W. Sixth (at West)	44
1100 W. Sixth (by Lamar)	42
1000 W. Sixth (at Lamar)	40
100 S. First (at Town Lake)	34
1200 W. Sixth (at Blanco)	34
11500 Burnet (east of Mopec Expressway)	31
1600 E. Riverside (off I-35)	29
600 Baylor (at Pecan)	25
Riverside and Tinnin Ford/Burton	19
600 Blanco (at Sixth)	19

Fargo, North Dakota

The Fargo Police Department was more than surprised when we called to check its drunk-driving statistics. A spokesman argued that Fargo has "an aggressive approach to DUI [driving under the influence] intervention."

And maybe they're right: Fargo experienced only five alcohol-related fatalities from 2003 to 2007. (Interestingly, four of those five took place in 2007 alone.)

So, why is Fargo on the drunkest-cities list with so few alcohol-related accidents? It probably has something to do with *why* the police are taking an aggressive stance against drunk driving: binge drinking. According to the CDC's 2007 Behavioral Risk Factor Surveillance System, North Dakota was the number

(continued)

DRUNKEST PLACES—*Continued*

two state (just behind Wisconsin) for binge drinking: 30.2 percent of males admitted having had five or more drinks on one occasion, and 16.5 percent of females had had four or more drinks on one occasion.

With all that binge drinking, you would expect more traffic fatalities, right? Well, Fargo officials are cutting to the chase and taking impaired drivers off the streets. In 2004, officials implemented sobriety checkpoints and boosted other police efforts to combat drunk driving: The police department reported that the number of DUI arrests went from 965 in 2005 to 1,028 in 2006.

So, kudos to Fargo for combating drunk-driving accidents, but that doesn't mean the basic problem has been solved.

In April 2008, the National Survey on Drug Use and Health issued a report entitled *State Estimates of Persons Aged 18 or Older Driving under the Influence of Alcohol or Illicit Drugs.* Guess where North Dakota fell? Number two . . . right behind Wisconsin again. Turns out, 24.9 of the drivers surveyed had driven under the influence over the course of a year. Guess they know their way around the checkpoints!

Anchorage, Alaska

Now, this one isn't a huge surprise. Alaska has had a long-term problem with alcohol abuse—but is Anchorage really the "drunkest" city in Alaska? Based on the 2000 census, the population of Anchorage is 260,283, and in 2007, the Anchorage Police Department reported 1,964 DUI arrests and 404 DUI accidents.

In reality, alcohol abuse is a major problem in Alaska's rural areas, particularly among the native population. Theories abound as to whether it's the cold weather, darkness, isolation, poverty, or all of the above, that leads to alcohol and drug abuse—but since access to health care can be limited in these communities, comprehensive statistics aren't available.

Alcohol abuse has become such a problem in some Alaskan villages and communities that they have become officially "dry," meaning that it's illegal to possess, buy, or sell alcohol there. Others are "damp," meaning residents can bring in alcohol from other communities but can't buy it in their own. With these restrictions, "wet" towns act as lightning rods for heavy binge drinking, like after a big event such as the Iditarod dogsledding race, which culminates in Nome.

Nome has a population of 3,500 and is surrounded by 15 mostly dry villages. In September 2007, Rachel D'Oro, an Anchorage-based Associated Press reporter, wrote about Nome, "It has six bars, four liquor stores and two private clubs that sell booze, and annual alcohol sales total $5.5 million, which is equal to more than half of the city's annual budget."

D'Oro painted a grim picture of Nome: "Day and night, drunks can be seen staggering along Front Street, slumped against buildings, and passed out near the tourist shops or along the seawall on the Bering Sea. . . . Some never make it out of Nome alive. . . . Over the past two decades, dozens have died of exposure or drowned."

So, while drunk driving in Anchorage is a concern, it isn't the only city with this kind of problem. Look at the map of all the dry cities and towns, then find another one nearby that's not dry, and stay away at all costs!

Are Smoking Bans Bad for Your Health?

This is one that the lawmakers didn't see coming. A study published in 2008 in the *Journal of Public Economics* entitled "Drunk Driving after the Passage of Smoking Bans in Bars" found that smoking bans actually increase drunk-driving fatalities by about 13 percent.

Researchers looked at data from 2,452 counties nationwide, comparing those with and without smoking bans in public places. In counties where the ban had been in place for more than 18 months, the accident rate went up by about 10 percent!

Why? Well, the theory is that people drive farther to find bars that let them smoke while they drink, whether they're heading to a nearby county that doesn't have a ban, to establishments with outdoor smoking areas, or to places that don't actively enforce the ban.

In Pennsylvania, for example, accidents in Delaware County went up by 26 percent when officials across the state line in Delaware enforced a smoking ban. Folks from the neighboring state came across the border to Pennsylvania to smoke while drinking. Similarly, fatal accidents in Jefferson County, Colorado, went up an astonishing 40 percent when neighboring Boulder County enforced a smoking ban.

In addition, the study pointed out, the National Institute on Alcohol Abuse and Alcoholism found that about 24 percent of licensed drivers who were of legal drinking age used both alcohol and tobacco in a 12-month period, and approximately 6.2 million adults claimed to have an alcohol disorder and nicotine dependence.

Translation? For many people, smoking and drinking go hand in hand, and they're not going to let pesky laws get in the way.

(continued)

DRUNKEST PLACES—*Continued*

Top Drinking Countries

You might be surprised to know that Russia is not the top consumer of alcohol. Luxembourg is! A 2006 survey by the Organization for Economic Co-Operation and Development tracked alcohol consumption and found that more than 15.5 liters of alcohol are consumed per capita each year in this tiny country. On its heels is Ireland, with an average per capita consumption of a staggering 13.3 liters a year, followed by Hungary, Moldova, and the Czech Republic.

Alcohol, Alcohol Everywhere . . . Even Under the Kitchen Sink

In 2007, a study by the London School of Hygiene and Tropical Health reported that 43 percent of all deaths among Russian men (of working age) are related to excessive drinking. A study conducted in the town of Izhevsk (the capital of Udmurtia, a Russian republic located about 800 miles southeast of Moscow) showed that it wasn't vodka that was killing them. Researchers found that residents were swigging cologne, alcoholic extracts used for medical purposes (which contained up to 90 percent alcohol), and even cleaning agents!

Who's Drinking Daily?

Each year in the United States, the CDC conducts its Behavioral Risk Factor Surveillance System, a national phone survey that assesses behavior such as exercise habits, tobacco use, and alcohol consumption. "Heavy" drinkers are identified as adult men having more than two drinks per day and adult women having more than one drink per day.

The following percentages of heavy drinkers among people surveyed may surprise you.

Hawaii 7.7

Guam 7.5

Vermont 7.2

Delaware 7.1

Nevada 7.1

Rhode Island 7.1

Wisconsin 6.7

Alaska 6.4

Maine 6.3

Chapter 13

BOTTLENECKS

REALLY BAD JAM SESSIONS

You can get there from here by car, but if you want to arrive sometime in this lifetime, it pays to know which roads and highways to avoid. Experienced drivers will tell you (as will the local police and highway patrol) that there are certain roads that will *always* be congested. So if your time and gas consumption are important to you, then why even attempt to drive on these roads?

First, some background. The American Highway Users Alliance (AHUA) tells us—and it stands to reason—that summertime marks the busiest travel season of the year for our roads, with 33 percent of all vacation travel occurring during that time. You might have guessed that July and August are the 2 months that see the most drivers on the road. Eighty-five percent of trips 100 miles or longer one-way are taken by car, while only 12 percent are taken via airplane and 3 percent in rental cars or on trains.

Okay, no real surprises there. But, despite the highest fuel prices in our history, we are still creatures of habit. There are more drivers on the road than ever. In fact, even lesser-known roads are witnessing an increase in traffic. From 1990 to 2002, the number of vehicles per lane mile on rural roads increased by 29 percent, whereas major urban roads saw only an 18 percent increase.

AHUA conducted a series of tests on various factors that cause delays in traffic, and found 233 bottlenecks in 33 states plus the District of Columbia. That's a 40 percent increase from the previous analysis, done in 1999.

It's not a pretty picture. Herewith, the places suffering from the worst bottlenecked roads in America.

The Hamptons, Long Island, New York

The Hamptons like to boast that they offer the quintessential upscale East Coast summer experience, and many people still diligently travel there despite increasingly horrific traffic.

Things started to get busy back in the 1970s, and traffic has continued to heighten, as this is still the place where celebrities and wannabes alike tend to their upscale aspirations. As a New Yorker, I can think of few less appealing things than fighting hours of traffic to get to a place where I'm going to see the very same people I've just seen all week and want desperately to avoid.

But the cars, and the people, keep coming.

New York's State Highway 27 is the only main route into the Hamptons, and it comprises the Sunrise Highway and the temperamental County Route 39 (a.k.a. the Shinnecock Squeeze). The real bottlenecks happen on Friday nights and Sunday afternoons—especially on Route 39.

My advice? Take the ferry from Connecticut, or the Long Island Rail Road to the Hamptons. It'll save you time, money, and a whole lot of hassle . . . and you'll have a much better view than looking at the rear end of a parade of SUVs.

Branson, Missouri

Surrounded by lakes and campgrounds, which are among the most desirable of summer attractions, this hot spot for music and entertainment in southwestern Missouri is especially susceptible to high-season traffic.

U.S. 65 and Missouri Highway 76 serve as major routes in and out of the Branson area, accommodating a broad mix of cars and RVs. According to the Missouri Department of Transportation, U.S. 65, which leads into Branson from the north, experiences a drastic jump in traffic from March through July and November to mid-December. But it's that month of July that you'll really want to watch out for, when traffic more than doubles. In January, the average daily number of vehicles on U.S. 65 is 6,384. In July, it skyrockets to 15,850 vehicles per day.

With an increase in traffic flow comes the need for roadwork, especially in a state like Missouri, which endures some of the harshest and coldest winters in the country, as well as heavy wear and tear in the summer. Branson is working on improving traffic flow: The road around the intersection of U.S. 65 and Highway 76 (the Strip) is being widened, and a connector road is being built between Roark Valley Road and West 76 at Fall Creek Road.

Additionally, the intersection of Highway 76 and Roark Valley Road has seen notable improvements, which are helping ease the east-west traffic flow out of Branson.

Keep an eye out around Forsythe Street, though, which connects Roark Valley Road with West 76 and is undergoing major improvements at private expense.

Presque Isle State Park, Pennsylvania

Located just north of Erie, Pennsylvania, and visited by about four million people each year, Presque Isle State Park is a 3,200-acre peninsula that arches directly into Lake Erie.

For Pennsylvania, that means traffic to Presque Isle is concentrated in the summer months, and starts to pick up as early as April or May. There is only one road leading into the entrance of the park, and that's Route 832 North.

Ed Bemis, a traffic control technician for the Department of Transportation (a.k.a. the guy in charge of counting all those cars), offered up some specific numbers regarding Route 832 in the month of June, when traffic starts to reflect the summer travel trends. And those numbers show you how bad it can get.

The data for the first week of summer 2007 show that northbound weekday traffic was highest on Wednesdays, with about 9,200 cars heading in. Thursday was the lightest day of the week for northbound traffic, dropping off sharply to about 7,000 cars per day. If we compare this with weekend traffic numbers, Saturday was the busiest day by far, with 12,349 cars. Peak times for weekend northbound traffic started around 1 p.m.

For southbound Route 832, traffic heading back out of the park, the weekday average was 7,490 cars; but for Sunday, when many people leave the park, the total number of cars jumped to 11,884. If you insist on driving on 832 on a Sunday in the summer, bring a book. You'll be reading it.

Provo Canyon, Utah

U.S. 189 winds through Utah's popular Provo Canyon, paralleling the Provo River. As one of the state's best fly-fishing locations and an easy access route to the Wasatch and Uinta mountain ranges, Provo Canyon sees some real congestion during the summertime.

The good news: U.S. 189 has recently undergone a 5-mile-long road-widening and reconstruction project between the Deer Creek Dam and the Sundance Resort turnoff. The project turned the two-lane road into four lanes, and the extra lanes should help with traffic flow.

Now the bad news: More cars are using the road, and the official speed limit has been *raised* to a whopping 55 mph (wishful thinking during the summertime). Oh, and don't forget about the avalanches: U.S. 189 is shut down periodically in the winter for transportation crews to conduct avalanche control.

Yosemite National Park, California

Yosemite is known as a climber's mecca, famous for Camp 4 on the valley floor but, more notably, for its gigantic granite monoliths and miles of hiking. It's become one of America's most crowded national parks . . . and whether you're a hiker, climber, or birder, you'll end up in Yosemite traffic if you go during its bottleneck season.

The park's heaviest traffic reflects the nationwide school system's vacation times. That means spring break and summer vacation are the absolute worst times to be in Yosemite. For example, in January 2007, the park saw a mere 104,213 visitors, but this number rose steadily to hit 871,728 in May and June alone—that's twice as many people in those 2 months as visit in January, February, and March combined. July and August are the busiest operating months for Yosemite, with more than a million visitors combined.

Of the park's five entrances, all but the Hetch Hetchy entrance have bad bottlenecks, the worst happening when you're trying to *leave* the park—when you're exhausted and just want to get home.

All the outgoing traffic from the park ends up in one single spot, and that is the intersection at Yosemite Lodge at the Falls, one of the most heavily congested areas in the park, with pedestrians crossing in hordes to get to the falls, and cars trying to maneuver around the people.

Below, the routes of Yosemite, explained.

HIGHWAY 140 gets you into the park from the west if you're coming from Modesto or Merced, peeling off Highway 99 (east of and parallel to the huge Interstate 5) in Merced. Highway 140 has the legitimately impressive Arch Rock entrance, which you get to drive right under. Delays at this entrance are normally only about 5 minutes but can be as bad as half an hour—especially in the peak months of July and August.

HIGHWAY 120 WEST, or the Big Oak Flat entrance, also takes you to the park from the west, but it comes in north of Highway 140 and is slightly less traveled.

Here's where it gets tricky: Highway 120 bisects the park, east to west, and is technically a state road when you're *not* in the park; however, when it reaches the park, it becomes a federal road known as Big Oak Flat Road, and then turns into Tioga Road (also federal) and eventually spits out as State Highway 120 East on the other side of the park. Tioga Road closes to cars in the wintertime but remains open to those who want to ski and snowshoe.

HIGHWAY 41 is the park's south and most popular entrance. This road has the heaviest traffic, as most of the people using it are coming from Fresno, Clovis, Oakhurst, and Los Angeles—and that's a lot of people. Traffic can get so bad here that cars will be lined up starting at Goat Meadow, about a mile south of the entrance. Park rangers have been known to just wave people through the entrance—no stopping to pay.

But if you want to avoid traffic *and* avoid paying, later is better. The park officials never really close the gates—there might be rangers collecting money until about 10 p.m., but after that, it's basically a free ride. So, if you come in after 10 p.m. and camp, you miss the crowds and skip the fees. Just make sure that you also leave after 10 p.m.

Finally, you've got the **HETCH HETCHY ENTRANCE VIA EVERGREEN ROAD**, which is the least traveled route to the park, mainly because Evergreen is the only road that does not lead to Yosemite Valley. Upon parting from Highway 120, you'll be on a route coming from the west through dense Forest Service land, eventually ending in the park—but *not* at Yosemite Valley. Evergreen Road dead-ends at the Hetch Hetchy Reservoir, which is fed by the Tuolumne River and, more significantly, is the historical proof of John Muir's lost battle to keep Hetch Hetchy from being dammed by the O'Shaughnessy Dam in the early 20th century.

Yellowstone National Park, Wyoming, Idaho, and Montana

Yellowstone is America's oldest national park, encompassing a large chunk of Wyoming, slivers of Montana, and bits of Idaho. In fact, this park was founded before those states were states.

As with Yosemite, the school calendar dictates crunch times on the roads to Yellowstone.

Cape Cod, Massachusetts

The Cape Cod Chamber of Commerce certainly kept things short and sweet when it came to giving advice on avoiding bottlenecks. Could it be that they were . . . stuck in traffic?

Best times to arrive at the Cape

Sunday through Thursday: Anytime

Friday: Before 2 p.m. or after 9 p.m.

Saturday: Before 8 a.m. or after 2 p.m.

Best times to leave the Cape

Monday through Friday: Anytime (except Monday holidays between 1 and 9 p.m.)

Saturday: After 2 p.m.

Sunday: Before 1 p.m. or after 9 p.m.

Travel times to avoid

Arriving: Friday, 2 to 9 p.m.; Saturday, 8 a.m. to 2 p.m.

Departing: Sunday, or Monday holiday, 1 to 9 p.m.

One area in which the Chamber of Commerce *did* open up a bit was in promoting a new flyover project at the Sagamore Rotary that can shave off up to 45 minutes from peak driving time.

The park gets inundated with 2.8 to 3.1 million visitors from June to September, and estimated driving distances and times can be deceiving. Once you're inside the park, there are much lower speed limits, not to mention the inevitable "animal jams"—bison, bear, deer, wolf, and moose, to name a few—and because of limited shoulders and pullouts, people stop in the middle of the road to take pictures. The average speed limit is between 30 and 45 mph, so don't plan to go anywhere quickly in Yellowstone.

Getting down to specifics, there are five entrances into Yellowstone: (1) the northeast entrance, off the Beartooth Highway; (2) the north entrance, in Gardner, Montana; (3) the west entrance, via West Yellowstone, Montana, which is the busiest; (4) the south entrance, at Grand Teton National Park; and (5) the east entrance, from Cody, Wyoming.

Of course, we can't forget Yellowstone's beloved geyser, Old Faithful, which brings in four out of every five visitors to the park. You can reach the geyser via any of the entrances, but the closest is the west entrance—which is probably why it's the busiest.

One of the least busy times to visit Yellowstone is September, in part because the little ones are back in school. Although the park has been seeing an increase of visitors (primarily older and younger couples) in that month, it remains one of the best times to go, as there are few people and little chance of snow. Just remember to bring a sweater—it can get cold at night.

Outer Banks, North Carolina

North Carolina's 130 miles of barrier islands, known as the Outer Banks, lend excellent views of prime Atlantic coastline, but with winding tributaries and estuaries tangling the area's roads, you're going to contend with some major bottlenecks if you go at the wrong time.

U.S. 158, also known as the Chesapeake Expressway, is the main route drivers take to reach the Outer Banks. Do make a note that Virginia's Route 168 turns into U.S. 158 East after you hit North Carolina. Despite being a comfortably sized four-lane road, this is the primary road from the mainland to the popular Kitty Hawk and Nags Head areas. Things get most crowded early Saturday morning in both directions, with travelers heading to and from their weekend homes and rental properties.

Traffic to all the Outer Banks islands reaches a peak in mid-June through the end of August. According to North Carolina's State Highway Administration, traffic volumes pick up as early as mid-April and stretch well into October, with the peak month being July.

The Highway Administration also mentions that in 2007, the Outer Banks saw the highest weekend traffic volumes for nonholidays in late July and early August. Take a look at traffic volumes for the last weekends of each summer month.

Thursday, June 21, through Sunday, June 24: 193,000 (one way)

Thursday, July 26, through Sunday, July 29: 196,000 (one way)

Thursday, August 23, through Sunday, August 26: 179,000 (one way)

What's happening is that traffic on Thursday and Friday evenings and Saturday mornings becomes crowded as drivers head east toward the beach. On Saturday mornings and afternoons and Sunday evenings, it's the westbound traffic you have to watch out for, as people drive back home.

But here's an insider tip: On Saturdays, the real crunch begins around 1 p.m., when vacation-home renters are returning from a morning at the beach and day-trippers are heading toward it. Congestion and delays can build in both directions well into the early evening.

Keep in mind that flying into the Outer Banks is not possible, because there is no commercial air service into or out of the area. You can, however, fly into Norfolk International, 82 miles north of the Outer Banks. Of course, you can fly into Raleigh, too, but then you face a 3-hour drive to the Outer Banks after your flight. So, either way, you're going to have to drive some distance.

And here's another tip: Peak bottleneck times vary on Sundays, but on that day, avoid driving anywhere near the areas of Duck and the Southern Shores.

Sun Valley, Idaho

Nestled in the middle of the Sawtooth Range in central Idaho, Sun Valley immediately grips visitors with impressive mountain panoramas. Between skiing in the winter and hiking in the summer, Sun Valley hosts its fair share of drivers. The one major downfall of this area is that State Highway 75 provides the only major access to the city.

State Highway 75 is the main route between Shoshone, Idaho, just south of Sun Valley, and Stanley, situated north of Sun Valley. A lot of out-of-staters take ID 75, the Sawtooth Scenic Byway, so it grows more crowded in the summer. In the winter, driving conditions from other parts of Idaho to Sun Valley are extremely weather dependent, and many people prefer to fly. In January 2007, ID 75 just south of Sun Valley had 11,895 vehicles, and in July of the same year, volume rose to 16,084 vehicles.

Another scenic byway breaks off in Stanley, on Highway 75: Idaho 21, also known as the Ponderosa Pine Highway, is your road of choice to avoid bottlenecks. It takes you about 20 miles north—in fact, you travel to the middle of nowhere—but then drops you back down to Boise via the Lucky Peak State Park and Reservoir.

The Idaho Department of Transportation maintains that ID 21 sees very few visitors, as it is more of a supplemental road than a main vein, and the numbers are there to prove it. In January 2007, the Banner Summit area on ID 21 saw a raging total of 80 cars; by July 2007, the number jumped to 1,076.

Myrtle Beach, South Carolina

Myrtle Beach and the generous stretch of beaches known as the Grand Strand claim to have it all: shopping, amusement parks, water sports, golf, fishing, and historic sites. But having it all inevitably means one thing: traffic. Situated about 60 miles east of I-95, Myrtle Beach is primarily fed by the punier but popular U.S. 501.

April marks the beginning of the traffic upswing, with an average of 56,192 cars jamming between the city of Conway and Myrtle Beach on U.S. 501 each day.

For a chance to avoid the traffic, use SC 22, the Conway Bypass, which peels off from U.S. 501 between Aynor and Conway. By taking drivers up to the north end of Myrtle Beach, SC 22 also grants access to SC 31, which heads north as well. In July 2007, SC 22's highest traffic month, it had only 33,975 cars, far fewer than U.S. 501.

An equally viable option for visitors is SC 544, which is longer but eventually gets you to the beach by hooking into Ocean Highway, U.S. 17. No matter what you decide, South Carolina is aware of Myrtle Beach's popularity, and the state plans to alleviate traffic by building I-73, which will connect I-95 to SC 22.

Oregon Coast

Known as one of the most beautiful drives in the nation—through wine country and rugged coastal mountains—the drive up the Oregon coast is a long-beloved route for road-trippers.

You would think that the main thoroughfares of U.S. 101, Interstate 5, and the Pacific Coast Highway up the Oregon coast would top the Don't Drive There List. Not so: It's Oregon's alternate routes of U.S. 26, SR 18, U.S. 20, U.S. 30, and SR 22 that are inundated with summer drivers.

These roads, which get you there via Oregon's Willamette Valley, have grown more popular with drivers who are meandering off the main roads to enjoy the scenic route.

You'll see loads of drivers on U.S. 26, which heads east off the coast's U.S. 101 just south of Seaside and eventually collides with Portland.

It's the same story with SR 18 between McMinnville and Lincoln City, which cuts away from the 101 near Otis. U.S. 20, from Corvallis into the coastal city of Newport, gets busy in July and August, and the same goes for U.S. 30 between Portland and Astoria.

But the one road to keep an eye on is U.S. 22, a major commuter route between Grand Ronde and Lincoln City, and the busiest route in summertime. So locals must also contend with summer travelers—especially during July and August, the heaviest traffic months.

In January 2007, when commuters still had to get to work despite temporary road closures on U.S. 22, drivers totaled 475,362, which is about 15,334 cars per day. However, in August of the same year, the monthly total jumped to 722,167, bringing the average daily traffic to 23,296 cars in the peak of summer. And that's exactly when you don't want to go there!

DON'T GO THERE THEN

We've all experienced it: the absolute excitement of visiting one of the great iconic travel monuments or destinations in the world. We've studied it in school, we've seen images in books, in magazines, on television. And then the moment arrives, and we're actually there. But suddenly we're surrounded by human locusts—swarms of tourists lining up, pushing, and crowding in vain to have the same unforgettable experience.

As you lean over to kiss your significant other on top of the Eiffel Tower, you notice the large group of schoolchildren openly gawking at you. Even worse, you miss seeing the *Mona Lisa* at the Louvre because the crowd you thought was waiting to see Da Vinci's masterpiece is actually the never-ending line for the women's restroom.

Nothing squashes special moments more than crowds.

My tried-and-true approach to seeing those special places is a contrarian tactic—and a contrarian time. When venturing out to those idyllic locales, I always hire a taxi or a private car to pick me up at 4:30 in the morning, arriving at the Taj Mahal, the Great Wall of China, or the Pyramids before the sun rises. No bus traffic. No hordes. No lines. Watch the sun rise and have that special moment without feeling as if you have to take a number and wait.

If your idea of vacation is sleeping in, then use the following as a guide to being a contrarian traveler. Essentially, it's about when *not* to go somewhere.

United States of America

Exploring our country from coast to coast may seem like an ideal vacation—until you factor in the millions of people a year who have the same idea.

New York, New York

With nearly 46 million visitors taking a big bite out of the Big Apple each year, it pays to know when *not* to go.

Do you really want to see the Christmas tree at Rockefeller Center or jam into Times Square for a claustrophobic, often nauseating, experience on New Year's Eve?

Trust me, you don't want to be in town during big holidays like Thanksgiving and Christmas, or you'll see the worst that the city has to offer in terms of crowds and expense. We're talking jam-packed sidewalks with gridlocked cars honking angrily, and hotel rates that are double—or triple—the off-season rates. And don't even *think* about stepping into Macy's to go Christmas shopping unless you want to get into an elbowing match with hardened city slickers.

Things get particularly bad around Times Square, where peak pedestrian counts are found during December and August. In the summer of 2006, 320,200 pedestrians walked through Times Square—and that's not counting the people stuck in taxis and other forms of public transportation. The area saw an 11.1 percent increase in pedestrian traffic from 2006 to 2008 (although vehicular traffic dropped).

If you still want to see New York City, fight the cold from January to March. After all, you're not visiting to get a suntan or hang by a pool. If your schedule will fit only a summer trip, go during a 3-day holiday weekend—the city empties out as locals get out of town. It's the best place to be and the best time to be there.

If you do end up choosing to brave a New York City winter, you'll have to wait only 30 minutes to enter the Statue of Liberty. On bad days, particularly during the summer months, expect to wait several hours—in 2007, an average of 11,500 to 12,000 people visited Liberty Island each *day* in July and August.

A better bet? Skip Ellis Island and Liberty Island altogether and take the Staten Island Ferry from downtown Manhattan. It's free, and you'll have an unbeatable view of the statue.

Don't Go There When . . .

It's always tempting to visit places during huge spectacles, festivals, and sporting events. If I've learned anything in my travels, it's that you go to New Orleans during Mardi Gras only *once.* You do Carnival in Rio and vow never to return during that time. And the Super Bowl? Sorry, but the wide-screen television in my living room is the best way to see the game.

There really are times *not* to go somewhere. For example, consider Las Vegas and these particular events to avoid if at all possible.

Traffic is already bad enough on the famed Las Vegas Strip. Now add to it the annual (and massive) International Consumer Electronics Show and the back-to-back Adult Video News Awards every January, when about 150,000 geeks and porn stars come to town. It's just not a pleasant place to be, so avoid going there during that time. New Year's Eve in Sin City is another must-miss evening—in 2007, roughly 300,000 people landed in Las Vegas on December 31.

No time is worse to be in Las Vegas than during a major sporting event. And that goes for any other host city, too. Out-of-control fans? Drunken brawls? Sore losers? Bashed automobiles? It's a perfect reason to run and buy an airline ticket for as far away as possible. For example, when Las Vegas hosted the NBA All-Star Game in 2007, things got totally out of control, and 1,379 arrests were made. If that game is ever played in Vegas again, do whatever you can not to go, unless you bring your lawyer.

But still, Las Vegas doesn't win the crown. The host cities of other major 2007 sporting events had it rough, too. During the Super Bowl in Miami, there were 690 arrests. Hockey fans were a little more violent during the NHL All-Star Game in Dallas, with 765 arrests. And let's not forget the NCAA Final Four played in Atlanta, which took the honors with 1,462 arrests.

Disney World, Orlando, Florida

Disney World's Magic Kingdom remains one of the most visited tourist spots in the world, with nearly 17.1 million visitors in 2007, up 2.5 percent from the previous year. A few steps behind is Epcot Center, with 11 million visitors, while Disney's Hollywood Studios and Animal Kingdom saw approximately 9.5 million visitors each in 2007.

There are several peak times throughout the year at Disney World, and they shouldn't come as a surprise: whenever school is out. We're talking Christmas through the New Year, Easter and spring break, and anytime between Memorial Day and Labor Day (plus another spike during the July 4th weekend).

Historically, the busiest days for the Magic Kingdom are Monday, Thursday, and Saturday. Somewhat surprisingly, the rest of the parks vary in terms of their most crowded days (perhaps because the bulk of visitors get their fill of the Magic Kingdom before heading to other parts of the complex). Epcot peaks on Tuesday and Friday; Hollywood Studios sees a surge on Sunday and Wednesday; and the Animal Kingdom has seen its heavier crowds on Monday, Tuesday, and Wednesday. Translation: Start your week on Tuesday and spend 2 days at the Magic Kingdom, followed by Epcot, then Hollywood Studios, and end your trip on Saturday at the Animal Kingdom (while the rest of the crowd is still in line to see Mickey).

Disney officials tout the Fast Pass as your ticket to skipping the lines, but during peak times, it's hardly worth it. Imagine bringing your kid to the Jungle Cruise and finding out that you have to return . . . 6 hours later! And you can hold only one Fast Pass at a time, meaning that ultimately you're going to have to wait in line somewhere.

And here's something you may not know: The parks close their doors when they reach capacity. So even if you have a pricey ticket in hand, you are not guaranteed admission!

Grand Canyon, Arizona

As one of America's most famous natural landmarks, the Grand Canyon attracts tourists all year round. However, you'll find a slight dip in crowds during early spring and late fall. Winter is the slowest season, especially during January and February, because freezing winter weather and snow will deter even the most determined travelers.

While the South Rim is open all year, the road to the North Rim closes down from late October to mid-May, due to heavy snowfall and other winter conditions. If you want to avoid tour groups, early October before the road closes is the opportune time.

Or, you can skip both rims and head west instead. Owned and operated by the Hualapai Tribe on their tribal lands, the Skywalk on the Grand Canyon West is a horseshoe-shaped glass walkway that allows you to walk 65 feet beyond the canyon's edge (4,000 feet up!). Since its grand opening in March 2007, the Skywalk has seen about 3,000 visitors a day during its busy season (late summer through early fall).

If you want to be suspended over the Grand Canyon, try visiting in the

10 Most Visited U.S. National Parks, 2007

1. Great Smoky Mountains (TN, NC)—9,372,253
2. Grand Canyon (AZ)—4,413,668
3. Yosemite (CA)—3,503,428
4. Yellowstone (WY, ID, MT)—3,151,343
5. Olympic (WA)—2,988,686
6. Rocky Mountain (CO)—2,895,383
7. Zion (UT)—2,657,281
8. Grand Teton (WY)—2,588,574
9. Cuyahoga Valley (OH)—2,486,656
10. Acadia (ME)—2,202,228

Want a (much) less crowded alternative? Check out the top 10 *least* visited national parks in 2007.

1. Kobuk Valley (AK)—847
2. National Park of American Samoa—6,774
3. Gates of the Arctic (AK)—10,942
4. Isle Royale (MI)—15,973
5. North Cascades (WA)—19,534
6. Dry Tortugas (FL)—60,895
7. Wrangell–St. Elias (AK)—61,085
8. Great Basin (NV)—81,364
9. Katmai (AK)—82,634
10. Congaree (SC)—115,524

first 2 weeks of December or in January or February. Also, contrary to popular belief, it's better to visit on the weekends, since most tour groups and excursions visit on weekdays.

France

It's the number one tourist destination in the world, with more than 60 million visitors descending upon France each year, so finding a time when it's not flooded with tourists is nearly impossible. But you might be able to catch a break or two if you time your visits wisely.

Eiffel Tower

In 2007 alone, 6,893,000 visitors climbed the Eiffel Tower, France's most famous landmark. So, on any given day, there could be close to 18,885 other people at the top of the tower with you. Although officials claim that the average wait time to get up there is just 30 minutes, usually that number really represents the wait time to board the elevators. The truth is that it can often take hours before you reach the top. To make things even more frustrating, there are two sets of elevators—once you finally step off the first one, you think you're there and . . . surprise! You get to wait in line for another one.

If you're planning to visit Paris between the end of May and the end of September, good luck—it happens to be the most crowded period at the Eiffel Tower. It's the worst during June, July, and August, so if you're looking for a romantic getaway, you might as well wave good-bye to it now. The average number of visitors in June between 2000 and 2007 reached about 622,000; 773,000 in July; and about 825,000 in August alone!

Instead, visit the City of Lights and the Eiffel Tower in November or December, particularly the week after Thanksgiving or the week after New Year's.

The Louvre

If you were one of the 7.7 million people who stopped by Paris's most renowned museum in 2007, you can probably testify as to how crowded things can get. They're exponentially worse in the summer and during holidays, when it seems like everyone has decided it's time to head overseas for a French vacation. Still worse are weekends at the Louvre—avoid them entirely. Instead, try midweek or Friday nights around 8 p.m., since most people don't know that the Louvre stays open until 10 p.m. every Friday.

If you can't go during those windows, here's my other suggestion: Avoid the Louvre entirely. No points will be deducted from your final score. Instead, visit the permanent collections at the City of Paris museums, which are free all year round. There are more than 14 of these municipal museums, including the Musée d'Art moderne, the Musée du Petit Palais, and the Musée Carnavalet.

Australia

For a country that has a population of 4.4 people per square mile, you'd be surprised how many people are around when you decide to visit the land Down Under.

Uluru (Ayers Rock)

Nestled in Australia's Northern Territory, one of the so-called must-see spots in Australia is Uluru, otherwise known as Ayers Rock, a large sandstone formation that is a sacred Aboriginal spot. However, once you find out that an average of 25,000 to 33,000 people visit Uluru each month, you'll probably want to visit some other rock in the middle of the desert.

So skip Uluru and head to the West MacDonnell Ranges, also in the Northern Territory. Spanning 250 miles on either side of Alice Springs, this mountain range has more than enough uncrowded spots from which to view the spectacular mountain scenery, ancient rock art, and deep gorges. The Devils Marbles Conservation Reserve is another good alternative: Naturally rounded granite boulders, a whopping 13 feet tall and up to 100 feet wide, sit precariously in the middle of the desert. This less-visited site is worthy of your footprints.

But if you still have your heart set on going to Ayers Rock, you might want to go during February, April, or December, because these months see fewer tourists. One other important note: Most people watch the sunsets and sunrises from designated viewing areas, so try to find a spot away from these to avoid the crowds. Also, since flights arrive and depart in the middle of the day, tourists are still getting situated between midmorning and midafternoon—so you may find the rock barren at those times.

Great Barrier Reef

The most extensive reef system in the world, stretching almost 1,500 miles along the east coast of Queensland in the Pacific Ocean, the Great Barrier Reef is one of Australia's most famous tourist destinations. And, despite its size, the Great Barrier Reef gets crowded . . . *very* crowded, with more than 1.8 million visitors descending upon it via cruises, glass-bottomed boats, semisubmersible vessels, and helicopters. My advice: Check out some other locations instead, such as Lord Howe Island or Dunk Island. Less crowded, and you might even have a more authentic experience.

Egypt

Try walking like an Egyptian when there are swarms of people ahead of you who are walking as fast as mummified corpses.

Pyramids of Giza

Since they're the last remaining member of the Seven Wonders of the Ancient World, it's no *wonder* that the Pyramids of Giza draw large crowds daily despite the dry heat of the Egyptian desert. The Pyramids see about three million visitors annually, and the most popular time to go is October through April, because of the cooler temperatures. Still, the Pyramids attract their fair share of visitors during the summer as well. If you want to avoid *all* the crowds, hire a car and driver to pick you up from your hotel at 4:30 a.m. and embark for Giza before dawn. Arrange with your hotel the night before for horses to be ready. You'll saddle up at 5:15 a.m. and head out to the desert, where you'll be out there, alone, with the Pyramids and the dawn. A staggering photo opportunity for you. When you head back into town, notice the caravan of crowded tourist buses trundling toward the Pyramids.

China

The land of more than one billion citizens gets about 131 million visitors annually, ensuring that there will be plenty of people to block your path.

The Great Wall of China

China's most famous monument is a must-see sight for you as a visitor. Unfortunately, everyone else has the same idea, making things quite crowded, and even worse on hot days. Like the Pyramids in Egypt, it's not about when you go to the Great Wall as much as what time of day you go, and once again, predawn wins.

The Great Wall doesn't actually run through Beijing, but the section at Badaling, the most popular segment of the wall, with about 10 million visitors a year, is within reasonable driving distance. This section has been fully restored and outfitted with cable cars and other tourist traps. It offers great views of the Chinese landscape, but it's often so overrun with tourists that you won't even be able to snap a photo without having at least 10 people walk in front of the camera.

My advice here parallels my tip on Egypt: Hire a car and driver to leave your hotel at 4:30 a.m. Within 45 minutes, you'll be climbing while the sun is rising. The only other people there at that time will be some elderly Chinese men practicing tai chi.

The Great Wall of China is not continuous, and there are many parts scattered throughout China. Other less popular yet developed portions of the wall include the sites at Mutianyu or Simatai, which draw crowds—but not as big as those at Badaling. If you want something more private, it's easy to find a taxi driver who will take you to a location like Huanghuacheng, a section of the wall that has not been retrofitted for tourists. Remember— since sections like this one haven't been renovated, they can be dangerous to walk on or around, making them popular for hikers but a challenge for the average visitor.

Some things to note: Locals may ask for "tolls" to get past areas around the wall. There's no such thing, so don't pay money to people who ask. Also, to ensure that your driver doesn't leave you stranded, pay no more than half the fare up front, and, if he's nice, you might want to bring him lunch and water while he's waiting for you. He may know more about the area and may share his valuable insights with you.

DANGEROUS THEME PARKS

Even if you're not afraid of heights or breakneck speeds, some theme-park rides are admittedly menacing—particularly when you know that previous riders blacked out or nearly suffered concussions while on board. Carnival-ride injuries and nausea from Disney's teacups seem like no-brainers, but what about injuries on permanent, solidly built and currently operating coasters at big theme parks?

In 2006, the International Association of Amusement Parks and Attractions (IAAPA) released the *Fixed-Site Amusement Ride Injury Survey,* a comprehensive study conducted by the National Safety Council. The study found that in 2005, more than 300 million guests visited U.S. amusement facilities and took 1.8 billion rides. That year, there were an estimated 1,783 ride-related injuries (5.2 per million guests). Of those injuries, 132 (about 7 percent) were reported as "serious," meaning that they required some form of overnight treatment at a hospital. In 2004, there were an estimated 1,637 ride-related injuries (5.2 per million guests); and in 2003, approximately 2,044 ride-related injuries were reported (7.0 per million guests). On average, IAAPA estimates that there have been four fatalities every year dating back to 1987.

You may remember the horrifying story of the 13-year-old girl whose feet were severed on a ride at Six Flags Kentucky Kingdom in 2007. The Superman Tower of Power, a 177-foot-high free-fall ride that drops passengers at speeds up to 50 mph, malfunctioned, and a cord that was part of the ride wrapped around the girl's feet, severing them at the ankle.

The girl gave an account of her terrifying experience in a deposition filed in the Jefferson Circuit Court, in which she wrote that the ride jolted after climbing only 20 feet. Two wire ropes were lifting the car, and one—the ride's side wire—snapped and fell on her and two friends, wrapping around their necks. The three friends and other passengers screamed for someone to stop the ride, but it continued moving up to the top. "I remember smoke and the smell of burning. I felt like I was going to die," she said. The three teenagers managed to pull the cables away from their necks, but when the ride dropped, the cord severed one girl's feet and broke her left femur. She was rushed to a hospital, where doctors were able to reattach her right foot, but her left foot was amputated below the knee.

Of course this kind of tragedy isn't commonplace on amusement-park rides, but it represents a larger issue here. According to a sworn statement given by the park's ride-maintenance manager, John Schmidt, ride technicians at Six Flags Kentucky Kingdom didn't follow instructions as recommended by the ride's manufacturer. And the Kentucky Department of Agriculture (KDA) agreed. The KDA released a report in May 2008 after intense analysis, blaming "cable fatigue" for the accident and noting that such fatigue would have been noticeable if inspections had been performed as instructed in the maintenance manual. The department also found that the injuries might have been "less severe" if the operator had pressed the emergency button, as trained, within the 10 seconds between the "loud noise followed by the cable falling and the freefall of the ride." The ride's 16-year-old operator delayed hitting the button in favor of calling the park's emergency number.

To date, the case is still tied up in the court system, but the KDA fined the park a whopping $1,000 . . . for violating the state law requiring that amusement-park rides be in good electrical and mechanical condition. Now, that's comforting.

But serious accidents at theme parks date back even further. In August 1999, the country was stunned when there were four fatalities in amusement parks in the course of 1 week. On August 22, a mother watched her 12-year-old son plummet 200 feet from the Drop Zone Stunt Tower at Paramount's Great America (now California's Great America) theme park in Santa Clara, California; the next day, a 20-year-old man fell from the Shockwave roller coaster at Paramount's Kings Dominion near Richmond, Virginia, after partially removing himself from the overhead harness; a week later, a mother and her 8-year-old child were killed at Gillian's Wonderland Pier in Ocean City, New Jersey, after their Wild Wonder roller-coaster car rolled backward, downhill, for 30 feet, throwing them both from the car.

Following the four deaths, U.S. Representative Edward Markey (D-Mass.) took action in the form of the National Amusement Park Ride Safety Act, which would have closed a current loophole that exempts thrill rides in amusement parks from federal safety regulations. The measure called for the Consumer Product Safety Commission (CPSC) to have jurisdiction over the fixed-amusement-park industry and would have established G-force limits on rides. The bill failed to pass in the House Energy and Commerce Committee in late 2007, but Markey was promised a congressional hearing in the future.

Though some have argued that federal regulation is not necessary and that Congressman Markey is overstating the ill effects of high-velocity rides, a 2007 letter to the congressman's office from an industry insider had some chilling insight:

"I am a former senior executive, board member and stockholder in the amusement park industry and a former board member of the International Association of Amusement Parks and Attractions," wrote Jim Prager. "But, because in my opinion the industry does not adequately protect children—its

(continued)

principal customers—against the risk of its ride attractions, I now support CPSC regulation of amusement park rides. Amusement park rides are often haphazardly conceived and designed and then engineered and manufactured by small firms with limited resources in states and in countries other than the communities where the rides are installed. . . . The cost-cutting of the last 25 years has reduced the industry capacity for safety."

But what you need to know is not your likelihood of getting injured, but rather, which ride you're likely to get injured on. The Amusement Safety Organization (ASO), a nonprofit organization that evaluates ride safety levels in amusement parks, has issued its 2008 list rating some of the riskiest rides in the country.

So before you hurl yourself on a coaster during your next theme-park retreat, beware of what body part(s) will ache postride.

Kings Island, Mason, Ohio

Though generally considered to be a "decent" venue, this park has one element that has some people running scared: a wooden coaster called Son of Beast.

Built in 2000, Son of Beast was touted as the only wooden coaster with a loop. (Its predecessor, the Beast, is the longest wooden coaster in the world.) However, Son of Beast lost its signature element after a serious incident took place on July 9, 2006, when 27 people were injured during one run of the ride. A bump in the track made the cars come to a quick halt toward the end of the ride, resulting in minor neck and chest injuries. The cause? A splintered timber that led inspectors to examine the ride's "structural integrity." (If that's not a scary enough problem for a roller coaster, I don't know what is.) After the incident, park officials removed the loop from the coaster for good.

Despite that precaution, in 2007 alone, there were at least 60 complaints of back and/or neck problems in the park, the majority of which stemmed from Son of Beast. Several other, more minor problems involved patrons biting down hard on their lips or cheeks during the ride.

ASO calls Son of Beast "one of the worst roller coasters we have come across. . . . The intensity of the injuries . . . makes us wonder how and why this roller coaster is still operating. Avoid this roller coaster."

Knott's Berry Farm, Buena Park, California

This 160-acre amusement park is located on what was once an actual berry farm in Southern California. Fun for many, but not so much for the people behind the 122 complaints filed in 2007. The vast majority of injuries involved back pain, along with about 24 head injuries (which can include bloody noses and severe bumps on the head). Most of the neck and back injuries came from one ride: GhostRider.

This wooden coaster boasts a 108-foot banked drop and some rough-and-tumble turns. One passenger complained of back and neck pain after the first drop, while another threw up and suffered from blurry vision immediately after stepping off GhostRider. One 46-year-old woman suffered "intense back pain" during the ride and wondered later how the ride could be so "rough and relentless." Here's one tip: Many of the complaints came from people sitting in the last two rows of GhostRider, so if you still feel inclined to ride it—don't sit there!

When ASO contacted Knott's Berry Farm about the complaints it had received on this particular ride, they were shuffled over to the park's headquarters, Cedar Fair Entertainment Company in Sandusky, Ohio, where they were stonewalled by the head honcho himself. ASO obtained an internal e-mail from Cedar Fair COO Jack Falfas instructing that no one in operations, maintenance, or marketing/PR respond to the inquiry . . . or presumably address the concerns of those 122 consumers who took the time to complain about their experiences.

Six Flags Magic Mountain, Valencia, California

The good news coming out of this park is that ASO has never received reports of neck injuries, and visitors have reported only four back injuries. Now the bad news: Other body parts may be bearing the brunt.

In 2000, Magic Mountain's new thrill ride, X, shocked the industry with an innovative new "four-dimensional" design in which the cars spin 360 degrees independently and without warning. But beware—X has reportedly caused males extreme scrotum pain. Riders complained of repeated slamming of their groin during the ride, making for quite an uncomfortable experience. Now, that's a guarantee that I won't go there! The good news is that X was upgraded in late 2007 to the new and improved X^2, though it's too early to tell whether riders are suffering the same consequences.

Meanwhile, other park-goers have flooded ASO with 67 reports of head injuries, particularly bloody noses, after riding the daunting Tatsu, known for its 263-foot elevation changes as it swoops from the peak of a mountain and into other parts of the park. Magic Mountain's macho coaster Goliath once held the world's title for longest (255-foot) and fastest (85 mph) opening drop after its debut in early 2000. That short-lived title did leave one legacy: According to ASO, "riders blacking out on Goliath during its final helix run are very common." In 2001, things took a tragic turn when a 28-year-old woman rode Goliath and died of a brain aneurysm, albeit due to a preexisting condition.

(continued)

Six Flags New England, Agawam, Massachusetts

Not only has the ASO labeled Six Flags New England's employees "apathetic," but the organization also recommends you "do something else when you're in southern Massachusetts."

Of the 75 injuries reported to ASO from this park in 2007, 56 stemmed from the Cyclone, so don't be surprised if you step off this bumpy, jolting wooden roller coaster with newfound back problems. In the recent past, Cyclone riders ranging from their late 20s to early 40s have complained of "extreme back pain," but luckily the thrill ride has yet to cause any major injuries. If you already suffer from back problems, though, this is one ride you need to skip.

In this East Coast park, you may also want to avoid the steel coaster called Flashback. It lives up to its name a little too much, leading to various, frequent head-related issues. Riders have complained about slamming their heads and ears into the restraint system, causing neck strain and ringing in the ear, while one 46-year-old reported upper-back pain due to the rough, jerky ride.

New York New York, Las Vegas, Nevada

Though it's not exactly in a theme park, the roller coaster that sits atop New York New York Hotel & Casino has led to a surprising number of complaints among passengers. Formerly known as the Manhattan Express, this bumpy and jarring ride spurred multiple complaints in 2007, including 60 neck and/ or back injuries, 14 head injuries, and other issues, such as blurry vision and headaches. Many reports have likened what is supposed to be a sleek, smooth steel ride to a rickety old wooden coaster.

Is the experience of zipping through a hotel at breakneck speeds and catching a view of a fake New York City skyline worth the $14 price of admission? Not if you want to get a doctor's bill to go along with it. Check out the Big Shot ride at the Stratosphere instead, which shoots riders a terrifying 1,081 feet above the Strip.

Six Flags Over Texas, Arlington, Texas

Texas summer temperatures can climb well into the 100s some days, so it's no surprise that complaints during these months skyrocket. Whether or not you take the coaster risk during that heat, keep well hydrated to avoid what ASO credits as one of the root causes of coaster blackouts: dehydration.

According to ASO, in 2007 Six Flags Over Texas visitors reported 38 back injuries and 11 neck/back injuries—all related to the Judge Roy Scream and Texas Giant roller coasters. The wooden coaster Texas Giant hits 62 mph and goes 14 stories in the air. Though it has been named one of the top wooden coasters on earth by industry insiders such as *Amusement Today* magazine and the National Amusement Park Historical Association, the title obviously didn't factor in the number of riders complaining of severe back pain. If you are going to take your chances on this one, ride in the first four rows—ASO reports that there haven't been complaints from riders in those seats.

But even worse than Texas Giant and Judge Roy Scream is Titan, which earned 79 complaints of "other" injuries (meaning not neck, back, or head). Alarmingly, all but seven of those involved blacking out, leg cramps, loss of feeling in extremities, nausea, and even vision problems after climbing Titan's 26 stories and dropping at 85 mph.

Six Flags Discovery Kingdom, Vallejo, California

Six Flags Discovery Kingdom, formerly known as Marine World, made the news in August 1999, the month that saw four amusement-park deaths in 1 week. The incident here, while nonfatal, left 28 riders on the seven-car Boomerang dangling 75 feet in the air . . . for nearly 4 hours! The coaster, which is made up of a series of loops and hills, stopped when a cable snapped loose, leaving several riders stuck at a 45-degree angle. The rest of the passengers were upright, but with temperatures reaching almost 100°F, several riders were later treated for heat exhaustion.

While the Boomerang hasn't had any reported mechanical troubles since, visitors still complain of back and neck injuries—49 complaints in all for 2007. In addition, 45 people reported head injuries that year, particularly after riding the Boomerang and another main coaster, Kong.

Kong, a steel coaster transplanted from its original home at Opryland USA, where it was known as the Hangman, drops passengers a heart-stopping 95 feet, followed by loops and twists. "This roller coaster is something to behold," reports ASO. "Pick a seat, any seat, and we have a story for you regarding riders and pain inflicted by this roller coaster." One 26-year-old rider complained of back pain due to the ride's "banging [him] around like a doll." According to ASO, "Complaints are so commonplace that we would advise that you skip this roller coaster."

DANGEROUS DESTINATIONS

YOU'D BETTER PACK MORE THAN SAMSONITE

Anytime you mention areas of high crime, locals immediately get defensive. I know. . . . I've done it myself: After all, I live in New York, Bangkok, and Los Angeles, and each has dangerous zones—places I would do everything possible to avoid or, at the very least, never send a friend. Indeed, it's arguable that along with vibrant, culturally rich cities come bad areas and crime-ridden zones. Historically, in many cities, the most dangerous neighborhoods remain the most dangerous—for years, even decades. And no one seems to be doing anything about it. As a result, it's my responsibility to give you my list of the most dangerous areas in America's most dangerous cities—the places you definitely want to avoid at all costs—and then . . . maybe . . . someone will pay attention.

U.S. Cities

Detroit, Michigan

Is Detroit really the most dangerous city in America? Yes, says research company Morgan Quitno, which regularly publishes a list of the 25 most dangerous cities in the United States. Morgan Quitno ranks the cities as "safest" and "most dangerous" using FBI statistics on murder, rape, burglary, robbery, aggravated assault, and motor vehicle theft, each weighted per capita.

Not surprisingly, the cities that make the "most dangerous" list slam it every time it's published, accusing the researchers of painting a negative picture based solely on numbers. Still, that doesn't change the fact that Detroit is blighted by heavy crime, urban flight, a lingering crack problem, and a depressed economy. First hurt by the continuing collapse of the auto industry, the city then earned the nickname "the Murder Capital of America" in the 1980s, when gun violence escalated. While Detroit has been struggling to rise above its reputation, it was hurt even further by the subprime mortgage crisis in 2007, which led to yet another nickname: "the Foreclosure Capital of America." It seems like Detroit just can't get a break.

Statistically, Detroit may be a lot safer than it was in the 1980s, but it's still no walk in the park. In 2006, the city saw 418 murders and nonnegligent manslaughters, 593 forcible rapes, and 13,143 aggravated assaults.

The preliminary stats for 2007 weren't much more promising: 383 murders, 344 forcible rapes, and 12,382 aggravated assaults.

But how does Detroit measure up to other cities? Look at the Motor City's 2006 statistics calculated per 100,000 people.

TYPE OF CRIME	NUMBER PER 100,000 PEOPLE	NUMBER NATIONALLY PER 100,000 PEOPLE
Murder	47.3	5.7
Rape	67.0	30.9
Robbery	818.6	149.4
Aggravated assault	1,486.0	287.5
Burglary	2,050.3	729.4
Larceny/theft	2,406.8	2,206.8
Motor vehicle theft	2,591.1	398.4

So, what areas do you want to avoid in Detroit? For one thing, when you're leaving town, don't plug the wrong airport into your GPS: The Detroit Metropolitan Airport is the international airport located southwest of the city; Detroit City Airport (officially known as Coleman A. Young International Airport) is a municipal airport on the east side. "Around the Detroit City Airport, it's very rugged, with a lot of drug use," said Joe Swickard, a staff writer for the *Detroit Free Press*.

If you're at all familiar with popular rap artist Eminem, you may be tempted to take a firsthand look at Eight Mile Road, his childhood neighborhood, immortalized in the film *8 Mile*. This 27-mile road is the literal and metaphorical boundary between northeast Detroit and the suburbs.

Though some parts are receiving a face-lift, it's not high on my list of places to explore.

Other spots you want to bypass on your next Detroit city tour: the neighborhoods of Brightmoor and North End. Despite the efforts of community leaders and an initiative by the mayor aiming to revamp these areas, suburban flight has transformed these once-historic middle-class neighborhoods into neglected, high-crime communities.

St. Louis, Missouri

Always a top contender among high-crime cities, St. Louis has struggled with its "dangerous" image for years. But are things getting any better?

In 2006, St. Louis had 129 murders and nonnegligent manslaughters, 337 forcible rapes, and 4,992 aggravated assaults. How did it compare with other cities that year?

TYPE OF CRIME	NUMBER PER 100,000 PEOPLE	NUMBER NATIONALLY PER 100,000 PEOPLE
Murder	37.2	5.7
Rape	97.2	30.9
Robbery	907.2	149.4
Aggravated assault	1,439.1	287.5
Burglary	2,453.3	729.4
Larceny/theft	6,802.4	2,206.8
Motor vehicle theft	2,492.2	398.4

Which areas are most affected? St. Louis is split in half by Delmar Boulevard, with the north side having higher crime rates than the south side. Locals point to north-side neighborhoods such as The Ville, Jeff VanderLou, and Walnut Park as areas to avoid after dark and when traveling solo.

My advice? If you're visiting St. Louis, exit the airport (located on the north side) and stay on I-70 heading south. Do not pass "go," do not stop until you're dumped off downtown. Same deal for I-55 and I-64/U.S. 40, which also converge downtown; just keep driving until you see the river.

Flint, Michigan

The city of Flint, Michigan, was put on the map—or, some might argue, taken off the map—by Michael Moore's 1989 documentary *Roger & Me,* chronicling the aftermath of the General Motors factory shutdown, which eliminated more than 30,000 jobs and left the one-industry town in dire straits.

After a massive surge in crime through the 1980s and 1990s, Flint's crime stats are only just starting to show some improvement. Locals credit a recent renaissance downtown and near the University of Michigan–Flint, and say that they feel perfectly safe walking around those areas late at night.

But does that mean Flint is a safe place to be? Not really. Large swaths of the city still experience tremendous poverty and gang activity. When you're in town, think of I-69 and the Flint River as natural barriers and stick to the downtown area in between—but avoid heading north (especially on foot and after dark!). For now, skip over the area known as Buick City—once it closed, the site of the GM-Buick headquarters was razed, leaving behind about 235 acres of empty land surrounded by depressed communities.

Check out the 2006 stats comparing Flint with the rest of the country.

TYPE OF CRIME	NUMBER PER 100,000 PEOPLE	NUMBER NATIONALLY PER 100,000 PEOPLE
Murder	45.7	5.7
Rape	120.9	30.9
Robbery	530.2	149.4
Aggravated assault	1,899.3	287.5
Burglary	2,585.9	729.4
Larceny/theft	2,991.8	2,206.8
Motor vehicle theft	1,286.2	398.4

Oakland, California

Oakland is no stranger to crime. News reports were buzzing after Oakland's homicide rate spiked from 93 murders in 2005 to 145 in 2006, making it the deadliest year in more than a decade.

But these 2006 statistics show that murder wasn't the city's only problem that year.

TYPE OF CRIME	NUMBER PER 100,000 PEOPLE	NUMBER NATIONALLY PER 100,000 PEOPLE
Murder	36.4	5.7
Rape	76.7	30.9
Robbery	886.1	149.4
Aggravated assault	906.1	287.5
Burglary	1,271.2	729.4
Larceny/theft	2,187.6	2,206.8
Motor vehicle theft	2,645.0	398.4

Richmond, California

If you don't even know where Richmond, California, is on a map, don't worry; you're not alone. It's basically a smaller version of Oakland (Richmond's population in 2006 was 103,106, and Oakland's was 398,834) immediately to the north, and it suffers from similar economic and social problems.

The great irony is, the city that proclaims itself to be the "City of Pride and Purpose" has an enormous problem with methamphetamine use and gang violence. In 2006, there were 42 murders, 41 rapes, and 637 aggravated assaults, and in 2007, homicides climbed to 47, the highest since the early '90s. Shootings in Richmond got so bad in 2007 that city officials called upon the California Highway Patrol to help police the streets.

A good rule of thumb when traveling through Richmond is that its high-crime neighborhoods—such as the Iron Triangle and nearby Coronado—are west of 23rd Street, which slices through the city and ends at I-580, so stay away from there. The Iron Triangle, a notoriously high-crime zone, is formed by three major railroad tracks, and the southernmost part consists of abandoned lots and run-down buildings. With luck, the ongoing Richmond Greenway Project will transform this abandoned zone into usable green space for locals.

These statistics are especially alarming if you don't know your way around town—particularly at night and while traveling alone. Crime is pretty much divided geographically: The most dangerous part of town is East Oakland, and the second most dangerous is West Oakland.

West Oakland, once a thriving African American middle-class community, has been declining for decades. Bordered by Interstates 880, 580, and 980, this district still reflects remnants of its former glory, with abandoned lots and crumbling Victorian homes.

Within East Oakland (geographically on the southeastern part of the L-shaped city), there are some trendy areas, such as Fruitvale, which are okay to check out, but avoid Oakland's deadliest area, between International Boulevard (formerly known as East 14th Street), Bancroft Avenue, and 66th Avenue. Oakland International Airport is just about 5 miles from here, so once you arrive, get on the I-880 freeway—don't follow Hegenberger Road, which will take you right into the heart of this area.

Camden, New Jersey

How do you spell *dangerous*? In New Jersey, it starts with a capital C, for Camden. Some say that the whole city is unsafe, and I may have to agree.

Newark, New Jersey

You know a city is in trouble when part of a public relations campaign brags that the place has gone 33 whole days without a murder . . . for the first time in 40 years! That was the announcement in Newark on February 15, 2008. And the worst part: This was considered startling news. Newark averages about two murders a week, and the last time it went for this long a stretch without a killing was in 1963.

And to think one of its more bizarre claims to fame is that it was the site of the first Church of Scientology. Who knew?

A once-impressive city post-WWII, Camden had begun to decline by the 1970s, when residents moved out to the suburbs and industry began disappearing. Now, outside of some revitalization on the waterfront, much of Camden is marked by block after block of abandoned buildings.

This is how Camden, with a population around 80,000, stacked up to other cities in 2006.

TYPE OF CRIME	NUMBER PER 100,000 PEOPLE	NUMBER NATIONALLY PER 100,000 PEOPLE
Murder	40.0	5.7
Rape	82.4	30.9
Robbery	965.4	149.4
Aggravated assault	1,026.6	287.5
Burglary	1,472.4	729.4
Larceny/theft	3,034.8	2,206.8
Motor vehicle theft	1,471.2	398.4

That year, Camden saw 32 murders, 66 rapes, and 822 aggravated assaults. Homicide rates in the beginning of 2008 were so jarring that the local *Courier-Post* even published its own handy "homicide map," marking where the first 42 murders of the year took place.

In short, unless you have a grandmother who set her roots in Camden and refuses to leave, there's not a lot of reason to visit.

Birmingham, Alabama

How's this for a front-page newspaper story? On October 4, 2007, Birmingham's *Black & White* posed the question "Right now, for a student at any

Birmingham city school, what are the better odds: being involved in a shooting (as a victim, witness, or perpetrator) before they reach the age of 20, or earning sufficient grades and SAT scores to enter a major university?"

Even though the question was rhetorical, I'm sure members of the city's chamber of commerce weren't too thrilled to read that in their morning paper.

Crime in Birmingham reached a critical point in the 1990s—in 1994, there were an astonishing 135 reported homicides and 4,237 aggravated assaults. Things tapered off later, but as reporter David Pelfrey of *Black & White* wrote in the October 4 piece quoted above, "In terms of pure numbers, it's true that crime is not as severe a problem right now as it was 10 years ago. It's merely a severe problem."

In 2004, there were 59 murders, and by 2006 the number had jumped to 104. That same year, there were also 220 rapes and 1,422 aggravated assaults. By 2007, the number of murders went back down—but not by much—to 93.

Here are all the city's 2006 stats.

TYPE OF CRIME	NUMBER PER 100,000 PEOPLE	NUMBER NATIONALLY PER 100,000 PEOPLE
Murder	44.5	5.7
Rape	94.2	30.9
Robbery	611.8	149.4
Aggravated assault	608.8	287.5
Burglary	2,060.6	729.4
Larceny/theft	5,185.9	2,206.8
Motor vehicle theft	890.9	398.4

Once a thriving steel and iron town (during its heyday it was known as "the Pittsburgh of the South"), Birmingham suffers from a lack of industry, a crumbling public school system, and high crime, so residents flee the urban center. As a result, there are large swaths of downtrodden areas that are only getting worse with time.

Despite that, there are parts of Birmingham, now driven financially by its enormous medical center and banking industry, that are perfectly safe—such as downtown and the area around the university. Both are an easy drive from the airport—just a straight shot on I-59, with little room to get lost.

The city is divided by the north-south I-65, and on the west side, Elyton Village is the starting point of some of the areas that you want to avoid at all costs. Ironically, Elyton Village was named after the Elyton Land Trust, which actually founded the city of Birmingham. In addition, the bustling entertainment district of Five Points South can be extremely risky for muggings and car break-ins after dark, while on the east side, areas adjacent to the airport are definitely not safe at night.

While in Birmingham, also keep in mind that the semirural areas on the outskirts of town can be just as dangerous as the inner city. Why? Well, meth production there now rivals the steel industry of the 1950s. While there aren't too many drive-by shootings or other urban-type crimes here, it's an ugly scene nonetheless.

North Charleston, South Carolina

Don't be fooled—North Charleston isn't part of the city of Charleston, and it's certainly not as nice and genteel. It may not be on your radar for a visit, but because of the similar names, you might end up wandering into the town by accident.

North Charleston became its own city in the early 1970s, and, according to some locals, the city of about 87,000 (as of 2006) is still struggling to find its own identity. Sadly, that identity now includes a lot of drug-related crimes: homicides, shootings, stabbings, robberies.

Police and city officials are fighting a public relations battle as high crime statistics cloud the city's reputation. In 2006, there were 28 murders, 81 forcible rapes, and 828 aggravated assaults. In 2007, the number of forcible rapes increased significantly, considering the size of the population.

Take a look at how North Charleston's crimes in 2006 stack up against those of the rest of the country—scary numbers, given it's such a small city.

TYPE OF CRIME	NUMBER PER 100,000 PEOPLE	NUMBER NATIONALLY PER 100,000 PEOPLE
Murder	31.9	5.7
Rape	92.4	30.9
Robbery	620.6	149.4
Aggravated assault	944.6	287.5
Burglary	1,518.5	729.4
Larceny/theft	5,749.8	2,206.8
Motor vehicle theft	1,253.8	398.4

Neighborhoods that you want to skip include Chicora-Cherokee, which suffers from the highest crime rate in the city; Ferndale; Charleston Farms; Dorchester Terrace; and Waylyn.

Memphis, Tennessee

A grisly March 2008 murder in Memphis's Binghamton neighborhood left four adults and two children dead and three other children in critical condition—prompting locals to wonder what caused the decline from a mixed-income community to a downtrodden, gang-ridden area with only a handful of redeeming places remaining.

Crime stats in Memphis show that in 2006, there were 147 murders, 425 rapes, and 7,661 aggravated assaults. Preliminary numbers for 2007 show that the trend continued, with 129 murders, 451 rapes, and 7,603 aggravated assaults.

As you can see from the 2006 crime statistics, violent crimes in Memphis are two to three times the national averages.

TYPE OF CRIME	NUMBER PER 100,000 PEOPLE	NUMBER NATIONALLY PER 100,000 PEOPLE
Murder	21.6	5.7
Rape	62.4	30.9
Robbery	780.1	149.4
Aggravated assault	1,125.2	287.5
Burglary	2,416.2	729.4
Larceny/theft	4,955.1	2,206.8
Motor vehicle theft	986.9	398.4

Ongoing efforts to revitalize downtown Memphis—including the Beale Street area—have been successful, with heavy police presence and the lowest crime rates in the city.

That's the good news. As for the rest of Memphis, it can get pretty rough out there. Avoid Binghamton, part of the blighted east side of town, and the depressed community of Frayser, north of I-40.

In East/Southeast Memphis, just south of I-40/Sam Cooper Boulevard, another neighborhood on a downward spiral is Hickory Hill, which began its decline almost immediately after being annexed by the city in 1998. This neighborhood, say locals, is riddled with crime and foreclosures.

Historic South Memphis, near the Mississippi border, has some mixed areas, but most of it is run-down and dilapidated, with abandoned businesses and factories. So, here's a tip: When you're visiting Graceland, bring your GPS navigator along. Elvis's mansion is located in the Whitehaven section of South Memphis, which is a lively commercial zone, for the most part—but one wrong turn and you'll end up in some much rougher areas.

Youngstown, Ohio

Just an hour away from Cleveland is Youngstown, Ohio. Organized crime, drug trafficking, car bombings, and government corruption in the 1960s earned it the moniker "Murder City, USA." And things haven't gotten much better.

In 2006, there were 32 murders, 48 rapes, and 555 aggravated assaults; compared with 2005, murders remained consistent, rapes went down significantly, but aggravated assaults jumped 14 percent. Given that Youngstown's population is under 100,000, it's pretty shocking to see that its murder rate is more than six times the national average, while rapes and aggravated assaults more than double the national average.

The last stronghold of safe neighborhoods in Youngstown is the West Side. The South Side is absolutely awful, while the north and east sides are just not good. (Use Youngstown State University as your central point.) So, what does that say for visitors? Stick with the downtown area and west of I-680, and well, that's about it. Youngstown ain't that big.

Cleveland, Ohio

Cleveland seems stuck somewhere between a Chicago-like renaissance and a Detroit-like decline. The booming Cleveland Clinic, among other health-care facilities, is helping turn the city into a 21st-century "hospital town," as opposed to a 20th-century "factory town." While the city was once a manufacturing base, many Cleveland businesses, such as Maytag and Whirlpool, have started outsourcing jobs to Mexico.

Cleveland crime got worse in 2007 with 90 homicides, up from 75 the year before. In 2006, there were 445 rapes and 2,196 aggravated assaults, which, compared with national averages, translates to . . .

TYPE OF CRIME	NUMBER PER 100,000 PEOPLE	NUMBER NATIONALLY PER 100,000 PEOPLE
Murder	16.6	5.7
Rape	98.3	30.9
Robbery	947.1	149.4
Aggravated assault	485.0	287.5
Burglary	2,131.4	729.4
Larceny/theft	2,658.4	2,206.8
Motor vehicle theft	1,443.2	398.4

It seems pretty easy to stay out of Cleveland's danger zones, because the city is essentially split in half by the Cuyahoga River (which famously caught fire in 1969, thanks to massive industrial pollution). As for areas to avoid, let's start east of the river, which one local police officer likens to a "war zone." Now, while some of the most famous tourist attractions, such as the House of Blues and several museums, also sit on that side of the river, they are technically located downtown. From there, you would have to drive several miles east before you ran into sketchy areas.

To get more specific, avoid one of the most dangerous neighborhoods in Cleveland: St. Clair–Superior, an area that stretches from East 70th Street to East 123rd, with St. Claire Avenue to the north and Superior Avenue to the south. If you're driving from Cleveland-Hopkins International Airport, St. Clair–Superior is only a couple of exits past downtown on I-90, so watch the road. Farther south, you also want to skip the stretch of Kinsman Avenue from about East 55th Street to 130th Street.

After the subprime meltdown, Cleveland earned the dubious honor of having the neighborhood with the most foreclosures in the nation: Slavic Village. The historic, working-class area was a Cleveland gem—settled by Czech and Polish immigrants—and *the* place to find traditional pierogies and polka. Today, the historic neighborhood is defined by more than 800 vacant homes stripped clean by looters and rampant crime.

Honorable Mentions

Washington, DC

Washington, DC, has come a long way since it earned the nickname "the Murder Capital of the United States" in the early 1990s. In 1991, the tiny district peaked at 482 homicides with a population of just 600,000—meaning that the homicide rate was 80 per 100,000 people.

That same decade, the crack epidemic reached astronomical proportions, even infiltrating the government—DC's own mayor, Marion Barry, was arrested for possession of crack cocaine during a sting operation in 1990.

Crime rates in the nation's capital have improved steadily over the years: In 2006, DC saw 8,408 violent crimes, 169 murders, 182 rapes, and 4,453 aggravated assaults. Compare that with 7 years earlier, when there were 239 homicides, 251 rapes, and 4,582 aggravated assaults. Or 1993, when there were 454 murders, 324 rapes, and a stunning 9,003 aggravated assaults.

Terrific news, right? Not quite. On July 11, 2006, following a surge in homicides, police chief Charles H. Ramsey declared a crime emergency in

DC, summoning increased police presence and later enacting a mandatory curfew. That month, 13 people were killed in less than 2 weeks, including the high-profile case of a 27-year-old British activist whose throat was slit in Georgetown. And, if that weren't bad enough, just hours after the crime emergency was declared, two groups of tourists were robbed at gunpoint at the National Mall. Talk about bad PR.

See how our capital city compares with the rest of the nation, based on 2006 crime statistics.

TYPE OF CRIME	NUMBER PER 100,000 PEOPLE	NUMBER NATIONALLY PER 100,000 PEOPLE
Murder	29.1	5.7
Rape	31.3	30.9
Robbery	619.7	149.4
Aggravated assault	765.7	287.5
Burglary	657.9	729.4
Larceny/theft	2,602.1	2,206.8
Motor vehicle theft	1,213.5	398.4

In the past 15 to 20 years, much of the city has been gentrified—and while that improves DC's reputation, it means that crime and gang activity have been pushed farther into Maryland suburbs such as Prince George. What remain are some crime-ridden pockets scattered throughout the city where intense gang activity continues.

So, what spots do you need to watch out for? Even trendy neighborhoods such as Adams Morgan see a lot of late-night petty crime, including muggings and drunken fistfights. But the real heavy-duty stuff takes place in the city's Ward 5, in the northeast quadrant, which includes neighborhoods such as Trinidad. Things have gotten really bad in the 5th District: 10 murders from January to June 2008. In the southeast quadrant, you want to skip the neighborhoods of Anacostia and Berry Farm.

Chicago, Illinois

What comes to mind when you think of Chicago? Blues, comedy, food . . . Eliot Ness? Well, sure, the city that spawned legendary names like Al Capone is deeply rooted in its criminal past, but how does that translate today?

Turns out gang activity is still a major problem in Chicago, according to Jim Wagner, a former FBI agent and the current head of the Chicago Crime Commission, a nonprofit crime-fighting organization established way back

Miami, Florida

Though it has moved past its *Miami Vice* image of bad fashion and a cocaine problem, large areas of this fast-growing city continue to suffer from overcrowding and petty crime. While cocaine abuse has abated somewhat, the city has seen a rise in heroin and designer drugs such as Ecstasy and Ketamine. The number of rapes dropped dramatically between 2006 and 2007, but burglaries went up by 8 percent, and robberies increased by a whopping 17 percent. Perhaps the most infamous neighborhood in all of Miami is Overtown, located just northeast of downtown. Though there are safe pockets, it's not a neighborhood that should be on your must-see list. If you take one wrong turn downtown, you can easily get stuck in this neighborhood along the many one-way streets.

in 1919. In 2006, the commission released *The Gang Book,* a detailed overview of street gangs and their areas of activity in the Chicago metropolitan area.

"It's very similar to the way that we'd look at organized crime in the 1970s," said Wagner, who is widely considered to be an expert on mob crime. "Gangs don't have the family structure, but their methods of operation are similar in the way that they control their territories." In the Capone era, branches of the mafia clashed over neighborhood "franchises" to peddle alcohol; today, gangs such as the Gangster Disciples and the Vice Lords peddle heroin, crack, and marijuana. "They're even starting to infiltrate the political spectrum. They're also moving toward other crimes to launder drug money, which includes financial crimes, mortgage fraud, and identity theft," explained Wagner.

If that's not scary enough, Chicago saw a spate of homicides in April 2008: In one weekend, nine people were killed in 36 shootings. Some specu-

Gary, Indiana

Though Michael Jackson was born in Gary, Indiana, and the city is mentioned in the musical *The Music Man,* little else makes this town a famous, must-visit destination. Known for its grimy steel-mill industrial-scape and trio of interstates, Gary remains riddled with crime and has been referred to as the state's redheaded stepchild.

lated that a crackdown in gang activity put the leaders behind bars, creating a vacuum in undisciplined gangs.

In 2006, Chicago saw 468 murders and 17,445 aggravated assaults. (Forcible rapes were not reported.) According to preliminary data from 2007, things were well on their way to matching those numbers, with 443 murders and 17,424 aggravated assaults.

The good news is that when you look at the 2006 crime statistics, Chicago actually stacks up pretty nicely compared with some other major cities: Its murder rate was *only* a little bit more than double the national average.

TYPE OF CRIME	NUMBER PER 100,000 PEOPLE	NUMBER NATIONALLY PER 100,000 PEOPLE
Murder	16.4	5.7
Rape	53.6	30.9
Robbery	558.0	149.4
Aggravated assault	613.6	287.5
Burglary	848.7	729.4
Larceny/theft	2,938.2	2,206.8
Motor vehicle theft	767.7	398.4

The high-crime areas in Chicago tend to be on the city's west side, where you should stay out of the Garfield Park and Lawndale neighborhoods, and the infamous South Side—don't go south of Roosevelt Road. The touristy

San Juan, Puerto Rico

When a destination calls itself "the Isle of Enchantment," I wouldn't expect to be stepping into one of the deadliest cities in America. Puerto Rico's capital city of San Juan, where 1.5 million of the island's 4 million residents live, is on the losing side of a bloody drug war. In 2007, San Juan saw 167 murders—down slightly from 174 murders in both 2006 and 2005. The city of Ponce also suffers from a high murder rate, with 59 homicides in 2007 and 62 in 2006 (though that's down from 2005, when a spike in murders shot to 101). The good news in all this? Because so much of the violence is drug-fueled, visitors generally don't get caught up in it. Still, you need to watch out for petty crimes such as mugging, carjacking, and theft. One tip: Leave the camera behind if you're visiting these urban centers. Not only can it get stolen, but you also don't want to inadvertently catch a drug deal on film.

zones are around the north fronts close to the lake, so while there's little likelihood of stumbling into the danger zones, be careful when you're driving south on the expressway from the Loop toward Indiana—one wrong exit and you could be in some dangerous territory.

International Destinations

Danger, of course, is a relative term. I've been to Iraq, but I think that bungee jumping and skydiving are dangerous. I'd probably go to Afghanistan before I'd stroll through Compton, California. And, not surprisingly, you probably have your own definition of what constitutes real danger.

One thing you may know about me is that I don't really trust State Department warnings regarding other countries. One reason is that if you applied to U.S. cities the same criteria the U.S. government uses to assess the danger of overseas destinations, we'd never leave our own homes.

And now there are dozens and dozens of advisories. "We have a responsibility to inform Americans about traveling and living safely overseas," says Doug Koneff, director of the Office of American Citizen Services and Crisis Management. "This came from the Pan Am 103 crash in Lockerbie—at that time, there were threats to commercial aviation that were not shared with the public. We now apply a firm policy, called the 'No Double Standard' policy, that information on risks shared with official Americans must be shared with private Americans as well. If we're telling embassy employees to avoid travel to a particular city, we have to notify private Americans, too."

Now, take a look at the State Department's warning on Afghanistan:

> The Department of State continues to strongly warn U.S. citizens against travel to Afghanistan. No part of Afghanistan should be considered immune from violence, and the potential exists throughout the country for hostile acts, either targeted or random, against American and other western nationals at any time. . . . There is an on-going threat to kidnap and assassinate U.S. citizens and Non-Governmental Organization (NGO) workers throughout the country. Travel in all areas of Afghanistan, including the capital, Kabul, is unsafe due to military operations, landmines, banditry, armed rivalry among political and tribal groups, and the possibility of terrorist attacks, including attacks using vehicular or other improvised explosive devices (IEDs). The security environment remains volatile and unpredictable.

Phew, just looking at that, of course I can understand not wanting to include Afghanistan in your next family vacation. But, according to some folks, travel to Afghanistan is a must-do experience . . . as long as you go to the right places. Janet Moore runs a company called Distant Horizons, which takes tour groups to Asia and the Middle East. "Our trips include countries like Iran and Libya, and our Afghanistan program covers Kabul, Herat, Mazar, and Bamiyan, but we never venture south of Kabul toward Kandahar." (Keep in mind, Distant Horizons was also the company that took a tour group to Saudi Arabia 3 weeks after 9/11!)

Jonathan Daniel, of Afghan Logistics & Tours, also takes groups to Afghanistan. "There are select areas that we visit, such as Bamiyan, Bandi-Amir, and the Shomali Plains," he reports, "but we take the appropriate security approach to each region." Those security measures include traveling in very small groups, usually three or fewer; always traveling with a driver/translator who is familiar with the area; and briefing travelers on Islamic culture and traditions.

That said, there are several countries that you should travel to only with an experienced tour company or private guide who knows the lay of the land. Afghanistan is one.

"Driving around by yourself without in-depth knowledge of the country, roads, etc., is not advised," says Daniel. "Bribery can be a big problem, and if you don't know what to do when a guard stops you at a checkpoint, or even at the airport, a novice might panic."

Another country that you don't want to travel to without an experienced guide is Iran—not because the country is so dangerous, but because the Iranian government requires that American visitors be accompanied by a guide. Make sure the guide is knowledgeable about the area and can translate for you.

Travel to Iran can be an incredibly rewarding experience—Tehran is extremely safe, and other parts of the country boast word-class skiing, subtropical rain forests, vast deserts (try camel trekking!), and water sports in some of the most pristine waters in the world. The places you probably want to avoid are in the southeastern part of the country, around the city of Zahedan, toward the Pakistani and Afghan borders. Kidnapping is a risk here for travelers, and the area has been infiltrated by drug smugglers. The northwestern part of Iran, toward Kurdistan (or northern Iraq), is also a problem area, but here an experienced guide can probably get you through police checks with little problem.

Travel to Iraq? Now, that's just crazy . . . or maybe not.

Turns out, there are parts of Iraq that are perfectly safe for travelers, and in fact, Americans are not only tolerated but welcomed. Kurdistan (don't call it northern Iraq to locals) is an autonomous region—it even has its own airport, Erbil International, which flies the Kurdish flag.

The key here is flying to Erbil, *not* Baghdad. In fact, Austrian Airlines—among other carriers—has regularly scheduled flights there from Vienna. "I would not be comfortable sending a group to Baghdad or even flying there, but the region of Kurdistan is perfectly and utterly safe," says Distant Horizons' Moore, who recently launched the first tour group to Kurdistan. Though solo travel to Kurdistan is permitted, and doable, I don't recommend it.

Okay, so now that I've cleared up all that confusion, let's focus on some real danger areas. I call them the access of evil.

Yemen

Yemen has had quite a reputation for kidnapping foreigners. In 1998, the world took notice when 16 travelers—12 Britons, two Australians, and two Americans—and four Yemeni drivers were taken hostage as they drove in the southern province of Abyan from Habban to Aden. A shootout the following day killed four of the victims—three Brits and one Australian.

The violent ending to this crisis, however, is something of an anomaly. The kidnappers in this case were Islamic militants, led by Abu Hamza, a Sunni Muslim leader and Al Qaeda supporter. What you hear about more often in this region is something called "tribal kidnapping," in which tribes snatch visiting foreigners to get the attention of the government in order to air their political grievances—demands have ranged from better health care and improved roads to pardoning prisoners. Most of the time, hostages are released, unharmed, within days, and many even report having had pleasant experiences with their kidnappers. There have even been travelers who actively sought out being kidnapped while traveling through the country! That practice, however, has decreased drastically since the 1998 killings.

The Web site Al-Bab.com counted 47 kidnappings in Yemen from 1996 to 2001, 21 of which involved travelers and 26 of which involved expatriates. The site's founder explained that he stopped tracking after 2001 because kidnapping had become a less important issue, although he pointed out that there have been incidents as recently as 2006, when tribesmen seized five Italian tourists and another group kidnapped five Germans on a family vacation.

If you are traveling in Yemen, avoid driving—even on that beautiful desert road from the capital city of Sana'a east to Seiyun. Trust me, you don't want to get involved in any kind of kidnapping situation—tribal or otherwise. The good news is, now you can fly between those two cities.

Tijuana, Mexico

Mexican border towns have historically had their share of problems, and Tijuana, in the state of Baja, is no exception. Though it's still a haven for hedonistic travelers seeking cheap tequila and a good party, there has been an alarming increase in crime against U.S. citizens. You know things are bad when drug cartels have ramped up the number of kidnappings and shootings—so much so that during recess, children in local schools are practicing how to survive a shootout.

There has been an alarming increase in kidnappings of American citizens—and it's not just random instances. Reports have revealed well-planned kidnappings of U.S. citizens for ransom. According to the FBI's San Diego office, in 2007, at least 26 residents of San Diego County were kidnapped and held for ransom in Tijuana, Rosarito Beach, or Ensenada, compared with 11 cases in 2006 and 10 in 2005. It should be noted that most of the victims did some sort of business in Mexico or had family members over the border, but that doesn't change the fact that it's happening. "It's happening for a number of reasons, but it appears that it's a successful profit-making venture for these kidnapping criminal enterprises," said Special Agent Darrell Foxworth, of the FBI's San Diego office.

Even though many kidnap victims tend to have some ties with Mexico, that doesn't mean you're out of the woods—there's also something in Tijuana and Mexico City called express kidnapping. . . . That's right.

"These are not planned and don't last very long," says David Robillard, deputy regional managing director of Kroll, a consulting firm that helps businesses, agencies, and individuals reduce their exposure to risk. "An express kidnapping typically lasts about 4 hours. [The kidnappers] will force you to take out as much money as you can from an ATM, then hold you for a few hours until after midnight, when you can take out your next daily limit. Then they probably dump you off somewhere far away." There are no official statistics available on how many express kidnappings take place in cities like Tijuana.

Also causing fear among would-be border crossers, in April 2008, Tijuana experienced one of its bloodiest killing sprees when a massive gang shootout near a shopping mall killed 13 people.

Common sense, of course, is key here. Don't go to an ATM late at night. Don't take a cab that has no meter, and carefully compare the photo ID (make sure there is one) with the driver—there have been many cases of set-up robberies in pirated cabs. Don't carry wads of cash or wear expensive jewelry. But, conversely, don't walk around with no cash at all—that will just anger your muggers. Keep about $200 in your wallet and you may be able to avoid an express kidnapping altogether.

São Paulo and Rio de Janeiro, Brazil

Violence and corruption have sullied Brazil's reputation for decades, and not without reason. In 2003, Amnesty International released a report that compared violence in São Paulo and Rio de Janeiro with that of war zones in Israel and the Palestinian territories!

However, if you travel there, your biggest concern in these two Brazilian cities remains petty crime, such as theft, and commonsense rules apply: Don't show up at the airport with a camera around your neck and flashing your expensive watch, or you just may find that a motorcycle-riding criminal has followed you to your hotel and will rip you off while the motorcycle is still moving.

Express kidnapping is also a concern here, although Brazilian officials wisely implemented a system that allows ATMs to dispense only about $70 per person between 10 p.m. and 6 a.m. (except at airports).

One of the really big issues in Brazil is not the criminals, but the people who are supposed to protect you! Corrupt police officers are a major problem in Rio—to the point that "thousands of people were killed in confrontations with the police, often in situations described by the authorities as resistance followed by death. Police were responsible for numerous killings in circumstances suggesting extrajudicial executions," reads the Amnesty International report.

According to Philip Alston, UN Special Rapporteur, in just the first half of 2007, it was estimated that 694 deaths caused by police were extrajudicial killings (without the permission of a court or legal authority). Bottom line? When in Brazil, don't go to the cops for help unless you're in an extremely touristic zone or are in dire need of help.

São Paulo is a sprawling metropolis, more popular with business travelers than with pleasure seekers. That means its financial center is well equipped with security cameras and enough police presence to deter criminals—in fact, crime has decreased drastically over the past 7 years. That hasn't stopped the U.S. Department of State from rating São Paulo's crime rate as "critical," pointing to evidence of violent crimes throughout the state with "various degrees of severity." But as a traveler, you really want to stay away from the suburbs.

In Rio, the problem is that the city's poshest districts nudge right up against some of its poorest neighborhoods (known as *favelas*). While there are parts of the West Zone that aren't too bad (like the newer Barra da Tijuca neighborhood), other parts are plagued by extremely high levels of violence and crime and packed with favela housing. The North Zone houses the main airport, the main state university, the national museum, and a few other notable attractions, but they're interspersed with slums in some areas. The South Zone is the area most tourists hit up and includes famous beaches such as Ipanema and Copacabana, but even this area is not free of crime by any means—although at night Ipanema is far preferable to Copacabana, where you are just asking to be mugged.

Wondering why you don't see too many convertibles in these cities, despite the perfect weather for it? Carjacking is a massive problem in Brazil. That's also why natives of the city, known as Cariocas, will ignore red lights if there's no traffic—they don't want to stop unnecessarily and open themselves to carjacking. Also watch out on major highways late at night. Why? Most are surrounded by favelas, making them prime targets for both gangland shootings and carjackings.

Johannesburg, South Africa

Though not quite as bad as the reputation it has acquired, South Africa's biggest city is still a dangerous, crime-ridden zone that has a very long way to go. You can have a wonderful experience here, given the huge array of restaurants, bars, galleries, and museums, but you need to have your defenses up at all times.

This is a city where violent crime continues to be a major concern for locals and visitors alike. One thing you'll notice when you visit Johannesburg is that it's a city of walls and gates. The rich and middle-class barricade themselves behind lines of defense, but break-ins and robberies are still common occurrences in these sectioned-off mansions.

Since you don't have portable walls around you for constant protection, it's not recommended that you walk even 5 minutes from your hotel to the restaurants down the street at night. Also, know that travelers have often been followed from the airport and robbed on their way to their hotels.

According to the South African Police Service, from April 2006 to March 2007, there were 611 murders. Carjackings, another common crime in Johannesburg, numbered a scary 2,332 incidents from 2006 to 2007, up from 2,112 the previous year. Locals drive with their cars locked, no matter what the time of day or which neighborhood they're in.

One of the lingering problems the city faces is violent sexual assault: From April to December 2007, there were 1,353 rapes and indecent assaults—slightly fewer than in previous years, but still a significant issue. In fact, the city has earned the unpleasant reputation of being South Africa's "rape capital." CIETafrica (Community Information and Epidemiological Technologies), an international group of epidemiologists and social scientists, released a report in 2001 entitled *Beyond Victims and Villains: South Johannesburg, 1997–2000*. The report found that one in five men said that they had had sex

Shadow Cities

There are subcultures of danger out there—and they sprout up all over the world. They are cities without titles. You won't find highway signs pointing you to their location. They are embarrassments to their governments as well as to the billion-plus people worldwide, known as squatters, who are forced to live there because they don't have any other choice. Considering the squalid living conditions, these neighborhoods are, by even the most basic definition, dangerous—to residents and visitors alike. Theft, gang-related homicides, drug dealing, and prostitution are just a few of the crimes that plague these "shadow cities."

Most people don't "visit" these places in cities such as Rio de Janeiro, Nairobi, Mumbai, and Istanbul . . . just to name a few. They stumble upon them. Every year, close to 70 million people leave their rural homes and head for cities in search of opportunities for a better life. Want to do the math? It works out to 130 people every single minute of every hour of every day. For example, already, one-fifth of the people of Rio are squatters; it's estimated that by the midpoint of this century, there will be *three billion* squatters in the world. That works out to more than one-third of all people on the planet. And since developers have shown no interest in building for the poor, the inevitable result of ongoing poverty is already with us—as well as the crime, pollution, and high murder rates that inevitably are attached when have-nots are forced to live in intolerable conditions.

with a woman without her consent. Eighty-five percent of men said that they knew someone who had been raped, 7 percent of those thought the woman enjoyed it, and 16 percent thought the woman "asked for it."

The bottom line is that you need to be careful in almost any Johannesburg neighborhood, from the inner-city neighborhoods, such as Berea and Hillbrow, all the way to the outskirts, from Alexandra in the northeast to the Soweto township in the southwest. It's a sprawling city, not unlike Los Angeles, so while you may find some safe little pockets to walk around in, keep your guard up and use your common sense.

Kingston–Spanish Town, Jamaica

Jamaica is one of those destinations that most visitors see through rose-colored (or alcohol-hazed) glasses. Travelers who don't venture beyond the resorts in Negril, Ocho Rios, and Montego Bay see only the white-sand beaches and beautiful waterfalls. But there's a whole different—dangerous—world that exists outside the resorts.

Murders, shootings, robberies, sexual assaults, and burglaries plague Jamaica. In 2007, the island saw a substantial rise in shootings (14 percent) and break-ins (11 percent), compared with 2006.

According to the Overseas Security Advisory Council, managed by the U.S. Department of State's Bureau of Diplomatic Security, the greater Kingston metropolitan area, which includes Kingston, St. Andrew, and St. Catherine, is the most dangerous part of the island. Now, while the Kingston police department is reluctant to divulge the number of murders that have occurred in the city, I can tell you that in 2007, there were 1,574 murders in Jamaica. (And, for the record, 146 of the victims were women and 65 were children.) This rate is up 17 percent from 2006, when there were 1,340 murders on the island.

Though Kingston is a sprawling city, the central part is broken into downtown and New Kingston. In short, don't go downtown, especially at night. Gang-ridden streets can unexpectedly erupt into violence, but the bigger risk for travelers is mugging and carjacking. Heading west toward Spanish Town means entering a war zone.

The outskirts of Jamaican cities are also of major concern. In Montego Bay, for example, the central city zone is chaotic with drug deals, street hustling, and muggings, but the real concern is when tourists drive their rental cars into the hilly outskirts. From Montego Bay up to Maroon Town, you might stumble into remote areas that are dominated by drug lords and gangs. Not exactly what you had in mind on your vacation—so the point is, stay within your resort, and don't go exploring the city and beyond.

Port-au-Prince, Haiti

Would I go to Haiti? Sure, but it sucks. It has almost always sucked, destroyed by a chronic history of violent crime and poverty. And, most recently, kidnappings.

That's right, as in Yemen, kidnapping is a big risk here. The only difference is that in Haiti, there are definitely no tourists looking to be kidnapped for the thrill of it. This is serious stuff. According to the U.S. State Department, kidnappings here usually involve physical and sexual assault, and victims are often killed. In June 2008, the UN reported that at least 169 people had been kidnapped in Haiti so far that year, primarily in the capital city of Port-au-Prince.

For some perspective on how bad things are, take American Airlines, which flies daily scheduled service from Miami to Port-au-Prince. Each flight lands as if it's in a war zone: The crew stays on the plane, and the aircraft tends to already have enough fuel to make the return trip—no refueling needed on the ground. And with good reason: The airline doesn't think Haiti is safe enough to leave either its planes or its crews overnight. The AA planes land, disgorge passengers, board new passengers, and fly back to Miami within an hour of the original arrival time. I've interviewed longtime American Airlines pilots who are veterans of the Haiti route and admitted to me that in all their time flying to Haiti, they have never left the airport.

That said, Haiti—the poorest nation in the Western Hemisphere—is a tropical Caribbean island, which means that the tourism industry is trying to get a piece of it. In fact, in 1986, Royal Caribbean took part of the north coast and made it its own private resort, called Labadee. High security and strict controls over which merchants can set up business in the resort keep this 260-acre area safe from crime. Though the local economy does, in fact, benefit from this kind of faux-paradise setup, you're not exactly going to depart Haiti feeling that you've had an authentic experience.

Not that many travelers would want to experience the real Haiti. Besides kidnapping, there's violence, prostitution, drug trading, overcrowding, political instability . . . you name it, and Port-au-Prince has it. If you do decide to go there, only a few sections of town stand out as being safe for travelers, notably Pétionville, which is actually a separate suburb and has a bustling nightlife that caters to tourists and expats.

HUMAN RIGHTS
AND CORRUPTION

HOMES OF THE BRAVE, LANDS OF THE FEE

When it comes to travel decisions, the subject of corruption confuses, frustrates, and often misleads many of us. If a country is corrupt, if it has a continuing legacy of human rights abuses, do you go there?

Some have argued—convincingly—that travel breaks down barriers and builds bridges of peace and understanding. But before you all break into a chorus of "Kumbaya," think about it another way.

Travel has a huge economic impact on individual economies, so where you have blatant examples of corruption or human rights abuses, I firmly believe that you can—and should—vote with your wallet. Don't go there.

What exactly constitutes a human rights violation? The definition goes back to 1948, when the General Assembly of the United Nations issued the Universal Declaration of Human Rights, stating that human rights are "a common standard of achievement for all peoples and all nations" and that "recognition of the inherent dignity and of the equal and inalienable rights of all members of the human family is the foundation of freedom, justice and peace in the world. . . . [A] world in which human beings shall enjoy freedom of speech and belief and freedom from fear and want has been proclaimed as the highest aspiration of the common people."

Sounds good. Except that 60 years later, dozens of countries still openly ignore the declaration.

2007 Corruption Perceptions Index

Each year, Transparency International (TI) releases its Corruption Perceptions Index, ranking 180 countries by their "perceived levels of corruption, as determined by expert assessments and opinion surveys." The list relies on 2 years' worth of data from 14 sources originating from 12 independent institutions. Experts on the countries evaluate the extent of corruption in each location and assign it a score from 0 to 10. The lower the score, the more corrupt the country. TI defines corruption as private gain being acquired by abuse of public office (such as embezzlement, bribery, kickbacks, and so on).

The most corrupt countries in the world in 2007 were . . .

COUNTRY	SCORE
Myanmar	1.4
Somalia	1.4
Iraq	1.5
Haiti	1.6
Tonga	1.7
Uzbekistan	1.7
Afghanistan	1.8
Chad	1.8
Sudan	1.8
Democratic Republic of the Congo	1.9
Equatorial Guinea	1.9
Guinea	1.9
Laos	1.9
Bangladesh	2.0
Cambodia	2.0
Central African Republic	2.0
Papua New Guinea	2.0
Turkmenistan	2.0
Venezuela	2.0
Zimbabwe	2.1

As for corruption, do we really need a United Nations definition of the word to be able to identify it around the world? You know it when you see it.

What places should you avoid? We checked in with organizations ranging from Amnesty International to Transparency International, a nonpartisan group leading the fight against corruption; Freedom House, a nonprofit, nonpartisan organization dedicated to promoting worldwide freedom; Human Rights Watch; and Reporters Without Borders.

Here is my ever-expanding list of corrupt and sanction-violating don't-go-there places.

Myanmar

Though Myanmar (formerly known as Burma) tied with Somalia as the number one most corrupt country in the world in Transparency International's 2007 Corruption Perceptions Index, it took a devastating natural disaster to spotlight the Burmese government as one of the worst violators of human rights in modern memory.

On May 2 and 3, 2008, Cyclone Nargis ravaged the country, killing upwards of 130,000 people and rendering another one million homeless. But that wasn't the biggest travesty of all. In the most critical days following the disaster, the notoriously paranoid and reclusive military government refused to accept foreign aid, seizing food and medical supplies while refusing citizens access to disaster relief experts and medical professionals. This blatant and unapologetic violation of human rights subjected thousands to the risk of starvation, injury, and disease. Reports of residents of the devastated Irrawaddy Delta being forced to work in exchange for food were just one example of the atrocities suffered by the Burmese population.

The military junta, which seized power of what was then Burma in 1988, is lead by General Than Shwe, who is considered one of the world's most secretive and repressive leaders. His citizens anxiously await the country's new constitution, which was promised to them 17 years ago. Examples of the military junta's ironhanded approach are manifold.

Burmese activist U Ohn Than, known for his solo and nonviolent protests, conducted a silent demonstration outside the U.S. Embassy in Rangoon in August 2007. The poster he held was mild in diction, calling for parliament to reconvene and for oil prices to be reduced. Ohn was hit with a fine of less than $1 and a life sentence in prison. He committed no known offense.

One month later, 31 peaceful activists were confirmed killed during a 5-day government crackdown on protests, but it's estimated that more than 100 people were actually killed, including several Buddhist monks. The crowd of demonstrators was attacked with batons, tear gas, and both rubber bullets and live rounds of gunfire. Thousands from the crowd were detained at deteriorating holding centers, where some reported being held in rooms meant for dogs. These secret centers fail to comply with international standards of prisoner treatment, reportedly withholding or giving inadequate amounts of food, water, blankets, sleeping space, sanitary conditions, and medical treatment. Throughout 2007, Myanmar denied the International Committee of the Red Cross access to the country to perform its core mandated activities.

Myanmar offers no safeguards for fair trials, and many detainees in general report having been tortured by being beaten, forced to "kneel barelegged for long periods on broken bricks," or made to stand on their tiptoes for hours at a time. Monks were forced to eat in the afternoon, which is sacrilege for them, and were stripped of their robes.

While all this was happening in 2007, the Pacific Asia Travel Association estimated that more than 248,000 tourists were visiting Myanmar. Those record numbers have been dropping steadily since the military crackdown and even further since the cyclone. The country's tourism sector has been dealt a major blow, but these days, I'm one of many travel professionals who are calling for a boycott of this brutal and corrupt regime by halting tourism until there is a change.

North Korea

Kim Jong Il is often on *Parade*'s list of the "most dangerous" dictators. And according to some accounts, his day-to-day behavior is irrational, unpredictable, a few might even say crazy. Since he inherited the position of "absolute ruler" of North Korea after his father's death in 1994, Kim's reputation as a booze-swilling playboy in his private life has been contrary to the behavior he exhibits in ruling his country.

"Lil' Kim" wears 4-inch platform shoes and his hair in a pompadour to hide his minuscule 5'3" stature. He consumes bottles of Hennessy cognac, each costing a whopping $630, and was reported to have spent $20 million on 200 Mercedes vehicles in 1998.

Oh, and Kim reportedly tested nuclear weapons in 2006.

Perhaps the worst of the dictator's violations are his flagrant human rights abuses. Citizens in North Korea may be more isolated from the world than those of any other country, earning it the nickname "the Hermit Kingdom." North Koreans live under the constant threat of famine, with 12 percent of the population suffering from severe hunger.

North Korea is a Communist state, but it follows the ancient ruling model of Confucianism, which is largely centralized and follows paternalistic leadership—more or less an authoritarian system. All social, political, and economic aspects of life are rigidly governed, and citizens are denied all basic rights. The state has complete dominion over all media, and televisions and radios are permanently stuck on state channels. Even though freedom of religion is a constitutional right, in reality it's nonexistent—citizens are able to participate only in state-sponsored religious organizations, such as the Korean Buddhists' Federation and the Christian Federation.

Thousands of political prisoners experience brutal treatment, and a common sentence is "collective punishment"—the imprisonment of an entire family if officials suspect even one member of dissent. Often, individuals convicted of petty crimes, such as stealing bread, are executed by hanging or by firing squad.

Cambodia

Transparency International notes that corruption has pervaded almost every sector of Cambodia, and much of it is fueled by travel-and-tourism money. Think of it as a pyramid, in which the lowest of public servants rely on bribes to earn their living, but the payments are passed on to the highest-ranking officials. Want to buy a train ticket? You may have to pay an "extra" fee. If you hire a driver, don't be surprised if you're pulled over by the police to pay a fine—and I wouldn't recommend refusing.

After trying to escape from North Korea to China, some citizens were forcibly returned, suffered torture or ill treatment, and were sentenced to up to 3 years' imprisonment. According to the most recent Amnesty International report, citizens have told of "enforced disappearances among families of North Koreans who left the country or were forcibly returned." The punishment of repatriation was the most horrendous for pregnant women, who were forced to have abortions in terrible medical conditions.

In recent years, the traditionally reclusive North Korea has opened its borders to U.S. citizens during restricted periods—namely in August during the Mass Games, also known as the Arirang, a colossal and patriotic choreographed performance. And in a move almost duplicating the ping-pong diplomacy in China in 1971, the New York Philharmonic was invited to perform in North Korea (and it did in February 2008).

China

This one is a tough call. When you consider the Chinese government's human rights violations against its own citizens and the people of Tibet, you've got the makings of a must-miss destination. Though an ongoing PR campaign to clean up its image—which went into full force to promote the 2008 Olympics—has built China into an even more highly touristed (and safe) destination, there are still flagrant issues that we should not ignore.

The U.S. State Department reports that China has violated 22 types of human rights during Hu Jintao's dictatorship, with such acts as torture, forced abortions, forced labor, detention of religious groups, government corruption, and speech and media restrictions. Curiously, though, no significant travel advisories or warnings have been issued to U.S. citizens, aside from earthquake-related warnings in May 2008—such is the economic power of this American trading partner.

In 2006, the Chinese government prohibited critics of the regime and thus detained and arrested dissidents, journalists, and lawyers. Violence erupted in November 2006 in Shunde, Guangdong Province, when outgoing crooked local officials didn't want to give up their power—they hired thugs to attack newly elected officials and anyone who supported them.

In 2007 and 2008, an increasing number of human rights activists were imprisoned or subjected to house arrest or surveillance. In China, an individual can be sentenced to death and executed for any one of 68 offenses—most of which are nonviolent crimes, such as corruption or drug-related

> ## When Corruption Leads to Tragedy
>
> Want a prime example of how government corruption can pervade even the most basic infrastructure in a country? It's all about corrupt building inspectors. Take the case of the magnitude-7.9 earthquake that struck China on May 12, 2008. Shoddily constructed schools collapsed while government buildings stood strong. Nearly 300 students died at a school in Juyuan, where the building had been constructed with prefabricated concrete slabs and the main classroom building lay parallel to the fault line.

offenses. In that same period, censorship of the Internet and other media became more prevalent, and around 500,000 people suffered punitive detention—without charge or trial. They were forced to participate in "reeducation through labor" or other types of punishment.

In Tibet, most of the human rights that we take for granted are denied. Tibet was once a free, independent kingdom until the Chinese Communist government came in and took control, restricting Tibetans' freedom of religion, expression, and association. Grisly forms of torture continue to be a widespread punishment for political activists: In September 2007, four schoolchildren 14 and 15 years old were beaten and tortured for allegedly writing "free Tibet" slogans on an Amdo region police station.

The people of Tibet revolted against the Chinese government in 1959, but the uprising failed, causing the Dalai Lama, the Tibetans' political and spiritual leader, to flee to India in exile, followed by 100,000 more Tibetans. About 3,000 Tibetans a year continue to escape the country by crossing the treacherous Himalayas through Nepal and into India, where a government in exile exists in Dharamsala. There have been multiple reports over the years of Chinese police shooting at fleeing refugees, while the Nepalese government is under increasing pressure to return fleeing Tibetans.

Egypt

In general, Egypt is safe for visitors, and in fact its government happily accepts American dollars as readily as it accepts Western tourists. But if you're gay or lesbian, you're probably not welcome. The primarily Muslim nation has strong homophobic beliefs, and in fact, consensual gay sex is punishable by law.

According to Amnesty International and Human Rights Watch, the Egyptian government has issued a crackdown on men who are believed to be HIV positive. Between 2007 and 2008, 12 men were arrested. So far, a total of nine of those 12 have been sentenced to prison on charges of "habitual practice of debauchery": Four are serving 1 year in prison, and five received 3-year sentences. Arrested men have reported being chained to beds and being forcibly tested for HIV, and even undergoing "forensic examinations" to determine whether they've had sex with other men.

Zahir Janmohamed, a Middle East specialist for Amnesty International, advises, first and foremost, don't go into a gay nightclub. They're frequently raided by police officials, and people suspected of being gay are often arrested at random. Similar raids have also happened at restaurants. Even something as seemingly innocuous as a man carrying a copy of *Cosmopolitan* (okay, your wife/girlfriend/best friend's copy) could arouse unwelcome suspicion.

"Arbitrary arrests, forcible HIV tests, and physical abuse only add to the disgraceful record of Egypt's criminal justice system, where torture and ill treatment are greeted with impunity," said a representative of Amnesty International's Middle East and North Africa Program.

But problems in Egypt go even deeper than gay rights. Egypt has been governed under "Emergency Law" with almost no break since 1967 and continuously since 1981, after the assassination of President Anwar Sadat. Emergency Law gives the government every right to arrest people—without stating charges against them. In May 2008, the state of emergency was renewed, despite urging for it to be rescinded.

Janmohamed notes that Egypt is a very safe country overall, especially since it is trying to rebuild its image by welcoming tourists. Just keep a low profile, respect the laws and social norms, and leave your racy magazines at home.

Iran

Mahmoud Ahmadinejad is Iran's president, but Ayatollah Khamenei and the Guardian Council—made up of 12 additional men—actually call the shots, controlling (and interpreting) the country's laws, not to mention its nuclear program.

Under the Guardian Council, freedom of expression is being suppressed more and more, and that includes sexual preference. Janmohamed says that the acceptance of gay, lesbian, and transgender travelers is a concern, and they may feel uncomfortable. In November 2006, an Iranian man was hanged because he was a homosexual.

If you're traveling as an unmarried couple, you could also be scrutinized. Hotel owners looking to stir up trouble (or induce a bribe) often harass travelers for proof of marriage. Even worse, an unmarried woman spending time with a married man could put both of them at risk legally, since under current law this can be considered a criminal offense. Mixed-gender interaction is highly discouraged, even if the relationship is platonic. It is still acceptable for women to be stoned to death for adultery, and also, perhaps not surprisingly, women are expected to dress modestly.

According to Amnesty International, a significant number of political prisoners and "prisoners of conscience" were still serving sentences after unfair trials that occurred before 2006. Many individuals were arbitrarily

Democratic Republic of the Congo

The Democratic Republic of the Congo has been torn apart by war for the past decade, resulting in widespread violence, disease, and malnutrition. On average, 45,000 people die each *month,* and a total of 5.4 million have died, mostly from disease and malnutrition, since conflict broke out in 1998. Though the Congo is one of the poorest nations in Africa, it is also one of the richest in terms of natural resources: namely diamonds, metals, and minerals. Congolese civilians have been killed, tortured, raped, or driven from their homes to secure rich swaths of land, while children as young as 12 have been forced into manual labor in the mines.

detained, including human rights defenders who were journalists, students, and lawyers.

Syria

President Bashar al-Assad may be more liberal than his dictator father, who preceded him, but Syria still has a long way to go when it comes to democratic principles and human rights.

When al-Assad senior died in 2000, the nation was one of the Arab world's poorest countries, largely due to the debilitating Ba'athist rule. The vaguely worded articles of the penal code, Emergency Rule, and a 2001 press statute leave locals and visitors at risk of being detained, especially if they are accused of attacking national unity or the state's image—so don't think you have freedom of speech here. Although Syria is a parliamentary republic, the country still is ruled by the Ba'ath Party, an authoritarian regime.

The key to understanding the dynamic of Syria is to remember that Emergency Rule, which has been used to suspend civil liberties, was imposed in 1963 and still remains in effect. The government limits freedom of expression, association, and assembly. Any verbal or written attack (or what is perceived to be an attack) on the country's leadership or image can be prosecuted.

Academic freedom is also highly controlled. Professors who express dissent in classrooms commonly are dismissed from state universities, and some even get thrown into prison. From January to March 2006, eight stu-

Zimbabwe

This war-torn nation is like the movie *Casablanca* on steroids, rife with chaos, corruption, instability, and absurdity—and there's no happy ending in sight. Inflation is so explosive that you almost need a wheelbarrow to hold enough Zimbabwean dollars to buy a decent dinner. To make matters exponentially worse, the country is struggling with drought, food shortages, and the ongoing HIV/AIDS pandemic. The government of long-standing president Robert Mugabe remains in power only by bribing lower-level government and police officials. Unless Mugabe leaves—either by legitimate electoral vote or by other means—and until some stability returns to the country, my vote is, don't go there.

Russia

It may come as no surprise that greasing a few palms is practically mandatory in many parts of Russia. Bribes, kickbacks, and so-called favors are often the routine for locals, and recently, a Russian prosecutor put a price tag on government corruption: He estimated that corrupt officials skimmed close to a third of the government's annual budget, or about $120 billion. But even visitors can be asked to hand over a few rubles to ease their way past airport security guards or to bypass corrupt cops.

President Dmitry Medvedev has made public vows to combat corruption, but how those words will translate into action remains to be seen. In fact, I'd bet more than a few rubles that nothing will happen, since this culture is so ingrained. Everything else being relative, there's some good news: Moscow has become one of the best cities in the world to secure your own personal bodyguard. That's right, the National Bodyguard Association of Russia has been in business since 1995, and personal protection will cost you only about $30 to $75 an hour.

dents attending universities were arrested, apparently because of their attempts to create a political reform youth movement on campus. Five are still in detention with no charges and are awaiting trial, two were charged with inciting unrest and are undergoing trial, and one was released with no charges.

In November 2007, the government shut down the popular social networking site Facebook, due to online discussions about the president. The following month, political dissidents were arrested in a government crackdown. Interestingly, in a move that showed that political activism can't always be tamped down, hackers managed to crack the Facebook ban, and within 5 months, the number of Syrian accounts rose from 28,000 to 34,000.

Human Rights Watch reports that the regime's human rights violations came to a head in 2006, following the Beirut-Damascus Declaration, which called for improved relations between Lebanon and Syria. Dozens of Syrians who signed the petition were arrested by security forces. Syrian activist Habib Saleh, a writer for the Lebanese newspaper *An-Nahar* who signed the petition, was arrested after criticizing the president and the government in open letters and online forums. Saleh was sentenced to 3 years in prison— his second arrest in 7 years.

Women's rights are also severely repressed in this Muslim country.

"Honor killings" are still prevalent in Syria, with perhaps as many as 300 girls killed each year by close family members. Males enjoy Penal Code provisions that reduce their sentences for killing a female family member who is thought to have committed adultery or to have had sexual relations. In March of 2006, it was reported that a young female was forced to marry the man who had raped her. The marriage was in accordance with Article 508 of the Penal Code—which absolved her husband of the crime.

United Arab Emirates

While the United Arab Emirates is a safe country, visitors definitely need to understand the local rules.

The UAE has some bizarre interpretations of drug laws, and there have been shocking cases that should make you paranoid. In one of the most extreme, a Swiss national ate a bread roll with poppy seeds at Heathrow Airport en route to the UAE. When he arrived at his destination, customs officers found three poppy seeds on his clothes, and he was ultimately sentenced to a 4-year jail term.

In what most people would view as a minor offense, Keith Brown, a British tourist, was sentenced to 4 years in prison for having a 0.003-gram trace of cannabis stuck to his shoe. According to Fair Trials International, a London-based legal charity, cases such as these are occurring more frequently. If you're sick, you may want to suffer the symptoms—if customs officers catch you carrying cold and flu medications, you could be hit with a mandatory 4-year prison sentence.

Amnesty International reports that countries within the UAE violate international human rights laws by not prohibiting "torture, or cruel, inhu-

Bangladesh

The good news is that Bangladesh has dropped from its 2003 first-place ranking in the Transparency International report. The bad news is that corruption continues to be pervasive, ranging from kickbacks on government contracts to misappropriation of public funds to criminals bribing public officials. As in most Islamic countries, expect to pay a small *baksheesh* (tip) in almost every exchange of money you encounter.

man and degrading treatment." Many crimes, such as sex out of wedlock, are subject to these types of punishments. In one case cited by Amnesty International in a July 2006 report, one visitor was sentenced to death by stoning. Was he a murderer? No, he was convicted of having sex with a female domestic worker, who received a flogging sentence of 100 lashes and 1 year of imprisonment. Fortunately, the man's punishment was reduced to 1 year in prison followed by immediate deportation to his home country of Bangladesh, but the woman's sentence was upheld.

The UAE is a business-traveler hot spot, and Dubai's hotel occupancy alone often runs at 85 percent, but if you plan on visiting, make sure to know the laws.

LAMEST CLAIMS TO FAME

Can you remember the name of the town with the biggest ball of twine? (Hint: It's in Kansas.) How about the "Salad Bowl of America"? Some places have so little going on that they have to rely on gimmicks, silly nicknames, and what I like to call . . . lamest claims to fame.

Silly Nicknames and "Capitals"

Gilroy, California

I have nothing against quaint little farming communities. But unless you really, really love garlic, there's not much else going on in Gilroy, a.k.a. the self-proclaimed "Garlic Capital of the World." And they've taken things a little too far. They even sell garlic ice cream in Gilroy. I'll take two scoops . . . *not*.

Delaware

Delaware is known as "the First State"—not because it *was* the first state, but because it was the first of the 13 original states to ratify the U.S. Constitution in . . . oh, sorry, I just fell asleep writing that. That's it? Is that all that Delaware could come up with? That's sad. . . .

Fountain, Minnesota

I think it's bad enough that the folks of Fountain, Minnesota, thought it was a great idea to print a brochure touting this place as the "Sink Hole Capitol [sic] of the USA." Then, they actually made things worse: To illustrate and support their claim, the brochure's cover sports little children riding bicycles. My advice: If you're still determined to go there, leave the bikes at home. The sink holes are "the most dominant land form in this area." And I'm quoting from the brochure!

Berrien Springs, Michigan

If you know what a Christmas pickle is, you're halfway there. It's great when towns hold on to their history, and the Christmas pickle (an ornament hidden in Christmas trees) is an old German-American tradition.

But if you somehow find yourself at the annual Christmas Pickle Festival, do me a favor and don't get so caught up in the action that you come home with a suitcase full of glass Christmas pickles. Trust me, they won't look so cute when you're outside of Berrien Springs.

Eau Claire, Michigan

Is there not enough to do in this part of Michigan? Eau Claire is a village located in east central Berrien County. It also claims to be the "Cherry–Pit-Spitting Capital of the World." And when you think about how lame that is, who would ever want to challenge that claim? Enough said. . . .

Battle Mountain, Nevada

In 2001, the *Washington Post* dubbed Battle Mountain, Nevada, "the Armpit of America." This tiny mining community (population: 2,871), located about 200 miles east of Reno, beat out other top contenders, such as East St. Louis, Illinois; Elizabeth, New Jersey; and Fargo, North Dakota. Well, the following year, Battle Mountain took ownership and threw—what else?— an Armpit Festival, sponsored by—who else?—Old Spice. The event drew thousands of participants and featured a deodorant-tossing competition and a "sweat" T-shirt contest. Out-of-towners, who obviously had nothing better to do, were welcomed by a billboard that read, "Make us your Pit Stop!" Sadly, at least for Battle Mountain, the once-annual event is now defunct, which means that there once again may be no reason to go to Battle Mountain.

Beaver, Oklahoma

The town of Beaver is proud of its title: "Cow-Chip-Throwing Capital of the World." If you have the desire to reach for the stars yourself, you can enter the World Championship Cow Chip Throw, held every April. Just don't be scared off by the statue of a plucky beaver clutching a giant cow chip.

Ashland, Virginia

Unless you can chart the entire universe and pinpoint Ashland, this city's claim to be the "Center of the Universe" has its flaws. And if it's true, then God has a wicked sense of humor indeed.

Fake European Towns

Some American towns strive to be anything but American. Solvang, California, is famous for its replicated Danish windmill and bust of fable writer Hans Christian Andersen. Leavenworth, Washington, has Bavarian storefront facades. Castroville, "the Little Alsace of Texas," prides itself on possessing an original 1600s Alsatian house that was relocated from Wahlbach, France. It may be worth visiting these pseudo-European towns for a day, but forget about wasting an entire weekend.

(continued)

LAMEST CLAIMS TO FAME—*Continued*

Stupid Events

Coalinga, California

Ribbit, ribbit! Do you like horned toads? Enough actually to watch horned toads race against one another? Coalinga, California, throws the Annual Horned Toad Derby, in which live horned toads compete. Unless you've already placed your bet, skip rooting for "Sir Toady."

International Falls, Minnesota

The Freeze Yer Gizzard Blizzard Run in International Falls, Minnesota, is just that: a frigid 5-K or 10-K run. But it also comes with other goodies, such as snow sculpting and—drumroll, please—frozen-turkey bowling.

Luling, Texas

Each year, Luling, Texas, hosts the Luling Watermelon Thump festival. It comes complete with magicians, mimes, fire-eaters, a champion melon contest and auction, a world champion seed-spitting contest, a melon-eating contest, and much, much more. Instead of seeing how far you can spit a watermelon seed, take my advice and buy some watermelon when you get home.

The World's Largest What?

Anniston, Alabama

You may have missed the announcement, but Anniston is the current reigning champion of the ongoing "World's Largest Office Chair" competition. This is a century-old battle, which started in Gardner, Massachusetts, in 1906 (12 feet). Thomasville, North Carolina, entered the fight with a chair that measured 13 feet, 6 inches. The title went from South to North and back again and again, breaking many a Guinness World Record. But the South rose again, and in 1981, Miller's Office Furniture of Anniston, Alabama, built a 31-foot-tall office chair that put the town on the map.

Kansas

It's hard to narrow down just which Kansas town has the lamest claim to fame. The world's largest ball of twine? Cawker City. Home to the world's largest hand-dug well? That title belongs to Greensburg. The world's largest easel? Goodland. The state with the motto "As Big As You Think" is so eager to be noticed that the Kansas Arts Commission gave a grant to World's Largest Things, Inc., a nonprofit organization that helps communities develop their own "largest thing." How about the world's largest absurd excuse for going somewhere?

Chepachet, Rhode Island

If, for some reason, you find yourself in Chepachet, Rhode Island, you'll be faced with a most perplexing statue in front of the town hall. Imagine that Mr. Potato Head and an elephant had a baby. Well, you don't have to imagine—it exists, and she's named Betty, the Learned Elephant. That's right, this 6-foot-tall statue was erected in 2000 as part of a statewide tourism campaign—"Rhode Island—The Birthplace of Fun"—which placed 47 Mr. and Mrs. Potato Heads all over the state. (To be fair, the Potato Head family was born in Pawtucket, Rhode Island.) So why an elephant? The real Betty was a pachyderm that arrived in Chepachet in 1822 from Calcutta, India, as part of a traveling circus, but was shot and killed 4 years later on a bridge over the Chepachet River. On the 150th anniversary of Betty's death—May 25, 1976—a day of observance was officially declared . . . Elephant Day!

Unnecessary Museums and Sites

Dongguan, China

Even though the South China Mall is the world's largest mall, you're probably better off shopping till you drop at your local shopping center. Dubbed "the Ghost Mall," this venue has space to hold 1,500 stores, but it houses fewer than 12. It does sound appealing, though, complete with bumper cars, a Venetian canal, an indoor rain forest, an outdoor roller coaster, and even an 85-foot replica of the Arc de Triomphe. But the place is so devoid of customers that some employees kill time by folding origami, while others simply sleep on the job!

Sedlec, Czech Republic

Most people feel pacified after visiting a heavenly sanctuary—be it a synagogue, church, mosque, or temple—but once you eye the Sedlec Ossuary chapel's chandelier, you're likely to experience nausea rather than enlightenment. Located in Sedlec, Czech Republic, this church's chandelier doesn't drip with crystals; instead, it's freakishly crafted out of bones—at least one of every bone in the human body is incorporated. The church's entire interior is decorated with the remains of more than 40,000 people. Talk about creepy!

Columbus, Georgia

Unless you have fond memories of your mom leaving little notes in your lunch pail and need to be a know-it-all about the history of toting school lunches, you might as well pass up the Lunchbox Museum in Columbus, Georgia. It features thousands of lunchboxes and items like thermoses, lunch trays, and coolers, but

(continued)

it's two sandwiches short of a picnic, so your best bet? Save the money you would have spent on admission and buy a PB&J.

Allenstown, New Hampshire

The Snowmobile Museum in Allenstown, New Hampshire, has—you guessed it—snowmobiles: big ones, small ones, old ones, new ones, a homemade one, and even a first-aid snow-cruiser emergency one. But if you're visiting New Hampshire during the winter holidays, wouldn't you rather *ride* a snowmobile?

Mitchell, South Dakota

Gaudy, clashing, and downright corny, the Corn Palace in Mitchell, South Dakota, is exactly what you would expect from the "Corn Capital of the World." Its fiasco of pseudo-Russian onion towers and mosaics—constructed out of thousands of bushels of corn, grain, wild oats, and other foodstuffs—makes this building an eyesore. The admission is free, but you're better off visiting the Mount Rushmore National Memorial.

Edinburgh, Scotland

Perhaps once state-of-the-art, the Edinburgh Dungeon traces the history of medieval torture devices, but the exhibits lack thrill, as they are merely dusty replicas. For example, Animatronic rats trapped in a metal cage pretend-gnaw on a mannequin's stomach—one technique for punishing a "criminal." And the "adventurous" water ride takes you what feels like 50 feet—basically a low-budget ride from one room to another.

These Places Just Suck

Clipperton Island

As "the world's most traveled man," Charles Veley, notes, Clipperton is one of the toughest places to visit, mainly because of its way-off-the-radar location: It's a whopping 700 miles off the Mexican Pacific coast. Known for its barren landscape of crags and caves, and the sheer, utter isolation that has driven even the burliest adventurers mad, this uninhabitable island makes Alcatraz feel like a cozy, welcoming getaway.

Atlantic City, New Jersey

Once hailed as the "Queen of the Coast" during the 1930s and '40s, Atlantic City, New Jersey, is overwhelmed with casinos, including three Trump Entertainment Resorts and four Harrah's Entertainment properties. No longer in its heyday, this gambling corridor is banking on building more casinos to entice travelers. But if you're going to chance breaking your own bank, you might as well visit world-famous restaurants, entertainment, and casinos in Las Vegas.

Elmira, New York

No more than a blip in the occasional New York State guidebook, Elmira is known as Tommy Hilfiger's birthplace and the burial place of Mark Twain. Perhaps the only intrigue for travelers is the Woodlawn Cemetery, where Twain's burial site resides. Elmira is also fraught with an extreme cat population problem, so much so that the state legislators are trying to give Elmira permission to trap, neuter or spay, and return the cats.

South of the Border, South Carolina

No, it's not in Mexico. This travesty of a tourist attraction is located on the border of North Carolina and South Carolina. It's a combination of a Mexican restaurant, theme park, and truck stop straddling the border—and it's the epitome of where *not* to go on a road trip.

Put simply, this decidedly unauthentic location is nothing less than a tourist trap marked by every racist stereotype you can imagine about the Mexican community.

Let's start with the attraction's Web site, Pedroland.com. Its welcome message is, verbatim: "BUENS DIAS, AMIGO! pedro VER' GLAD YOU COME!! pedro got 112 meelion amigos, who stay weeth heem, opp teel now all satisfy come back, send frans . . . thees make pedro ver' HAPPEE . . . like for frans come back all time . . . pedro hope YOU make 112 meelion and wan happee amigos! you come back soon, too, yes?"

It doesn't end there. The stock image of Pedro? A sombrero-wearing man snoozing soundly against a cactus.

Pedroland Park is a lame assortment of bumper cars, a Ferris wheel, and a rousing glass elevator ride up the 200-foot-tall Sombrero Tower. (But, hey, according to its brochure, "pedro has sometheeng for every juan." Get it? Every juan?)

Oh, and if you're so inclined, you can putt a round or two at the Golf of Mexico. There are also six forgettable restaurants (if you eat there, there's a possibility you really will feel Montezuma's revenge) and, of course, a plethora of chintzy souvenir shops with appealing names such as Myrtle Beach Shop, El Drug Store, and the Leather Shop (don't ask).

If you're driving down Interstate 95, you definitely cannot avoid the countless billboards announcing that South of the Border is up ahead. But you can—and should—avoid South of the Border itself, unless you really want your picture taken under the giant Pedro in the oversize sombrero next to a plastic pink flamingo.

SEE, I'M NOT ALONE

LEGENDARY ROAD WARRIORS WEIGH IN

This book would not be complete without checking in with some other megatravelers to get their lists of places they don't want to go or return to. Toward that end, I asked five legendary road warriors to weigh in.

CHARLES VELEY

If you think I travel a lot, meet Charles Veley, who holds the distinct title of being the most traveled man in the world, according to Guinness World Records, *among other "most traveled people" lists.*

Since 1999, Veley has been dedicated to going "everywhere." He's cajoled his way onto expedition ships, jumped islands illegally in West Africa, and bribed his way into Chechnya. He's already visited 629 of 673 unique countries, territories, autonomous regions, enclaves, geographically separated island groups, and major states and provinces of the world. And yes, he has his Don't Go There List, which he defines as "places that are difficult to get to, and once you get there, you wish you were gone."

Lagos, Nigeria
Every place has neighborhoods you should avoid, but Lagos is a whole city that you shouldn't go into. It was built for about half a million peo-

ple, and now it's got about 15 million people fighting for scarce resources. Add to that a tropical climate, not a lot of money, massive corruption, and tribal rivalries—and you get a real pit.

The thing I remember most about going through Lagos is that the garbage piles up in some places, and people were shoveling paths through neighborhoods and streets. Sometimes, garbage was piled higher than my head. I also remember broken sewer-line pipes with massive flooding—every kind of chaos you can imagine.

What sets Lagos apart is that it's an isolated urban area. If you travel 20 miles out of the city, you're in the unpopulated countryside. It's an example of all that's wrong in the current migratory patterns. People in villages know that there is opportunity elsewhere, so they overcrowd the cities.

In Lagos, if they see that you're white, practically anyone in uniform will ask to see your papers and then ask for money to give those papers back. You have to be on heightened alert at all times, because people are looking to rip you off. Travelers aren't recommended to walk alone, because you're likely to get robbed. The standards in Lagos have deteriorated, and everyone is just too busy, or too apathetic, to help you out.

Amur Highway, Russia

The Amur Highway runs for 1,300 miles from Chita to Khabarovsk and is a section of the Trans-Siberian Highway—an east-west network of federal highways that runs for about 7,000 miles, connecting Russia to Asia.

There are sections of the Amur Highway that have been under construction since the 1970s. In 2004, President Putin officially "opened" the highway with a ribbon-cutting ceremony and a projected completion date of 2008. That's now been pushed back, again, to 2010.

My friend Misha and I were driving around Russia in 2007, trying to visit every state and territory. He said, "There's supposed to be this road. It was impassable previously, but it should be drivable, and I've heard that people do it."

Well, the condition of the road was horrible. In some places the bed wasn't even complete, and about a third of it wasn't paved. It's the vastest countryside in the world, with only one road going across . . . and it's not even a road yet.

In the United States, a construction zone has detours and signage, but here, once in a while there would be a little hand-drawn sign. Other times you'd drive and then stop at a cliff. We were going through some of the most remote areas in the world, with few villages and towns along the way.

We stopped for a night in a little town called Mogocha. In the United States or Europe, when you get off a main road, there will be signage to lead you into town. Russian towns are not like that at all. Here, you have roads that just end. We finally found our way there after midnight, and the whole experience truly felt like purgatory.

Bouvet Island

For extreme travelers who are trying to go "everywhere," Bouvet Island, literally the world's most isolated piece of land, is sort of a holy grail, and it's a requirement for the Guinness Record. It's an uninhabited sub-Antarctic volcanic island that is a dependent of Norway.

The closest port is about 1,500 miles away in Cape Town, South Africa; the nearest piece of land is the uninhabited Queen Maud Land, Antarctica, just over 1,000 miles away. Or you can depart from the Tristan da Cunha islands in the South Atlantic, the most remote archipelago in the world, which is about 1,400 miles away from Bouvet Island.

It took us 5 days to sail there from Cape Town, and Bouvet is one of the most difficult places to land. You need weather suitable to fly a helicopter. The day I went, there were 50-knot winds—and they said that was a calm day.

We were there for a total of about 3 hours, and it was just as gloomy as I had imagined, with dark, volcanic cliffs, massive glaciers, and huge waves. Once you get there, it's freezing cold, with horrible weather. Oh, and it stinks from the seals and penguins that make their way to the edges of the island.

Sahrawi Republic

The Western Sahara is a scorching desert that was abandoned by Spain in the 1970s and is now mostly occupied by Morocco. But the native Sahrawi people, and the liberation group known as the Polisario Front, have been battling for the independence of the Western Sahara since 1973.

There is a 1,700-mile sand wall known as the Berm of Western Sahara that separates the Moroccan-controlled desert on the west from Polisario-controlled land on the east. The east side, which is called the Free Zone, is where the Sahrawi people and the government in exile, the Sahrawi Arab Democratic Republic, exist entirely in refugee camps.

In the far northeastern corner of the Free Zone, looking in from Algeria, there's a gap in the wall where we entered the refugee camps and saw terrible living conditions. These camps have a hundred thousand people living on nothing but rocks and dirt. The temperature can reach well into the hundreds and then drop down to freezing; there are sandstorms and floods that can wipe out everything. Essentially, there's no will to live on the eastern side of the wall.

Shanxi Province, China

Shanxi Province is located in the northern part of China. It is the country's largest coal reserve and produces about 580 million tons of coal annually.

Shanxi Province is sort of the epicenter of China's pollution problems. Because it's coal country, the air pollution is even worse there than in the rest of China. I remember it as a dismal gray zone where a thick layer of coal dust coated everything. The poor rural landscape was completely devoid of color (not that you could see more than 50 feet in front of you), and people had masks on their faces. Very apocalyptic.

It has hills like West Virginia's, but the infrastructure isn't there. We're talking about dirt roads, mud huts, and basic brick buildings, all covered with gray coal dust blocking out the sun. Beijing is a green paradise compared with Shanxi.

Russian Caucasus

The Russian Caucasus is some of the most rugged terrain in the world, separating Europe and Asia. What was once all Soviet is now separated into northern Russian territory and the country of Georgia, on the south.

The farther south and the closer to the mountains you go, the more corrupt it gets. For an outside traveler, it's a nightmare. There are police at every intersection, and if these guys recognize that you're from out of town, they'll probably pull you over and take money. You need to be traveling with a local who can communicate and haggle with them just to get through without being arrested.

The deeper we went, the worse it got. My friend Misha, his father, and I were driving from west to east; at this point we were around Nal'chik, on our way to Vladikavkaz. It was already our fourth police stop of the day. The policeman who stopped us was drunk, swinging his baton and looking like Porky Pig with his belly hanging out.

Misha went over to talk to him, and the police officer said, "So-o-o, do you have something for me to drink? I'm feeling a bit thirsty." I happened to have a bottle of vodka, so we gave it to him. But so that it wouldn't be a bribe, he said to us, "I have a gift for you." And he handed us a ziplock bag full of melted vanilla ice-cream cones! Guess the last guy he stopped didn't have any vodka on him.

Fanning Island

Fanning Island is located in the Pacific, a good 1,250 miles southwest of Hawaii. It seems unbelievable that anyone would even find this 9-mile-wide atoll.

I went in October 2003 as part of a boat journey to visit the region— an extremely poor area, with just a few villages. The thing that makes Fanning Island such a strange destination is that Norwegian Cruise Lines pumped in a couple of million dollars to build a beachfront facade.

It's absolutely bizarre. It's a completely false little playground beach creation. The ship comes in, and cruisers step off the tenders in their stretchy shorts and tennis shoes, kind of blinking in the sunlight. The cruise line makes it seem like an exotic port of call on a Hawaiian itinerary, but it's all artificial.

The strangest part is that Norwegian has a stop here at all. Foreign-flagged ships, which are registered in another country, have to sail to an international destination—they can't just cruise amongst the islands of Hawaii. So at least a day and a half is spent sailing on the open sea, more than 1,000 miles, just to get to Fanning Island. They sail all the way down here and stop for about 7 hours.

The good news is that now Norwegian has U.S.-flagged ships that can cruise just around the Hawaiian Islands, so you don't have to go to Fanning Island—and as of now, Norwegian has put a halt to this itinerary. But if it comes back, don't be fooled by that "international" call.

Kingman Reef

Few people have ever been here, and it's not hard to see why. On the surface, it's a pretty lame destination, but Kingman Reef is definitely on the list for people who want to go everywhere. It's located in the Pacific Ocean, about halfway between Hawaii and American Samoa.

Almost everyone agrees that this is not only an island, it's a distinct territory. It's just about 200 meters' worth of coral stone thrown together—like walking on a gravel pile. The patch where we landed is about a quarter mile long, shaped like a starving yin-yang paramecium, varying in width from a few inches to about 50 feet, and covered with bleached coral and plastic ocean detritus. It just seems kind of pointless.

But there is one silver lining to this very, very dark cloud called Kingman Reef: One thing I could not believe was that somehow coconuts had floated from another island—and were sprouting up on top of the mounds. Coconuts need fresh water, but this is just an isolated dead beach, so these random coconuts, with no roots, would fill up with rainwater and consume themselves for nourishment. Of course, they would eventually die, but for a time, those sprouting coconuts showed that life always does find a way.

Turkmenistan

The nation of Turkmenistan is everything that is bad about Nevada with none of the good stuff. Desert wasteland, mining, and that's about it.

Things in Turkmenistan have been very strange since the Soviet Union fell. The country was ruled until 2006 by "President for Life" Saparmurat Niyazov, who nicknamed himself Turkmenbashi ("Chief of the Turks") and was deeply corrupt. Despite the country's oil wealth, it's extremely poor, and Niyazov spent amazing amounts of money in the capital. He put up golden statues of himself and constructed a series of fountains in the middle of the city, despite limited water supplies!

The thing that struck me is the beautiful market outside of town, like a giant desert swap meet. People wear the most colorful robes, doing all they can to combat the blandness of the desert, the gray sameness of Soviet bureaucracy.

I don't have a burning desire to go back, but it might be interesting to see whether it's changed since Niyazov's death. But it's also one of those places that you don't want to support with your dollars, because of the human rights violations and the exploitation of its environment and its people.

Nicobar Islands

The Nicobar Islands are an island chain southeast of India, in the Bay of Bengal, toward Asia. They are off-limits to most foreign visitors, but I've been trying to get there since 2002. They're usually considered part of the territory Andaman, which I had been to before, but I found out that some groups call the Nicobar Islands a separate destination. So I had to go. . . .

There is a helicopter that leaves for the Nicobar Islands from Port Blair, the capital city of Andaman, but before I went, I had to get the government's permission. The remote, 1950s-style, bureaucratic Indian offices were all working against a customer-service-oriented experience.

Everyone in the Port Blair office wanted to help me, but it's so bureaucratic they just shuffled me on to the next person. I was approved to fly on the helicopter—but not to leave the area, so I found the helicopter pilots and had some beers with them. They finally said I could fly on standby, but because it was soon after the 2004 tsunami, everything was full for a long time. I couldn't stay there, so I said, "Remember me and I'll be back."

I went back the next year, and their jaws dropped. There was availability on the helicopter, but I needed approval from Delhi, so I flew back there to deal with another layer of bureaucracy.

I finally got into a private meeting with the man who could approve my permit. He started out really gruff, at first saying no, but then I explained that I'm trying to set a world record, and his expression changed. He said, "This young man, his eyes are kind, like John Travolta. Let's give him what he wants."

Next, I had to return to Port Blair to get approval from the police department *and* the helicopter company. I set up a meeting with someone that evening; and just as he was about to hand me the permit, an assistant came out of nowhere, whispered in his ear, and handed him a fax.

It was from the local Indian intelligence. It said something like, "Please be advised that Mr. Veley is not allowed to go to the Nicobar Islands. If he already commenced his travel, he must return immediately on the next flight."

This was the last hurdle in a thousand hurdles. There I was, in this blazing heat, and I said, "Okay, I'll give up. For now."

ARNIE WEISSMAN

Arnie Weissman is editor in chief of Travel Weekly, *the national newspaper of the travel industry. Here's his list of 10 Places I Would Rather Die Than See Again, in descending order.*

Ganges River, Varanasi, India

I was thrilled by the holy sites and spiritual feel of this sacred Hindu city but was unprepared for an early-morning boat ride on the Ganges. My guide had not warned me we'd be rowing past bloated human bodies serving simultaneously as a means of conveyance, and breakfast, for crows. The guide said that these were bodies of paupers; the workers who were supposed to transport them to a communal pyre for cremation had instead pocketed the cremation fee and just dumped the bodies in the river.

Viewing the floating bodies with the crows pecking at them was bad enough; seeing people brushing their teeth in the water not 10 feet away secured Varanasi's place on this list. For the rest of my time in that city, I would drink only sodas bottled in some distant place—preferably a town upstream.

Tunnels of Cu Chi, Vietnam

These narrow tunnels were escape routes for the Vietcong during the Vietnam War. The Vietcong knew which way to go, but anyone who followed and didn't know the layout would probably make a wrong turn into a booby-trapped diversion.

Odd as it may seem, these tunnels are now a tourist attraction. And those willing to pay a small fee will have the opportunity to slither along on their bellies for 100 yards or so through a tunnel. When I did it, it wasn't the claustrophobia, discomfort, or total darkness that got to me—it was the dozens of centipedes I saw when I finally decided to turn on my flashlight.

The Campgrounds of Europe

Camping in Europe, I learned, is less about communing with nature than about trying to replicate urban density in a park setting.

On my first day camping in Spain, I was delighted to find that I had the campgrounds to myself—and had my choice of secluded spots.

I found a corner at a far end, set up my tent, and left the campground to get some groceries. When I returned a half hour later, I saw that two other tents had gone up—one on either side of mine. They were so close that our guy wires intertwined.

I also learned that the Spanish habit of eating dinner around 11 p.m., so quaint when I was able to shut the window of my hotel room to muffle the noise of the street below, was decidedly less charming when only a micron-thin piece of nylon separated me from clanking dishes, crying babies, and barking dogs.

The Cities of Morocco

It's sometimes hard to appreciate the stunning beauty of Fez, Marrakech, and other Moroccan cities, because every child in the street wants to be your guide. You can tell them no, you don't want a guide, but they will continue to hound you with entreaties to let them escort you.

As it turns out, there is method in their pestering. As soon as you walk into a shop to escape them, they stand in the doorway and signal the owner to indicate that they brought you into the store. This automatically raises the price of anything you might buy, since the owner now has to tack on the cost of the commission.

Once I figured this out, I brought the shopkeeper to my would-be guide and said, "He did not bring me here. If I buy anything, he is not to get any commission."

The infuriated "guide" waited for me and, as I left the store, fell in step with me. But instead of pleading for me to let him show me around, he let loose with invective, ending with "And you're a racist! A racist! You're as bad as the Jews!"

He finally peeled away, only to be replaced, 30 paces later, by another would-be guide.

The Mail Boat between New Providence and Eleuthera Islands, Bahamas

I once booked passage on a mail boat making an overnight run between New Providence and Eleuthera in the Bahamas. A mail boat is often an economical and traditional way to get around this area, and at first, all was fine. The moon was bright, the waters calm, the atmosphere peaceful. I went to sleep shortly after dark, but then woke up, wondering if we were approaching our destination. I walked up to the pilothouse to ask the captain and saw that, although we were moving fairly briskly, no one was at the wheel.

I hurriedly looked for someone, anyone, who was awake. I found a crew member and alerted him that no one was steering. He was nonplussed and reassured me that yes, the captain was asleep, but would surely wake up before we reached land.

From that point on, the captain may have slept well, but I no longer could.

U.S.–Chiang Kai-shek War Crimes Museum (a.k.a. Martyr's Memorial), Chongqing, China

When I first saw the name of this museum, I felt it had loads of promise. I was hoping for strident Communist rhetoric on the display labels and perhaps a "Grandma went to the U.S.–Chiang Kai-shek War Crimes Museum, and all I got was a lousy T-shirt" shirt in the gift shop. To my great disappointment, both museum and shop were profoundly boring.

Gatlinburg, Tennessee

If dictionaries needed a photo to accompany the definition of *tourist trap*, a panorama of Gatlinburg, Tennessee, would get my vote.

Tea Warehouses, Darjeeling, India

Hilly Darjeeling, India, is a beautiful place. You can arrive via a winding, small-gauge railroad called the "toy train" and relax in this hill station that used to be a favorite among the families of British bureaucrats during the Raj. The famous tea bearing the town's name is indeed grown in nearby plantations, which can be toured. At the conclusion of a tour, I wandered into a warehouse where piles of leaves were drying—and, I observed, occasionally being remoistened by dogs roaming freely in the building.

I used to enjoy drinking Darjeeling tea.

West Sea Barrage, near Nampo, North Korea

When you arrive in North Korea and meet your guide, you begin to worry not that you will be brainwashed or jailed as a spy, but that you will be bored to death. My itinerary, recited staccato by my guide, Kim, sounded dreadful: "We will go to Kim Il Sung Square. We will go to Kim Il Sung Stadium. We will visit the Revolutionary Martyrs Cemetery. We will inspect the West Sea Barrage. We will see the Kim Il Sung International Friendship Exhibition. We will see the Tower of the Juche Idea. . . ."

As it turns out, the Revolutionary Martyrs Cemetery is fascinating. In fact, almost all of it is fascinating. Almost. The day's excursion to the West Sea Barrage, a dam near Nampo, had no redeeming value whatsoever. I'm guessing even an ardent student of dams would be bored. On this excursion, you'll be shown how "Dear Leader" Kim

Jong Il, the son of "Great Leader" Kim Il Sung, drew a line across a map of the West Sea inlet to show exactly where the dam should go. And you'll see the dam. And you'll see a lot of water. And you'll have wasted the better part of a day.

Tamanrasset, Algeria

In all my travels, one place alone stands out as being an exclusively negative experience. Tamanrasset, Algeria, a southern oasis on the route transiting the Sahara in western Africa, is a singularly unattractive outpost that's populated by the most gratuitously hostile people on earth.

It's near a beautiful part of the Sahara, where dunes are broken up by volcanic stumps. Tuareg camel trains pass through the scenery, and there's a monastery atop one of the volcanic stumps, which is where I, along with a group of 10 other Westerners, was heading to spend the night.

We stopped on the outskirts of Tamanrasset to fill our jerricans with what proved to be nearly undrinkable, mineral-saturated water. But we were told that the canned mango nectar in town was outstanding. So we trekked in to get some.

Tamanrasset is in a very conservative part of the country. It's the only place I've been where I've seen absolutely no women on the streets at all, not even women fully covered in burkas. About half our group were female, all with limbs and heads covered, but as we walked along the street, young men would approach us menacingly and simply pantomime the most obscene acts they could think of, reaching out as if to grope the women, tongues lapping wildly. It was a weird cultural moment, to be sure. Perhaps they felt the women's presence was so offensive that offense without limit was the only appropriate response. As great as the mango nectar was (and it was great), I know I'm not going back. It creeped me out.

To put my list in perspective, I'll mention that, before I embarked on a 100-day overland camping expedition through 10 countries in Africa, my travel agent, who had made a similar trip, told me, "I wouldn't do it again for a million dollars, tax free. But I wouldn't give up my memories of that trip for a million dollars, either."

Which is, of course, how I feel about the places on this list.

Except Tamanrasset.

You keep the memories, I'll take the million.

KEITH BELLOWS

Keith Bellows, editor in chief of National Geographic Traveler, *has a different approach to his Don't Go There List. Like many world travelers—including me—he says, "There's nowhere I wouldn't go . . . after all, any given place can be bad at any given time."*

But Bellows has his own suggestions as to destinations that might easily be on most people's "bucket lists," and yet, for reasons he'll now explain, you still shouldn't go there.

Machu Picchu, Peru

If you look at Machu Picchu, it is arguably one of the greatest places on earth. But it hasn't been managed properly. It's geologically unstable, and the nearby rivers are polluted. And if you go by road, you'll have to survive the most outrageous hairpin turns known to man.

Ten years ago, 4,000 people a week visited the area. Now it's 4,000 a day, so you have a situation where, on one hand, it's one of the greatest places in the world, but on the other hand, going will mean you'll be cheek by jowl with thousands of other tourists.

In the end, the bottom line is that you won't learn about this place. You shouldn't go there until they figure out how to preserve and present the site properly.

Easter Island, Chile

It was on the World Monument Fund's list of most endangered sights in 1996 and 2000. And now there's talk of putting a casino on the island, followed by cruise ship ports. Run the numbers and you can see where we're going. Five thousand people visited Easter Island in 1990. Now, it's up to 52,000 per year. And no real protective strategies are being applied, so you've got a situation where those world-renowned monuments are at high risk.

Great Barrier Reef, Australia

This area is incredibly vulnerable to oil spills; the corals are dying, and in the future, the habitat isn't likely to be sustainable. While the potential for ecological decline is more related to global warming than to tourists, the bottom line is that if you decide to take a trip to the reef, you won't see the reef you've imagined, because it isn't like that anymore, and the places where it *is* like that are inaccessible. The ads show you one thing, but you can't get there.

Angkor Wat, Cambodia

This temple is one of the great missed opportunities to promote Khmer culture, but that's not the biggest problem. Angkor Wat is one of the greatest World Heritage sites in the world—and the most visited. This results in a poor country having to leverage everything it possibly can to make money—more and more hotels, more and more ticky-tacky tourist stuff . . . people clambering up ancient rock faces, every single day degrading the culture. There are water shortages and pollution, and untreated sewage is dumped into the river by hotels and guest houses. Tourism here tends to benefit the corrupt officials and hotels but not the locals.

Chengdu, China

Another World Heritage site, Chengdu is also the financial hub of western China, and home to Qingcheng Mountain, the birthplace of Taoism. This legendary and mythical place is where people go to see pandas, not to mention 32 different species of mammals, 43 species of birds, seven types of fish, more than 4,000 flowering plants, and 110 other plants that have been discovered there. It's a botanical hot spot, the richest site of any temperate region in the world, and now . . . there's tourism, growing rampantly with 22,000 visitors a day (though that number has decreased, for now, since the May 2008 earthquake). Five years ago, no one went there—no one even knew about it. And now it's a place that China wants to create as a mecca for tourism, neglecting its enormous fragility. Though it is beautiful, this place could well be trashed in 5 years.

Lhasa, Tibet

Tibet's economy has grown by more than 12 percent each year in the past 5 years, and Lhasa has become a dumping ground for Chinese development. Resource extraction is extreme, and there is no controlled development. The domain of snow leopards, blue sheep, and, now, deforestation has lost its spirit of place. Tourism, souvenir shops, plastic palm trees, and cartoon cutouts have become the vernacular of one of the great treasured places of the world. The homeland of the Dalai Lama is gone. The Chinese are invading Tibet with tourism . . . and as a result, its unique culture is disappearing.

Taj Mahal, India

Forty percent of the tourists who travel to India go to the Taj Mahal—the biggest industry in Agra. It wasn't too long ago that private enterprise wanted to build a huge development there. It desperately needs landmark preservation, which may be its only salvation. The white marble has deteriorated, acid rain has denigrated the quality of the Taj . . . and don't get too close. It also stinks. Garbage is everywhere. Everyone feels they have to see the Taj, but it could easily turn into an amusement park. This is a magical place in the world—a place we all must see, but let's not go there now.

Serengeti, Tanzania

It is one of the world's last great wilderness areas. Tanzania has been about as smart as any government in limiting access and development, but still, the numbers are killing them.

Twenty-four percent, almost a quarter, of all the tourists to the area stop at the Ngorongoro Crater. In 1983, 35,000 people went there. In 2005, more than 300,000 people showed up, and they keep coming. It doesn't take a brain surgeon to run those numbers and figure out what's going to happen if this continues. It's impossible to deny the country the opportunity of leveraging one of its greatest tourist assets, but if you go there, you're contributing to its demise.

Pyramids of Giza, Egypt

Some folks think that many of the world's monuments will be gone in 50 years. And the number one challenge is tourism. For example, until recently, at least 4,000 people saw the tomb of King Tut every day, though the number is now limited to 1,000. And, to Egypt's credit, it has shut down many of the other tombs.

The amazing thing is that it's believed that only 30 percent of Egypt's archaeological wonders have even been discovered. But tourism is the enemy of archaeology—it's estimated that 16 million people will visit Egypt by 2014. If you look at that number, something has to give. Do you deny access in order to preserve sustainable tourism? Do you want five million "good" tourists willing to pay a hefty price to see these wonders, or 50 million folks who will visit and ruin the country?

Marrakech, Morocco

Drought and urbanization are wiping out what we like to think of as Morocco. One indication is that the date harvest dropped by 35 percent—something in which the growth of tourism has played a huge role.

In 2001, the king of Morocco proposed a master plan for monetizing tourism (including golf courses that the country can't sustain), which is supposed to draw 10 million tourists by the end of the decade. In the center of Marrakech, you want to see the medina, the culture, the snake handlers, but it's turned into a mall—authenticity has diminished. The one place where everyone wants to go—Marrakech—has become a disappointment. They're putting on a show more than anything that's genuine or authentic.

We are in very grave danger from a cultural survival perspective as much as we are threatened by global warming. Whether we want to admit it or not, we are in the midst of a process of destroying culture, language, and places themselves. And when the Chinese and the Indians start to travel, they'll also want to see the Grand Canyon and the Pyramids, and we could all be underwater, one way or another.

Okay, I've painted a very bleak picture. Am I saying don't go there? If you don't understand the negative impact you can have simply by being there, I guess I *am* saying not to go.

COSTAS CHRIST
Costas Christ is chairman of the World Travel & Tourism Council Tourism for Tomorrow Awards, which recognize best practices in green travel, as well as global travel editor for National Geographic Adventure *magazine. For the past 30 years, he's been at the leading edge of the green travel movement, since way before it was ever called "green" or even a movement. Here's his top-10 must-avoid list.*

Cancún, Mexico
What was once a small coastal island in the 1970s, with fishermen, local merchants, and a few small pensions, today is a stretch of high-rises sporting some 30,000 hotel rooms. Mangrove forests were cut to accommodate this megadevelopment, clear-water lagoons were filled in, and wildlife disappeared, along with any sense that you are still in Mexico. Stand on Cancún's miracle mile of tourism, and wet T-shirt contests and Jell-O shot bars pass for today's local culture. This country is one of the greatest travel destinations in the world, but Cancún is pure generic mass tourism.

Santorini, Greece

One of the most beautiful islands in the Mediterranean has become a textbook example of paving paradise. Sure, it has amazing views and spectacular sunsets—just be prepared to share them with as many as 15,000 cruise ship passengers, all off-loading at the same time and pushing past each other for the best spot to take a photo. Condo, hotel, and tourist sprawl is spreading like a fungus over the landscape. Talk about killing the goose that lays the golden egg—find your Greek island inspiration elsewhere.

Orlando, Florida

It really is a small world after all, and every family in America would do better to see it firsthand by having a genuine cross-cultural experience of learning and discovery, rather than get taken for a ride by the marketing engine of overdeveloped and environmentally unfriendly theme parks.

Kuta, Bali

Take an unspoiled tropical beach, add a vibrant ancient culture, cap it off with friendly local villagers eager to share their rich heritage, and then trample it all with a parade of western brands such as Hard Rock Cafe, T.G.I. Friday's, and KFC. Certainly, tourism destinations change over time, but that does not mean they should be trashed beyond recognition. Skip this one and instead consider Bali's artistic capital, Ubud, where a more balanced path embraces the local culture rather than conquers it.

Dubai, United Arab Emirates

Just one of Dubai's golf courses requires a million gallons of desalinated water a day to keep the grass green under the scorching desert sun. And it takes more than a gallon of crude oil to make 1 gallon of desalinated water. And that is before powering the air-conditioned indoor ski slopes, the gilded shopping malls, and the giant man-made islands shaped like a palm tree just offshore that are causing sedimentation runoff onto fragile coral reefs. Is this really the way to make the desert bloom? Seek an alternative.

Myanmar

Aung San Suu Kyi, the Noble Peace Prize winner living under house arrest for courageously opposing one of the most brutal military regimes in history, has called for international travelers to boycott Myanmar. Nelson Mandela did the same while under arrest during the height of apartheid rule in South Africa. Some tour operators run trips to Myanmar (formerly Burma) with the justification that giving the local people an opportunity to interact with the outside world is a good thing; meanwhile, they are making a business profit. Follow the real leaders and respect the travel boycott.

Antarctica

This is a "must-see" on everyone's travel list, and that's the problem. Rapidly increasing tourism—some 40,000 tourists in 2008—to one of the most fragile and untouched environments on the planet could have a devastating impact. For instance, 49,000 gallons of fuel spilled into the waters of Antarctica when one cruise ship sank. (No one was hurt.) Another ship ran aground. Now major cruise companies want to bring in even more tourists on ever-larger ships—Princess Cruises' *Star Princess* carries 3,800 passengers to Antarctica in one voyage. Time to call on the 46-nation Antarctic Treaty System to set limits before it's too late. Until then, think twice before making the trip.

China Beach, Vietnam

Local and foreign investors have scooped up nearly the entire vast tract of beautiful China Beach in central Vietnam, including ancestral burial grounds found there. Villagers have been forced to break open the coffins of their ancestors and take out the remains before the bulldozers level and bury the place, all in the name of building a parade of new mass tourism resorts. Do you really want to sleep in a hotel built right on top of a traditional burial ground where villagers honored dead ancestors for centuries, and then, grief-stricken, were forced to remove the remains? Things did not have to go this route, so let's not reward it.

Costa Rica's Overdeveloped Coast

There is a battle going on in Costa Rica—once the darling of ecotourism—between those who are working overtime to make the country a true green travel destination, and unscrupulous developers who like marketing the green label but couldn't care less about practicing the principles. The latter are winning in Tamarindo, Jaco, and a string of other coastal areas that have succeeded in carving up the landscape into large condos and megahotels. Your travel choice makes a difference in this struggle. The Costa Rican Certification for Sustainable Tourism (CST) helps identify the good guys.

Ngorongoro Crater, Tanzania

Definitely stay on the crater rim in one of the great safari lodges and sip a gin and tonic while looking down into what naturalists have called the Eighth Wonder of the World—an ancient, unflooded, collapsed caldera that forms a natural zoological garden—if it survives, that is.

Don't drive into the crater, unless you like your wildlife viewing in a parade of 4x4 vehicles. Save the up-close wildlife encounters for the 5,700 square miles of neighboring Serengeti National Park and let the inner crater have time to heal from tourism's wounds.

RICHARD BANGS

Last but not least, my friend and world adventurer Richard Bangs, who admits to having a problem with his Don't Go There List. "When I thought about the task," he says, "I realized that I have never really had a bad trip, or a disappointing destination. . . . I suffer from some sort of rare disease in which I like every place I visit." So, Bangs decided to turn my assignment on its head and list the 10 places he thought would be bad, but turned out to be delightful, at least for him.

But one important note: Remember that we all have a variety of different reasons why we don't go to a certain place, or will never go back. And despite Bangs's love affair with the following list, he did save the worst for last: Seal River, in Manitoba. But first . . .

Ghat, Libya

The ancient entrepôt of Ghat, near the Algerian border in southwestern Libya, was a trading center for the great camel caravans of lore, bringing ivory, gold, salt, and slaves from the sub-Sahara. Dusty and desultory, it lies some 30 miles northeast of Djanet, where 31 European tourists were kidnapped a few years back by an Islamic extremist group believed to have ties to Al Qaeda. I stayed at the Ghat Hotel, an unlovely affair with a gleaming cappuccino machine that belongs in a Paul Bowles novel. Out back is a mud-walled camel stable with a very low door, making it difficult for camels to wander out. My bed was an orgy of leaping bugs, but the evening was among my most memorable when I dropped into a hookah bar and whiled away the night smoking ornate, waist-high narghiles—puffing fruit-flavored tobacco through long, flexible hoses—and watching *Pan Arabic Idol* on TV. By 2 a.m., I felt truly Libyrated.

Kigali, Rwanda

It was here that the genocide of 1994 began, in which the ruling Hutu set out to kill neighbors, families, and friends, anyone with rival Tutsi heritage, and killed up to a million people in just over 3 months. And it was on a nearby volcano that Dian Fossey, the infamous researcher on gorillas, was hacked to death with a machete in her bed in 1985. So, it was with some trepidation that I set out following a group of local guides (and actress Daryl Hannah), slashing through the rain forest with their machetes on a trek to see the mountain gorillas. But after a successful sighting, we headed down the mountain and built a cistern for a local school. Afterward, the whole of the region showed up for a party of dancing, singing, and local wine, and I felt like I was at the premiere of *Silverback Mountain*.

Sarajevo, Bosnia

The Bosnia we know from images of the war—the bombed and bullet-ridden buildings, the scars from the 1,200-day siege of Sarajevo—has kept from view a Bosnia we don't know, a place where nature has been bighearted with its gifts. The country, described sometimes as the heart between the mouths of two lions, hosts one of the two greatest tracts of primeval forest in Europe, daunting mountain faces yet to be climbed, wild rivers with water so pure you can cup your hand and drink it, some of the highest concentrations of wildlife, and perhaps the last highland tribes of seminomadic peoples on the Continent.

Mount Hagen, Papua New Guinea

There's been much reportage about the "raskols" of New Guinea, modern versions of tribal warriors who drink too much and run amok attacking passersby. And it's true; if you take a taxi down the Highlands Highway, the car is likely to be completely covered in protective metal grids, and almost every window you pass is barred, every cinder-block building topped with razor wire and fronted with armed guards. There are villages where cannibalism is still practiced, and some of the more ambitious are always trying to get ahead. But, once you're off the main road and into the valleys, it is paradise, and the folks as friendly as family. I was invited and initiated into one clan, and still have the scar to prove it.

Granada, Nicaragua

It was definitely contra to what I expected. The Nicaragua that capers in my mind is from potent images from the late '70s, a country then bleeding in civil war. The conflict ended with the Sandinistas' 1979 overthrow of the Somoza family's corrupt, 4-decades-long regime. Then came a dozen years of postwar fighting as American-backed contra rebels—with the assist of a U.S. embargo—tried to push the Sandinistas out of power. Now, though, it is a peaceful place, poised to be the next Costa Rica.

Granada was gutted by William Walker, the American filibuster who declared himself president of Nicaragua in 1856 and was shot by firing squad 4 years later. The city has been given a face-lift, freshly painted in mustard, peach, and salmon, and looks more like a colonial city than in its heyday.

Granada has today transformed from a hot zone to a hot destination. And I had my own transformation there when I stopped at the 007 Barbershop and sat down in a torn red vinyl chair. My barber, Luis, in his bleached white guayabera, pulled out a straight razor and sharpened it on a belt. "What do you want cut?" Caught up in the moment, I looked in the mirror and saw a mustache I had sported for 30 years . . . disheveled, streaked with gray, with wild hairs leaping out in all directions. "Shave it off," I said. Before I could reconsider, it was gone. By twinkling transmutation, a barbershop in Nicaragua became a magic glass into which I stepped, and then stepped out with a past elided, and a future thick with facial possibilities.

Annapurna, Nepal

In recent years, Annapurna became the heart of Maoist-controlled country, and trekkers have been held up and forced to pay a "rebel toll" for passage. At least two tourists were blown up by land mines. But I went with climber Ed Viesturs to base camp as he attempted to become the first American to climb all 14 of the peaks in the world over 8,000 meters. (This was his last.) I loved the fact that on the trek in, we passed not a single foreigner, though we did almost fall down a couple of precipitous passes. It was as though we had the whole of the Himalayas to ourselves. Ed, by the way, was successful, which made the trip that much sweeter.

Lake Kariba, Zimbabwe

Despite the corruption and inflation, or perhaps because of it, this is a peaceful retreat alongside one of the largest man-made lakes on the continent, with rock shanties in the shade, vervet monkeys frolicking for entertainment, giant crocodiles lurking in the shallows, and million-dollar views everywhere. But then almost everyone is a millionaire here: $35 U.S. is a million Zimbabwe dollars at this writing. On the border crossing to Zambia, I was shaken down with a bogus claim that my visa, which I had obtained hours before, was invalid. It cost me $20 U.S., but it was worth it. Hey, I'm a billionaire in Zimbabwe.

Darien Gap, Panama/Colombia

The jungle-wrapped isthmus that separates Central and South America is one of the great modern smuggling corridors—everything from gold to cocaine to hot iPods. In a long dugout canoe called a *cayuco,* I headed up the Rio Mogue through a tangled fantasy of black mangrove toward an Emberá Indian village. My guide told me about the many deadly creatures along this waterway, from vipers to cats to crocodiles and caimans, and even the insects—apparently in the late '80s, a boatload of adventure tourists was attacked by African killer bees. The boat flipped in the mayhem, and two drowned.

As we pulled into an embankment at the village of Paraíso Mogue, we were greeted by an ambuscade of Emberá Indians, once warriors who painted themselves with the juice of the jagua fruit in jagged patterns meant to frighten enemies. When their ancestors were forced to work in the Spanish gold mines of the Darien, they sometimes fought alongside British pirates, using poison-tipped blowgun darts and primitive weapons to beat back the conquistadors.

The Emberá met us with the same war paint, but also music: drums, maracas, and a groovy flute in a combo that sounded like jungle jazz. The women and girls were bare-chested, wearing only palm-fiber skirts and bandoliers of silver coins. This was my kind of place.

West Bank, Palestine

I drove west into the Judaean hills, up an irrigation aqueduct, and met Mohammed Saaydeh, a Palestinian field researcher for Friends of the Earth Middle East. Mohammed took me up the Jordan valley, past children sliding down a sluiceway through citrus orchards, past banana groves and fields of red poppies, to the headwaters of a dancing, clearwater creek rimmed with green tamarisk. This was the only oasis on the West Bank with year-round water that flowed to the Jordan, and it was blissfully beautiful. Mohammed, in concert with other environmentalists, is lobbying for the village of Auja to become a proper nature reserve, one that would be administered by Palestinians, attract eco-tourists from around the world, and provide an alternative livelihood for local farmers so they could give diverted water back to the Jordan. This may be, Mohammed believes, a form for a balance between nature and man in this region, a formula in some measure for the bracing air of peace.

Seal River, Manitoba, Canada

It has a reputation for its swarms of mosquitoes—so many that one has to wear special mosquito-net hats, coats, gloves, and pants. I took my then wife on a canoe trip down this scenic corridor and was indeed lost in the blizzards of mosquitoes; but then I saw and enjoyed more wildlife than in almost any other basin. We had black bears, an arctic wolf, even a polar bear come into camp. There were bald eagles swooping over our tents. We passed thousands of seals, and at the river's mouth, at the Hudson Bay, we canoed over dozens of beluga whales, which rolled next to the canoe and winked at me. It was the most delightful river trip for me; my wife thought it the worst trip of her life. When we got home, we divorced.

Chapter 1: Air Pollution

U.S. CITIES

State of the Air: 2008, American Lung Association, May 2008, stateoftheair.org/2008/states/california

U.S. Environmental Protection Agency, epa.gov

Arvin, California

Central Valley Air Quality Coalition (CVAQ), calcleanair.org

"Arvin, California: Home to the Most Polluted Air in America," Associated Content, August 2007, associatedcontent.com/article/345375/arvin_ california_home_to_the_most_polluted.html?cat=5

Bakersfield, California

"Digging Up Trouble: The Health Risks of Construction Pollution in California," compiled by Union of Concerned Scientists, November 2006: 1–3, 7, 8, ucsusa.org/assets/documents/clean_vehicles/ Digging-up-Trouble.pdf

"School Construction Following Population Surge," Gregg Aragon, California Construction, December 2005, california.construction.com/features/archive/0512_ Feature1.asp

"Number of Building Permits, Bakersfield, CA," Economagic, economagic.com/em-cgi/data.exe/ cenc40/12540u01

Fresno, California

State of the Air: 2008, American Lung Association, stateoftheair.org/2008/states/california/fresno-06019. html

1,000 Friends of Fresno, 1000friendsoffresno.org/ airquality.html

"Fresno, CA: Where Breathing Is like Smoking without Filters," Sierra Club, sierraclub.org/comunidades/ingles/ fresno.asp

Los Angeles, California

State of the Air: 2008, American Lung Association, stateoftheair.org/2008/states/california/ los-angeles-06037.html

"The 'Sootiest City' Is...Not Los Angeles," Tami Abdollah, *Los Angeles Times,* May 2008, latimes.com/ news/local/la-me-lungs1-2008may01,0,2646636. story

"Pittsburgh and Los Angeles—The Most Polluted US Cities," *Forbes,* May 2008.

Birmingham, Alabama

State of the Air: 2008, American Lung Association, stateoftheair.org/2008/states/alabama/ jefferson01073.html

"Birmingham: Economy: Major Industries and Commercial Activity," City-Data.com, city-data.com/ us-cities/The-South/Birmingham-Economy.html

Detroit, Michigan

State of the Air: 2008, American Lung Association, stateoftheair.org/2008/states/alabama/ jefferson-01073.html

"In Pictures: America's Dirtiest Cities," Robert Malone, Forbes.com, March 21, 2007, forbes.com/ logistics/2007/03/21/americas-dirtiest-cities- biz-logistics-cx_rm_0321amdirt_slide_8. html?thisSpeed=15000

Box: Top Asthma Capitals in 2008

Asthma and Allergy Foundation of America, asthmacapitals.com

Pittsburgh, Pennsylvania

State of the Air: 2008, American Lung Association, stateoftheair.org/2008/states/pennsylvania/ allegheny-42003.html

"It's No Dirty Secret—Pittsburgh Air Ranked among Nation's Worst," Karen Roebuck, *Pittsburgh Tribune,* 2003, pittsburghlive.com/x/pittsburghtrib/s_150808. html

"Pittsburgh Takes Sooty Air Crown from L.A.," CBS News, May 1, 2008, cbsnews.com/ stories/2008/05/01/tech/main4061365.shtml

Box: Eternal Flames

"The Unforgettable Fire," Jason Zasky, *Failure Magazine,* January 2001, failuremag.com/arch_science_centralia_ unforgettable_fire.html

INTERNATIONAL CITIES

"The World's Worst Polluted Places: The Top Ten of the Dirty Thirty," Blacksmith Institute, September 2007, blacksmithinstitute.org/wwpp2007/final Report2007.pdf

Tianying, China

"The World's Worst Polluted Places: The Top Ten of the Dirty Thirty," Blacksmith Institute, September 2007, blacksmithinstitute.org/wwpp2007/finalReport2007.pdf

"The World's Most Polluted Places," *Time,* September 2007, time.com/time/specials/2007/ article/0,28804,1661031_1661028_1661017,00.html

Chongqing, China

"The World's Worst Polluted Places: The Top Ten of the Dirty Thirty," Blacksmith Institute, blacksmithinstitute. org/wwpp2007/finalReport2007.pdf

"CCCEH Research: Chongqing, China," Columbia Center for Children's Environmental Health, ccceh.org/ research-chongqing.html

"Big, Gritty Chongqing, City of 12 Million, Is China's Model for Future," Howard W. French, *New York Times,* June 1, 2007, nytimes.com/2007/06/01/world/asia/01chongqing.html

Box: Beijing, China

"Citing Pollution, Gebrselassie Opts Out of Olympic Marathon," Katie Thomas, *New York Times,* March 11, 2008, nytimes.com/2008/03/11/sports/othersports/11olympics.html

"An Olympic Farewell for Haile Gebrselassie," John Leicester, Associated Press, United States Olympic Committee, August 17, 2008, teamusa.org/news/article/5360

"Breathing in Beijing: Environmental Quality and the 2008 Summer Olympics," Steve Cohen, Columbia University's Earth Institute, August 14, 2008, observer.com/2008/green/breathing-beijing-environmental-quality-and-2008-summer-olympics

Cairo, Egypt

"Cairo, Egypt Statistics," cairotourist.com/cairostatistics.htm

"Air Pollution in Cairo—The Cost," Salah Hassanein, Arab World Books, arabworldbooks.com/articles1.html

"Living in Cairo Is the Same as Smoking a Pack a Day," Leslie-Ann Boctor, IPS News, October 23, 2007, alternet.org/healthwellness/65852/

"Slow but Sure Environmental Progress in Cairo," Liane Hansen, NPR, May 4, 2008, npr.org/templates/story/story.php?storyId=90109734

Delhi, India

World Bank Statistics, April 2007, siteresources.worldbank.org/DATASTATISTICS/Resources/table3_13.pdf

"New Delhi Air Quality Is Worsening, Group Says," Amelia Gentleman, *New York Times,* November 7, 2007, nytimes.com/2007/11/07/world/asia/07delhi.html

"The Health Effects of Air Pollution in Delhi, India," Maureen L. Cropper, Nathalie B. Simon, Anna Alberini, and P. K. Sharma, December 1997, ideas.repec.org/p/wbk/wbrwps/1860.html

"Air Pollution Making Delhi Children Asthmatic: Survey," Headlines India, February 2008, delhi.headlinesindia.com/index1.jsp?news_code=69716

Center for Science and Environment press release, May 23, 2008, cseindia.org/AboutUs/press_releases/press_20080523.htm

Centre for Science and Environment press release, June 2, 2008, cseindia.org/AboutUs/press_releases/press_20080602.htm

Calcutta, India

"Kolkata Now India's Pollution Capital," *Times of India,* May 2008, timesofindia.indiatimes.com/Earth/Kolkata_now_Indias_pollution_capital/articleshow/3078902.cms

World Bank Statistics, April 2007, siteresources.worldbank.org/DATASTATISTICS/Resources/table3_13.pdf

"Air Pollution Suffocates Calcutta," Subir Bhaumik, BBC News, May 2007, news.bbc.co.uk/2/hi/south_asia/6614561.stm

"Oxygen Supplies for India Police," Subir Bhaumik, BBC News, May 2007, news.bbc.co.uk/2/hi/south_asia/6665803.stm

Box: Windsor, Ontario, Canada

"Windsor 'the Most Polluted City in North America': RFK Jr.," Trevor Wilhelm, *Windsor Star,* April 27, 2008,

canada.com/windsorstar/story.html?id=4cb4ab4f-772e-47fc-8a01-3e0621454330&k=93563

Mexico City, Mexico

"Air Pollution: Mexico City," July 29, 2003, pulseplanet.com/dailyprogram/dailies.php?POP=2977

"Basin Traps Air Pollution in Mexico City: International Study Has Implications for U.S. Cities," EurekAlert!, September 9, 1997, eurekalert.org/pub_releases/1997-09/PNNL-BTAP-090997.php

"Luisa, Mario Molina Battle Air Pollution in Mexico City," Nancy Stauffer, Laboratory for Energy and the Environment, MIT News, April 2, 2003, web.mit.edu/newsoffice/2003/mexico-0402.html

Box: Who's Smoking the Most?

"Where There's Smoke: Emerging World: WHO to Offer a Road Map to Combat Tobacco Use; Sales Up in Poorer Nations," Betsy McKay, *Wall Street Journal,* February 7, 2008, online.wsj.com/article/SB120235550960649857.html?mod=googlenews_wsj

Chapter 2: Water Pollution

U.S. SITES

Great Pacific Garbage Patch

"Big Island Beach Attracts Plastic Trash," Howard Dashefsky, KHNL NBC 8, November 9, 2007, khnl.com/global/story.asp?s=7334574

"Plastic Debris in the World's Oceans," Michelle Allsopp, Adam Walters, David Santillo, and Paul Johnston, Greenpeace, oceans.greenpeace.org/raw/content/en/documents-reports/plastic_ocean_report.pdf

Box: Shark Attacks

"International Shark Attack File," Florida Museum of Natural History, flmnh.ufl.edu/fish/sharks/statistics/2006attacksummary.htm

Onondaga Lake, Syracuse, New York

Onondaga Lake Partnership, onlakepartners.org

Onondaga Nation, People of the Hills, onondaganation.org

Lake Pontchartrain, Louisiana

"Lake Pontchartrain's Toxic Brew," Sewell Chan and Andrew C. Revkin, *International Herald Tribune,* September 8, 2005, iht.com/articles/2005/09/07/news/pollute.php

Lake Champlain, Vermont

Conservation Law Foundation, clf.org

Vermont Natural Resources Council, vnrc.org

Box: You Left Your *What* in San Francisco?

"2.7 Million-Gallon Sewage Spill in Richardson Bay," Peter Fimrite, Marisa Lagos, Jill Tucker, and Chronicle staff writers, SFGate, February 2, 2008, sfgate.com/cgi-bin/article.cgi?f=/c/a/2008/02/02/MNSTUQQO6.DTL

Gulf Coast States

Texas Department of State Health Services

Florida Department of Health

"*Vibrio vulnificus*," Centers for Disease Control and Prevention (CDC), Division of Foodborne, Bacterial and Mycotic Diseases, updated March 27, 2008, cdc.gov/nczved/dfbmd/disease_listing/vibriov_gi.html

Phyllis Kozarsky, MD, Division of Global Migration and Quarantine, CDC; professor of medicine and infectious diseases, Emory University School of Medicine

Box: Lake Washington, Mississippi
Mississippi Department of Environmental Quality, deq.
state.ms.us
"Lake Washington—No Longer Muddying Up the
Waters," U.S. Environmental Protection Agency,
February 25, 2008, epa.gov/nps/Section319I/MS.html
Anacostia River, Washington, DC
"America's Great Outdoors: District of Columbia:
Anacostia River," Sierra Club, sierraclub.org/
greatoutdoors/dc
"America's Most Endangered Rivers 2007," American
Rivers: Thriving by Nature, americanrivers.org
Santa Fe River, New Mexico
"America's Most Endangered Rivers 2007," American
Rivers: Thriving by Nature, americanrivers.org
Iowa River, Iowa
"America's Most Endangered Rivers 2007," American
Rivers: Thriving by Nature, americanrivers.org
"Iowa River Pollution Draws Calls for Action," Matt
Nelson, *Daily Iowan,* April 19, 2007, media.www.
dailyiowan.com/media/storage/paper599/
news/2007/04/19/Metro/Iowa-River.Pollution.Draws.
Calls.For.Action-2851549.shtml
Kinnickinnic River, Wisconsin
"America's Most Endangered Rivers 2007," American
Rivers: Thriving by Nature, americanrivers.org
Box: Before You Go to Any Beach . . .
*Testing the Waters: A Guide to Water Quality at Vacation
Beaches,* Mark Dorfman and Kirsten Sinclair Rosselot,
National Resources Defense Council, July 29, 2008,
nrdc.org/water/oceans/ttw/ttw2008.pdf
CDC Health Information for International Travel 2008, ed.
Paul M. Arguin, MD, Phyllis E. Kozarsky, MD, and
Christie Reed, MD, Atlanta: Elsevier Publishing, 2008:
44–49
Neuse River, North Carolina
"America's Most Endangered Rivers 2007," American
Rivers: Thriving by Nature, americanrivers.org
Neuse River Foundation, neuseriver.org

INTERNATIONAL SITES
Aral Sea, Uzbekistan
"White Gold: The True Cost of Cotton: Uzbekistan,
Cotton and the Crushing of a Nation," Environmental
Justice Foundation, ejfoundation.org/pdf/white_gold_
the_true_cost_of_cotton.pdf
King River, Australia
"State of the Environment Tasmania: King River,"
Resource Planning and Development Commission, soer.
justice.tas.gov.au/2003/casestudy/16/index.php
International POPs (Persistent Organic Pollutants)
Elimination Network, ipen.org
Groundwater and Coastal Water, Bangladesh
Local Environment Development and Agricultural
Research Society (LEDARS), Mohon Kumar Mondol,
executive director
"A Guide to Arsenic Pollution of Groundwater in
Bangladesh and West Bengal," John McArthur, *ECG
Bulletin,* University College London, January 2006, rsc.
org/images/BangladeshGuide_tcm18-58881.doc
Citarum River, Jakarta, Indonesia
"ADB Funds Water Quality Study in West Tarum Canal,"
Asian Development Bank, February 15, 2007, adb.org/
Media/Articles/2007/11510-indonesian-water-qualities-
studies/default.asp

"Is This the World's Most Polluted River?" Richard
Shears, *Daily Mail,* June 5, 2007, dailymail.co.uk/news/
article-460077/Is-worlds-polluted-river.html
Sarno River, Italy
"The Case of Sarno River (Southern Italy). Effects of
Geomorphology on the Environmental Impacts,"
Tommaso de Pippo, Carlo Donadio, Marco Guida, and
Carmela Petrosino, Earth Science Department,
University of Naples Federico II, April 2004
More Efficient Transnational Technology Transfer in the
Environmental Sector (METTTES), Regional Demand
Profile, April 2007, metttes.innovationmalta.com

Chapter 3: Toxic Places
U.S. SITES

Cancer Alley
Rick Hind, legislative director, Greenpeace, greenpeace.
org
Louisiana Cancer Control Partnership, lcltfb.org/laccp
Hanford, Washington
"Hanford Likely Caused Cancer Downwind, Jury
Decides," Warren Cornwall, *Seattle Times,* May 20,
2005, seattletimes.nwsource.com/html/
localnews/2002281825_downwinder20m.html
"An Overview of Hanford and Radiation Health Effects,"
Washington State Department of Health, doh.wa.gov/
Hanford/publications/overview/overview.html
Department of Energy, Hanford Site, www.hanford.gov
Hanford Public Tours, Department of Energy, www5.
hanford.gov/publictours
Indian Point Nuclear Power Plant
Citizens Awareness Network, nukebusters.org
Department of Energy, Energy Information Administra-
tion, www.eia.doe.gov
"Chernobyl on the Hudson? The Health and Economic
Impacts of a Terrorist Attack at the Indian Point Nuclear
Plant," Edwin S. Lyman, Union of Concerned Scientists,
commissioned by Riverkeeper, Inc., September 2004,
riverkeeper.org/document.php/317/Chernobyl_on_th.pdf
Box: Apex, North Carolina
Dr. Daniel Horowitz, Director of Congressional, Public,
and Board Affairs, U.S. Chemical Safety Board
"Hazmat Sites Often 'Forgotten,'" Toby Coleman, *News &
Observer,* October 15, 2006, newsobserver.com/front/
story/498961.html
Box: Butte, Montana
Berkeley Pit Public Education Committee, pitwatch.org
Box: Love Canal, New York
"The Love Canal Tragedy," Eckardt C. Beck, *EPA Journal,*
January 1979, epa.gov/history/topics/lovecanal/01.htm
Picher, Oklahoma
"Pollution Brings End to Mining Town in Oklahoma,"
Justin Juozapavicius, Associated Press, Boston.com,
May 10, 2008, boston.com/news/nation/
articles/2008/05/10/pollution_brings_end_to_mining_
town_in_oklahoma/
"FEMA, EPA Visit Tornado-Ravaged Oklahoma Town,"
Murray Evans, Associated Press, *Seattle Times,* May 12,
2008, seattletimes.nwsource.com/html/
nationworld/2004409134_apsevereweatheroklahoma.
html
"Heroes Among Us: Prescription for Kindness,"
Richard Jerome, *People* 67, no. 21 (May 28, 2007),

people.com/people/archive/article/0,,20062329,00.html

Toms River, New Jersey
"Citizen's Guide to the Childhood Cancer Incidence Update: A Review and Analysis of Cancer Registry Data, 1979–2000, Dover Township (Ocean County), New Jersey," January 2003, www.state.nj.us/health/eoh/hhazweb/case-control_pdf/cg_cancerpdate_99_00.pdf

Box: Sylvester, West Virginia
Joel Finkelstein, End Mountaintop Removal, ilovemountains.org/memorial/c295/39

INTERNATIONAL SITES

Bhopal, India
"India: Summary of Clouds of Injustice—Bhopal Disaster 20 Years On," Amnesty International, November 29, 2004, amnesty.org/en/library/info/ASA20/104/2004/en
"Bhopal—The World's Worst Industrial Disaster," Greenpeace, greenpeace.org/international/photosvideos/slideshows/bhopal-the-world-s-worst-ind
Aquene Freechild, Environmental Health Fund

Chernobyl, Ukraine
"Chernobyl: The True Scale of the Accident," World Health Organization, September 5, 2005, who.int/mediacentre/news/releases/2005/pr38/en/index.html
"Health Effects of the Chernobyl Accident and Special Health Care Programmes," Report of the UN Chernobyl Forum Expert Group "Health," ed. Burton Bennett, Michael Repacholi, and Zhanat Carr, World Health Organization, Geneva, 2006, who.int/ionizing_radiation/chernobyl/WHO%20Report%20on%20Chernobyl%20Health%20Effects%20July%202006.pdf
Fred A. Mettler Jr., MD, MPH, chairman, UN Chernobyl Forum, World Health Organization

Dzerzhinsk, Russia
"The World's Worst Polluted Places: The Top Ten of the Dirty Thirty," Blacksmith Institute, September 2007, blacksmithinstitute.org/wwpp2007/finalReport2007.pdf
"Polluted Places: A Project of the Blacksmith Institute," pollutedplaces.org/region/e_europe/russia/dzerzhinsk.shtml

Kabwe, Zambia
"The World's Worst Polluted Places: The Top Ten of the Dirty Thirty," Blacksmith Institute, September 2007, blacksmithinstitute.org/wwpp2007/finalReport2007.pdf

La Oroya, Peru
"The World's Worst Polluted Places: The Top Ten of the Dirty Thirty," Blacksmith Institute, September 2007, blacksmithinstitute.org/wwpp2007/finalReport2007.pdf
"Crisis Deepens in La Oroya," Oxfam America, December 20, 2004, oxfamamerica.org/newsandpublications/news_updates/archive2004/news_update.2004-12-20.4019587716
"Call for Clean Up in La Oroya," Oxfam America, January 11, 2006, oxfamamerica.org/newsandpublications/news_updates/archive2006/news_update.2006-01-11.8660175981

Linfen, China
"The World's Worst Polluted Places: The Top Ten of the Dirty Thirty," Blacksmith Institute, September 2007, blacksmithinstitute.org/wwpp2007/finalReport2007.pdf
"Air Pollution Grows in Tandem with China's Economy," *All Things Considered*, NPR, May 22, 2007, npr.org/templates/story/story.php?storyId=10221268

Sukinda and Vapi, India
"The World's Worst Polluted Places: The Top Ten of the Dirty Thirty," Blacksmith Institute, September 2007, blacksmithinstitute.org/wwpp2007/finalReport2007.pdf
"Integrated Environmental Epidemiology Study in Identified Critically Polluted Areas in the Country: Report on Vapi (Gujarat)," Ministry of Environment and Forests, blacksmithinstitute.org/docs/vapiScan1.pdf

Sumgait, Azerbaijan; Norilsk, Russia; and Mailuu-Suu, Kyrgyzstan
"The World's Worst Polluted Places: The Top Ten of the Dirty Thirty," Blacksmith Institute, September 2007, blacksmithinstitute.org/wwpp2007/finalReport2007.pdf
"Cancer Incidence and Mortality in the Industrial City of Sumgayit, Azerbaijan: A Descriptive Study," James Andruchow, University of Alberta, World Health Organization, and UN Development Programme, January 2003, csih.org/what/schip/cancerworkshop.pdf

Box: Mercer's Dirtiest Cities
Health and Sanitation Rankings, 2007 *Quality of Living* survey, Mercer Human Resource Consulting

Box: Most Depressed and Depressing Destinations

Introduction
"Suicide Prevention" report, World Health Organization, who.int/mental_health/prevention/suicide/suicideprevent/en/
"U.S. Suicide Statistics (2005)," CDC, suicide.org/suicide-statistics.html#2005

AMERICA'S SUICIDE CAPITALS

Montana
"U.S. Suicide Statistics (2005)," Centers for Disease Control, suicide.org/suicide-statistics.html#2005
Missoula City-County Health Department Suicide Prevention Network
2006 Montana Vital Statistics, Office of Vital Statistics, Montana Department of Public Health and Human Services
"2000–2006 Rate of Suicide for Montana Counties," 2006 Montana Vital Statistics, Office of Vital Statistics, Montana Department of Public Health and Human Services, co.missoula.mt.us/measures/PDF2000.06%20suicide%20rate%20by%20county.pdf

Nevada
"U.S. Suicide Statistics (2005)," CDC, suicide.org/suicide-statistics.html#2005
"Suicide in Nevada Fact Sheet 2007," Nevada Office of Suicide Prevention, dhhs.nv.gov/Suicide/DOCS/Suicide%20in%20Nevada%20Fact%20Sheet%20Public.pdf
"The Suicide Capital of America," CBS News, February 9, 2004, cbsnews.com/stories/2004/02/09/health/main599070.shtml

Alaska
"U.S. Suicide Statistics (2005)," Centers for Disease Control, suicide.org/suicide-statistics.html#2005
Alaska Suicide research, Critical Illness and Trauma Foundation/Alaska Injury Prevention Center, citmt.org/research.htm
Alaska Department of Health and Social Services
"Alaska Suicide Follow-back Study Final Report," Suicide Prevention Council, 2006, www.hss.state.ak.us/suicideprevention/pdfs_sspc/sspcfollowback2-07.pdf

New Mexico and Wyoming

"U.S. Suicide Statistics (2005)," CDC, suicide.org/suicide-statistics.html#2005

New Mexico Suicide Prevention Coalition

"Governor Richardson's Youth Suicide Prevention Task Force: Preventing Youth Suicide," New Mexico Department of Health, January 7, 2005, www.sprc.org/stateinformation/PDF/resources/nm_recs.pdf

"Suicide Remains a Disturbing Problem in Wyoming," Wyoming Department of Health, September 5, 2007, wdh.state.wy.us/news.aspx?NewsID=106

"Wyoming State Suicide Prevention Information," Wyoming Suicide Prevention Resource Center, www.sprc.org/stateinformation/statepages/showstate.asp?stateID=50

Suicide Bridges

"The Bridge of Death," ABC News, October 20, 2006, abcnews.go.com/2020/story?id=2592841&page=1

"Residents Welcome Aurora Bridge Barrier," Casey McNerthney, Seattle Post Intelligencer, January 30, 2008, seattlepi.nwsource.com/local/349490_bridge31.html

"Through the Air into Darkness," Suzy Hagstrom, San Diego Weekly Reader, October 12, 2000, sandiegoreader.com/news/2000/oct/12/through-air-darkness/

"Suicide Magnet," Randy Dotinga, VoiceofSanDiego.org, May 1, 2008, voiceofsandiego.org/articles/2008/05/01/news/01suicide050108.txt

Manhattan Tourism Sites

"Some 'Tourists' Choose City Landmarks for Suicide," Jordan Lite, New York Daily News, November 21, 2007, nydailynews.com/news/2007/11/01/2007-11-01_some_tourists_choose_city_landmarks_for_-1.html

"Suicide Tourism in Manhattan, New York City, 1990–2004," C. Gross, T. M. Piper, A. Bucciarelli, K. Tardiff, D. Vlahov, and S. Galea, Journal of Urban Health 84, no. 6 (2007): 755–765, electronic publication September 21, 2007, Department of Psychiatry, Weill Cornell Medical College, Cornell University, ncbi.nlm.nih.gov/pubmed/17885807

"Suicide Tourism in Manhattan, New York City, 1990–2004," Journal of Urban Health, November/December 2007, nyam.org/news/2990.html

DEPRESSION AND SUICIDE ABROAD

"More Killed by Suicide Than War," BBC News, September 8, 2004, news.bbc.co.uk/2/hi/3639152.stm

Lithuania

"News Review for Lithuania," Central Europe Review, April 3, 2000, www.ce-review.org/00/13/lithuanianews13.html

"Lithuania's Suicide Epidemic," Justin Webster, Insight News TV, insightnewstv.com/d74/

Russia

"Perestroika and Suicide," Harvard University School of Public Health, www.hsph.harvard.edu/research/hicrc/success-stories/violence/index.html

"Heavy Drinking and Suicide in Russia," William Alex Pridemore, Indiana University, September 2006, pubmedcentral.nih.gov/articlerender.fcgi?artid=1642767

Belarus

"Looking Back on 2007," Annette Beautrais, Crisis: The Journal of Crisis Intervention and Suicide Prevention 28, no. 4 (2007): 159–164, hogrefe.com/index.php?mod=journals&action=1&site=crisis

"Suicide and Alcohol Psychoses in Belarus 1970–2005," Yury E. Razvodovsky, Crisis 28, no. 2 (2007): 61–66, lib.bioinfo.pl/pmid:17722686

Estonia

"Suicide among Russians in Estonia: Database Study Before and After Independence," Airi Värnik, Kairi Kõlves, and Danuta Wasserman, BMJ 330 (2005): 176–177, bmj.bmjjournals.com/cgi/content/full/330/7484/176

Hungary

"For Which Strategies of Suicide Prevention Is There Evidence of Effectiveness?" World Health Organization, November 1, 2004, www.euro.who.int/HEN/Syntheses/suicideprev/20040712_2

"Hungary Seeks Way to Cut High Suicide Rate," Henry Kamm, New York Times, July 30, 1987, query.nytimes.com/gst/fullpage.html?res=9B0DE0DF153CF933A05754C0A961948260

China

"Traditions Weigh on China's Women," Christopher Allen, BBC News, June 19, 2006, news.bbc.co.uk/2/hi/programmes/5086754.stm

"Suicide and Attempted Suicide—China, 1990–2002," Morbidity and Mortality Weekly Report 53, no. 22 (June 11, 2004), CDC, cdc.gov/mmwr/preview/mmwrhtml/mm5322a6.htm

"Risk Factors for Suicide in Adults Aged 30–49: A Psychological Autopsy Study in Hong Kong," Paul Wai-Ching Wong, ePublications@Bond University, p. 6, epublications.bond.edu.au/theses/wong

Chapter 4: Places That Really Stink

FACTORY FARMS

"What's Wrong with Factory Farming?" Center for Food Safety, centerforfoodsafety.org/pubs/FactoryFarmingFactSheet.pdf

"Boss Hog," Pat Stith, Joby Warrick, and Melanie Sill, News & Observer, February 19–28, 1995, pulitzer.org/works/1996,Public+Service

"Concentrated Animal Feeding Operations (CAFOs)," CDC, cdc.gov/cafos/about.htm#concerns

Box: Factory Hog Farms

"Factory Farm Pollution in the United States," Food & Water Watch, factoryfarmmap.org

Putnam County, Missouri

Scott Dye, national program director, Sierra Club Water Sentinels Program, sierraclub.org

Box: Tour de Stench

Aloma Dew, Sierra Club, sierraclub.org/factoryfarms/tour_de_stench/

Hereford, Texas

"The Old Philosopher," Clint Formby, KPAN Radio, kpanradio.com/krew/oldphilo.htm

"The Smell of Money," Larry Stalcup, Corn & Soybean Digest, February 15, 2002, cornandsoybeandigest.com/mag/soybean_smell_money/index.html

"Shrinking Ethanol's Carbon Footprint," Jerry W. Kram, Ethanol Producer Magazine, July 2007, ethanol-producer.com/article-print.jsp?article_id=3092

New Bern, North Carolina

Rick Dove, former riverkeeper, Waterkeeper Alliance, riverlaw.us

"Hogs and CAFO's: Hog Facts: All the Poop on Swine," Neuse River Foundation, www.neuseriver.org/hogsandcafos.html

Box: Bridgewater, Maine
"Outhouses: Nostalgia Replaces Privies," Tom Bell, *Portland Press Herald*, July 14, 2002, mainetoday.com/census2000/news/020714outhouse.shtml

FACTORIES AND INDUSTRY
Cedar Rapids, Iowa
"Methane Energy Recovery on Iowa Farms," Iowa Department of Natural Resources, 2003, alliantenergy.com/docs/groups/public/documents/pub/p012042.pdf
"Formerly Closed Landfill Easing Flood Clean Up Job," Dave Franzman, KCRG-TV9, July 9, 2008, kcrg.com/news/local/24273839.html
"Cedar Rapids Flood Debris Could Fill More Than Four Football Fields," Mark Geary, KCRG-TV9, June 23, 2008, kcrg.com/floodwatch/cleanup/20725114.html
Box: Ogden, Utah
"City Sniffs Out Odors at Pet Food Factory," Itchmo: News for Dogs and Cats, September 18, 2007, itchmo.com/city-sniffs-out-odors-at-pet-food-factory-2912
Spring Valley Lake and Victorville, California
Violette Roberts, Mojave Desert Air Quality Management District, mdaqmd.ca.gov
"Residents Complain about Odors from Nutro Products Pet Food Plant," Emily Huh, Itchmo: News for Dogs and Cats, September 28, 2007, itchmo.com/residents-complain-about-odors-from-nutro-products-pet-food-plant-3129
Lewiston, Idaho
"Health Consultation: Evaluation of Air Exposure, Potlatch Pulp Mill, Lewiston, Nez Perce County, Idaho," Agency for Toxic Substances & Disease Registry, www.atsdr.cdc.gov/HAC/PHA/potlatch/ppm_p1.html
"Air Pollution: The 'Feds' Move to Abate Idaho Pulp Mill Stench," Bryce Nelson, *Science,* September 1967: 1,018–1,021
Williamsburg, Michigan
Bill O'Brien, business editor, *Traverse City Record-Eagle*
"Processing Plant's Environmental Issues Linger," Bill O'Brien, *Traverse City Record-Eagle,* January 30, 2006, archives.record-eagle.com/2006/jan/29wrs.htm

INTL. HONORABLE MENTIONS
Taean County, South Korea
"South Korea Cleans Up Big Oil Spill," Choe Sang-Hun, *New York Times,* December 10, 2007, nytimes.com/2007/12/10/world/asia/10skorea.html?_r=1&scp=5&sq=stench&st=nyt&oref=slogin
"South Korea Arrests Two Captains in Huge Oil Spill," Agence France-Presse, *New York Times,* December 25, 2007, nytimes.com/2007/12/25/world/asia/25skorea.html?scp=1&sq=Taean+County+south+korea+and+oil+spill&st=nyt
Box: Naples, the Stinkiest Place on Earth? Sometimes
"Naples Trash Crisis Gets Personal," CNN, January 4, 2008, edition.cnn.com/2008/WORLD/europe/01/04/naples.protest.ap/index.html
"European Commission Sues to Force Italy to Take Out the Garbage," Ian Fisher, *New York Times,* May 7, 2008, nytimes.com/2008/05/07/world/europe/07italy.html?_r=1&oref=slogin
Dharavi Slum, Mumbai, India
"Life in a Slum," BBC, 2006, news.bbc.co.uk/2/shared/spl/hi/world/06/dharavi_slum/html/dharavi_slum_intro.stm

"A Flourishing Slum," *Economist,* December 19, 2007, economist.com/world/asia/displaystory.cfm?story_id=10311293
"Alternative Tourist Trail: Slumming It in Mumbai," Justin Huggler, *Independent,* July 25, 2006, independent.co.uk/travel/news-and-advice/alternative-tourist-trail-slumming-it-in-mumbai-409227.html

Chapter 5: Natural Disasters
Jay Gulledge, PhD, senior scientist, Pew Center on Global Climate Change, pewclimate.org/
John Leslie, National Oceanic and Atmospheric Administration, Satellite and Information Service (NOAA), noaa.gov
Kevin Krajick, Earth Institute at Columbia University, www.earth.columbia.edu
Dr. Stephen P. Leatherman, Laboratory for Coastal Research, Florida International University, Miami, www.ihc.fiu.edu

HURRICANES
Outer Banks, North Carolina
Jim William, editor, HurricaneCity.com
Sandy Semans, editor, *Outer Banks Sentinel*
National Park Service, Cape Hatteras National Seashore, nps.gov/caha
Dorothy Toolan, Replace the Bridge Now, replacethebridgenow.com
South Florida
Ken Kaye, senior writer, South Florida *Sun-Sentinel*
City ranking, HurricaneCity.com, hurricanecity.com/Rank.htm
"Sketches of a Catastrophe," *Miami Herald,* May 7, 2006
Bahamas
Superclubs Hurricane Guarantee, superclubs.com/guarantee
Galveston, Texas
Galveston: A History of the Island, Gary Cartwright, TCU Press, 1998
Heber Taylor, editor, *Galveston County Daily News*
Box: Indianola, Texas
"Indianola, Texas, 1846–1886: Texas Ghost Town," Texas Escapes Online Magazine, texasescapes.com/TexasGhostTowns/IndianolaTexas/IndianolaTx.htm
Grand Cayman
"Grand Cayman: Devastation Beyond Imagination," Cayman Net News, September 13, 2004, caymannetnews.com/2004/09/738/imagination.shtml
City ranking, HurricaneCity.com, hurricanecity.com/Rank.htm

TORNADOES
Oklahoma City–Moore, Oklahoma
Gary England, meteorologist, KWTV Channel 9
Anniston, Alabama
"Compressed Air: When Local Media Isn't There for the Public," John Fleming, *Anniston Star,* March 5, 2008, www.annistonstar.com/showcase/2008/as-open-0305-jflemingcol-8c05k1127.htm
John Fleming, editor at large, *Anniston Star*
Jackson, Tennessee
Dr. Jeff Masters, director of meteorology, Weather Underground
Box: Aurora, Nebraska
Aurora, Nebraska, City Hall Information Center, cityofaurora.org

Kurt Johnson, publisher, *Aurora News Register*

"Climate of 2003 Annual Review: Significant U.S. and Global Events," National Climatic Data Center, National Oceanic and Atmospheric Administration, January 15, 2004, www.ncdc.noaa.gov/oa/climate/research/2003/ann/events.html

FLOODS

Tuvalu Islands

"Stop My Nation Vanishing," Saufatu Sopoanga, *Our Planet: The Magazine of the United Nations Environment Programme* 15, no. 1: 9–10, unep.org/ourplanet/imgversn/151/sopoanga.html

San Francisco Bay, California

Will Travis, executive director, San Francisco Bay Conservation and Development Commission, www.bcdc.ca.gov/index.php

"Sea Level a Rising Threat," Mike Taugher, *Contra Costa Times,* January 26, 2007, contracostatimes.com/specialreports/ci_5434856

Box: Shishmaref, Alaska

Dr. Jeff Masters, director of meteorology, Weather Underground

Shishmaref Erosion & Relocation Coalition, shishmaref relocation.com

INTERNATIONAL RISKS

Bangladesh

Natural Disaster Hotspots: A Global Risk Analysis, Maxx Dilley, Robert S. Chen, Uwe Deichmann, Arthur L. Lerner-Lam, and Margaret Arnold, Washington, DC: World Bank Publications, 2005, www.ldeo.columbia.edu/chrr/research/hotspots

Art Lerner-Lam, director, Center for Hazards & Risk Research at Columbia University

Indonesia

Natural Disaster Hotspots: A Global Risk Analysis, Maxx Dilley, Robert S. Chen, Uwe Deichmann, Arthur L. Lerner-Lam, and Margaret Arnold, Washington, DC: World Bank Publications, 2005, www.ldeo.columbia.edu/chrr/research/hotspots

"Indonesia's Mud Volcano Wreaking Havoc," Chris Brummitt, Associated Press, *Washington Post,* September 28, 2006, washingtonpost.com/wp-dyn/content/article/2006/09/28/AR2006092801232.html

Art Lerner-Lam, director, Center for Hazards & Risk Research at Columbia University

India

Natural Disaster Hotspots: A Global Risk Analysis, Maxx Dilley, Robert S. Chen, Uwe Deichmann, Arthur L. Lerner-Lam, and Margaret Arnold, Washington, DC: World Bank Publications, 2005, www.ldeo.columbia.edu/chrr/research/hotspots

Art Lerner-Lam, director, Center for Hazards & Risk Research at Columbia University

MOST OVERDUE FOR A POUNDING

New York, New York

"National Assessment of Coastal Vulnerability to Future Sea-Level Rise," U.S. Department of the Interior, U.S. Geological Survey, June 2000, pubs.usgs.gov/fs/fs76-00/fs076-00.pdf

"Waiting for Hurricane X," Erik Larson, *Time,* June 24, 2001, time.com/time/magazine/article/0,9171,139890,00.html

"Saving New York from a Major Hurricane," staff writers, New York (AFP), Terra Daily, Jun 28, 2006, terradaily.com/reports/Saving_New_York_From_A_Major_Hurricane_999.html

"Hurricane Danger Zone: N.Y.C.," Nicholas Coch, CUNY Lecture Series podcast, August 28, 2007, www1.cuny.edu/forums/podcasts/?m=200708

Southern California

"The Big One: Earthquake Risk in Southern California," San Diego State University, advancement.sdsu.edu/marcomm/features/2007/earthquake.html

Leslie Gordon, U.S. Department of the Interior, U.S. Geological Survey

Cumbre Vieja, Canary Islands

"5 Natural Disasters Headed for the United States," Jim Gorman, *Popular Mechanics,* October 2006, popularmechanics.com/science/earth/3852052.html

Dr. Simon Day, associate researcher, Benfield UCL Hazard Research Centre

Yellowstone National Park, Wyoming

"Yellowstone Is Rising on Swollen 'Supervolcano,'" Richard A. Lovett, *National Geographic News,* November 8, 2007, news.nationalgeographic.com/news/2007/11/071108-yellowstone.html

"Yellowstone Volcano: Is 'the Beast' Building to a Violent Tantrum?" StandardNET, *National Geographic News,* August 30, 2001, news.nationalgeographic.com/news/pf/65133666.html

Mount Taranaki, New Zealand

"Mt Taranaki 'Overdue' for Eruption," Physorg.com, October 25, 2005, physorg.com/news7537.html

Shane Cronin, PhD, lecturer, Soil and Earth Sciences Group Institute of Natural Resources, Massey University

Himalayas

"Massive Himalayan Earthquake Overdue, Scientists Conclude," Kate Wong, *Scientific American,* August 27, 2001, sciam.com/article.cfm?id=massive-himalayan-earthqu&print=true

"Himalayan Seismic Hazard," Roger Bilham, Vinod K. Gaur, and Peter Molnar, *Science,* August 24, 2001, sciencemag.org/cgi/content/summary/293/5534/1442

Box: Is Anywhere Safe?

"Where to Hide from Mother Nature," Brendan I. Koerner, Slate.com, September 15, 2005, slate.com/id/2126321

Chapter 6: Disease Capitals

CDC Health Information for International Travel 2008, ed. Paul M. Arguin MD, Phyllis Kozarsky, MD, and Christie Reed, MD, Mosby, 2007

Phyllis Kozarsky, MD, Division of Global Migration and Quarantine, CDC; professor of medicine and infectious diseases, Emory University School of Medicine

Introduction

"Cumulative Number of Reported Probable Cases of SARS, From 1 Nov 2002 to 6 June 2003," World Health Organization, who.int/csr/sars/country/2003_06_06/en/index.html

"Cumulative Number of Confirmed Human Cases of Avian Influenza A/(H5N1) Reported to WHO, 19 June 2008," World Health Organization, who.int/csr/disease/avian_influenza/country/cases_table_2008_06_19/en/index.html

"Known Cases and Outbreaks of Ebola Hemorrhagic Fever, in Chronological Order," CDC, August 25, 2006, cdc.gov/ncidod/dvrd/spb/mnpages/dispages/ebola/ebolatable.htm

HIV/AIDS
"UNAIDS/WHO AIDS Epidemic Update: December 2005," Joint United Nations Programme on HIV/AIDS (UNAIDS), World Health Organization (WHO), unaids.org/epi/2005/doc/report_pdf.asp

"Eastern Europe and Central Asia AIDS Epidemic Update Regional Summary," UNAIDS, March 2008, data.unaids.org/pub/Report/2008/jc1529_epibriefs_eeurope_casia_en.pdf

"HIV/AIDS in Russia, Eastern Europe & Central Asia," AVERT, avert.org/eurosum.htm

"Sub-Saharan Africa," UNAIDS, unaids.org/en/CountryResponses/Regions/SubSaharanAfrica.asp

Cholera
Cholera Fact Sheet, World Health Organization, who.int/topics/cholera/en/

"Severe Acute Watery Diarrhoea with *V. cholerae* positive cases in Viet Nam," World Health Organization, who.int/csr/don/2008_04_22/en/index.html

Dengue Fever
Dengue Fever Fact Sheet, World Health Organization, who.int/topics/dengue/en/

"2008: Number of Reported Cases of Dengue and Dengue Hemorrhagic Fever (DHF), Region of the Americas (by Country and Subregion)," Pan American Health Organization, paho.org/English/AD/DPC/CD/dengue-cases-2008.htm

Malaria
"World Malaria Report 2005," World Health Organization, rbm.who.int/wmr2005/

"Malaria's Sting Spreads As Temperatures Rise—In Kenya's Highlands, Where It Once Was Rare, Africa's Biggest Killer Has Found New Territory," Edmund Sanders, *Los Angeles Times,* July 22, 2007, articles.latimes.com/2007/jul/22/world/fg-malaria22

"The Effect of Deforestation on the Human-Biting Rate of *Anopheles darlingi,* the Primary Vector of Falciparum Malaria in the Peruvian Amazon," Amy Yomiko Vittor, Robert H. Gilman, James Tielsch, Gregory Glass, Tim Shields, Wagner Sánchez Lozano, Viviana Pinedo-Cancino, and Jonathan A. Patz, *American Journal of Tropical Medicine and Hygiene* 74, no. 1 (2006): 3–11, www.ajtmh.org/cgi/content/abstract/74/1/3

"Jamaica Fights Malaria Outbreak," BBC Caribbean, December 6, 2006, bbc.co.uk/caribbean/news/story/2006/12/061206_malariaupdate.shtml

Hepatitis B
Hepatitis B Fact Sheet, World Health Organization, who.int/mediacentre/factsheets/fs204/en

Meredith Bergin, special projects coordinator, Asian Liver Center, Stanford University School of Medicine, liver.stanford.edu/Education/faq.html

Hepatitis C
Hepatitis C Fact Sheet, World Health Organization, who.int/mediacentre/factsheets/fs164/en

"Hepatitis C Program in Egypt," Sustainable Sciences Institute, ssilink.org/index.php?option=displaypage&Itemid=79&op=page&SubMenu=

Lyme Disease
"Learn about Lyme Disease," CDC, cdc.gov/ncidod/dvbid/Lyme/

"Travelers' Health: Yellow Book, CDC Health Information for International Travel 2008: Lyme Disease," wwwn.cdc.gov/travel/yellowBookCh4-LymeDisease.aspx

Toxoplasmosis
"The 'Cat Lady' Conundrum," Rebecca Skloot, *New York Times,* December 9, 2007, nytimes.com/2007/12/09/magazine/09_10_catcoat.html

"Parasite Makes Men Dumb, Women Sexy," *Sydney Morning Herald,* December 26, 2006, smh.com.au/news/national/parasite-makes-men-dumb-women-sexy/2006/12/26/1166895290973.html

"Alley Cats & Sex Kittens," Nicky Boulter, *Australasian Science,* January/February 2007

Box: Delaware's Cancer Battle
"Eight Cancer Clusters Discovered in Delaware," Delaware Online, April 24, 2008, delawareonline.com/apps/pbcs.dll/article?AID=/20080424/HEALTH/804240339/1006/NEWS

Box: Supersize Me . . . Not
Greenville, North Carolina
"Top 10 Fast-Food Markets 2007," Sandelman & Associates, sandelman.com/store/ProductInfo.aspx?productid=REPORTS-RANKINGS-2007

Greater Greenville Chamber of Commerce, greenvillechamber.org/

Hardee's nutritional information, hardees.com/nutrition/

Greenville Convention & Visitors Bureau, visitgreenvillenc.com/news/article_view.asp?article_id=63

McAllen, Texas
"Top 10 Fast-Food Markets 2007," Sandelman & Associates, sandelman.com/store/ProductInfo.aspx?productid=REPORTS-RANKINGS-2007

CNN Money, "10 Fastest Growing Real Estate Markets," CNN.com, May 15, 2008, money.cnn.com/galleries/2008/moneymag/0805/gallery.resg_gainers.moneymag/

"Steady Labor Market Midland, Odessa Continue to Lead State in Job Growth," Mella McEwen, *Midland Reporter-Telegram,* April 19, 2008, mywesttexas.com/articles/2008/04/20/news/top_stories/midland_unemployment.txt

Oklahoma City, Oklahoma
"Top 10 Fast-Food Markets 2007," Sandelman & Associates, sandelman.com/store/ProductInfo.aspx?productid=REPORTS-RANKINGS-2007

Sonic nutritional information, sonicdrivein.com/pdfs/menu/SonicNutritionGuide.pdf;jsessionid=2D911B0BB961785F888EF6177D62422A.sonic-prod

OKC Million, thiscityisgoingonadiet.com

El Paso, Texas
"The Fittest & Fattest Cities in America, 2008," *Men's Fitness,* March 2008: 85–91

"Texas! Bringing Healthy Back," Texas Department of State Health Services, February 6, 2008, www.dshs.state.tx.us/obesity/default.shtm

"Globesity: The Crisis of Growing Proportions," Donna Eberwine, *Perspectives in Health Magazine* 7, no. 3 (2002), www.paho.org/English/DPI/Number15_article2_5.htm

"Special Report: How Safe Is Your Food?" Stephanie Sanchez, *El Paso Times,* April 20, 2008, elpasotimes. com/dining/ci_8987102

More Fast-Food Tidbits

"Fast-Food Ban Proposed in South Los Angeles," Mandalit del Barco, *All Things Considered,* NPR, September 16, 2007, npr.org/templates/story/story. php?storyId=14459040

"Prevalence of Overweight among Children and Adolescents: United States, 1999–2002," CDC, cdc. gov/nchs/products/pubs/pubd/hestats/overwght99.htm

"The World Health Organization Warns of the Rising Threat of Heart Disease and Stroke As Overweight and Obesity Rapidly Increase," World Health Organization, September 22, 2005, who.int/mediacentre/news/ releases/2005/pr44/en/index.html

"Obesity and Overweight," World Health Organization, September 2006, who.int/mediacentre/factsheets/ fs311/en/index.html

"McDonald's Restaurants (Most Recent) by Country," NationMaster.com, nationmaster.com/graph/foo_mcd_ res-food-mcdonalds-restaurants

Map provided by Ian Spiro, FastFoodMaps.com

Chapter 7: Worst Airlines

On-Time Arrival Rates

"Number of Reported Flight Arrivals and Percentage Arriving On Time, by Carrier and Airport (Reportable Airports Only)," Table 2, Air Travel Consumer Report, Office of Aviation Enforcement and Proceedings, U.S. Department of Transportation, June 2008, airconsumer. ost.dot.gov/reports/2008/June/200806atcr.pdf

Box: Worst On-Time Arrivals

"Overall Percentage of Reported Flight Operations Arriving On Time and Carrier Rank, by Month, Quarter, and Data Base to Date," Table 1A, Air Travel Consumer Report, Office of Aviation Enforcement and Proceedings, U.S. Department of Transportation, June 2008, airconsumer. ost.dot.gov/reports/2008/June/200806atcr.pdf

The Lost-Luggage Blues

"January–March Mishandled Baggage Reports," Air Travel Consumer Report, Office of Aviation Enforcement and Proceedings, U.S. Department of Transportation, May 2008, p. 28, airconsumer.ost.dot.gov/ reports/2008/May/200805atcr.pdf

"Air Transport Users Council Delayed Baggage Table for 2007," www.caa.co.uk/docs/306/AUC%20press% 20release%20(2).pdf

Most Delayed Flights

"List of Regularly Scheduled Flights Arriving Late 80% of the Time or More," Table 5, Air Travel Consumer Report, Office of Aviation Enforcement and Proceedings, U.S. Department of Transportation, May 2008, airconsumer. ost.dot.gov/reports/2008/May/200805atcr.pdf

Bumped Passengers

"January–March, Passengers Denied Boarding by U.S. Airlines," Air Travel Consumer Report, Office of Aviation Enforcement and Proceedings, U.S. Department of Transportation, July 2008, airconsumer.ost.dot.gov/ reports/2008/July/200807atcr.pdf

Box: Don't Let Fido Go There

"April 2008 Airline Reports to DOT of Incidents Involving the Loss, Injury or Death of Animals during Air Transportation," Air Travel Consumer Report, Office of Aviation

Enforcement and Proceedings, U.S. Department of Transportation, June 2008, airconsumer.ost.dot.gov/ reports/2008/June/200806atcr.pdf

"March 2008 Airline Reports to DOT of Incidents Involving the Loss, Injury or Death of Animals during Air Transportation," Air Travel Consumer Report, Office of Aviation Enforcement and Proceedings, U.S. Department of Transportation, May 2008, airconsumer. ost.dot.gov/reports/2008/May/200805atcr.pdf

"February 2008 Airline Reports to DOT of Incidents Involving the Loss, Injury or Death of Animals during Air Transportation," Air Travel Consumer Report, Office of Aviation Enforcement and Proceedings, U.S. Department of Transportation, April 2008, airconsumer. ost.dot.gov/reports/2008/April/200804atcr.pdf

"January 2008 Airline Reports to DOT of Incidents Involving the Loss, Injury or Death of Animals during Air Transportation," Air Travel Consumer Report, Office of Aviation Enforcement and Proceedings, U.S. Department of Transportation, March 2008, airconsumer.ost.dot.gov/reports/2008/march/ 200803atcr.pdf

The Bottom Line on Airline Seats

Seatguru.com

Spirit Airlines aircraft information, spiritair.com/Aircraft. aspx

American Airlines aircraft seating chart, aa.com/aa/ i18nForward.do?p=/aboutUs/ourPlanes/ATR72.jsp

"Aerospatiale/Alenia ATR-72 1988," All the World's Rotorcraft, aviastar.org/air/inter/atr-72.php

Northwest Airlines seat maps, nwa.com/travel/trave/ seatm/dc930/index.shtml

"Northwest Speeds Up DC-9 Reduction," Ben Mutzabaugh, *USA Today,* January 22, 2008, blogs. usatoday.com/sky/2008/01/nwa-dc9.html

"Ryanair 'to Cut Frills Further,'" BBC News, February 15, 2004, news.bbc.co.uk/2/hi/business/3489761. stm

Banned Airlines

International Aviation Safety Assessments (IASA), Federal Aviation Administration, faa.gov/safety/ programs_initiatives/oversight/iasa/

"List of Airlines Banned within the EU," European Commission, ec.europa.eu/transport/air-ban/list_en. htm

Chapter 8: Worst Airports

DOMESTIC

Chicago, Illinois: O'Hare International

Chicago O'Hare International Airport (ORD), ohare.com

Year-to-date statistics, Flychicago.com, flychicago.com/ statistics/stats/1207SUMMARY.pdf

Miami, Florida: Miami International

"County Adds $503 Million to North Terminal Budget," Wayne Tompkins, *Miami Today,* May 24, 2007, miamitodaynews.com/news/070524/story1. shtml

Miami International Airport (MIA), miami-airport.com

Cincinnati, Ohio: Cincinnati/Northern Kentucky International

"Domestic Airline Fares Consumer Report—Third Quarter 2007 Passenger and Fare Information," Department of Transportation, April 2008, ostpxweb.dot.gov/aviation/ domfares/web073.pdf

Atlanta, Georgia
"America's Most Time-Draining Airports," Rebecca Ruiz, *Forbes,* June 3, 2008, forbes.com/home/2008/06/02/aviation-travel-delays-biz-logistics-cx_rr_0603travel.html

Box: **The Most Delayed Airports**
April: "Percentage of All Carriers' Reported Flight Operations Arriving on Time, by Airport and Time of Day (Reportable Airports Only)," Table 3, Air Travel Consumer Report, Office of Aviation Enforcement and Proceedings, U.S. Department of Transportation, June 2008, airconsumer.ost.dot.gov/reports/2008/June/200806atcr.pdf

March: "Percentage of All Carriers' Reported Flight Operations Arriving on Time, by Airport and Time of Day (Reportable Airports Only)," Table 3, Air Travel Consumer Report, Office of Aviation Enforcement and Proceedings, U.S. Department of Transportation, May 2008, airconsumer.ost.dot.gov/reports/2008/May/200805atcr.pdf

February: "Percentage of All Carriers' Reported Flight Operations Arriving on Time, by Airport and Time of Day (Reportable Airports Only)," Table 3, Air Travel Consumer Report, Office of Aviation Enforcement and Proceedings, U.S. Department of Transportation, April 2008, airconsumer.ost.dot.gov/reports/2008/April/200804atcr.pdf

January: "Percentage of All Carriers' Reported Flight Operations Arriving on Time, by Airport and Time of Day (Reportable Airports Only)," Table 3, Air Travel Consumer Report, Office of Aviation Enforcement and Proceedings, U.S. Department of Transportation, March 2008, airconsumer.ost.dot.gov/reports/2008/march/200803atcr.pdf

December: "Percentage of All Carriers' Reported Flight Operations Arriving on Time, by Airport and Time of Day (Reportable Airports Only)," Table 3, Air Travel Consumer Report, Office of Aviation Enforcement and Proceedings, U.S. Department of Transportation, February 2008, airconsumer.ost.dot.gov/reports/2008/february/200802atcr.pdf

November: "Percentage of All Carriers' Reported Flight Operations Arriving on Time, by Airport and Time of Day (Reportable Airports Only)," Table 3, Air Travel Consumer Report, Office of Aviation Enforcement and Proceedings, U.S. Department of Transportation, January 2008, airconsumer.ost.dot.gov/reports/2008/january/200801atcr.pdf

INTERNATIONAL

Manila, Philippines: Ninoy Aquino International Airport
The Guide to Sleeping in Airports, sleepinginairports.com/list.asp?region=6&country=Philippines&city=Manila&terminal=Ninoy+Aquino+International
"NAIA 3 Opening Seen Mid-2008," Tarra Quismundo, *Philippine Daily Inquirer,* January 14, 2008, newsinfo.inquirer.net/breakingnews/metro/view_article.php?article_id=112162

Dakar, Senegal: Leopold Sedar Senghor International
"A Filthy Lobby, Sullen-Faced Employees, No Place to Sit, and a Vague Sense of Danger All Add Up to the World's Worst Airport," Patrick Smith, Salon.com, May 25, 2007, salon.com/tech/col/smith/2007/05/25/askthepilot233/print.html

Box: **The World's Scariest Runways**
"Aargh—Here We Go Again," *Sunday Times,* July 13, 2008, timesonline.co.uk/tol/travel/article4315480.ece

São Paulo, Brazil: Congonhas International
Aviation Safety Network, aviation-safety.net/database/record.php?id=20070717-0

Box: Expensive Cities
2008 *Quality of Living* survey, Mercer International, mercer.com/qualityofliving
"Cost of Living Comparison for Selected Cities," provided by Mercer International
"Big Mac Index," *Economist,* February 1, 2007
"Average Travel Costs in Selected Cities," provided by Runzheimer International, runzheimer.com

Chapter 9: Worst Hotels

Introduction
"Look Out for That 'Rustic Ambiance,'" Charles Hillestad, *Hotel Secrets from the Travel Detective,* Peter Greenberg, New York: Villard, 2004
"South Jersey Hotel Settles Fraud Lawsuit," New Jersey Department of Law and Public Safety, Division of Consumer Affairs, March 31, 2003, www.state.nj.us/oag/ca/press/diamond.htm

Legionnaires' Disease
"Hotel Closes over Legionnaires' Disease," WKMG Orlando, March 14, 2008, local6.com/health/15595503/detail.html
Orange County, Florida, Health Department
"Legionnaires Disease Associated with Potable Water in a Hotel—Ocean City, Maryland, October 2003–February 2004," CDC, February 25, 2005, cdc.gov/mmwr/preview/mmwrhtml/mm5407a1.htm
Maryland Department of Health
"Cortina Inn Closed after Tests Show Legionnaires' Disease," Rutland Herald Online, April 4, 2008, rutlandherald.com/apps/pbcs.dll/article?AID=/20080404/NEWS04/804040378/1002/NEWS01
"Killington Inn Closed a Second Time for Bacteria," *Boston Globe,* June 19, 2008, boston.com/news/local/vermont/articles/2008/06/19/killington_inn_closed_a_second_time_for_bacteria/
"Embattled Hotel Files for Bankruptcy," Times Argus Online, June 22, 2008 timesargus.com/apps/pbcs.dll/article?AID=/20080622/NEWS02/806220407/1003/NEWS02
Vermont Department of Health
"Two Cases of Legionnaires' Disease Force the Seagarden Inn in Daytona Beach Shores, Florida to Voluntarily Close," Willoughby Mariano, *Orlando Sentinel,* February 4, 2006
Matthew Freije, president, HC Information Resources; consultant, *Legionella* risk assessments, management plans, investigations, and remediation

Dirtiest Hotels
TripAdvisor's Top 10 Dirtiest Hotels 2008, April 23, 2008, tripadvisor.com/TravelersChoice-c1
Brooke N. Ferencsik, TripAdvisor.com
New York City Department of Health and Mental Hygiene
New York City Department of Housing Preservation and Development
Nashville Environmental Health Services

Florida Department of Business & Professional Regulation, Broward County, Florida, https://www.myfloridalicense.com/inspectionDetail.asp?InspVisitID=2800723&id=2142476

Florida Department of Business & Professional Regulation, St. Johns County, Florida, https://www.myfloridalicense.com/inspectionDates.asp?SID=&id=2245739

New Jersey Department of Community Affairs, Bureau of Housing Inspections

Pennsylvania Department of Health, Lancaster County

Los Angeles County Environmental Health Department

Box: Osaka's Love Hotels

"Osaka Love Hotels: The Room Menu," HotelChatter, March 8, 2005, hotelchatter.com/story/2005/3/8/101028/4318/hotels/Osaka_Love_Hotels:_The_Room_Menu

Better Business Bureau Complaints

Alison Preszler, Council of Better Business Bureaus media relations specialist, Better Business Bureau

Better Business Bureau Northwest Florida

Interview with Kaycee Chapman, filed with Northwest Florida Better Business Bureau

Wisconsin Better Business Bureau

Interview with Joy Williams, filed with Wisconsin Better Business Bureau

Sauk County (Wisconsin) Health Department

Bed Bugs!

Clint Briscoe, Terminix

Breaking Legal News release, "One of the World's Premier Luxury Hotels, Mandarin Oriental Hyde Park in London, Rented Bed Bug-Infested Room . . ." Robertson Freilich Bruno & Cohen, January 15, 2007, prforlaw.com/news/Bluming_v_Mandarin_News Release_FINAL_20070115.pdf

Rosanna Crawley, Mandarin Oriental

"Woman Sues Motel for Bed Bugs," *Morning News* (Northwest Arkansas), March 8, 2007, nwaonline.net/articles/2007/03/09/news/030907bzbedbugs.txt

"Another Bed Bug Lawsuit: The Stone Inn, Siloam Springs, Arkansas," Bedbugger, March 10, 2007, bedbugger.com/2007/03/10/another-bed-bug-lawsuit-the-stone-inn-siloam-springs-arkansas

Arkansas Department of Health

New York City Department of Health and Mental Hygiene

New York City Department of Housing Preservation and Development

Los Angeles County Environmental Health Department

Chapter 10: Worst Cruises

Introduction

Cruise Lines International Association, cruising.org

Cleanliness Is Next to Godliness

Vessel Sanitation Program, CDC, cdc.gov/nceh/vsp/

"CDC's Investigation of Gastroenteritis on the *Royal Odyssey* Cruise Ship, March 4–14, 1997," cdc.gov/nceh/vsp/surv/outbreak/1997/royal.htm

"Outbreak Updates for International Cruise Ships," CDC, cdc.gov/nceh/vsp/surv/GIlist.htm

"Green Sheet Report: A List of the Most Recent Inspection Scores," CDC, wwwn.cdc.gov/vsp/InspectionQueryTool/Forms/InspectionGreenSheetRpt.aspx

Box: "All Hurl the Queen!"

"Sickness Strikes Camilla's Cruise Ship," Natalie Paris and agencies, *Daily Telegraph,* December 31, 2007,

telegraph.co.uk/news/uknews/1574000/Sickness-strikes-Camilla's-cruise-ship.html

Pillage and Steal: The Modern-Day Jack Sparrow

Piracy and Armed Robbery against Ships, International Chamber of Commerce International Maritime Bureau, Annual Report, January 1–December 31, 2007

Piracy and Armed Robbery against Ships, International Chamber of Commerce International Maritime Bureau, Annual Report, January 1–June 30, 2008

Nickel-and-Diming on Cruise Ships

Onboard Experiences information, Royal Caribbean, royalcaribbean.com/findacruise/experiencetypes/home.do;jsessionid=0000x8ybm5O79PdimTkPlWUSajA:12hdhubrs?cS=NAVBAR

Shore Excursions information, Norwegian Cruise Line, ncl.com/nclweb/shorexLanding.html

Safety on Cruise Ships

"Testimony of Ross A. Klein, PhD, before the Subcommittee on Surface Transportation and Merchant Marine Infrastructure, Safety, and Security, Senate Committee on Commerce, Science, and Transportation," hearings on "Cruise Ship Safety: Examining Potential Steps for Keeping Americans Safe at Sea," June 19, 2008, rainn.org/pdf-files-and-other-documents/Public-Policy/Issues/Ross-A-Klein-Testimony.pdf

"Rep. Doris Matsui Amends Legislation to Keep Americans Safe on Cruise Ships," U.S. Rep. Doris Matsui, April 24, 2008, matsui.house.gov/index.php?option=com_content&task=view&id=359&Itemid=50

"Are You Safer Today on a Cruise Ship Than in 1999?" Ross Klein, CruiseJunkie.com, April 2, 2007, cruisejunkie.com/Editorial%20-%20Sexual%20Assaults.html

Ross Klein, CruiseJunkie.com

The Cruise Industry and Pollution

"A Global Perspective on the Challenges of Coastal Tourism," Fareedali Kanji, Coastal Development Centre, Faculty of Fisheries, Kasetsart University, Jatujak, Bangkok, Thailand, November 16, 2006, cdc.fish.ku.ac.th/work%20on%20web/Global%20coastal%20tourism.pdf

"Congressional Research Service Report for Congress: Cruise Ship Pollution: Background, Laws and Regulations, and Key Issues," Claudia Copeland, Congressional Research Service, February 6, 2008, ncseonline.org/NLE/CRSreports/07Dec/RL32450.pdf

"Land, Air and Water: Cruise Ships," Friends of the Earth, action.foe.org/content.jsp?content_KEY=2716&t=2007_Peoples-Resources.dwt

"Ocean Pollution—Global Shipping and the Cruise Industry," Earthjustice, earthjustice.org/library/background/ocean-pollution-global-shipping-and-the-cruise-industry.html

"Large Environmental Fines ($100,000 or More)," CruiseJunkie.com, cruisejunkie.com/largefines.html

"Attorney General Janet Reno Press Conference on Environmental Crimes by Royal Caribbean Cruises Ltd.," U.S. Department of Justice, July 21, 1999, usdoj.gov/archive/ag/speeches/1999/royalcaribbean.htm

Division of Water, Cruise Ship Program, Alaska Department of Environmental Conservation, dec.state.ak.us/water/cruise_ships

"Dickerson Cruise Ship Bill Passes House Unanimously," Washington State Legislature, March 11, 2005,

housedemocrats.wa.gov/members/Dickerson/
cruise-house.asp
"Cruise Bill Clears Committee," Kimi Yoshino, *Los Angeles Times,* April 09, 2008, articles.latimes.com/2008/apr/09/business/fi-cruise9

Chapter 11: Dangerous Trains
Train Derailments
"China Train Crash Kills 70 and Injures Hundreds," Guo Shipeng and Nick Macfie, Reuters, April 28, 2008, reuters.com/article/topNews/idUSPEK34967020080428?feedType=RSS&feedName=topNews
"Train Accidents: Derailment," Federal Railroad Administration, Office of Safety Analysis, safetydata.fra.dot.gov/OfficeofSafety/publicsite/Query/inctally1.aspx
Railroad Accident Report, "Derailment of Southern Pacific Transportation Company Freight Train on May 12, 1989," National Transportation Safety Board, pstrust.org/library/docs/ntsb_doc26.pdf
"Train Accidents: Texas," Federal Railroad Administration, Office of Safety Analysis, safetydata.fra.dot.gov/OfficeofSafety/publicsite/Query/inctally1.aspx
"Train Accidents: Illinois," Federal Railroad Administration, Office of Safety Analysis, safetydata.fra.dot.gov/OfficeofSafety/publicsite/Query/inctally1.aspx
"Train Accidents: California," Federal Railroad Administration, Office of Safety Analysis, safetydata.fra.dot.gov/OfficeofSafety/publicsite/Query/inctally1.aspx
Texas Transportation Institute

Trespassing Accidents
"Trespasser Casualties," Federal Railroad Administration, Office of Safety Analysis, safetydata.fra.dot.gov/OfficeofSafety/publicsite/Query/castally4.aspx
"Lawsuit in Train Deaths Is Beating the Odds," Nancy Bartley, *Seattle Times,* May 3, 2006, seattletimes.nwsource.com/html/localnews/2002968329_train03m.html
"Appeal from the United States District Court for the Western District of Washington," Barbara Jacobs Rothstein, District Judge, Presiding, filed April 6, 2005, www.ca9.uscourts.gov/coa/memdispo.nsf/pdfview/040605/$File/03-35718.PDF
"Trespasser Casualties: California," Federal Railroad Administration, Office of Safety Analysis, safetydata.fra.dot.gov/OfficeofSafety/publicsite/Query/castally4.aspx
"Trespasser Casualties: Texas," Federal Railroad Administration, Office of Safety Analysis, safetydata.fra.dot.gov/OfficeofSafety/publicsite/Query/castally4.aspx

Box: Are You Fit for Train Travel?
"HK Man's Death on Tibet Railway Kept under Wraps," Carrie Chan and Leslie Kwoh, *Standard,* August 29, 2006, thestandard.com.hk/news_detail.asp?pp_cat=11&art_id=26092&sid=9631674&con_type=1

Box: There's *What* Riding on That Train?
"Train Derailment, Acid Leak Forces La. Evacuation," Melinda Deslatte, *USA Today,* May 17, 2008, usatoday.com/news/nation/2008-05-17-train-derailment-leak_N.htm

Highway-Railroad Grade Crossings
"Highway-Rail Accidents by State/Railroad," Federal Railroad Administration, Office of Safety Analysis, safetydata.fra.dot.gov/OfficeofSafety/publicsite/Query/gxrabbr.aspx
Vicky Moore, Angels on Track, angelsontrack.org
"Guarded Crossings: An In-Depth Analysis of the Most Effective Railroad Crossing Protection," W. L. Farnham, October 18, 2000, www.angelsontrack.org/images/guardedcrossings.doc

Box: Truth and Consequences
"Unsafe Crossings: The Failure to Protect Railroad-Highway Intersections," *The Long Term View* 5, no. 2 (Summer 2001), Massachusetts School of Law at Andover, angelsontrack.org/unsafecrossings.html

Box: When Stupidity Leads to Tragedy
"Man Accused in Train Crash Faces Murder Charges," CNN, January 27, 2005, cnn.com/2005/US/01/27/train.derailment/
"Alvarez Sentenced to 11 Life Prison Terms for Metrolink Crash," KNBC News, August 20, 2008, knbc.com/news/17244102/detail.html?rss=la&psp=news

On-Time Train Performance
Amtrak route performance, amtrak.com/servlet/ContentServer?pagename=Amtrak/Page/OTP_Route_List&cid=1202243059386

Chapter 12: Highways of Death
DANGEROUS RURAL ROADS
"Growing Traffic in Rural America: Safety, Mobility and Economic Challenges in America's Heartland," The Road Information Program (TRIP), March 2005, tripnet.org/RuralRoads2005Report.pdf

Alabama
Alabama Department of Transportation

South Carolina
"Getting Home Safely: An Analysis of Highway Safety in South Carolina," The Road Information Program (TRIP), February 2008, tripnet.org/SouthCarolinaSafetyReport-Feb2008.pdf
South Carolina Department of Transportation

North Carolina
"NC 2006 Total Crashes, Fatalities by County Miles Traveled," AAA Carolinas, aaacarolinas.com/Media/Releases/attachments/NCDangerousCO_2.xls
"New Hanover Tops List of North Carolina's Most Dangerous Counties for Crashes, Graham Is Most Deadly for Fatal and Injury Crashes," AAA, February 01, 2008, aaacarolinas.com/absolutenm/templates/releaseTemplate.asp?articleid=605&zoneid=2
North Carolina Department of Transportation

Montana
"County Leads State in Roadway Fatalities," *Daily Inter Lake,* April 10, 2008, dailyinterlake.com/articles/2008/04/10/news/news01.txt
Larry Stroklund, Montana American Legion

HAZARDOUS HIGHWAYS
Florida
Florida Highway Patrol
Florida Department of Transportation

Box: Road Rage
"In the Driver's Seat 2008 AutoVantage Road Rage Survey," from press release, Auto Vantage, https://www.autovantage.com/global/scripts/promo.asp?ref=avAUTVANonlgs01

Arizona
Arizona Department of Transportation

California
California Department of Transportation
California Highway Patrol

Colorado
Colorado Department of Transportation
Nevada
"Getting Home Safely: An Analysis of Highway Safety in Nevada," The Road Information Program (TRIP), March 2008, tripnet.org/Nevada_Safety_Report_March2008.pdf
Nevada Department of Transportation
According to Truckers
"Highway Report Card," *Overdrive,* January 2008: 42
"Keystone Drama," Todd Dills, *Overdrive,* January 2008: 38–41
Pennsylvania Department of Transportation
Box: United States Road Assessment Program
United States Road Assessment Program, usrap.us

INTERNATIONAL ROADS
Association for Safe International Travel (ASIRT) statistics, www.asirt.org/GlobalSafety/Issues/tabid/97/Default.aspx
Rochelle Sobel, founder, ASIRT
"Global Status Report on Road Safety," World Health Organization, who.int/violence_injury_prevention/road_traffic/global_status_report/en/index.html
"Road Safety Overseas," U.S. State Department, travel.state.gov/travel/tips/safety/safety_1179.html
"Driving Overseas: Travelers at Risk," *Today* show, July 6, 2007, http://video.msn.com/?mkt=en-us&brand=msnbc&fg=&vid=1ee1af92-522a-4daa-9cbf-38a12e0afd0b&from=00
North Yungas Road, Bolivia
"The World's Most Dangerous Road," Mark Whitaker, BBC News, November 11, 2006, news.bbc.co.uk/2/hi/programmes/from_our_own_correspondent/6136268.stm
"Briton among Nine Killed on Bolivia's 'Road of Death,'" Guardian.co.uk, April 25, 2008, guardian.co.uk/world/2008/apr/25/bolivia.travelnews
Michael Liebreich, chairman and CEO, New Energy Finance
Box: Dangerous Curves Ahead
"Sexy Sign Language," Courtney Scott, Abroad'r View, March 15, 2008, abroadrview.blogspot.com/2008/03/sexy-sign-language.html
Nairobi, Kenya
Channa Commanday, chair, ASIRT Kenya
Mexico
"I'll Never Go to Baja Again," Scott Bass, *Surfer,* June 2007, surfermag.com/features/onlineexclusives/carjackedmexicobaja

HONORABLE MENTIONS
South Africa
Accident Statistics/Crash Data & Statistics in South Africa, Arrive Alive, arrivealive.co.za/pages.asp?mc=info&nc=AccidentCrashStats
Spain
"Road Safety Report: Spain," ASIRT
Highway 16, Canada
"Stolen Sisters: Discrimination and Violence against Indigenous Women in Canada, A Summary of Amnesty International's Concerns," Amnesty International, October 2004, p. 6, amnesty.ca/stolensisters/concerns_photos.pdf
Highwayoftears.com

Box: Drunkest Places
Alcohol-Related Car Accidents
"Youth and Road Safety," World Health Organization, 2007, whqlibdoc.who.int/publications/2007/9241595116_eng.pdf
Fatality Analysis Reporting System, National Highway Transportation Safety Administration, www-fars.nhtsa.dot.gov/Main/index.aspx
"Dangerously Drunk" Cities
"Most Dangerously Drunk Cities," *Men's Health,* December 2007
Austin, Texas
Public Information Office, Austin Police Department
Fargo, North Dakota
Public Information Office, Fargo Police Department
Anchorage, Alaska
Public Information Office, Anchorage Police Department
"In Remote Alaska, Wet Towns Draw Heavy Drinkers," Rachel D'Oro, *USA Today,* September 6, 2007, usatoday.com/news/nation/2007-09-06-alaska_N.htm
Are Smoking Bans Bad for Your Health?
"Drunk Driving after the Passage of Smoking Bans in Bars," S. Adams and C. Cotti, *Journal of Public Economics,* June 2008: 32
Top Drinking Countries
"The World's Hardest-Drinking Countries," Robert Malone and Tom Van Riper, *Forbes,* November 28, 2007, forbes.com/2007/11/27/drinking-europe-alcohol-biz-commerce-cx_tvr_1128drinking.html
Alcohol, Alcohol Everywhere . . . Even Under the Kitchen Sink
"Alcohol Blamed for Half of Russia's Premature Deaths," Jeremy Laurance, *Independent,* June 15, 2007, independent.co.uk/life-style/health-and-wellbeing/health-news/alcohol-blamed-for-half-of-russias-premature-deaths-453197.html
Who's Drinking Daily?
"Alcohol Consumption," Behavioral Risk Factor Surveillance System, 2007, CDC, apps.nccd.cdc.gov/brfss/page.asp?cat=AC&yr=2007&state=All#AC

Chapter 13: Bottlenecks
Introduction
"Unclogging America's Arteries: Effective Relief for Highway Bottlenecks, 1999–2004," American Highway Users Alliance, highways.org/pdfs/bottleneck2004.pdf
The Hamptons, Long Island, New York
New York State Department of Transportation
Branson, Missouri
Missouri State Department of Transportation, Springfield
Presque Isle State Park, Pennsylvania
Presque Isle State Park Department of Conservation and Natural Resources
Pennsylvania State Department of Transportation
Provo Canyon, Utah
Utah Office of Tourism

Yosemite National Park, California
Yosemite National Park Office of Tourism
Yellowstone National Park, Wyoming, Idaho, and Montana
Yellowstone National Park Office of Tourism
Box: **Cape Cod, Massachusetts**
Cape Cod Chamber of Commerce
Outer Banks, North Carolina
North Carolina State Highway Administration
Sun Valley, Idaho
Idaho Department of Transportation
Myrtle Beach, South Carolina
South Carolina Department of Transportation
Oregon Coast
Oregon Department of Transportation

Chapter 14: Don't Go There Then

UNITED STATES
New York, New York
Times Square Alliance for Times Square
Statue of Liberty National Monument (U.S. National Park Service)
Box: **Don't Go There When . . .**
"The ESPN 100: The Biggest Sports Stories of 2007," *ESPN The Magazine,* December 31, 2007: 72
Disney World, Orlando, Florida
TEA/ERA Attraction Attendance Report 2007, April 21, 2008, parkworld-online.com/news/fullstory.php/aid/762/Disney_does_it_again!.html
Grand Canyon, Arizona
Grand Canyon Tourism
Box: **10 Most Visited U.S. National Parks, 2007**
National Park Service, nature.nps.gov/stats/park.cfm

INTERNATIONAL
France
Maison de la France/French Government Tourist Office
Australia
Tourism Australia
Egypt
Egyptian Tourist Authority
China
"Off the Brochure: Beijing," Mike Day, PeterGreenberg.com, October 18, 2007, petergreenberg.com/2007/10/18/off-the-brochure-beijing/

Box: Dangerous Theme Parks
"Fixed-Site Amusement Ride Injury Survey, 2005 Update," National Safety Council, September 2006, nsc.org/downloads/documents/pdf/fap_906.pdf
"Amusement Ride–Related Injuries and Deaths in the United States: 1987–2000," Consumer Products Safety Commission, August 2001, cpsc.gov/LIBRARY/Amus2001.pdf
"Teen: 'I Felt Like I Was Going to Die,'" Jason Riley, *Courier-Journal,* January 31, 2008, courier-journal.com/apps/pbcs.dll/article?AID=/20080131/NEWS01/801310390
"Excerpts of Kaitlyn Lasitter's Deposition," *Courier-Journal,* January 30, 2008, courier-journal.com/apps/pbcs.dll/article?AID=/20080130/NEWS01/80130056

"Amusement Ride Incident of June 21, 2007, Six Flags Kentucky Kingdom, Louisville Kentucky," Final Report of the Kentucky Department of Agriculture, May 30, 2008, www.kyagr.com/documents/SFKKINCIDENTREPORT212.pdf
RideAccidents.com
Amusement Park Ride Safety information, U.S. Rep. Edward Markey, markey.house.gov/index.php?option=com_issues&task=view_issue&issue=44&parent=14&Itemid=35
Letter from Jim Prager to U.S. Rep. Edward Markey, December 7, 2007, markey.house.gov/docs/consumer_protection/Amusement%20Park%20Ride%20Safety—Letter%20to%20Congressman%20Markey%2012-7-07.pdf
"2008 Amusement Ride Safety Tracker," Amusement Safety Organization, amusementsafety.org/tracker_2008.asp
All theme park reports provided by Amusement Safety Organization, amusementsafety.org
"Venues to Watch in 2008," Amusement Safety Organization, amusementsafety.org/venue_info_example.asp

Chapter 15: Dangerous Destinations
"Most Dangerous Cities," Morgan Quitno, cqpress.com/docs/City%201%20-%20Top%20and%20Bottom%20025_14E.pdf
Ben Krasney, Marketing Communications, CQ Press
FBI crime statistics, www.fbi.gov/ucr/ucr.htm

U.S. CITIES
Detroit, Michigan
FBI crime statistics, www.fbi.gov/ucr/ucr.htm
Detroit Police Department
Joe Swickard, staff writer, *Detroit Free Press*
NEXT Detroit Neighborhood Initiative, www.ci.detroit.mi.us/Home/NextDetroit/tabid/1521/Default.aspx
City Data Detroit, city-data.com/city/Detroit-Michigan.html
St. Louis, Missouri
FBI crime statistics, www.fbi.gov/ucr/ucr.htm
St. Louis Metropolitan Police Department
Alderman Sam Moore, Fourth Ward
City Data St. Louis, city-data.com/city/St.-Louis-Missouri.html
Flint, Michigan
FBI crime statistics, www.fbi.gov/ucr/ucr.htm
City Data Flint, city-data.com/city/Flint-Michigan.html
Oakland, California
FBI crime statistics, www.fbi.gov/ucr/ucr.htm
Oakland Police Department
Stephen Buel, editor, *East Bay Express*
City Data Oakland, city-data.com/city/Oakland-California.html
Box: **Richmond, California**
FBI crime statistics, www.fbi.gov/ucr/ucr.htm
Stephen Buel, editor, *East Bay Express*
Camden, New Jersey
FBI crime statistics, www.fbi.gov/ucr/ucr.htm
Box: **Newark, New Jersey**
"Newark Goes 33 Days Without a Murder," CNN, February 15, 2008, cnn.com/2008/CRIME/02/15/no.homicides.ap/index.html

Birmingham, Alabama
FBI crime statistics, www.fbi.gov/ucr/ucr.htm
"Crime by the Numbers," David Pelfrey, October 4,
2007, bwcitypaper.com/1editorialbody.lasso?-token.
subpub=&-token.story=203997.112112&-token.
folder=2007-10-04
David Pelfrey, editor, *Black and White*
City Data Birmingham, city-data.com/city/
Birmingham-Alabama.html

North Charleston, South Carolina
North Charleston Police Department

Memphis, Tennessee
FBI crime statistics, www.fbi.gov/ucr/ucr.htm
Bill Dries, reporter, *Memphis Daily News*
City Data Memphis, city-data.com/city/
Memphis-Tennessee.html

Box: **Youngstown, Ohio**
Youngstown Police Department

Cleveland, Ohio
FBI crime statistics, www.fbi.gov/ucr/ucr.htm
Mike Tobin, assistant metro editor, *Cleveland Plain Dealer*
City Data Cleveland, city-data.com/city/Cleveland-Ohio.
html

Washington, DC
FBI crime statistics, www.fbi.gov/ucr/ucr.htm
City Data Washington, DC, city-data.com/city/
Washington-District-of-Columbia.html

Chicago, Illinois
FBI crime statistics, www.fbi.gov/ucr/ucr.htm
Jim Wagner, president, Chicago Crime Commission
City Data Chicago, city-data.com/city/Chicago-Illinois.
html

Box: **San Juan, Puerto Rico**
"Violence in Puerto Rico," University of Puerto Rico,
Commission for the Prevention of Violence, May 2,
2008, tendenciaspr.com/Ingles/Violence.html

INTERNATIONAL DESTINATIONS
Introduction
Doug Koneff, director, Office of American Citizen
Services and Crisis Management
Travel Warning: Afghanistan, U.S. State Department,
updated February 6, 2008, travel.state.gov/travel/cis_
pa_tw/tw/tw_2121.html
Janet Moore, public relations manager, Distant Horizons
Jonathan Daniel, Afghan Logistics & Tours

Yemen
"Kidnapping of Tourists, 28–29 December 1998,"
February 16, 1999, www.al-bab.com/yemen/hamza/
hostage.htm
Gregory D. Johnsen, PhD candidate, Near Eastern
Studies, Princeton University
Al-Bab.com

Tijuana, Mexico
"Kidnappings of U.S. Citizens on Rise: Sophisticated
Mexican Groups Plot Abductions," Tony Manolatos,
Union-Tribune, February 6, 2008, signonsandiego.com/
news/mexico/tijuana/20080206-9999-1m6kidnap.
html
Special Agent Darrell Foxworth, FBI, San Diego Division
David Robillard, deputy managing director and head of
Kroll Mexico

São Paulo and Rio de Janeiro, Brazil
Laurence Casagrande Lourenço, Kroll São Paolo

Professor Philip Alston, Special Rapporteur of the United
Nations Human Rights Council on Extrajudicial,
Summary or Arbitrary Executions, Brasilia, November
14, 2007, extrajudicialexecutions.org/news/Brazil_
November_2007_Press_Statement.pdf

Johannesburg, South Africa
South African Police Service, www.saps.gov.za/
"1997–2000 Surveys of Sexual Violence," CIETafrica,
ciet.org/en/documents/projects_library_
docs/2006224131250.pdf

Box: **Shadow Cities**
Shadow Cities: A Billion Squatters, A New Urban World,
Robert Neuwirth, New York: Routledge, 2005

Kingston–Spanish Town, Jamaica
"Jamaica 2008 Crime & Safety Report," Overseas
Security Advisory Council, March 10, 2008, https://
www.osac.gov/Reports/report.cfm?contentID=80861
Karl Angell, director of communications, Jamaica
Constabulary Force

Port–au–Prince, Haiti
Travel Warning: Haiti, U.S. State Department, April 30,
2008, travel.state.gov/travel/cis_pa_tw/tw/tw_917.html
Royal Caribbean, royalcaribbean.com/findacruise/ports/
group/home.do?portCode=LAB

Chapter 16: Human Rights and Corruption
Introduction
Universal Declaration of Human Rights, adopted by UN
General Assembly Resolution 217A (III) of December
10, 1948, un.org/Overview/rights.html

All Countries
"Who Is the World's Worst Dictator?" David Wallechinsky,
Parade, February 11, 2007, parade.com/articles/
editions/2007/edition_02-11-2007/Dictators
"The Worst of the Worst: The World's Most Repressive
Societies, 2007," Freedom House, www.freedomhouse.
org/uploads/special_report/58.pdf
"Amnesty International Report 2008: State of the
World's Human Rights," Amnesty International,
thereport.amnesty.org

Box: **2007 Corruption Perceptions Index**
"2006 Corruption Perceptions Index," Transparency
International, November 6, 2006, transparency.org/
news_room/in_focus/2006/cpi_2006__1

Myanmar
"Silent Burmese Protester Jailed," Jonathan Head, BBC
News, April 4, 2008, news.bbc.co.uk/2/hi/
asia-pacific/7330797.stm
"Myanmar Seizes U.N. Food for Cyclone Victims and
Blocks Foreign Experts," Seth Mydans, *New York Times,*
May 10, 2008, nytimes.com/2008/05/10/world/
asia/10myanmar.html

Box: **Papua New Guinea**
"Policing Papua New Guinea's 'Raskols,'" Nick Squires,
BBC News, December 9, 2004, news.bbc.co.uk/2/hi/
programmes/from_our_own_correspondent/4081685.stm

North Korea
"N.Y. Philharmonic Tunes Up in N. Korea," CNN,
February 25, 2008, cnn.com/2008/WORLD/
asiapcf/02/25/nkorea.nyphilharmonic/index.html

China
*Civil and Political Rights, Including the Question of
Torture and Detention: Mission to China,* Manfred

Nowak, March 10, 2006, www.freetibet.org/files/file/about/Nowak%20report.pdf

"China Earthquake Kills Thousands," Mark Tran, Elizabeth Stewart, and agencies, *Guardian,* May 12, 2008, guardian.co.uk/world/2008/may/12/china

Egypt
"The Baksheesh Diaries," Rolf Potts, Salon.com, April 11, 2000, archive.salon.com/travel/diary/pott/2000/04/11/baksheesh/print.html

Iran
"Iran: Who Holds the Power?" BBC News, news.bbc.co.uk/2/shared/spl/hi/middle_east/03/iran_power/html/guardian_council.stm

Box: Democratic Republic of the Congo
"Crisis Caused 5.4 Million Deaths in Congo, Report Says," CBC News, January 22, 2008, cbc.ca/world/story/2008/01/22/congo.html

Syria
"Summary of Human Rights Violation in Syria—January 2008 Digest," Syrian Human Rights Committee, February 2, 2008, shrc.org/data/aspx/d2/3462.aspx

"Syria Blocks Facebook in Internet Crackdown," Khaled Yacoub Oweis, Reuters, November 23, 2007, reuters.com/article/worldNews/idUSOWE37285020071123

"Honour Crime Fear of Syria Women," Lina Sinjab, BBC News, October 12, 2007, news.bbc.co.uk/2/hi/middle_east/7042249.stm

Box: Russia
"Russia's $120 Billion Elephant: Corruption," Vidya Ram, *Forbes,* June 6, 2008, forbes.com/2008/06/06/russia-corruption-business-markets-face-cx_vr_0606auto facescan01.html

"If You'll Be My Bodyguard," David Perry, Dealmaker Daily, April/May 2008, dealmakerdaily.com/magazine/article/17202.html

United Arab Emirates
"Tourists Warned of UAE Drug Laws," BBC News, February 8, 2008, news.bbc.co.uk/2/hi/uk_news/7234786.stm

Fair Trials International, fairtrials.net

Box: Lamest Claims to Fame

Gilroy, California
City of Gilroy, www.ci.gilroy.ca.us

Berrien Springs, Michigan
Berrien Springs Chamber of Commerce, berriencounty.org

Eau Claire, Michigan
Eau Claire Area Chamber of Commerce, eauclairechamber.org

Fountain, Minnesota
City of Fountain, bluffcountry.com/fountain.htm

Battle Mountain, Nevada
"Why Not the Worst?" Gene Weingarten, *Washington Post,* December 2, 2001, washingtonpost.com/ac2/wp-dyn/A31628-2001Nov28?language=printer

Beaver, Oklahoma
Town of Beaver, beaveroklahoma.net

Ashland, Virginia
Town of Ashland, town.ashland.va.us

Fake European Towns
Solvang (California) Convention and Visitors Bureau, solvangusa.com

Leavenworth (Washington) Chamber of Commerce, leavenworth.org

City of Castroville, Texas, castrovilletx.com

Coalinga, California
City of Coalinga

International Falls, Minnesota
International Falls Area Chamber of Commerce, internationalfallsmn.us/iceboxdays.shtml

Luling, Texas
Luling Chamber of Commerce, watermelonthump.com

Anniston, Alabama
"World's Largest Chair: The Battle Rages," Roadside America, roadsideamerica.com/set/CIVIchair.html

Chepachet, Rhode Island
"Little Bett," Roadside America, roadsideamerica.com/pet/littlebet.html

Dongguan, China
"South China Mall: The Largest (Ghost) Mall in the World," Cory Doctorow, Boing Boing, June 15, 2008, boingboing.net/2008/06/15/south-china-mall-the.html

Sedlec, Czech Republic
Kostnice Ossuary Beinhaus, kostnice.cz

Columbus, Georgia
"Lunch Box Museum," Roadside America, roadsideamerica.com/story/7077

"World's Largest Lunch Box Museum," lunchboxmuseum.com

Allenstown, New Hampshire
New Hampshire Snowmobile Museum Association, nhsnowmobilemuseum.com

Mitchell, South Dakota
Corn Palace Convention & Visitors Bureau, cornpalace.com

Edinburgh, Scotland
The Dungeons, thedungeons.com

Clipperton Island
Charles Veley, *Guinness Book* Record Holder, World's Most Traveled Man

Atlantic City, New Jersey
Atlantic City Tourism, atlanticcitynj.com

Elmira, New York
City of Elmira, cityofelmira.net/

South of the Border, South Carolina
South of the Border, Pedroland.com

Index

Underscored references indicate tables or boxed text.